ALASKA

CANADA

International Date Line

ALEUTIAN ISLANDS

Seattle

U. S.

San Francisco

Los Angeles

MIDWAY IS.

Dec. 6

Dec. 7

Pearl Harbor

HAWAIIAN ISLANDS

EQUATOR

PEARL HARBOR:
WARNING AND DECISION

ROBERTA WOHLSTETTER

PEARL HARBOR
WARNING AND DECISION

STANFORD UNIVERSITY PRESS
STANFORD, CALIFORNIA

To my favorite *Magician*

FOREWORD

It would be reassuring to believe that Pearl Harbor was just a colossal and extraordinary blunder. What is disquieting is that it was a supremely *ordinary* blunder. In fact, "blunder" is too specific; our stupendous unreadiness at Pearl Harbor was neither a Sunday-morning, nor a Hawaiian, phenomenon. It was just a dramatic failure of a remarkably well-informed government to call the next enemy move in a cold-war crisis.

If we think of the entire U.S. government and its far-flung military and diplomatic establishment, it is not true that we were caught napping at the time of Pearl Harbor. Rarely has a government been more expectant. We just expected wrong. And it was not our warning that was most at fault, but our strategic analysis. We were so busy thinking through some "obvious" Japanese moves that we neglected to hedge against the choice that they actually made.

And it was an "improbable" choice; had we escaped surprise, we might still have been mildly astonished. (Had we not provided the target, though, the attack would have been called off.) But it was not all *that* improbable. If Pearl Harbor was a long shot for the Japanese, so was war with the United States; assuming the decision on war, the attack hardly appears reckless. There is a tendency in our planning to confuse the unfamiliar with the improbable. The contingency we have not considered seriously looks strange; what looks strange is thought improbable; what is improbable need not be considered seriously.

Furthermore, we made the terrible mistake—one we may have come close to repeating in the 1950's—of forgetting that a fine deterrent can make a superb target.

Surprise, when it happens to a government, is likely to be a complicated, diffuse, bureaucratic thing. It includes neglect of responsibility, but also responsibility so poorly defined or so ambiguously delegated that action gets lost. It includes gaps in intelligence, but also intelligence that, like a string of pearls too precious to wear, is too sensitive to give to those who need it. It includes the alarm that fails to work, but also the alarm that has gone off so often it has been disconnected. It includes the unalert watchman, but also the one who knows he'll be chewed out by his superior if he gets higher authority out of bed. It includes the contingencies that occur to no one, but also those that everyone assumes somebody else is taking care of. It includes straightforward procrastination, but also decisions protracted by internal disagreement. It includes, in addition, the inability of individual human beings to rise to the occasion until they are sure it *is* the occasion—which is usually too late. (Unlike movies, real life provides no musical background to tip us off to the climax.) Finally, as at Pearl Harbor, surprise may include some measure of genuine novelty introduced by the enemy, and possibly some sheer bad luck.

The results, at Pearl Harbor, were sudden, concentrated, and dramatic. The failure, however, was cumulative, widespread, and rather drearily familiar. This is why surprise, when it happens to a government, cannot be described just in terms of startled people. Whether at Pearl Harbor or at the Berlin Wall, surprise is everything involved in a government's (or in an alliance's) failure to anticipate effectively.

Mrs. Wohlstetter's book is a unique physiology of a great national failure to anticipate. If she is at pains to show how easy it was to slip into the rut in which the Japanese found us, it can only remind us how likely it is that we are in the same kind of rut right now. The danger is not that we shall read the signals and indicators with too little skill; the danger is in a poverty of expectations—a routine obsession with a few dangers that may be familiar rather than likely. Alliance diplomacy, interservice bargaining, appropriations hearings, and public discussion all seem to need to focus on a few vivid and oversimplified dangers. The planner should think in subtler and more variegated terms and allow for a wider range of contingencies. But, as Mrs. Wohlstetter shows, the "planners" who count are also responsible for alliance diplomacy, inter-service bargaining, appropriations hearings, and public discussion; they are also very busy. This is a genuine dilemma of government. Some of its consequences are mercilessly displayed in this superb book.

Center for International Affairs   THOMAS C. SCHELLING
Harvard University

PREFACE

This study is primarily based on the thirty-nine volumes of the *Congressional Hearings* on the Pearl Harbor attack, published in 1946; on memoirs published since 1941 by both Japanese and American statesmen and military leaders; and on secondary accounts by historians—in particular such excellent, objective studies as the Army World War II series and the works of Robert Butow, Herbert Feis, William Langer and Everett Gleason, Walter Millis, and Samuel Eliot Morison. I have consulted some private, unpublished sources, including papers of Franklin D. Roosevelt in the Hyde Park Collection and the transcript of the Japanese War Crime Trials in the Treasure Room of the Harvard Law School. Interviews with American Army and Navy participants in the events of 1941 have proved useful in establishing the atmosphere of bureaucracy at the time and in defining the live lines of communication as opposed to those charted on paper. These oral interviews have not been used, however, to establish exact dates or timing on any of the controversial subjects, since human memory is notoriously fallible.

The initial stimulus for the book came from my friend, Andrew W. Marshall. For constant encouragement and advice through five years of research I am especially grateful to him and to Bernard Brodie and Harvey DeWeerd. The study has also profited from the suggestions of two long-term analysts of surprise attack and accidental war: Henry Rowen and Albert Wohlstetter. A number of other experts in economics, engineering, history, law, and strategy have provided valuable help. I am indebted in particular to Michael Arnsten, James Digby, A. M. Halpern, Solis Horwitz, Victor Hunt, William W. Kaufmann, and F. M. Sallagar.

Thanks are due to Adolf A. Berle, Jr., for allowing me to peruse his diaries on the period covered and for giving me permission to quote from them; and to Herman Kahn for permission to consult papers at the Franklin D. Roosevelt Library, Hyde Park, and for his criticism of the chapter on the decision to warn the theaters. Kent Roberts Greenfield, Chief of the Office of Military History, kindly gave me access to the files of his office. I am grateful to Israel Wice of that office for guiding me to the relevant sources, and to the historian, Stetson Conn, for his comments on the manuscript. Admirals Robert G. Lockhart, Stuart S. Murray, and Harry Sanders, Capt. Charles L. Freeman, Col. George C. Reinhardt, and Gen. Kenneth P. Bergquist were very helpful in elucidating certain technical aspects of the organization and capabilities of the U.S. Navy and Army in 1941.

Of the many persons I was fortunate enough to interview, I would like to thank in particular Admirals Edwin T. Layton and A. H. McCollum —Admiral Layton for his special insight into local problems in Honolulu and for his detailed criticism of the material on Hawaii, and Admiral McCollum for clarification of obscurities in the Naval *Hearings* and for his special knowledge of the workings of Washington bureaucracy.

And, finally, I must thank the brilliant cryptanalyst Col. William F. Friedman and the Army and Navy teams whose dedicated efforts resulted in our ability to read MAGIC messages. Though Colonel Friedman could not, for obvious security reasons, comment on any aspects of the cryptanalytic material presented in this book, he gave liberally of his time, wit, and wisdom. To him and to other unnamable magicians who pulled this rabbit out of their hat, I sound this note of admiration and thanks.

It has been a pleasure to work with Eleanor Harris, whose editorial assistance was invaluable in the preparation of the manuscript for publication.

For permission to quote from copyright material I wish to acknowledge the following publishers: Harper & Brothers for quotations from Robert E. Sherwood's *Roosevelt and Hopkins: An Intimate History* (1948); Duell, Sloan and Pearce, Inc. for quotations from *F.D.R.: His Personal Letters: 1928–1945*, Vol. II (1950), edited by Elliott Roosevelt and Joseph P. Lash;

Simon & Schuster, Inc. for quotations from Harold L. Ickes' *The Lowering Clouds* (1954), Vol. III of *The Secret Diary of Harold L. Ickes*; and also Shigenori Togo's *The Cause of Japan* (1956); and the U.S. Naval Institute for quotations from the *Proceedings*: Mitsuo Fuchida's "I Led the Air Attack on Pearl Harbor" (Vol. 78, September, 1952); Shigeru Fuku-dome's "Hawaii Operation" (Vol. 81, December, 1955); and Koichi Shimada's "Japanese Naval Air Operations in the Philippine Invasion" (Vol. 81, January, 1955).

Los Angeles, California   Roberta Wohlstetter
April, 1962

CONTENTS

MAPS AND CHARTS

NOTE ON RANK

In the following text, ranks of Army, Navy, and Air Force personnel designate military status in 1941. By the time of the formal inquiries, 1942 to 1946, most of the ranks had been advanced, which accounts for the apparent discrepancies when military witnesses are addressed with contemporary rather than 1941 titles at the hearings. Wherever possible, first textual references include full name and 1941 rank; thereafter a simplified form is used. (For example, Lieutenant Commander A. D. Kramer, thereafter Commander Kramer.) Where the 1941 rank is in doubt, the organization chart submitted by the services to the congressional investigation has been used. (See *Hearings*, Part 21, pp. 4552*ff*.)

The question of affixing the correct rank in the Navy is somewhat complicated by the fact that a naval officer can hold two ranks simultaneously. The "permanent" rank may be different from the "temporary" rank, as in the metaphysical distinction between the "real" and the "apparent." Kimmel, for example, had the permanent rank of Rear Admiral in 1941. However, as Commander-in-Chief of the Pacific Fleet, he was a full Admiral. When he stepped down from this post in December, 1941, he reverted to his permanent rank of Rear Admiral. The author has tried to select the rank assigned to the office, rather than the permanent rank.

This double standard of the Navy was not shared by the Army. Indeed, Lieutenant General Short of the Hawaiian Department of the Army resented the fact that his one rank was higher than Kimmel's permanent rank, but lower than Kimmel's temporary rank. In the matter of social protocol, this ordering meant that Kimmel had priority over Short. Unfortunately, it is such small irritants as these that affect the larger pattern of human relations and communication.

PEARL HARBOR:
WARNING AND DECISION

INTRODUCTION

Pearl Harbor provides a dramatic and well-documented example of an attack presaged by a mass and variety of signals, which nonetheless achieved complete and overwhelming surprise. Many analysts and historians have examined the evidence, some to assign or disprove personal or party guilt, others to consider the role of Pearl Harbor in the larger context of foreign affairs. This book, by contrast, is concerned almost exclusively with the facts of warning and surprise and their implications for today. It has proceeded from an interest in the functioning of American decisionmaking during 1941 and even more in the contemporary relevance, in the era of the H-bomb, of surprise attack.

Today a thermonuclear surprise attack not only might kill tens of millions, but also might cripple both the immediate military response of the attacked nation and its chances of slowly mobilizing a war potential. For this reason an attempt to reduce the likelihood of a surprise attack has in recent years been near the center of the West's negotiations with Russia, at least beginning with President Eisenhower's "Open Skies" proposal. Pearl Harbor may therefore be illuminating at this time as a case history on the conditions of surprise.

We shall ask first of all some relatively simple questions about information and its communication. We shall look specifically at the detection and communication of signals. (In this book the word "signal," while inspired by and compatible with its usage in the contemporary theory of information, can be understood in its nontechnical sense. It stands for a clue or a sign or a piece of evidence that tells about a particular danger or a particular enemy move or intention.)

Second, we shall examine how such information affected our actions. We want to know what happened to a signal from the moment it was picked up to the moment it arrived at a center of decision. Specifically we want to find answers to the following questions:

> What signals of an impending Japanese attack on a U.S. possession were available in our information system in 1941? That is, what signals had been collected by all our agencies, military and civilian, both in Honolulu and in Washington, D.C.?
>
> How much of this information was available to the military commands in Honolulu? How much of it was forwarded from Washington and how much arose locally? How much of it traveled from Honolulu to Washington?
>
> How good were our secret, as compared with our public, sources?
>
> How many signals were lost or missed? Were they long-term or last-minute signals or both?
>
> What signals reached the people who had the authority to act?
>
> How were these signals interpreted and used in decision?
>
> With all the information available, in what sense were our leaders surprised?

And finally,

> What does Pearl Harbor tell us about the possibility of a surprise attack today—with possible consequences of an even greater, and perhaps fatal, magnitude?

In trying to answer these questions, we shall describe how signals were received and decisions were made in the Hawaiian theater by Army and Navy Headquarters, and in Washington by the staff and top command of the War and Navy Departments and by the State Department and the White House. We shall examine the sources and knowledge available to these agencies, as well as the means, the frequency, and the types of communication between the operational branches of the military services and the top decisionmaking levels of the civilian government.

The popular view endows the activity of obtaining secret information with great risks and considerable drama. The hazards of interpretation, of selecting the relevant signs from the wealth of public and secret data, are scarcely understood. The leap of inference, however, if less dramatic, has great perils of its own.

In particular, the public image of warnings for the impending Pearl Harbor disaster appears to be highly simplified, with outlines clearly marked and with few shadings. The record is full of references to supposedly unambiguous indications of the Japanese plan. The MAGIC message "East Wind Rain" is one of the most famous. But, in fact, the signal picture in the limited locale of Honolulu is amazingly complex, and the mass of signals grows increasingly dense and freighted with ambiguities as we move to the larger assemblage of agencies in Washington. In both places signals announcing the Pearl Harbor attack were always accompanied by competing or contradictory signals, by all sorts of information useless for anticipating this particular disaster. We refer to these competing signals as "noise." To understand the fact of surprise it is necessary to examine the characteristics of the noise as well as the signals that after the event are clearly seen to herald the attack.

If it does nothing else, an understanding of the noise present in any signal system will teach us humility and respect for the job of the information analyst. In 1941, for example, he was confronted by trumpetings of danger from the Panama Canal and from San Diego, San Francisco, Vancouver, South America, the Caribbean, and the Philippines, to say nothing of a tremendous bulk of danger signals from the Atlantic and European areas. At Pearl Harbor a history of earlier alerts had created a local background of noise. In addition, the problems of training and of reinforcing the outlying islands served to divert attention from the pertinent signs. In Washington attention had been distracted by European and Atlantic alarms, and within the Far Eastern signal pattern itself, a large group of competing signals was announcing Japanese preparations to move north and attack Siberia. Looking back years later, we can see signs that were missed, but unfortunately the problem for those with the power of decision is anticipation, not retrospect. What we want to recreate now is the signal picture as it looked in 1941.

There have been many accounts of Pearl Harbor that deal with the gradual buildup to explosion during 1940–41 and include all the intricacies of diplomatic maneuver and the shifting pressures of European and Far Eastern interests. For the sake of simplicity we start in reverse and exclude this background. This account opens with the local scene in Honolulu and with the last few hours before the attack.

1 ▸ SIGNALS FOR HONOLULU

In the last few hours of peace, the detection and communication of warning signals depended most desperately on the speed and efficiency of technical facilities and on the reaction time of the individual observer. During the night and early morning of December 6–7, what were the provisions in Honolulu for receiving and sending last-minute signals of an impending attack? What were the signals and who got them?

RECEIVING AND SENDING LAST-MINUTE SIGNALS

Army Inshore Air Patrol

The Army was responsible for the inshore air patrol and the installation of a radar net, and the Navy for inshore ship patrols and distant reconnaissance. This division of reconnaissance duties went back to the days of Lt. Gen. Charles D. Herron's command of the Hawaiian Department, and it was confirmed by the Joint Coastal Frontier Defense Plan of April 11, 1941, which set up the joint Army and Navy responsibilities for the defense of Pearl Harbor. General Herron explained its origin as follows:

> ...the Navy was getting very jealous of the Army flying over the water, and of course we had to fly over the water out there in order to go up and down the Islands.
> Now, then, a reconnaissance such as we could perform with the number of planes we had, had no military importance except for this: it could scout for submarines, and the Navy were very anxious to have us watch the close-in waters for submarines. Well, now, in order to avoid coming to grips with

the Navy definitely, we worded it that they would be responsible for distant reconnaissance, which of course is logical, as they had the only planes that could go out and stay out; and in order to assure that we could fly over the water we put ourselves down for close-in reconnaissance, without defining that, but actually it amounted to trying to train our people to spot hostile submarines which came in close to shore. It had no military significance otherwise.[1]

Herron had figured the inshore air patrol to extend 40 miles offshore. Major General F. L. Martin, head of the Hawaiian Army Air Corps at the time of the attack, figured it to extend 4 or 5 miles offshore. Both officers limited its search to detection of "suspicious looking objects" under the water or on the surface.[2] With Martin the inshore patrol always functioned as part of another mission; it was "incidental to . . . training" and "not a well-organized reconnaissance for the area."[3] It had never discovered any submarines, but the line of communication provided was first to Hawaiian Air Force Headquarters, then to the Department of the Army, and then to the Navy. How this line would have functioned in an emergency it is difficult to say, since it was never used, but it seems probable that it would have taken a good half-hour for a message to reach the Navy. Whatever such a patrol might have discovered in the way of a hostile air attack would have provided at most a few minutes' warning for Air Force Headquarters. On the morning of December 7 it was not functioning. There were no Army aircraft in the air.

Army Aircraft Warning Service

On December 7 the AWS consisted of an information center at Fort Shafter on Oahu, which had just been built, and several mobile radars (SCR-270's) mounted on trucks and located at Kawailoa, Kahuku Point (or Opana), Kaaawa, Koko Head, the rear of Fort Shafter, and perhaps Waianae.[4] (See Fig. 1.) These radars were operated by motor gener-

---

[1] *Hearings before the Joint Committee on the Investigation of the Pearl Harbor Attack*, Part 27, p. 118*f*. Hereafter cited as *Hearings*.

[2] *Ibid.*, Part 28, p. 964.

[3] *Ibid.*, p. 954.

[4] Testimony and evidence on the location and number of mobile radars is conflicting. The text follows the chart in *Hearings*, Part 12, p. 322.

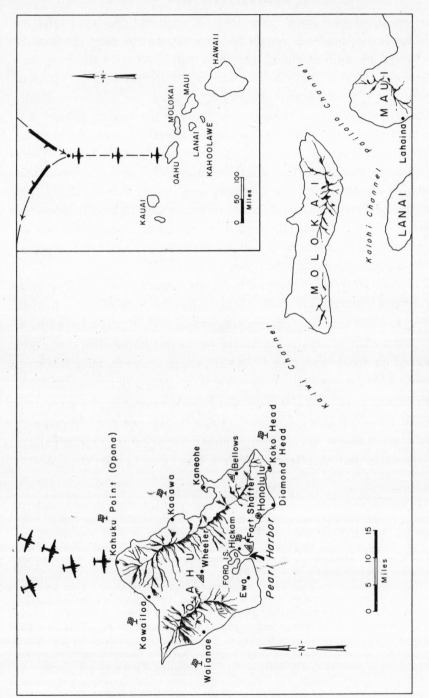

Fig. 1. Army Aircraft Warning Service on Oahu, December 7, 1941

ator sets that broke down under frequent use,[5] and they were effective only for high altitudes at ranges between 30 and 130 miles. They could not detect low-altitude flights nor those within 30 miles of the radar.[6] There was also one totally blank sector of 20 degrees north of Molokai, which was discovered after December 7, when the sets were finally calibrated. On Oahu, communication between the radar operators and the information center was by commercial telephone; from the outlying islands communication was by radio and was "unsatisfactory." There were no communication lines from the information center to the various operating centers, except for one telephone line to Wheeler Field, and tests during November established that contact with fighters could not be maintained for a distance of more than 5 miles offshore. There was no system of ground observers, though the Army's antiaircraft posts reported to the information center when they were manned.

The Aircraft Warning Service had been operating on a training basis for several months. The mobile radars had been received in August, 1941,[7] and had been operating in conjunction with a temporary information center. The plotting table for the permanent information center was installed on about November 17, when the permanent building was completed. After its installation the officers in charge discovered that the table took in a radius of 200 miles, which made the central plotting section for the Hawaiian area too small in scale. It took one week to make an overlay on a smaller radius, then another week to get the overlay painted on the table and to give the plotters some practice. By December 7,

[5] The motor generator sets were replaced after December 7 by commercial power.

[6] In 1941 it was believed that the higher the radar set was located, the better would be the reception. Later it was discovered that the ground clutter, which made the first 30 miles unreadable in the Hawaiian sets, could be eliminated by placing the radar low, with hills at the back. These particular radars were stationed at high points around the islands. Partly because of ground clutter and partly because of the curve in the earth's surface, they could not pick up a low-altitude flight.

[7] Three fixed radar sets (SCR-271's) had been received in July, 1941, but the buildings in which to house them were nowhere near completion. Authorization to start construction had been given by Washington on January 6, 1941, after approximately a year of discussion and correspondence; all the designs and various steps of approval for two of the sites had been completed by March, and those for the one site requiring approval from the Department of the Interior, by May 29. But the Army Engineers had been somewhat distracted by the resort features of the island. The testimony of Col. Theodore Wyman, District Engineer of the Army in charge of completion of the AWS installations, amounts to a long confession of the graft and inefficiency that explain this particular failure at Pearl Harbor.

however, according to the testimony of Comdr. William Taylor (a radar expert lent to the AWS by the Navy in the middle of November), "the plotters were reasonably well trained to watch and able to do checking without any controller on the plane."[8] There had been several drills involving both the Army and Navy in November, 1941. No drill had been complete, since not all radar centers had been manned at any one time. Identification and interception, however, had been considered satisfactory —enough so for Lt. Col. C. A. Powell, head of the Army Signal Corps in Hawaii, to report the success of the drills in a memorandum forwarded on November 19 to Secretary Stimson's special assistant, Harvey H. Bundy.[9] Even earlier, on August 5, Lt. Gen. Walter Short wrote to Adm. Husband E. Kimmel that the AWS was "rapidly nearing completion." Whether Short intended it or not, his letter left Kimmel with the impression that by the fall of 1941 the AWS would be completed and functioning as part of the Interceptor Command.

The men who operated the AWS understandably had a less rosy view than General Short or Admiral Kimmel. They were not only having trouble with low-priority ratings in getting equipment, and with the mechanics of radar (such as unidentifiable blips, interference from the hills encircling the islands, and breakdowns in power). They were also experiencing difficulties stemming from essentially human failings. The AWS was still operating on a training basis because Colonel Powell, as head of the Signal Corps, had "operational control" of the unit as long as it was in training, and he was unwilling to relinquish this control. Major Kenneth P. Bergquist, Operations officer of the Hawaiian Interceptor Command, was in charge of training the pursuit pilots and believed that all personnel were ready for the Air Corps to take control in November. The testimony indicates a good deal of bickering on this question of control between the Air Corps and the Signal Corps, and the Signal Corps won. For this reason the center and the radar sets were not being operated on a regular 24-hour basis on December 7. For the same reason there were no liaison officers present or even assigned, and therefore there was no possibility of correct and rapid identification and interception of aircraft. The requests for liaison officers had evidently carried little weight because

[8] *Hearings*, Part 27, p. 560.
[9] *Ibid.*, Part 18, p. 3187.

there was no recognized commander of the whole operation. Though the Navy had lent a radar expert it had not designated a liaison officer; nor had the Marine Corps, the Bomber Command of the Army, or the Federal Communications Commission, though officers from all these organizations had been present at the drills. Even with these officers present at the drills, there had been "considerable confusion,"[10] because of the great number of aircraft operating around the islands at all times, none of them equipped with IFF, and because of the requirement, instituted by the Commander-in-Chief of the U.S. Fleet, that all aircraft maintain radio silence during joint exercises. As General Frank of the Army Pearl Harbor Board put it: "It strikes me that right within the Army itself you had a situation between the Air Force and the Signal Corps where this AWS was operating on a cooperative basis rather than on a positive command basis."[11] This remark, of course, strikes at the central confusion in the defense plan of Pearl Harbor: no one knew who possessed the final command responsibility for defense of the Hawaiian Islands in the event of an enemy attack.

On the morning of December 7, the AWS radar centers were manned from 4 to 7 A.M. These hours had been instituted by General Short on November 28, in response to a war-warning message from Washington. Before that date the hours had been 6 to 11:30 A.M., plus a few hours in the afternoon, but Short figured the period from 4 to 7 A.M. to be "the most dangerous hours" for an attack by aircraft taking off from Japanese carriers. Evidently he did not communicate his reasons for changing the hours to anyone in charge of the AWS, so everyone assumed it was to reduce wear and tear on the equipment. There was no noticeable change in the alert conditions of the service. The AWS merely started operating a little earlier, and training continued until 11 A.M., except on Sundays.

Major Bergquist testified that he did not know why the hours had been changed, remarking that the service was under Signal Corps control, and he had not been informed. Brigadier General Howard C. Davidson of the Army Air Corps, who was slated to take over the command of AWS, when questioned about the sabotage alert[12] instituted by Short on

---

[10] Commander Taylor's testimony, *ibid.*, Part 27, p. 558.

[11] *Hearings*, Part 27, p. 274.

[12] For Short's alert numbers and procedures, see the Appendix.

November 28, said: "As a matter of fact, I wasn't here when No. 1 [the sabotage alert] was put into effect. I went to the United States on October 15 to study the interceptor command setup and didn't return until [December] the third, so I never gave it a thought as to why it was . . . . the only effect . . . on us was to double our guard, practically."[13] Colonel Powell was similarly uninformed about the background for the alert. He had been traveling with Davidson and had returned to Hawaii at the same time. On the reasons for the alert he testified: "All I know was what I read in the papers on the mainland on that subject."[14] Colonel Powell and Major Bergquist had both been urgent and energetic in getting the AWS under way, but the No. 1 alert had not conveyed any feeling of imminent danger even to them. Their subordinates naturally were less aware.

On the morning of December 7,[15] the Opana radar station was manned by Pvt. Joseph L. Lockard, the operator, and Pvt. George E. Elliott, the plotter. Instead of closing promptly at 7 A.M., as the other stations did, they stayed on because Elliott wanted further instruction in the operation of the oscilloscope. He was at the controls at 7:02 A.M. when "something completely out of the ordinary" appeared on the screen.[16] Lockard took over the controls, while Elliott plotted the flight starting at 137 miles north of Oahu and telephoned the switchboard at the information center. The telephone operator said he didn't know what to do because there was nobody at the information center, but a few minutes later the center called back and Lt. Kermit Tyler, an Air Corps officer in training who had been assigned by Bergquist to a 4 to 8 A.M. tour of duty there, told the two privates to forget it. They nevertheless continued to plot the flight until 7:30 A.M. (at which time it was about 30 miles from Oahu), because it was a "fine problem."[17]

[13] *Hearings*, Part 22, p. 110.

[14] *Ibid.*, p. 213.

[15] The morning of December 7 was the first Sunday morning in six weeks that the Interceptor Command had not directed a drill for the Army Antiaircraft Artillery Corps with the Fleet Air Arm. (See General Burgin's testimony, *ibid.*, Part 28, p. 1357.) In some ways this was fortunate, since no live ammunition was provided for the drills anyway, and it would have taken longer to get it to the guns when they were out in position.

[16] *Hearings*, Part 27, p. 520.

[17] Samuel Eliot Morison claims, on the authority of Rear Admiral Inglis, that from 6:45 to 7 A.M. these two operators had also "tracked one of the cruiser float planes that was reconnoitering ahead of the bombers, and reported it properly; the watch officer heard but did nothing." (*The Rising Sun in the Pacific: 1931–April 1942*, p. 138.)

Lieutenant Tyler's assignment was "pursuit officer at the interception control board, Fort Shafter." The AWS personnel at the control board had packed up and left at 7 A.M., but Tyler was on orders to remain until 8 A.M. General McNarney of the Army Pearl Harbor Board asked him later: "Were you acting both as controller and as pursuit officer?" Tyler replied: "Well, sir, I did not know what my duties were. I just was told to be there and told to maintain that work."[18] He had had no previous experience at the job. He had once "walked through the installation and had the situation explained."[19] He was evidently there to learn and to keep the station open until some relief arrived. When the Opana station had telephoned at 7:20 A.M., he decided in spite of his inexperience that what they were seeing were friendly craft, probably the flight of B-17's from the mainland that was due that morning and in fact arrived in the middle of the Japanese attack. At about 7:55 A.M. he stepped outside to witness what he took to be "Navy bombers in bombing practice over at Pearl Harbor."[20]

If this service had been operating on a 24-hour basis, under the most favorable conditions, it would probably have provided a 45-minute warning to the Army, and perhaps a 30-minute warning to the Navy.

Navy Patrols

The Navy maintained an inner air patrol of sorts, which covered only the fleet operating areas around the islands. These areas shifted from day to day. Outer patrols had been sporadic and largely for training, except in the case of alerts. For example, in the week prior to December 7, from Monday to Thursday, scouting patrols had been sent out each day on different sectors to the north and northwest to a distance of 300 to 400 miles. These missions had been largely to train the pilots and to break in a batch of recently arrived PBY aircraft. On week ends, including Fridays, these aircraft would return to base for maintenance. They were being saved to initiate action against the Japanese Mandates,[21] as pre-

---

[18] *Hearings*, Part 22, p. 223.

[19] *Ibid.*

[20] *Ibid.*, p. 221.

[21] The Caroline Islands, the Marianas, and the Marshalls, formerly German colonies, were mandated to Japan by the League of Nations after World War I. The term "Mandates" will be used in this study to describe these islands collectively.

scribed by U.S. naval war plans in the event of a declaration of war with Japan.

There had never been any attempt to cover the full 360 degrees around the islands by long-distance reconnaissance, though it was well recognized that such a long-range patrol to a distance of 800 miles was necessary in order to report the presence of enemy carriers in time to intercept the aircraft that they would launch. This had been pointed out quite clearly by General Martin, Commander of the Hawaiian Army Air Corps, and by Rear Adm. Patrick Bellinger, Commander of the Hawaiian naval patrol aircraft, in a joint report of March 31, 1941, in which they analyzed and in fact predicted in some detail the circumstances of the December 7 attack. However, for adequate air reconnaissance of this sort, Martin and Bellinger would have needed, and had requested, 180 more B-17's than they already had—more indeed than the entire number then in the United States. Since these aircraft had not been forthcoming, Bellinger evidently gave up the idea of trying to patrol effectively and concentrated on what he believed to be the job next in importance, that of expansion training.[22] His immediate superior, Rear Adm. C. C. Bloch, Commandant of the 14th District, and the Commander-in-Chief, Admiral Kimmel, also realized that a complete patrol was impossible under the circumstances, and agreed with Admiral Bellinger's course of action.

On the morning of December 7, the Navy had a number of patrol aircraft in the air. The dawn patrol, consisting of 3 PBY's (Patrol 14 of Patwing 2, under the command of Admiral Bellinger), was making its daily search of all fleet operating areas for that day. These aircraft carried live depth charges and were under orders to sink any submerged submarine sighted outside the submarine sanctuary and without a close escort. In addition 4 PBY's were cooperating with some submarines off Kaneohe in training exercises for communication and recognition. They were searching the area toward Lahaina Roads. Five PBY's left Midway at dawn to search the sector from 120 to 170 degrees on a radius of 450

---

[22] The Navy at Pearl Harbor was engaged in expansion training, operational training, and specific operations. According to Commander Ramsey, Operations officer for Bellinger, in "expansion training we were required to train complete flight crews for detachment, to be sent back to the United States to form the nuclei of squadrons just being commissioned .... it involved a tremendous training program, and the vitalization of the Naval Base Defense Air Force would have involved a practical cessation of that effort." (*Hearings*, Part 32, p. 449*f*.)

miles; 2 more PBY's left Midway at the same time to rendezvous with the carrier *Lexington* and serve as escorts for its Marine scouting planes. This made 14 aircraft in the air from Bellinger's command, but he knew that Task Force 8 under Vice Adm. William F. Halsey was returning that day to Pearl Harbor from Wake Island and that this force would send out a routine scouting flight. A squadron of Halsey's planes took off approximately 215 miles west of Pearl Harbor with orders to search the sector ahead through 045 to 135 degrees for a distance of 150 miles and proceed to the Ewa Marine Base. (Seven aircraft from this squadron were shot down by the Japanese on their arrival at Pearl Harbor.) Halsey's expedition had been well protected, and the western sector out of Hawaii was quite well covered on December 7, as it had been for a week beforehand. The northern sector was not covered, and for this reason the Japanese task force was able to approach unobserved from the north.[23]

In addition to these air patrols, the 14th District maintained a constant harbor patrol, besides a special boom patrol; 3 Coast Guard cutters and 1 destroyer always stood by on ready duty; 2 minesweepers made a routine daily sweep of the entrance. Nearly two months before the Japanese attack, Admiral Kimmel, in a confidential letter to his staff,[24] had stressed the probability of a Japanese surprise attack, and had added to his list of instructions in case of submarine attack:

> It must be remembered that a single attack may or may not indicate the presence of more submarines waiting to attack.
>
> It must be remembered, too, that a single submarine attack may indicate the presence of a considerable surface force probably composed of fast ships accompanied by a carrier. The Task Force Commander must therefore assemble his Task Groups as quickly as the situation and daylight conditions warrant in order to be prepared to pursue or meet enemy ships that may be located by air search or other means.[25]

Perhaps it is significant that he did not go so far as to say that the mere *sighting* of a single hostile submarine in the defensive sea area might indicate the proximity of an enemy task force; the evidence, he said, would be "a single submarine *attack* [author's italics]." Whatever the purpose behind this phrasing, Kimmel's directives were carefully read by

[23] For Japanese radio plotting of U.S. reconnaissance flights, see p. 379.
[24] Confidential letter 2CL-41 (rev.), October 14, 1941, in *Hearings*, Part 33, p. 1162.
[25] *Ibid.*

his staff and interpreted as applying to the situation after war had been declared.

In the early hours of December 7, the duty destroyer, U.S.S. *Ward*, was patrolling off the Pearl Harbor entrance. The 2 minesweepers, *Condor* and *Crossbill*, were making their routine nightly sweep of the entrance. At about five minutes to four the *Condor* signaled the *Ward* by blinker light that she had spotted a submerged submarine. There was a brief radio conversation between the two ships; the *Ward* was unable to get a sound contact; so Captain Outerbridge of the *Ward* retired after thanking the *Condor* and giving orders for the search to continue. Neither ship reported the incident to the Harbor Control Post in the Operations office of the 14th District.

This post was the nerve center for the network of signals that would have to be sent by the Navy in case of an emergency. Ordinarily it was manned by two watch officers and a telephone operator. During drills it was manned by "all the officers available, including all the teletype operators" and Army liaison. On the morning of December 7 one watch officer, Lt. Harold Kaminski, was on duty alone, with an assistant telephone operator, who was "perfectly useless and had not been instructed."[26] Kaminski was under orders, in case of an attack, to call the Chief of Staff and the Commandant's aide.

Apparently when this station was fully manned under drill conditions, communication was adequate. The major errors had been eliminated in a series of drills from the middle of April to the middle of October, and no special improvements had been noted since then.[27] Several complaints, however, had been registered orally by the men who had to operate under routine conditions, although only written complaints would have carried weight according to testimony after the event. Lieutenant Paul Bates, senior watch officer on December 7, though not on duty that day, testified that he had been trying to get more assistants: "We were supposed to call up about ten different places on a dial telephone in case of an attack, and we had one assistant who was a territorial reserve down at the section base at a time. He stood watch on the field telephone. That's the only

---

[26] *Hearings*, Part 23, p. 1036.
[27] According to the testimony of Captain Ramsey.

assistant we had...."[28] Lieutenant Kaminski agreed: "I felt that the station could not function efficiently with just myself.... I had complained about the man they had on the telephone watch, and they had Hawaiians there who were not able to speak English and they did not receive the proper instructions at the telephone ... they did not understand the teletype there, and I felt there was too much responsibility for one person."[29]

Lieutenant Kaminski's office went into action on Sunday at 6:53 A.M. on receipt of a message from the U.S.S. *Ward*. The *Ward*, continuing her patrol of the harbor, had spotted the conning tower of a submarine in the wake of the U.S.S. *Antares*. This time there was no doubt. At 6:45 A.M. Captain Outerbridge ordered his gunners to open fire and at 6:51 A.M. he radioed the 14th District station: "We have dropped depth charges upon sub operating in defensive sea area." Then, to make sure that there would be no doubt in the minds of the recipients that this was a hostile submarine and not a blackfish or a whale, he sent a second message at 6:53 A.M.: "We have attacked fired upon and dropped depth charges upon submarine operating in defensive sea area."

Lieutenant Kaminski had no doubt that we "were in it." He tried first to reach the Commandant's aide and couldn't. He got in touch with the fleet duty officer, then on his own initiative sent a message to the ready duty destroyer to "get under way immediately and contact U.S.S. *Ward* in defensive sea area." He instructed the communication office to send a copy of this message to the *Ward*. He then got the Chief of Staff, Capt. John B. Earle, who requested confirmation from the *Ward*. Kaminski never received this confirmation, but he did receive a third message from the *Ward* saying: "We have intercepted a sampan. We are escorting this sampan into Honolulu. Please inform Coast Guard to send cutter [to] relieve us of sampan." Kaminski called the Coast Guard and the War Plans officer and then started calling all department heads. Before he had reached all of these, the first attack had started, at 7:55 A.M. Neither he nor anybody else tried to get a report to Army Headquarters.

Kaminski's reaction to the *Ward*'s message was unique. Everyone else refused to believe that it was a submarine, or that the encounter indicated

[28] *Hearings*, Part 23, p. 1033.
[29] *Ibid.*, p. 1036.

any immediate danger. Captain Outerbridge, who had been careful to make clear that he had fired on a submarine, was convinced that he had sunk it. He was vaguely disturbed by the behavior of the sampan, whose captain had waved a white surrender flag at him, but when he heard the noise of the attack he said to his lieutenant commander: "I guess they are blasting the new road from Pearl to Honolulu."[30]

Captain Earle, on receipt of the information from Kaminski, "called the Commandant of the 14th Naval District, Admiral Bloch, informed him of what had been done, and talked the situation over with him for some time with a view to deciding what other action should be taken. Our reaction was that it was probably a mistake as we had numerous reports of sighting of submarines, but that if it were not a mistake, the *Ward* could take care of the situation and the relief destroyer could lend a hand, while the Commander-in-Chief had the necessary power to undertake any other action which might be desired. Mainly we were trying to definitely determine what had happened." "We were vaguely alarmed," Earle went on, "but could see no specific threat involved. . . . We couldn't imagine that the *Ward*, having actually attacked a submarine, would leave her post to proceed to Honolulu if it were a real attack . . . we felt that by referring the matter to the Commander-in-Chief that we had done all that we possibly could even if the attack were real."[31] In other words, the matter was now in the hands of higher authority. But even higher authority doubted the report. At 7:55 A.M. Admiral Kimmel was still waiting for confirmation from the *Ward*.

The Navy's dawn air patrol went through a similar experience. At 7:00 A.M. on that Sunday morning, one of its aircraft sank an enemy submarine a mile off the Pearl Harbor entrance.[32] The pilot radioed the staff duty officer of the Naval Air Force in code, which meant that the message was not ready for circulation until 7:30 A.M. (Kimmel testified later that the pilot had violated his staff instructions, which specified only plain language in an emergency.)

At 7:30 A.M. the staff duty officer telephoned the message to Comdr. Logan C. Ramsey, Operations officer for Admiral Bellinger, who relayed

---

[30] *Ibid.*, Part 36, p. 59.

[31] *Ibid.*, pp. 268–270.

[32] It is not clear from the records whether this was the same submarine as the one fired on by the *Ward*, or another one.

the information to the staff duty officer of the Commander-in-Chief. Admiral Kimmel received the information at 7:40. No report ever reached the Army.

Commander Ramsey was also incredulous. He

> asked ... if the message had been properly authenticated, because there was in the back of my mind the feeling that it was quite possible that it was a mistake, a drill message of some variety that had gotten out by accident. ... I went immediately to the Command Center and for no reason that I know of, drew up a search plan for our aircraft under the conditions prevailing that day. ... Meanwhile I was waiting for an authentication of the message.[33]

When he saw the first aircraft diving on Ford Island he started to make out a report of violation of flight rules, since he assumed that it was a young pilot "flathatting." Then the bomb detonated and Ramsey dashed into the radio room and ordered a broadcast on all frequencies in plain English: "Air Raid Pearl Harbor. This is no Drill."[34]

Ramsey's testimony on the efficiency of the communications system bears out the complaints of Bates and Kaminski. He described the system as follows:

> ... where planes were actually in the air, we used radio. For planes of the Marine Corps, based on Ewa, we had to communicate by telephone—field telephone set with specially strung wires. For Army bombardment aviation, we had a field telephone set which had been installed by the Army units, and which was our own direct means of communicating to the Army bombardment aviation. We had no means of direct communication, except through the Pearl Harbor, Ford Island, Hickam Field telephone exchanges, to the search and attack groups of the Naval Base Air Defense. It was very difficult to communicate with General Davidson, who had command of all fighter aircraft on Kaneohe. Our only means of direct communication was the telephone through the Pearl Harbor Exchange. In addition to that we had two or three—I forget which now—teletype page printer circuits, which ran to various localities, but which not on all outlying stations were continuously manned.[35]

On the morning of December 7 the system of naval inshore patrol might have provided, then, approximately one hour of warning.

---

[33] *Hearings*, Part 32, p. 444.
[34] *Ibid.* Drill messages were regularly required to begin with the word "Drill."
[35] *Ibid.*, p. 440*f*.

Provisions for Long-distance Reconnaissance

The question that occurs next, of course, is, Granted technical deficiencies, shortage of personnel, and inadequate training, why the almost total inertia in the face of these last-minute danger signals? This is a long story, which will take us into the field of intelligence and decisionmaking in Honolulu and Washington. But before we leave the local last-minute situation, let us look at the Hawaiian facilities and responsibilities for communicating a warning in 1941 as they appeared on paper, and let us take here the example of long-distance reconnaissance.

On paper the assignment of responsibility was something like this. On April 11, 1941, General Short, head of the Hawaiian Department of the Army, and Admiral Bloch, Commandant of the 14th Naval District, signed a document known as the "Joint Coastal Frontier Defense Plan." This was based on the "Joint Army and Navy Basic War Plan Rainbow No. 1" and a document of 1935 entitled "Joint Action of the Army and Navy." The document of April 11 opened with the general statement that "the method of coordination will be by mutual cooperation . . . until and if the method of unity of command is invoked."[36] It assigned to the Army the following general task: "To hold Oahu against attacks by sea, land and air forces, and against hostile sympathizers [i.e., fifth columnists]; to support the naval forces." It assigned to the Navy this general task: "To patrol the Coastal Zone and to control and protect shipping therein; to support the Army forces." Specifically, it required the Army to establish "an inshore aerial patrol of the waters of the Oahu D.C.A. in cooperation with the Naval Inshore Patrol . . . and an aerial observation system on outlying islands, and an Aircraft Warning Service for the Hawaiian Islands."[37] To the Navy it assigned an inshore patrol, an offshore patrol, and distant reconnaissance. Annex No. VII to this document gave a few details on command for joint air operations:

> Joint air attacks upon hostile surface vessels will be executed under the tactical command of the Navy. The Department Commander will determine the Army bombardment strength to participate in each mission. With due consideration to the tactical situation existing, the number of bombardment airplanes released to Navy control will be the maximum practicable. This

[36] *Ibid.*, Part 15, p. 1430.
[37] *Ibid.*, p. 1432.

force will remain available to the Navy, for repeated attacks, if required, until completion of the mission, when it will revert to Army control.

Defensive air operations over and in the immediate vicinity of Oahu will be executed under the tactical command of the Army. The Naval Base Defense Officer will determine the Navy fighter strength to participate in these missions. With due consideration to the tactical situation existing, the number of fighter aircraft released to Army control will be the maximum practicable. This force will remain available to the Army for repeated patrols or combat or for maintenance of the required alert status until, due to a change in the tactical situation, it is withdrawn by the Naval Base Defense Officer (Commandant, 14th Naval District), and reverts to Navy control.[38]

Annex No. VII, sometimes referred to as the "Joint Air Agreement," was drawn up by General Martin, Commanding General of the Army Air Force in Hawaii, and Admiral Bellinger, Commander of the naval patrol aircraft, and was signed by Admiral Bloch and General Short on March 28, 1941. It was in effect on December 7, 1941. A further operations agreement (Naval Base Defense Air Force Operation Plan No. A-1-41), signed by Martin and Bellinger on April 9, 1941, provided more detail on such matters as conditions of readiness for the aircraft and priority of targets.[39]

Provision for communication of signals was also set forth in several different documents. Annex D to Operation Plan 1-41, March 5, 1941, had established a Harbor Control Post in the Operations office, 14th Naval District. This post was to man and operate the following direct telephone connections:

> Harbor Control Post to—
> Headquarters, Hawaiian Dept., Fort Shafter
> Headquarters, HSCAB, Fort Derussy
> Command Post, Fort Kamehameha
> Command Post, Hickam Field
> Commander, Patrol Wing Two
> SOPA[40] (if at dock)
> Navy Yard Signal Tower
> Navy Yard Power House

In conjunction with Army and Navy reporting, communication, and intelligence agencies, the Harbor Control Post was to "be prepared to

---

[38] *Ibid.*, p. 1435.
[39] *Ibid.*, Part 22, pp. 348*ff.*
[40] Senior Officer Present Afloat.

'alert' Army and Navy forces against aircraft, or other surprise attack, and assist in coordinating their defense measures," and to "direct the Yard Power House when to sound air raid and blackout alarms and the secure signal."[41] It was further to

> Report promptly any action taken to immediate Superiors in Command, Army and Navy, and keep them advised of all known developments.
>
> In conjunction with Commander Inshore Patrol, Captain of the Yard, and District Public Works Officer keep the Army Harbor Defenses informed of authorized ship movements within the Control Post Area.
>
> . . . .
>
> Obtain from Commander Inshore Patrol the day-by-day list of patrol and minesweeping vessels under this command. Maintain up to date data on Army-Navy defenses and Conditions of Readiness.

The following conditions of readiness were prescribed for the Harbor Control Post:

Condition I: Post fully manned and ready to operate in all respects.

Condition II: Post manned by Army and Navy watch officers, telephone and teletype operators on watch.

NOTE: Conditions I and II are "Alert" conditions.

Condition III: Normal condition. Telephone operator on watch. District and Yard Duty Officer on call.

On December 7, as we have seen, the Harbor Control Post was in Condition III; it was manned by a reserve officer and his untrained telephone operator.

Annex E to the Operation Plan (added on July 19, 1941)[42] was a communication plan listing the radio frequencies and signals to be used, and providing for "instant" communication by radio between the information center at Fort Shafter (at that time under Army Antiaircraft) and the Commandant of the 14th Naval District. The Aircraft Warning Service was not yet in operation. In April, however, Annex VII had provided reassuringly that

> Upon establishment of the Aircraft Warning Service, provision will be made for transmission of information on the location of distant hostile and friendly aircraft. Special wire or radio circuits will be made available for

[41] *Hearings*, Part 33, p. 1305.
[42] *Ibid.*, p. 1306.

the use of Navy liaison officers, so that they may make their own evaluation of available information and transmit them to their respective organizations. Information relating to the presence or movements of hostile aircraft off-shore from Oahu which is secured through Navy channels will be trans-mitted without delay to the Aircraft Warning Service Information Center.

. . . .

During the period prior to the completion of the AWS installation, the Navy, through use of Radar and other appropriate means, will endeavor to give such warning of hostile attacks as may be practicable.[43]

At this point anyone in Washington who looked over the paper arrange-ments for Hawaiian defense could find little cause for alarm. He might pause at the spectacle of aircraft passing from Army to Navy control and back again, depending on how "the immediate vicinity of Oahu" was defined. But looking a little further, he could rest assured that this sort of detail would be ironed out by the provision for weekly air drills conducted by Bellinger and Martin.[44]

On February 14, 1941, Bloch and Short had issued an order for a joint committee to study and prepare plans for a series of weekly joint exercises to ensure the readiness of joint defensive measures against surprise air-craft raids. Short, in a separate memorandum of February 17, had set forth all the details for "fully satisfactory communications between all Army and Navy air activities, both in the air and on the ground," for determining the degree of responsibility under various conditions, for effective and instantaneous air alarm arrangements, coordination of ship and shore antiaircraft gunfire, restriction of American aircraft to specific operating areas to facilitate detection of enemy planes, etc. It would be difficult to mention a contingency that he failed to consider.

A Washington observer might well have gone on to question the absence of working details for the Navy's long-distance reconnaissance program. He might have inferred some information, however, from the Joint Estimate prepared by Martin and Bellinger on March 31, 1941—a

[43] *Ibid.*, Part 15, p. 1435f.

[44] The testimony read by the author indicates that the officers who had participated in these drills were subsequently under the impression that they had been holding these drills every week and that the system was working smoothly with the aircraft available. Actually, the first joint air-raid drill was held on April 24 and the last on November 12, and there were only thirteen joint drills in all for the year 1941. A drill had been scheduled for November 29, but it was canceled because of a sortie. A Washington observer would not have known about this discrepancy between theory and practice.

theoretical projection of possible methods of enemy attack against Oahu
and how best to meet them. Here the two air officers declared:

a.) A declaration of war might be preceded by:
   1. A surprise submarine attack on ships in the operating area.
   2. A surprise attack on Oahu including ships and installations in Pearl
      Harbor.
   3. A combination of these two.

b.) It appears that the most likely and dangerous form of attack on Oahu
would be an air attack. It is believed that at present such an attack would
most likely be launched from one or more carriers which would probably
approach inside of three hundred miles.

c.) A single attack might or might not indicate the presence of more submarines or more planes awaiting to attack after defending aircraft have been
drawn away by the original thrust.

d.) Any single submarine attack might indicate the presence of a considerable
undiscovered surface force probably composed of fast ships accompanied by
a carrier.

e.) In a dawn air attack there is a high probability that it could be delivered
as a complete surprise in spite of any patrols we might be using and that it
might find us in a condition of readiness under which pursuit would be slow
to start. . . .

Action open to us

a.) Run daily patrols as far as possible to seaward through 360 degrees to
reduce the probabilities of surface or air surprise. This would be desirable
but can only be effectively maintained with present personnel and material
for a very short period and as a practicable measure cannot, therefore, be
undertaken unless other intelligence indicates that a surface raid is probable
within rather narrow limits.[45]

Material readiness and degree of readiness were established in the Martin-
Bellinger estimate for all available aircraft, but the authors pointed out
that normal training programs would be drastically curtailed if the degree
of readiness were less than 2 hours and if more than one-quarter of the
aircraft were kept available for search and attack.

Since Oahu was being used as a training base for the Philippines, and
since there were not enough aircraft for both training and reconnaissance,
a Washington observer might have inferred that long-distance reconnaissance, though desirable, was not actually in effect, and that before

[45] *Hearings*, Part 15, p. 1437*f*.

instituting such reconnaissance, Admiral Bellinger would wait for an alert order based on up-to-the-minute intelligence. Such an observer might have derived some small comfort, however, from the realistic reasoning on enemy action in the Joint Estimate.

Now, if the Navy had been alerted to an imminent enemy attack, what officer would institute this 360-degree reconnaissance? Or would it be an automatic result of the alert? The answer is not on paper before December 7. After the event, inquiring congressmen naturally turned for information to the Naval Air Defense officer, Admiral Bellinger, who, after some research, was able to clarify, in his own mind, as well as in theirs, his various command responsibilities. It appeared that even though he was to direct the patrol aircraft, he did not have the authority to order such reconnaissance. This could have been done only by Admiral Bloch, who though not an airman, was supposed to designate the conditions of readiness for the aircraft and therefore had what he called a "supervisory control" over Bellinger.

Bellinger's jurisdiction was as follows: First, he was Commander, Hawaiian Based Patrol Wings, and Commander, Patrol Wing 2. (Included in the larger command were the patrol squadrons and aircraft tenders attached to Patrol Wings 1 and 2.) Second, he was Commander, Task Force 9. This comprised Patrol Wings 1 and 2 with attending surface craft and such other units as might be assigned by the Commander-in-Chief, Pacific Fleet. Third, he was Commander, Fleet Air Detachment, Pearl Harbor. The responsibilities of this function included administrative authority in local matters over all aircraft actually based on the Naval Air Station, Pearl Harbor, but did not include operational authority. Fourth, he was responsible for liaison with the Commandant, 14th Naval District, for aviation development within the district, including Midway, Wake, Palmyra, and the Johnston Islands. Fifth, he was Commander, Naval Base Defense Air Force.

In his various capacities Bellinger functioned under the following senior officers:

1. Commander, Aircraft Scouting Force, who as type commander for patrol wings was based at San Diego.
2. Commander, Scouting Force, the force command of which Patrol Wings 1 and 2 were a part.

3. Commander-in-Chief, Pacific Fleet. Bellinger in his capacity as Commander, Task Force 9, was directly under this officer.
4. Commanders of Task Forces 1, 2, and 3 for operation of patrol planes assigned those forces for specific operations.
5. Commandant, 14th Naval District, who was Bellinger's senior officer when Bellinger was performing duties as Commander, Naval Base Defense Air Force.

Senator Ferguson, in his cross-examination of Rear Adm. William W. Smith, Kimmel's Chief of Staff, asked, in relation to Bellinger's duties: "did you ever find these men getting tangled up in these orders?" Admiral Smith said: "No, they were able to keep everything in mind."[46]

Bellinger testified further—and this was something that could not possibly have been inferred by our hypothetical Washington observer— that the "Naval Base Defense Force was a paper organization . . . not . . . specifically manned and equipped to perform a definite job. It existed only when called into being by proper authority [Joint Army-Navy action] . . . or by an actual emergency. . . . Its composition was variable." Even when the Naval Base Defense Force was activated under drill order conditions Bellinger's authority extended "only over the search and attack groups of the Naval Base Defense Air Force and was nonexistent concerning Army pursuit aviation and Navy fighter aviation which were to function under the Army air command."[47] Admiral Bloch, Commandant of the 14th Naval District, referred to the Naval Base Defense Force as "a volunteer fire department."

Bellinger of course was free to recommend long-distance reconnaissance at any time, but he had never been informed of any war-warning dispatches. "During October, November, and December," he testified at the hearings, "my only information concerning our relation with Japan and the imminence of war came from the Honolulu newspapers. . . . The information available to me—limited and unofficial as it was—did not indicate that I should recommend to the commander in chief, Pacific Fleet, that distant patrol plane search for the security of Pearl Harbor be undertaken at that time."[48]

[46] *Ibid.*, Part 8, p. 3544.
[47] *Ibid.*, p. 3452.
[48] *Ibid.*, p. 3455.

The two men who were informed, Bloch and Kimmel, did not see fit to discuss the subject of reconnaissance on receipt of the November 27 warning, or to bring up the matter with Bellinger, though Admiral Bloch thought Bellinger would hear about any decision they might make on reconnaissance.[49]

General Martin, who was Admiral Bellinger's opposite number in the Army when Bellinger was acting for the Naval Base Defense, knew that naval air reconnaissance was not sufficient. He also knew that the paper plans for joint operation did not represent the organization in action. However, he shared with other Army officers a great deal of confidence in the Navy's ability to perform this mission by other means.

Under the Joint Air Agreement, General Martin was to lend all his available aircraft for long-distance reconnaissance whenever the Navy requested them. On December 7 he would have been able to lend only six aircraft capable of long-range patrol, i.e., six B-17's that he was currently using to train crews for the Philippine Air Force. But in any case Admiral Bloch did not request any. In the absence of such a request, both General Short and General Martin were confident that the Navy was somehow taking care of this job. Short knew that the Navy had a traffic analysis unit that kept them informed of the location of the Japanese Fleet. He knew that some American ships were equipped with radar; in fact some of his own officers had been given radar instruction on board these ships during the summer of 1941. He knew that the task forces always sent out scouting missions and that a good deal of reconnaissance was performed in this way, although he was not informed about the schedules and locations of these ships. And finally, he agreed with his Air Corps Commander, General Martin, that the presence of the Navy at Pearl Harbor was a form of security in itself, "that the Navy was strong enough and the task forces were strong enough to be such a threat against any concentration excepting the entire Japanese fleet . . . that it would be a very decided deterrent to the Japanese ever sending a task force into that area."[50]

[49] Senator Ferguson asked: "How? Did they have rumours that they relied upon?" The background information of the top staff will be discussed in detail below.

[50] *Hearings*, Part 28, p. 972. Cf. Short's testimony, *ibid.*, Part 27, p. 192.

Major General Henry T. Burgin, who commanded the Army Antiair-craft Artillery, shared General Short's confidence in Navy reconnaissance: "These [air] patrols were seen to go out every morning, come back late afternoon. I was never shown or didn't attempt to see what routes they took, where they went, or what sectors were covered, but in my mind, and I am sure, in that of General Short's was the idea that the Navy was doing the scouting, and that from the Navy we would get our information, should the enemy approach."[51]

Whatever the attitudes and estimates of its individual officers, the Navy had accepted on paper the responsibility for long-distance recon-naissance. The Army had therefore some basis for feeling secure. But what about the other means for reconnaissance available to the Navy that may have bolstered this feeling of security in the Army? No ship's radar would function within the harbor because of the surrounding hills. A new type of "gunnery radar," which had recently been installed aboard ship, was practically useless for detection of aircraft, according to Kimmel's protests to Washington.[52] The scouting missions of the task forces could not cover the semicircle north of Pearl Harbor because the Chief of Naval Opera-tions in Washington had issued orders on October 16 and again on November 25 to divert all traffic to the south. As for radio traffic analysis, this is another story of signals received that failed to communi-cate a warning to the officers who had the power of decision. We shall tell this story in connection with that of the whole intelligence structure for both the Army and the Navy in the Hawaiian Islands.

Army confidence in the Navy seems to have been matched by a kind of good-natured contempt on the Navy's part for Army performance. Naval fliers regarded most Army pilots as poorly trained; Naval Intelligence expected nothing from G-2 (Army Intelligence), and was constrained by a Washington directive from giving G-2 any of its privileged informa-tion.[53] This attitude in the Navy, which spread from the lowest ranks to the highest, of self-sufficiency combined with zealous security measures, may have done much to encourage the Army's illusions.

[51] *Hearings*, Part 28, p. 1356.
[52] Letter from Kimmel to Stark, October 22, 1941, *ibid.*, Part 33, p. 1172.
[53] Interview with Adm. Edwin T. Layton, July 11, 1956.

Admiral Kimmel was perhaps an exception to the rule of self-sufficiency in the Navy attitude, but what he said at the hearings in this regard may have been rationalization after the event. He testified that he had depended on the AWS to detect the approach of hostile aircraft. None of his subordinates had expected anything from this service. Bellinger, for example, did not even bother to telephone the information center after the attack. Many of them did not know of its existence.

At any rate, Army officers did nothing to challenge the Navy's attitude. It was General Short's policy not to inquire of Admiral Kimmel about any naval details, and Admiral Kimmel kept the same respectful distance from General Short. "As a Senior Admiral," General Short remarked, "Kimmel would have resented it if I had tried to have him report every time a ship went in or out, and as I say, our relations were such that he gave me without any hesitancy any piece of information that he thought was of interest."[54] The importance of cordial relations with the Navy had been underlined by Marshall in his first instructions to Short, and Short had carried out both the letter and the spirit of Marshall's advice. Interservice cordiality was evident on the golf course as well as in official interviews, but this was not equivalent to a free exchange of information.

THE INTELLIGENCE ORGANIZATION AT PEARL HARBOR

The Navy had three intelligence divisions in Hawaii: Combat Intelligence under Lt. Comdr. Joseph J. Rochefort, Fleet Intelligence under Lt. Comdr. Edwin T. Layton, and Counterespionage under Capt. Irving Mayfield. Mayfield was the 14th District Intelligence officer and reported directly to Admiral Bloch, Commandant of the 14th Naval District. Rochefort's unit was also under the command of the 14th District; Layton was in Kimmel's command. (See Fig. 2.)

On December 7, 1941, Commander Layton had been in his job one year to the day. Rochefort had started his assignment about May 15, 1941; Mayfield, on March 15, 1941. Rochefort was regarded as one of the most experienced cryptanalysts the Navy had produced. From 1925 to 1927 he had been "in charge of all cryptographic work for the Navy Department in Washington." He had spent three years in Japan as a language officer,

[54] *Hearings*, Part 27, p. 194.

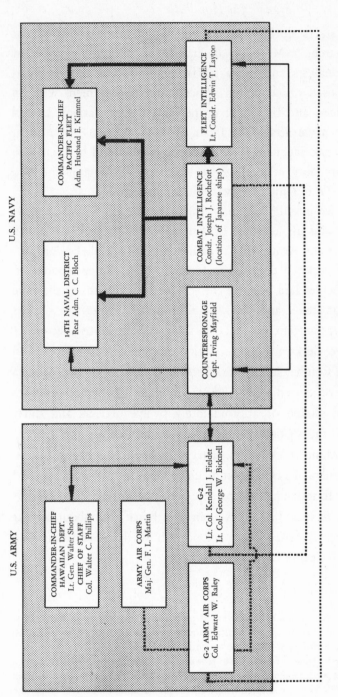

U.S. ARMY

U.S. NAVY

COMMANDER-IN-CHIEF
HAWAIIAN DEPT.
Lt. Gen. Walter Short
CHIEF OF STAFF
Col. Walter C. Phillips

ARMY AIR CORPS
Maj. Gen. F. L. Martin

G-2
Lt. Col. Kendall J. Fielder
Lt. Col. George W. Bicknell

G-2 ARMY AIR CORPS
Col. Edward W. Raley

COMMANDER-IN-CHIEF
PACIFIC FLEET
Adm. Husband E. Kimmel

14TH NAVAL DISTRICT
Rear Adm. C. C. Bloch

FLEET INTELLIGENCE
Lt. Comdr. Edwin T. Layton

COMBAT INTELLIGENCE
Comdr. Joseph J. Rochefort
(location of Japanese ships)

COUNTERESPIONAGE
Capt. Irving Mayfield

MAIN CHANNELS OF COMMUNICATION

——— INFORMATION ON COUNTERINTELLIGENCE AND ESPIONAGE

━━━ INFORMATION ON STRATEGIC INTELLIGENCE

••••••• OCCASIONAL CONTACT (CONFLICTING TESTIMONY ON FREQUENCY AND CONTENT OF COMMUNICATION)

FIG. 2. ARMY AND NAVY INTELLIGENCE GROUPS IN HAWAII

and "on various staffs during various war problems had carried out cryptographic research."[55] Moreover he had in his charge a number of well-trained cryptanalysts and radio traffic analysts. His unit at Pearl Harbor was composed of about ten officers and twenty men, with an additional ten officers and fifty to sixty men in outlying stations. Layton had been assistant naval attaché in Japan from April, 1937, to March, 1939, and could speak Japanese fluently. Captain Mayfield had had two weeks of temporary duty in intelligence work in Washington and two years as naval attaché in Chile. He was not a Japanese linguist.

The Army had two intelligence units: the main G-2 unit under Lt. Col. Kendall J. Fielder and his assistant Lt. Col. George W. Bicknell, and a special G-2 unit for the Army Air Corps headed by Lt. Col. Edward W. Raley. Fielder and Bicknell reported to General Short; Raley reported to General Martin. Fielder had been on the job for four months at the time of the Pearl Harbor attack, and "had had no prior G-2 experience."[56] His organization at Fort Shafter consisted of a small Administrative section of one officer and two clerks, a Public Relations section of two officers and three clerks; and a Combat Intelligence section, consisting of two officers and several clerks, organized to expand rapidly in an emergency. Another Counterintelligence section of approximately twelve officers and thirty agents, known as the "Contact Office," was located in the city of Honolulu, with Colonel Bicknell in charge. Bicknell had begun his assignment under General Herron's command in October, 1940, and so had had approximately fourteen months of experience before the Pearl Harbor attack. Raley had headed G-2, Hawaiian Air Force, for about a year preceding December 7, 1941. There are no published records indicating the character of Raley's unit.[57]

[55] *Ibid.*, Part 10, p. 4673.

[56] *Ibid.*, Part 35, p. 88.

[57] Judging from the records on Pearl Harbor, the amount of experience on the job has a good deal to do with the ability to recognize a warning signal when it is available. Layton and Rochefort interpreted their raw data with authority and precision and were explicit in their hypotheses. Bicknell came off next best. However, this impression may have arisen partly from the fact that we have much more testimony from Layton and Rochefort than from any other Intelligence officers. They testified before all the investigating committees except the Clarke Committee.

Navy Intelligence

The Combat Intelligence unit of the 14th Naval District (Com 14) under Commander Rochefort was one of two Far Eastern field units whose main office was in Washington. The other field unit was in Cavite in the 16th Naval District (Com 16). Both field units received their orders from Washington, and sent their material back there to the Chief of Naval Operations, as well as to each other and to the Commander-in-Chief, Asiatic Fleet, and the Commander-in-Chief, U.S. Fleet. Important messages were sent either by radio in their own cryptographic system or by airmail in a locked pouch. All old information went by naval transport. The primary business of the 14th District unit was radio traffic analysis to determine the location of Japanese ships. The 16th District unit in addition to this kind of analysis was charged with interception and decoding of Japanese diplomatic traffic (known as MAGIC). With few exceptions it sent the coded messages directly to Washington. After July, 1941, no diplomatic traffic went directly from Com 16 to Com 14, though it did go directly to Adm. Thomas C. Hart and General MacArthur.

Rochefort's immediate sources were four direction-finding stations at Dutch Harbor, Samoa, Oahu, and Midway; one radio unit at Aiea for intercepting all encoded Japanese naval traffic except for one system being processed in Cavite and Washington; and one radio unit for getting all information available on the Japanese by means other than cryptanalysis. He also received information from the local Army G-2 section; from the FBI and FCC in Hawaii; from the other two Naval Intelligence officers, Commander Layton and Captain Mayfield; and from the ONI in Washington. His unit's function was regarded as technical and limited: "We provided intelligence only of a particular and rather narrow type, and I did not expect—nor would I expect now—that all information bearing on any foreign country would be sent to my office."[58]

Of the naval traffic intercepted, Rochefort testified that his unit was able to decode and understand about 10 per cent. Neither unit had been able to break any high-priority naval code.[59] Rochefort's unit did not

[58] *Hearings*, Part 32, p. 369.

[59] Captain L. F. Safford claims that the unit at Cavite could read the Japanese naval code, JN 25, at least partially, in November, 1941. A new system of keys had been introduced on December 4, 1941, and was reported by Com 16, but carryover of the old code made solution simple. Safford's is the only testimony to this effect. (*Ibid.*, Part 18, p. 3335.)

attempt to intercept and never did intercept any encoded Japanese diplomatic traffic, but any encoded diplomatic material intercepted would have been forwarded to Washington for processing there, and the translations would not have been returned to Com 14. If necessary, Rochefort's unit could have read the simplest Japanese diplomatic code, PA-K2, but it was not requested to do so until December 3.

Radio traffic analysis was a difficult and somewhat inexact art at this time. As Commander Layton explained to the congressional committee, the analysts had to read the enemy's radio signals "without reading his messages and by taking who does things as a rule and how he does it as a rule and using that as a thumb rule to find out what he is doing now."[60] On November 30, 1941, they had deduced the presence of a carrier division in the Japanese Mandates, but, as it turned out, they were wrong. Layton explained this as follows:

> The Japanese naval organization was so set up that originally the carriers or carrier divisions had been assigned to both First and Second Fleets. Sometime in the middle of 1941 this organization was apparently dissolved. It took us some time to find it out for sure. The carriers were lumped under one organization. But one of the Japanese tendencies had been to keep plane guard destroyers with the same carrier division and when they moved over from the First and Second Fleet into the Carrier Fleet they took their plane guard destroyers with them.
>
> The presence of a plane guard destroyer in the Mandates would be the first and probably the only tip-off under normal circumstances if they were under radio silence that a carrier might be there too. It wouldn't prove that the carrier was there, but under normal circumstances it would be logical to assume it.... This plane guard destroyer division, it later turned out, had been detached from the carriers and had gone to the Mandates to reinforce the Mandate Fleet.[61]

Radio traffic intelligence was a highly guarded secret at Pearl Harbor, Cavite, and Washington. Its existence was not officially revealed to any Army officer in Hawaii except General Short. In Washington this unit's operation was so shrouded in mystery that many members of the Navy Department, to say nothing of top-ranking officers in the War Department, thought of it as a kind of secret weapon, and assumed that Pearl

[60] *Ibid.*, Part 10, p. 4836.
[61] *Ibid.*

Harbor was intercepting and decoding all sorts of codes, including diplo-matic, and had a trained staff of 400 men.[62]

Rochefort gave out daily information, both oral and written, to Com-mander Layton for Admiral Kimmel, to Admiral Bloch, and very occasionally to Admiral Kimmel directly. He gave no information to the third Naval Intelligence officer, Captain Mayfield. Rochefort testified that he did have contact "perhaps twice a week" with the head of the Hawaiian G-2, Colonel Fielder.[63] Rochefort did not say what he gave Fielder, but asserted that it had not included anything that he regarded as "ultra." As Rochefort testified, Fielder "was not on the list of personnel that I had, which indicated those that were entitled to receive ultra." The following exchange ensued:

Q.—Well, who made that list?
A.—That list was maintained in our office and was made up initially by the officer in charge and was passed on to succeeding officers in charge.
Q.—Who was the officer in charge?
A.—I was from June 1941 on, sir.
Q.—Then while you held this position it was solely within your province to determine who in the Army should or should not receive this secret information?
A.—Yes sir; unless I received contrary orders from either Washington or from Admiral Kimmel.[64]

It was only in the final congressional investigation that this questioning made clear that it was Rochefort's own decision to deny important in-formation to Fielder, or to withhold the source so that Fielder had no means of evaluating the information. There is evidence, however, that a Washington directive, not produced at the hearings, specifically had ordered him to limit the distribution to a few naval officers.[65] Rochefort had no contact with any other Army officer; and according to Fielder's testimony—in flat contradiction to Rochefort's—Rochefort had no contact even with Fielder.

Commander Layton was Admiral Kimmel's Fleet Intelligence officer. He reported directly to Kimmel, to his Chief of Staff, his Chief of War Plans, and his Operations officer. He also made up written bulletins for distribution to Fleet High Commands and the Chief of Naval Operations

[62] See Chap. 3 for details.
[64] *Ibid.*, p. 4703.
[63] *Hearings*, Part 10, p. 4675.
[65] Interview with Layton, July 11, 1956.

in Washington. His sources were the FBI (local and in Washington), the ONI, the other two Naval Intelligence officers, British intelligence sources in the Far East, American naval attachés and observers, consuls and State Department representatives in the Far East, and unnamed sources that he had found to be "completely reliable" or "generally fairly reliable."

Layton could remember no occasion when he had been called in to present the intelligence picture to Short and Kimmel alone. He could remember several occasions when Short had been present at conferences where he had briefed Admiral Kimmel and the task force commanders who had just returned to Pearl Harbor. He had never had any contact with Colonel Fielder, Short's head of G-2. Once in October or November, 1941, he had talked with Colonel Bicknell, who was Fielder's assistant.[66] He had had some contact with Colonel Raley, who was the Intelligence officer for General Martin of the Air Corps. He had imparted to Raley certain selected, carefully paraphrased, top-secret material, without disclosing his sources. He had "presumed . . . he [Raley] was then representing the Army."[67] It was on Raley's initiative that contact had been established and according to Layton this happened only three months before the attack. Layton also thought that during October he had seen Raley twice a week and that for the ten-day period prior to Pearl Harbor he had seen Raley every other day.

In 1945 Raley remembered his relations with Layton in this way:

> On 7 Dec. 1941 and for about one year preceding I was G-2, Hawaiian Air Force. Shortly after assuming these duties, I established . . . some form of contact with the Navy, through then Comdr. Layton, USN. I told Comdr. Layton that my contact was for the Hawaiian Air Force. During this period of about one year I had not more than six conversations with Comdr. Layton concerning the subject of my contact. These conversations were spread out during this period. As nearly as I can recall the last conversation I had with Comdr. Layton before 7 Dec. 1941, was about October 1941.
>
> The information given me by Comdr. Layton was my only Navy source. He stated that if there was any Navy movement by Japan, coming to his knowledge, and which might imperil the Hawaiian Islands, he would inform

[66] Many years later Layton informed the author that he had met with Bicknell "much more than once." (Interview, July 11, 1956.)

[67] Affidavit for Col. Henry C. Clausen, April 25, 1945, in *Hearings*, Part 35, p. 51.

me. The only specific information he gave me in this regard were studies he made of a possible Japanese Malay hostility and of Japanese fleet installations in the Mandates. I believe this was at least two months before 7 Dec. 1941.[68]

Layton does not mention ever receiving or requesting any information from Army sources, nor does he even imply that it might have been valuable (with the possible exception of fuller information on enemy troop movements). He obviously, and correctly, regarded his own sources as superior. His responsibility ended with his reports to Kimmel, the Fleet High Commands, and Washington. He assumed that Kimmel was forwarding all important naval information to Short as well as to his various task officers, and that the third Naval Intelligence officer, Captain Mayfield, was doing the same at a lower level through liaison with the Army G-2.[69]

Captain Mayfield was the 14th District Intelligence officer, responsible to Admiral Bloch, Commandant of the 14th Naval District, and to the Director of ONI for all intelligence matters, including countersabotage and counterespionage ashore in the 14th District. His sources were Robert Shivers of the local FBI, Colonel Bicknell of Army G-2, RCA files on messages going to and from the Japanese consulate after December 1, 1941 (sent over to Rochefort for decoding and translating), and inter-

[68] Affidavit for Col. Henry C. Clausen, March 11, 1945, *ibid.*, p. 38*f*. These affidavits taken by Clausen are notoriously unreliable, and the impression one receives from Layton's testimony is that contact between Raley and Layton was actually more frequent than Raley states.

[69] In answer to the question, "Who was your opposite number in the Army in Pearl Harbor?" Layton replied in part: "My liaison [with the Army] ... was ... through Capt. Mayfield. ... There were meetings between the Army and FBI and himself every week or more. I attended one of them shortly after I reported just to let them know I was there, and to say that I was willing to cooperate in all matters. But for anyone to imply that I had to search out and find an opposite number, or that the G-2 of the Hawaiian Department should be dependent upon me for sources of information, is rather unusual, for the simple reason the Army and Navy in Washington have close agreement, and have worked in close liaison for years in intelligence, that the Navy passed it down and disclosed it to the Army and the Army disclosed it to the Navy, and in case there was an occasion in which we wanted to consult one another in the field, we consulted then with each other in the field." And again, "if Fielder for one minute was not satisfied with what he was getting from Washington— and I did not know that he was getting anything or nothing—then, he could certainly establish liaison with me." (*Hearings*, Part 10, p. 4865.) Since Layton was frequently at sea, under radio silence, regular liaison with Fielder would have been somewhat impractical.

Unfortunately most members of the ONI and Washington G-2 carried in their heads the same complacent view of Army-Navy liaison in the theaters as Layton did of the liaison in Washington.

ceptions from tapping the telephone wires to the Japanese consulate for twenty-two months prior to December 2, 1941, when the practice stopped. He had conversations with Admiral Bloch and Commander Layton on counterespionage matters; he never discussed the probability of war except in this context and only with these two officers; and he did not remember receiving any information from them. He received no information from Rochefort. His exclusive Army contact was Colonel Bicknell.

Army Intelligence

Colonel Fielder, as head of G-2 for the Hawaiian Department, held weekly meetings with Short's Chief of Staff, Col. Walter C. Phillips, and with the other department heads. This was a routine matter, and his "part of it consisted of bringing the staff officers up to date on world conditions."[70] About once a month he submitted written reports "of the local situation which covered economy and communism, racial disorders and things like that."[71] At no time prior to December 7 did he submit a written strategic estimate, though he did so every week thereafter. He did not remember receiving from Washington any information on the international situation, but testified that "the only source of information we had [as to possible Japanese naval or military activity] was through the Navy,"[72] though he went on to say that he did have access to War Department and Navy Department information. His other sources were interviews with prominent travelers returning from the Orient, and the local FBI. He specifically excluded newspapers as a source. On liaison with Navy Intelligence locally, he testified that it was "very close insofar as counterintelligence was concerned. The investigations and the suspect list [of local Japanese] were discussed regularly every week. But insofar as combat intelligence [Rochefort] and my associations and relationships with the fleet-intelligence officer [Layton], they were not very close because we had practically nothing in common. There was no combat at that time."[73]

---

[70] *Ibid.*, Part 28, p. 1555.
[71] *Ibid.*, p. 1551.
[72] *Ibid.*, p. 1544.
[73] *Ibid.*, p. 1561. According to Fielder, "from the Army viewpoint there is no combat intelligence unless there is combat." (Fielder's statement to Clausen, May 11, 1945, *ibid.*, Part 35, p. 88.)

In an affidavit to Colonel Clausen, Fielder stated that he had never at any time received any information from Rochefort or Layton, and his other testimony is consistent with this statement. He evidently could have had access to whatever information Layton was willing to impart to Raley by way of General Martin, but he did not hear of this liaison before December 7. There is furthermore no evidence to indicate that Fielder would have liked to know more than he did; he never requested more information of any sort from Washington or from the Navy locally. Evidently both he and Layton were satisfied that Army-Navy liaison was provided at the Bicknell-Mayfield level and at the Short-Kimmel level, and that anything further was none of their business, since inadequacies would doubtless be resolved in the central liaison of Army and Navy Intelligence in Washington.

Colonel Bicknell became assistant G-2 in October, 1940. He testified at the hearings that he had had "immediate liaison with the FBI, the District Intelligence officer of the Navy [Captain Mayfield], the FCC, and all Territorial and Federal Departments such as customs, immigration and Treasury." His principal sources were businessmen returning from the Orient, interviews with British officials and the military representatives of other nations who came through Hawaii, intercepts of all Japanese plain-language radio broadcasts, Japanese-language newspapers available locally, and some newspapers from the Orient. Beginning in September, 1941, he wrote up fortnightly international estimates for dissemination through all branches of the Hawaiian Department and also presented his views orally at the weekly staff meetings. In his first estimate he predicted war with Japan by the end of November, or barring that, in April. Short never questioned him on any of his intelligence estimates, and Bicknell subsequently stated that "it was rather uncommon not to have questions asked . . . by the department commander."[74] However, it was very unusual for Short even to be present at the staff conferences. Bicknell did know of the Raley-Layton liaison and got all of Layton's information from Raley.[75]

Colonel Raley unfortunately was not examined by anybody except Colonel Clausen, who obtained the affidavit already quoted. Raley had reported directly to General Martin. He mentioned one joint meeting with

[74] *Hearings*, Part 10, p. 5119.
[75] *Ibid.*, p. 5112.

Bicknell and Layton in October, 1941, but did not mention Fielder or Short.

What records exist substantiate the view that the major work of the Hawaiian G-2 concerned sabotage and subversion and was dictated primarily by Army G-2 tradition and incidentally by the presence of a large local Japanese population. All three Army Intelligence officers were relying on local Navy sources and on Washington for international information indicating danger of a surprise attack or an outbreak of war.

The general picture is one of close communication between Layton, Rochefort, and Kimmel, between Bloch and Mayfield, and between Mayfield and Bicknell. Since Mayfield dealt only with counterespionage, any information on the international picture would have had to go from Kimmel to his naval officers and to Short. Kimmel, however, assumed liaison between Bloch and Short; while Bloch, like Layton, assumed liaison between Short and Kimmel. Actually the line of communication to Short was primarily through Bicknell, since nobody talked to Fielder. According to Fielder, Raley was "honor-bound" to report only to Martin what Layton revealed to him, and what Martin revealed to Fielder or Short is nowhere stated. In any case, communication between Layton and Raley was evidently infrequent and limited in content.

We see then that Army-Navy liaison in the matter of communicating essential international information was extremely tenuous. There was no basis whatsoever for Short or his G-2 to assume that the Navy would give them information of this character, which they needed and expected. In the matter of counterespionage ashore and in the fleet, liaison was fairly close. But no matter how much Mayfield and Bicknell may have talked, little illumination of the international scene or of such subjects as the probability of attack would have resulted, because even Mayfield was denied the major sources of Navy Intelligence.

It is interesting to observe that of these six officers only Layton has left any recorded complaint about receiving inadequate information or being inadequately staffed.[76] Even in Rochefort's unit, evidently no shortage was felt of trained cryptanalysts and linguists for the job assigned. The major obstacles to efficient work were the American laws that forbade censor-

[76] Honolulu G-2 did not even spend all of the money allotted to it ($15,000) for 1940–41 for extra clerks and for buying information.

ship or wiretapping or supervision of Japanese communications to the homeland, or locally within Hawaii. The Navy and the FBI had thrown such legal scruples to the winds, but G-2 kept to the letter of the law.

Layton's complaint is interesting. It was directed at a point of policy on circulation of intelligence information to the theaters, which we shall deal with later in discussing the intelligence organization in Washington. Layton had received information in February and July, 1941, based on the Japanese PURPLE[77] diplomatic code system, which had told him what the Japanese were going to demand of Vichy and what they were going to do if Vichy did not accede. He had also written earlier to Comdr. A. H. McCollum, head of ONI's Far Eastern Division, to urge him to continue sending him information based on decoded diplomatic traffic. Commander McCollum's reply sets down succinctly the Washington point of view:

> I thoroughly appreciate that you would probably be much helped in your daily estimates if you had at your disposal the DIP [diplomatic intelligence].
> This, however, brings up matters of security, et cetera, which would be very difficult to solve. While I appreciate your position fully in the matter, still I cannot agree that this material should be forwarded to you in the way you suggest. It seems reasonable to suppose that the Department should be the origin for evaluated political situations as its availability of information is greater than that of any command afloat, however large, its staff is larger and it should be able to evaluate the political consequences. Therefore it would seem that the forces afloat must rely on the Department for evaluated views of political situations.
> I should think that the forces afloat should, in general, confine themselves to the estimates of the strategic and tactical situations with which they will be confronted when the time of action arrives. The material you mentioned can necessarily have but passing and transient interest as action in the political sphere is determined by the Government as a whole and not by the forces afloat.
> It does not seem to me to be very practical to build up an organization afloat which will merely duplicate the efforts of the Intelligence Division in the Department. I appreciate that all this leaves you in rather a spot as naturally people are interested in current developments. I believe, however, that a sharp line should be drawn and a distinction continuously emphasized between information that is of interest and information that is desirable to have on which to base action.

[77] PURPLE was the name used to designate the top-priority Japanese diplomatic cipher. It is usually referred to in the *Hearings* as the "PURPLE code," and that is the terminology adopted in this study.

In other words, while you and the Fleet may be highly interested in politics, there is nothing you can do about it. Therefore, information of political
significance, except as it affects immediate action by the Fleet, is merely of
interest to you and not a matter of utility.[78]

McCollum's position here is thoughtful, but perhaps not entirely consistent. He suggests first that the diplomatic traffic might be useful in
making daily estimates, but that the security risk in sending it would
exceed the possible gain. His second argument is that Layton's evaluation
would merely duplicate the work of Washington, and is therefore unnecessary. Finally he says that MAGIC might be interesting to Layton, but
not useful, because it is relevant only to action in the political sphere,
which belongs to the government as a whole. The first argument is difficult to dismiss: there is a real dilemma here. But the last argument neglects
the fact that knowledge of political acts can be a basis for seeking and
observing local signals and for correctly interpreting them. One might
question whether MAGIC's possible usefulness to Layton would exceed its
cost, but the usefulness is hardly in doubt.

For the immediate purpose of this study it is significant that McCollum,
while rejecting Layton's request, expressed some ambiguity as to the basis
for limiting information. His letter, despite its successive approximations
to a decisive negative, led Layton to believe that he would receive any
essential action information based on PURPLE. After the event, he said he
was "outraged" at being shortchanged.

LATE SIGNALS

Now that we have in mind a picture of the local intelligence structure,
we can ask, How did these six officers and their staff handle the signals
that were arriving during the critical weeks prior to December 7? Who
received what information and forwarded it to whom? Was there anybody
in Hawaii who got all the signals?

Navy Intelligence

On November 1, 1941, Rochefort's unit reported to Layton in its daily
written summary that the Japanese had changed their call signs. On De-

[78] Letter from McCollum to Layton, April 22, 1941, in *Hearings*, Part 10, p. 4845*f*.

cember 1, they changed them again. The communication intelligence summary from Rochefort's office for December 1, 1941, read:

All service calls of forces afloat changed promptly at 0000, 1 December. Previously, service calls changed after a period of six months or more. Calls were last changed on 1 November 1941. The fact that service calls lasted only one month indicates an additional progressive step in preparing for active operations on a large scale.[79]

The closeness of these two changes constituted a warning in itself. According to Rochefort, such a rapid change had never happened before in his experience. Furthermore, these changes had made identification very difficult.[80] By the end of November, however, some progress had been made and, on November 25 and again on November 30, Rochefort's unit had reported a concentration of submarines and at least one carrier division in the Marshalls. The 16th District unit had agreed about the submarines and disagreed about the carriers (correctly, as it later appeared, for there was no carrier division in the Mandates). Because its radio stations reported no contact, this unit believed that all known carriers of the First and Second Japanese Fleets were in home waters in the Kure-Sasebo area.[81] Around the middle of November, Washington had decided that the 16th District unit had more reliable information than Com 14, and therefore relied on the Com 16 report.[82] After the second change in Japanese call signs, Rochefort's unit reported on December 2: "Almost a complete blank of information on the Carriers today."[83] On December 3

[79] *Hearings*, Part 17, p. 2636.

[80] Layton, in referring to the new difficulties in identification on December 2, testified that "this was only the second day of a change of call signs, which will run somewhere around 20,000 calls. You never could do it [identify them] if you had all the men in the world, because there isn't any way of doing it. It is only after many days of traffic that you can lay the traffic down and identify it. Even in those days, you see, commanders had several call signs, but the ships had only one." (*Ibid.*, Part 36, p. 134.)

[81] These carriers, *Akagi* and *Kaga* (Cardiv 1), *Hiryu* and *Soryu* (Cardiv 2), and *Shokaku* and *Zuikaku* (Cardiv 5), constituted the most important element of the Pearl Harbor task force.

[82] Dispatch of November 24, in *Hearings*, Part 14, p. 1405*f*. Com 16 was considered more reliable because of its better radio reception and because it was reading the Japanese naval code JN 25 and exchanging information and translations with the British C.I. unit in Singapore, according to Capt. Laurence F. Safford. (*Hearings*, Part 18, p. 3335.) This ability to read JN 25 was denied in the testimony of the officer in charge of radio traffic analysis at Cavite. There is no evidence in the records to indicate which of these statements is correct, but it seems likely that the officer in charge would be in a better position to know.

[83] *Ibid.*, Part 17, p. 2638.

it reported: "No information on submarines or Carriers."[84] From that date until December 7, there was no noticeable change in traffic volume, and no carrier traffic was intercepted.[85]

Admiral Kimmel had been disturbed by the loss of radio contact with the carriers (they had been lost since November 16), and on December 1 he had asked his Fleet Intelligence officer to make out a location sheet on the Japanese Navy and to check with Cavite (Com 16). Cavite's response had reassured him, although when he reviewed the location sheet on December 2, he remarked jokingly to Layton: "What, you don't know where the carriers are? Do you mean to say they could be rounding Diamond Head and you wouldn't know it?" Layton replied that he hoped they would be sighted before that.

This atmosphere of geniality and security is understandable. There had been many times in the course of 1941 and earlier when not only carriers but battleships, cruisers, and other warships were not located by radio intelligence traffic. Layton explained:

> This is because when carriers or other types of vessels go into home waters, home ports, home exercise areas, they use low power radio direct with shore stations. This is then handled normally on telegraphic land lines to prevent our direction finder stations and intercept stations from hearing their traffic. During such periods as that we have always carried those units as "home waters."[86]

This had been the policy, and in the past it had always been justified by events. As Layton reasoned:

> Had these carriers or carrier-division commanders or the carrier commander-in-chief been addressed in any messages of the thousands and thousands that came out from the Naval General Staff, regardless of the silence of carriers, then the thought of radio silence would have been paramount, but the fact they were never addressed, not even once, led to the belief that they were in the same situation as the carrier divisions were in July 1941 when the Japanese had a task force go down with their ultimatum into French Indochina.[87]

[84] *Ibid.*, p. 2639.

[85] This is an extremely simplified account of the radio intelligence traffic for December 1–7. For a full analysis, see the reprint of Layton's testimony at the Hewitt inquiry, *ibid.*, Part 36, pp. 116–141.

[86] *Hearings*, Part 10, p. 4838.

[87] For more details on the Indochina crisis, see Chap. 2.

At that time the carriers remained in home waters . . . in case we took counter-action.[88]

In making his deductions in July, 1941, Layton had had the benefit of a series of decoded messages sent by the Japanese in their top-priority diplomatic code, PURPLE. The information contained in PURPLE (and in the other Japanese codes that we collectively termed "MAGIC") was extremely detailed and accurate, and it confirmed his hypotheses about the location of the carriers. In December, 1941, Layton had only two items of information based on PURPLE (contained in three messages from the CNO). He had "reports from shore observers in China, assistant naval attachés, merchant skippers, consular authorities, that they had seen these ships loading and going out, that they had been sighted going south, the merchant marine ships stating that they were going south in a convoy, and the entire movement was noted as going south."[89] Layton had in addition a message received on the morning of December 6 from the Commander-in-Chief, Asiatic Fleet, giving the sightings of Japanese naval and auxiliary units in the Gulf of Siam and Camranh Bay by his reconnaissance forces. These sightings were also confirmed by one British report and a report from an assistant naval attaché in Shanghai. When Layton delivered this message personally to Vice Adm. W. S. Pye on his flagship, the *California*, on the same morning that he had received it, he remarked that the movement into the Gulf of Siam was "very significant and that the only problem remaining was whether or not they would leave us on their flank as a menace or take us out on the way down."[90] And by "us" he meant the Philippines and Guam, not Pearl Harbor. As Layton summed it up:

> I did not at any time suggest that the Japanese carriers were under radio silence approaching Oahu. I wish I had. . . . My own personal opinion, and

[88] *Hearings*, Part 10, p. 4839. Later, more emphatically, Layton stated: "The fact that ships could go under radio silence was well known but never in the history of the Japanese naval communications that I had observed over a period of years had such a phenomenon [a complete absence of messages either from or to the ships] occurred." (*Ibid.*, p. 4904.) Layton believed that contrary to the testimony of the Japanese, the ships that attacked Pearl Harbor were never addressed after November 16, and that the code signal for attack, "Climb Mount Niitaka," had never been sent. (*Ibid.*, p. 4906.)

[89] *Ibid.*, p. 4835. (See Exhibit No. 27, *ibid.*, Part 37, pp. 789*ff.* The reports reprinted in this exhibit are only a small selection from the file.)

[90] *Hearings*, Part 10, p. 4859.

that is what we work on, when making estimates to ourselves, was that the carriers were remaining in home waters preparing for operations so that they would be in a covering position in case we moved against Japan after she attacked, if she did, in southeast Asia.[91]

This opinion of Layton's was in agreement with Rochefort's summary statement for the month of November that a "strong force may be preparing to operate in Southeastern Asia while component parts may operate from Palao and the Marshalls."[92]

What signals did Layton receive up to December 7 that further confirmed this estimate? He was probably better informed than any other Intelligence officer at Pearl Harbor. As he testified, he had "all of the available information that came to Pearl Harbor."[93]

First of all, there were two warning dispatches directed to the Commander-in-Chief, Pacific Fleet, one of November 24 and the so-called war warning of November 27. They read as follows:

Nov. 24, 1941

FROM: Chief of Naval Operations

ACTION: CinCAF, CinCPAC, Com 11, Com 12, Com 13, Com 15

INFO: Spenavo London Cinclant

242005[94]

Chances of favorable outcome of negotiations with Japan very doubtful. This situation coupled with statements of Japanese Government and movements their naval and military forces indicate in our opinion that a surprise aggressive movement in any direction including attack on Philippines or Guam is a possibility. Chief of Staff has seen this dispatch concurs and requests action adees [addressees] to inform senior Army officers their areas. Utmost secrecy necessary in order not to complicate an already tense situation or precipitate Japanese action. Guam will be informed separately.

Copy to WPD, War Dept. and Op-12 but no other distribution.[95]

---

[91] *Ibid.*, p. 4840.

[92] *Ibid.*, Part 6, p. 2815.

[93] *Ibid.*, Part 10, p. 4859.

[94] These digits give the date and naval time of sending from the Naval Communications Office in Washington. The digits 242005 mean November 24, 20:05, which is 8:05 P.M. Washington time.

[95] *Hearings*, Part 14, p. 1405.

Nov. 27, 1941
FROM: Chief of Naval Operations
ACTION: CinCAF, CinCPAC
INFO: Cinclant, Spenavo
272337

This dispatch is to be considered a war warning. Negotiations with Japan looking toward stabilization of conditions in the Pacific have ceased and an aggressive move by Japan is expected within the next few days. The number and equipment of Japanese troops and the organization of naval task forces indicates an amphibious expedition against either the Philippines, Thai or Kra Peninsula or possibly Borneo. Execute an appropriate defensive deployment preparatory to carrying out the tasks assigned in WPL 46. Inform district and Army authorities. A similar warning is being sent by War Department.

Spenavo inform British. Continental districts Guam, Samoa directed take appropriate measures against sabotage.

Copy to WPD, War Dept.[96]

Layton's reaction to the November 24 message was that

they have the same information we have; they note this southern movement as we do, and they have found in their judgment that the Japanese may not leave us on their flank either. . . . It was my personal impression, and I so stated, that Japan had never yet, with the exception of Russia, left a strong enemy on a flank. . . . My estimate was there were two task forces under CinC Second Fleet, one proceeding down South from the Formosa-Hainan-Bako area into the South China Sea, and aiming at the Kra Isthmus or its vicinity, the Gulf of Siam. The other task force was proceeding via Palao in the Western Carolines with the intention perhaps of threatening Timor, Celebes, or other Dutch holdings in that general zone. . . . should they leave us on their flank, our position in the Philippines would be a threat to their line of communications should we decide to take action in assistance to Great Britain or French Indochina or the Thai operations, as the case might be.[97]

Layton's reaction to the November 27 message was that

it certainly fitted the picture up to date, and that we would be at war shortly if Japan would decide not to leave her Philippine flank open and proceed southward, hoping meanwhile to mollify us through a compromise deal with

[96] *Ibid.*, p. 1406. WPL 46 provided that the Pacific Fleet move against the Marshalls on outbreak of war in the Far East.
[97] *Ibid.*, Part 36, p. 144*f*.

Kurusu-Nomura negotiations. It made me feel that the picture we had was a good picture, and perhaps complete, and that the times were critical and perhaps the Department hoped for a last minute compromise in view of their statement that nothing should be done to aggravate an already serious situation.[98]

He recalled the fact that there had been comment on the omission of Guam in the second message and someone had remarked facetiously: "I guess they thought Guam was going to fall, anyway, so it would not be worthwhile to put it in."[99]

Again and again there is this reaction, that certainly the outbreak of war with Japan was to be expected at any moment after November 27, but not to be expected at Pearl Harbor. The other signals received by Layton all added up to this, and his estimate still seems to be a reasonable one in the light of the information available to him.

Another dispatch confirming the November 27 warning went out on November 28 and gave the full text of the Army warning. Much has been written about the "do-don't" character of the Army dispatch, about its cautions not to alarm the civil population, its insistence on making sure that Japan should commit the first overt act, etc. In this second naval warning the Navy also emphasized letting Japan commit the first act, but Layton does not lay claim to any bewilderment or doubt engendered by it. The November 28 dispatch read as follows:

FROM: Chief of Naval Operations

ACTION: Com Pnncf, Com Psncf

INFO: Cincpac Com Pncf

Refer to my 272338 [the naval sabotage warning].[100] Army has sent following to commander western defense command.

Negotiations with Japan appear to be terminated to all practical purposes with only the barest possibilities that the Japanese Government might come back and offer to continue. Japanese future action unpredictable but hostile action possible at any moment. If hostilities cannot repeat not be avoided the United States desires that Japan commit the first overt act. This policy should not repeat not be construed as restricting you to a course of action that might jeopardize your defense. Prior to hostile Japanese action you are directed to

[98] *Ibid.*, Part 10, p. 4860.

[99] *Ibid.*, p. 4867.

[100] *Ibid.*, Part 14, p. 1406. This was not sent to Kimmel's Command, but to continental districts, Guam, and Samoa.

undertake such reconnaissance and other measures as you deem necessary but these measures should be carried out so as not repeat not to alarm civil population or disclose intent. Report measures taken. A separate message is being sent to G-2, Ninth Corps Area re subversive activities in the United States. Should hostilities occur you will carry out the tasks assigned in Rainbow five so far as they pertain to Japan. Limit dissemination of this highly secret information to minimum essential officers. Unquote. WPL 52[101] is not applicable to Pacific area and will not be placed in effect in that area except as now in force in southeast Pacific sub area and Panama naval coastal frontier. Undertake no offensive action until Japan has committed an overt act. Be prepared to carry out tasks assigned in WPL 46,[102] so far as they apply to Japan in case hostilities occur.[103]

On the evening of November 27 Layton saw the Army "take their condition of readiness, trucks moving, troops moving, and I thought I saw weapons moving into the street and I presumed that they were going into full condition of readiness, including the emplacement of anti-aircraft and other mobile weapons around Pearl Harbor and other important points on Oahu."[104] Layton was not alone in this assumption. The Navy had three conditions of alert, No. 1 being a full alert condition, No. 2 and No. 3 tapering off toward routine conditions. The Navy always went into a full alert and tapered off. The Army's alert system worked in reverse. It started low with an alert No. 1, which covered sabotage; No. 2 was designed for an air attack; and No. 3 was a full alert.[105] The fact that Army and Navy alert practices in this respect had nothing in common was just one more detail in the picture of respectful and cordial, but empty, communication between the two services.

What Layton observed that evening was the setting in motion of General Short's No. 1 sabotage alert. Admiral Bloch was fully satisfied when he heard the Army was on Alert No. 1, since he made the same false assumption. In fact there is no testimony from any Navy officer to

[101] WPL 52 was Navy Western Hemisphere Defense Plan No. 5, under which the Atlantic Fleet had shooting orders for destroying German and Italian naval, land, and air forces encountered in the Western Atlantic.

[102] WPL 46 provided that the Pacific Fleet move against the Marshalls on outbreak of war in the Far East.

[103] *Hearings*, Part 14, p. 1407.

[104] *Ibid.*, Part 10, p. 4860.

[105] See the Appendix for General Short's alert procedures.

indicate that any other assumption was entertained.[106] Why the Navy should have universally assumed that the Army had gone on full alert, when they themselves had not, naturally aroused the curiosity of some inquiring congressmen. Under their questioning, it became clear that the ships in harbor were operating under the limited alert conditions that had always been observed while in harbor during 1941.

It may be convenient at this point to summarize the signals so far described in the order of their occurrence:

NOVEMBER 1—Change of Japanese call signs.

ENTIRE MONTH OF NOVEMBER: Reports by observers of ships going south.

NOVEMBER 16—United States loses track of Japanese carriers.

NOVEMBER 24—First Navy dispatch on "Surprise aggressive movement in any direction."

NOVEMBER 25—Com 14 reports one carrier division in Marshalls; Com 16 disagrees.

NOVEMBER 27—Naval war warning. (Received November 28.)

NOVEMBER 28—Naval transmission of Army war warning. (Received November 29.)

NOVEMBER 30—Com 14 reaffirms one carrier division in Marshalls.

DECEMBER 1—Change of Japanese call signs, combined with other indications of radio secrecy. Evaluated as extremely unusual after the November 1 change, and indicative of war preparations.

DECEMBER 6—Message from Commander-in-Chief, Asiatic Fleet, on sightings of Japanese ships in Camranh Bay.

Layton had received other signals in addition to these, some confirming the likelihood of war within a matter of days, and others pointing to Southeast Asia as the place of outbreak. There were the three messages based on MAGIC. The first of these, received on December 1, outlined a Japanese plan to entice the British to invade Thailand and thereby permit Japan to enter that country in the role of defender. It was based on an

106 See *Hearings*, Part 6, p. 2853*f.* for Kimmel's testimony on this.

intercepted radio message of November 29 from the Japanese ambassador in Bangkok to Tokyo.[107] This message reinforced the numerous reports of movements to the south ("South of French Indochina, South of Formosa, South of Hainan"[108]) and the predictions from observers of an attack on the Kra Isthmus. For an attack on Kra "the Thai airfield at Singora on the very southern tip of Thailand and only a few miles from the border [of Malaya], being a good beach area, presented an ideal point for amphibious landings."[109] Layton went over this point with Admiral Kimmel in his morning conference of December 6.

The other two messages derived from MAGIC and sent on December 3 gave notice that most Japanese diplomatic codes had been destroyed. The second message was sent out five minutes after the first. These messages were quoted many times in the course of the congressional investigation, since many officers in Washington regarded them after the event as the most significant tip-off to the American theater commanders, and an unambiguous signal for a full alert.

3 Dec. 1941

FROM: Opnav

ACTION: Cincaf, Cincpac, Com 14, Com 16

INFO:

Ø3185Ø

Highly reliable information has been received that categoric and urgent instructions were sent yesterday to Japanese diplomatic and consular posts at Hongkong, Singapore, Batavia, Manila, Washington, and London to destroy most of their codes and ciphers at once and to burn all other important confidential and secret documents.

3 Dec. 1941

FROM: Opnav

ACTION: Cincaf, Com 16

INFO: Cincpac, Com 14

Ø31855

Circular twenty four forty four from Tokyo one December ordered London, Hongkong, Singapore and Manila to destroy Purple machine.

---

[107] Dispatch No. 011400, Opnav to Cincaf, info Cincpac, December 1, 1941, *ibid.*, p. 2540. See *Hearings*, Part 12, p. 203, for the original intercept.

[108] *Ibid.*, Part 10, p. 4882.

[109] *Ibid.*

Batavia machine already sent to Tokyo. December second Washington also
directed destroy Purple. All but one copy of other systems. And all secret
documents. British Admiralty London today reports embassy London had
complied.[110]

These two messages were followed by a copy of an order to Guam
from Opnav on December 4, for the information of Cincpac and Com 14,
directing Guam to destroy all secret and confidential publications and
retain only minimum cryptographic channels for essential communications.
On December 6 Layton received the following message for Kimmel:

FROM: Opnav

ACTION: Cincpac

INFO: Cincaf

Ø61743

In view of the international situation and the exposed position of our outlying Pacific islands you may authorize the destruction by them of secret and
confidential documents now or under later conditions of greater emergency.
Means of communication to support our current operations and special intelligence should of course be maintained until the last moment.[111]

Layton also knew that the Navy had directed the naval attaché in Tokyo
and other U.S. naval establishments in China, such as the one at Tientsin,
to destroy their cryptographic material. On December 5 he received their
plain-language message, "Boomerang," which was the code word indicating that all codes and papers had been destroyed.

In addition to the code-destruction orders emanating from Washington
and the Far East, Layton also had on December 6 the information that
the local Japanese consulate had been burning papers for the past two
days. Rochefort initiated a message to Washington over Bloch's signature
to this effect: "Believe local consul has destroyed all but one system
although presumably not included your eighteen double five of third [the
earlier notice of code burning]."[112] Layton did not see this message but

110 *Ibid.*, Part 14, p. 1407*f*.

111 *Ibid.*, p. 1408. It is not clear whether Kimmel saw this message before or after the
attack. There are no records as to when it was received. (*Ibid.*, Part 9, p. 4288.) It was sent
by deferred status, and Kimmel thought he might have seen it but considered it unimportant
because it was sent deferred. (*Ibid.*, Part 6, p. 2829; cf. *ibid.*, Part 11, p. 5498.) The order
for messages was urgent, priority, routine, and deferred.

112 *Ibid.*, Part 14, p. 1409.

was "informed of its purport" by Rochefort, who had received notice from Mayfield, who had it from the local FBI.

Layton had also been informed by Rochefort of a November 28 directive to his unit from Naval Communications in Washington to monitor all Japanese shortwave broadcasts 24 hours a day for the so-called winds-execute message. On November 19 Tokyo had sent two messages to Washington in their J-19 code. J-19 messages were always set aside for translation after PURPLE; so these two were not processed by the Navy until November 26 and November 28. Com 16 also intercepted the same sort of message on the Tokyo-Singapore circuit, and two additional confirmations came in from officers in the Netherlands East Indies and Java. These five messages form the evidence for the winds-code setup. The Tokyo-Washington messages read as follows:

Circular #2353

> Regarding the broadcast of a special message in an emergency.
>
> In case of emergency (danger of cutting off our diplomatic relations), and the cutting off of international communications, the following warning will be added in the middle of the daily Japanese language short wave news broadcast.
>
> (1) In case of a Japan-U. S. relations in danger: HIGASHI NO KASEAME [east wind rain].
>
> (2) Japan-U. S. S. R. relations: KITANOKAZE KUMORI [north wind cloudy].
>
> (3) Japan-British relations: NISHI NO KAZE HARE [west wind clear].
>
> This signal will be given in the middle and at the end as a weather forecast and each sentence will be repeated twice. When this is heard please destroy all code papers, etc. This is as yet to be a completely secret arrangement.
>
> Forward as urgent intelligence [Translated November 28].[113]

Circular #2354

> When our diplomatic relations are becoming dangerous, we will add the following at the beginning and end of our general intelligence broadcasts:
>
> (1) If it is Japan-U. S. relations, "HIGASHI."
>
> (2) Japan-Russia relations, "KITA."
>
> (3) Japan-British relations, (including Thai, Malaya and N. E. I.), "NISHI."
>
> The above will be repeated five times and included at beginning and end.

[113] *Ibid.*, Part 12, p. 154.

Relay to Rio de Janeiro, Buenos Aires, Mexico City, San Francisco [Translated November 26].[114]

Rochefort testified consistently that his unit had never intercepted an execute of the winds code. He said further that he had never heard of any message from Washington G-2 instructing Hawaiian G-2 to contact him about weather broadcasts. And he had received no information from Washington of receipt of a winds-code execute.

Whatever the truth may be about the receipt in Washington or elsewhere of a winds-code execute before December 7, it is not relevant to the point we want to make here. The winds-code setup we do have in evidence, and as a warning signal it was comparable to the other notices of code destruction and preparation for code destruction.

Layton and Kimmel discussed "very briefly" the two messages of this sort based on MAGIC. Neither Layton nor Kimmel knew what the word PURPLE referred to, and on inquiring of Lt. Comdr. Herbert M. Coleman, fleet security officer for Kimmel, they learned that it was "an electric diplomatic coding machine" of the Japanese. Layton recalled that during their conversation "stress was laid on the fact that the word [used in the dispatch from CNO] was 'most,' meaning most of their codes and ciphers"; and Kimmel in his testimony before the congressional committee made the same point, that not all of the Japanese codes were being destroyed, and therefore he "didn't consider that [message] of any vital importance when [he] . . . received it."[115] Previously Kimmel had said that "At that time it indicated to me, in conjunction with the other messages I had that Japan was taking precautionary measures preparatory to going into Thai, and because they thought that the British or the Americans, or both of them, might jump on them and seize their codes and ciphers after they went into Thailand."[116] Because this was not new or vital information, Kimmel did not pass it on to General Short. The fact that he had received an order to authorize the outlying islands to destroy their secret papers did not mean much to him either. "One of the reasons that they [Washington] authorized that was because they found my communications set-up had given them [the islands] some very secret codes and they

114 *Ibid.*, p. 155.
115 *Ibid.*, Part 6, p. 2764.
116 *Ibid.*, p. 2596.

wanted them destroyed right away because they never should have had them."[117] As for the Japanese consulate's burning of papers, Kimmel testified:

> Such reports had been made to me three or four times in the course of the year. The first time I received such a report I was considerably concerned and attempted to find out all I could about it and on succeeding reports of that nature I also attempted to find out about it.
>
> . . . .
>
> Now, whether or not they were destroying codes, I do not know. There was nothing definite that came to me that they were destroying codes. The report that came to me was that they were burning papers once more.[118]

Kimmel's reaction, then, was considerably more relaxed than Rochefort's, for Rochefort had initiated the message to Washington, quoted above, which said that codes, not just papers, were being burned at the Honolulu consulate. Layton, it is presumed, drew some of his own conclusions on the basis of these judgments by Kimmel. At least it would be fair to assume that his own anxiety and sense of urgency on receipt of some of these signals may have been tempered by Kimmel's confidence in the accuracy of the prediction of a southeastern advance. At any rate, he could not remember whether he had informed Kimmel of Rochefort's message. At the time he regarded it simply as "additional evidence of code burning."

We have to add then to our earlier list of signals in Honolulu (see page 48) the following items:

NOVEMBER 28—Order to Rochefort to monitor for winds-code execute.

DECEMBER 1—MAGIC message on Japanese intrigue in Thailand to provoke British invasion.

DECEMBER 3—Two messages based on MAGIC of code-machine and secret-paper destruction by Japanese in major embassies.

DECEMBER 4–6—Receipt of notice to Guam to destroy codes and papers. Receipt of notice of U.S. code destruction in other danger spots (Tokyo, Tientsin, Chungking, Hong Kong, Saigon, Hanoi, Bangkok).

[117] *Ibid.*, p. 2765.
[118] *Ibid.*, p. 2793.

DECEMBER 6—Order to Kimmel to authorize outlying islands to destroy codes and secret papers.

DECEMBER 6—Notice from FBI that local Japanese consul was burning papers.

In addition, there were three signals available locally that did not reach Fleet Intelligence in Hawaii. Only one of these, according to Layton, might have influenced his estimate of the probability of an attack on Pearl Harbor. This was a sighting by the U.S.S. *Wright* of an unidentified ship in Hawaiian waters on December 6, 1941.[119] The captain was under orders for radio silence and did not report this sighting. Another unreported sighting was made toward the end of November when the *Boise* identified enemy ships in American waters adjacent to Guam. Layton said this would have added nothing new to the picture of Japanese ships heading toward Palau. The third signal was an intercepted transoceanic telephone call between a Japanese dentist named Dr. Mori[120] in Honolulu and someone in a Tokyo newspaper office. The transcript of this call by the local FBI came to the attention of Captain Mayfield on December 6, and he arranged to show it to Layton the next morning.[121] The call contained a good deal about flying conditions and Japanese-U.S. relations in Hawaii, but the suspicious sections about certain varieties of flowers in bloom at that time still defy interpretation today. It is doubtful that Layton would have interpreted this call to mean an imminent attack on Oahu.

There were other signals available in Washington, which we shall discuss later. They were not passed to any Intelligence officer in the theaters, or for that matter, to anyone in the Army or Navy in Honolulu. During 1941 Kimmel was alone among military officers in Hawaii in receiving a series of estimates on the international situation based on an official source. These were contained in his private correspondence with Adm. Harold R. Stark, the Chief of Naval Operations. They came in the form of informal disclosures of Stark's own personal opinions on the course of events and were scarcely equivalent to the full set of indicators collected in Washington.

[119] *Ibid.*, Part 17, p. 2829.
[120] Or his wife, Mrs. Mori.
[121] Layton has stated that he saw only the Japanese version, since no translation had yet been made in the Navy.

The list of signals available to Layton, as we scan them today, indicates war in a matter of days, probably breaking over the week end of November 30, and when that did not happen, over the week end of December 7. The targets of attack would be in Southeast Asia, with possible diversionary attacks on Guam and the Philippines, perhaps even on the outlying islands off Hawaii. An attack on Hawaii itself would have been, to use Kimmel's phrase, "national suicide" for the Japanese. Even today on the basis of these signals, one is tempted to predict that the major Japanese effort would be (or ought to have been) directed at Great Britain, particularly in Malaya, and not at the United States. This was the view of Layton and Kimmel on December 6 and in the terms of their evidence, it was a reasonable view. What was unreasonable was the failure under such conditions to consider seriously some less reasonable or less probable, but more damaging, eventualities.

If hindsight makes us critical of the Kimmel-Layton estimate, we must remember that it was made against a background of "buzzing and blooming confusion." The brief list of signals described above has been lifted out of a murky context of questions and answers provided by seven different investigating committees and one individual investigator (Clausen). In judging the contemporary estimate, one must bear in mind the background of noise or useless information that confronted intelligence. Layton had received at the time "probably fifty messages from Chinese sources and diplomatic sources . . . consuls and assistant naval attachés, Chiang Kai-shek's representative, and so forth, saying that the Japanese are positively going to invade Russia next week."[122] Every week Rochefort's unit discarded reams of transcripts of local Japanese broadcasts; Mayfield's unit was busy verifying numerous tips about sabotage and trying to interpret local Japanese telephone calls. The amount of material that had to be weighed and discarded must always be remembered, and the discarded items (with a few exceptions) do not appear in the record.

A part of the confusion was caused by the distraction of local military activities in Hawaii. Short and Kimmel and their respective staffs had conferred once again on the morning of November 27 and several times thereafter on the pressing problem of reinforcing Wake and Midway.

[122] *Hearings*, Part 10, p. 4856.

They were tangled in a number of details as to who would supply what, and who retain command, and the business of thrashing out these responsibilities assumed an inordinate importance in addition to focusing attention on the outlying islands rather than on Hawaii. There was also the delicate task of working out with the Army a reconnaissance mission over the Japanese Mandates, for the purpose of providing some sorely needed military information and incidentally settling the dispute between the radio intelligence units of Com 14 and Com 16 as to the presence of Japanese carriers. We must remember, too, the number of warnings received during 1941, which may have added up to a feeling of "cry wolf."[123]

To discriminate significant sounds against this background of noise, one has to be listening for something or for one of several things. In short, one needs not only an ear, but a variety of hypotheses that guide observation. We have so far ignored the variety of military and political hypotheses that were entertained by top officials before Pearl Harbor. These were not always made explicit to their subordinates, including Intelligence officers. It is true that Layton had merely to recognize certain activities—such as the direction of ships and conditions of radio secrecy or the destruction of diplomatic codes—as indicators of hostile intent, and that he needed to know only one simple equation: the enemy equals Japan, and the enemy implies a "surprise aggressive movement in any direction." Reality, however, is much more complex than the set of stimuli we have set down. No matter what official Washington might say about it, any Intelligence officer interested in his job would necessarily become involved in speculations and hypotheses about Japanese and American psychology and political behavior. And here it was necessary to reckon with such delicately balanced elements as the composition of the Japanese Cabinet, the predispositions and power of the Emperor and of the Japanese military clique, the influence of the American public and the State Department on the President, etc. If Washington had really been serious about sending only action information to the theaters, then a simple alert formula was required, rather than a set of speculations about what the Japanese might or might not do.

[123] We shall discuss these warnings later in connection with the alerts initiated during 1940 and 1941.

For his policy information Layton had to rely on inferences from Kimmel's conversation and facial expressions, local newspaper and magazine accounts of political developments, and certain political rumors current in the fleet. For example, when Layton was asked if he knew what the U.S. government's policy was in case Japan made a direct attack only on the British, he replied, No, he was not on that "level of high policy." In this connection, however, he had heard Kimmel say at least four or five times: "I wish I knew what we were going to do," and he had also heard a rumor, which he passed on to Colonel Raley, that

> there was some geographic limit drawn, that only the high authorities knew it; that if the Japanese went beyond that limit, action would be taken by either the British or the Dutch or ourselves, perhaps. There was no specific paper, or conversation by anyone in authority. It was one of those corridor gossip things that you pick up, but I passed it on to Colonel Raley for what it was worth.[124]

Mr. Murphy, the Representative from Pennsylvania, reproachfully summarized the situation: "In other words, you, as the chief intelligence officer for the fleet at Hawaii, were obliged to be passing corridor gossip." At that moment Mr. Murphy may have forgotten that he was speaking to the only Intelligence officer who had access to all the information available at Hawaii. The other Intelligence officers received less.

Moreover, in actual practice, Layton was not responsible for estimating U.S. or enemy political intentions; he was supposed to leave that sort of thing alone. Here again there was a discrepancy between the practice and the paper delineation of the duties assigned to a particular job. According to the Staff Instructions, Commander-in-Chief, U.S. Pacific Fleet, dated 1941, under which Layton was functioning, his duties were outlined as follows:[125]

214: Intelligence Officer—25

(a) Directs assembly of Enemy Information and evaluates same, disseminating to various members of staff, indicating where action is required.

(b) Provides Operation Officer and War Plans Officer information essential for current estimates (monograph material).

---

[124]*Hearings*, Part 10, p. 4995. This is a reference to the August 11, 1941, agreement between Churchill and Roosevelt. Roosevelt passed on the warning to Ambassador Nomura on August 17.

[125]*Ibid.*, Part 37, p. 812.

(c) Maintains Section II (a), (b), (c), (e), (f), and (g) of Estimate of Situation (Enemy Forces). Maintains location plot of fleets of possible enemy or allies.

(d) Directs counterespionage and counter information.

(e) Maintains intelligence records.

(f) Evaluates Intelligence Information received of procedures or practices of other navies and prepares definite recommendations as to any action to be taken within own Fleet.

(g) Prepares Fleet Intelligence Bulletins.

(h) In charge of censorship.

(i) Internal Security of ships.

(j) Supervises reconnaissance photographic activities.

His assistant (26) had the following duties:[126]

In addition to assisting "25" in all duties of the Intelligence Section, performs the following additional assignments:

(a) Maintains Merchant Marine plot and analysis.

(b) Prepares silhouettes of own and enemy ships and planes for dissemination to Fleet.

(c) Assembly, evaluation and dissemination of enemy information.

(d) Maintenance of current Estimate of Situation (Enemy Forces) and location plot of fleets of possible enemy or allies.

The use of the phrase "evaluate" enemy information, "indicating where action is required," in 214(a), above, would seem to require of Layton more than mere collection. However, once again, we must remember that this is a paper description of his duties. In reality, Layton was not expected to "formulate possible enemy courses of action,"[127] but rather to detail the composition of enemy forces, in particular, their fleet. (His information on land and air forces he regarded as "lacking considerably in detail,"[128] but this was also to be included.) Strictly speaking, he would have been trespassing on the purlieus of War Plans if he had attempted to predict enemy action on the basis of the composition of forces. Moreover, he testified that it would have been very "presumptuous" of him to indicate "where action is required."[129] And he never did so. He passed on his information to Operations and War Plans, and any action indicated was to come from them. As far as provisions for receipt of last-minute signals, Layton did not know that the Army had radar and he had never

126 *Ibid.*
128 *Ibid.*, p. 147.
127 *Ibid.*, Part 36, p. 146.
129 *Ibid.*, p. 154.

seen any part of the Joint Coastal Frontier Defense Plan or its annexes because "it was produced in another command."[130] He did not regard it as being within his province to recommend aerial reconnaissance or any changes in reconnaissance on the basis of the enemy information he collected.

All of these qualifications to the paper description of his duties came out in his testimony before Admiral Hewitt in answer to questions by Mr. Sonnett. Fortunately Layton's grasp of radio intelligence and his understanding of contemporary political events were much wider than the boundaries of enemy information delimited for him. As we have seen in the letter from McCollum, there is also some indication that he chafed under the restrictions.

Rochefort was next among the Naval Intelligence officers in the completeness of his information. Since he was in charge of radio intelligence, he had all of these signals: change of call signs, loss of the carriers, and general movement to the south. He did not see the message of November 24 from the Navy Department, but he saw the more crucial warning of November 27. He also saw the major notices of Japanese and American code destruction, and the message about the Thailand intrigue. He was informed by Mayfield of the destruction of papers at the local Japanese consulate and drew the inference that the consulate had destroyed all but one code system. He knew of course about the winds-code setup: four of his officers were monitoring this on a 24-hour basis. The only signals Layton had that Rochefort did not have were the message of November 24 and the order of December 6 to Kimmel to destroy the codes on the outlying islands.

Captain Mayfield was not so well off. Since he dealt in counterespionage, he evidently had the status of an Army G-2 officer, and only a very few items of "ultra" information ever filtered down to his unit. He did not receive directly or indirectly any reports of the location of Japanese Fleet units or any other radio intelligence. He did not know about the winds-code setup. He knew nothing about the messages of November 24 and 27. What he did have was one paraphrased notice that the Japanese were destroying most of their codes, a notice from the local FBI that the Japanese consulate was burning papers, and a transcript of the Mori tele-

---

[130] *Ibid.*, p. 147.

phone call also delivered by the FBI on the morning of December 6. The latter he thought was "somewhat curious" and "disconnected." Dr. Mori "seemed to be somewhat at a loss," and Mayfield thought at the time that the call merited further study. However, it gave him no cause for immediate alarm, and he did not report it to Admiral Bloch before December 7. Mayfield's own focus was on local espionage, and one of his closing statements in the Hewitt inquiry indicates that he thought entirely in these terms:

> *Mr. Sonnett*: What, if any, conversations did you have, Admiral, with Admiral Kimmel, Admiral Bloch, Captain Layton, or Commander Rochefort during the period of November 27 to December 7, concerning the likelihood of war between Japan and the United States?
>
> *Mayfield*: I do not remember, nor do I believe, that I had any conversations on this subject with Admiral Kimmel. I did have conversations with Admiral Bloch and Commander Layton on intelligence matters, with particular relation to counterespionage work, but I have no recollection of any statement to me that war was imminent. I do recollect that we discussed the increasing tension, particularly with relation to counterespionage measures.[131]

Mayfield did not recall any conversation at any time concerning the likelihood of attack on Pearl Harbor.

Army Intelligence

The G-2 Hawaiian Department enjoyed in effect about the same amount of knowledge as the least-informed Naval Intelligence officer, Captain Mayfield. Colonel Fielder and Colonel Bicknell did have the advantage of hearing the Army warning message[132] read aloud at the November 27 staff conference, whereas Mayfield disclaimed any knowledge of the parallel Navy warning. Bicknell had a "vague recollection" of having seen a paraphrase of the November 24 message to the Navy, but he did not know about the wording of the November 27 naval war warning. (Fielder mentioned neither of these.) Mayfield did not pass on his information about code burning to anyone in G-2, but Bicknell picked up a few rumors on his own about code burning by the Japanese in other parts of the world. He did not state his source, but in any case he did

131 *Ibid.*, p. 338.
132 Same text as that quoted earlier (see pp. 46–47) in separate dispatch to the Navy.

not convey any of this information to Colonel Fielder, because he could not substantiate it. As Senator Ferguson suggested, and he agreed, "it had never reached even a good rumor stage."[133] He did get from the FBI the information about paper burning at the local Japanese consulate, and passed this on to the staff at the December 6 staff conference. Evidently the reaction of Short and Fielder to this item of news was similar to that of Kimmel: A routine matter, we burn secret papers ourselves every so often.

Bicknell's testimony, though somewhat incoherent, throws some interesting light on the way in which this signal was discovered:

> Captain Mayfield, district intelligence officer, called Mr. Shivers, I believe somewhere around the third or fourth of December, and asked him if he knew that the Japanese consuls were burning their codes. The FBI did not know about it and thought he meant the local consulate. They redoubled their efforts and observation of the local consulate and then discovered that the local Japanese consulate was burning their codes. That was turned back to the Navy as confirmation that they were burning the codes, but at that time the FBI did not know that Captain Mayfield was talking about another message.[134]

The source of the FBI verification was not visual observation, since the papers were burned *inside* the consulate, but an intercepted telephone call from the Japanese cook in the consulate to someone in Honolulu, reporting in great excitment that they were burning all major documents. Bicknell did not know about this telephone call before December 7, and evidently he also assumed that it was another instance of back yard burning of secret papers, which could be observed visually. This notice, however, combined with other rumors, evidently led him to believe that "something warlike" was going to happen somewhere, and soon.[135] As an indicator, this particular FBI notice would have been much easier to evaluate if the source had accompanied the information. Moreover, if Mayfield had passed on his information on code burning in the form of a paraphrase rather than a query, the FBI and Army G-2 would have had

---

[133] *Hearings*, Part 10, p. 5113.

[134] *Ibid.*, p. 5111. The confusion between the local consulate and consulates throughout the world is reproduced in this statement by Bicknell in his plural references to a single consulate.

[135] *Ibid.*, Part 35, p. 30.

two signals instead of one. With respect to code burning, no one in the Hawaiian G-2 was informed that the United States also had started to destroy codes in some of its own outlying possessions.

On December 2 or 3 Bicknell also received from the British representative in Honolulu a dispatch from Manila concerning Japanese troop reinforcements in Indochina, accompanied by an estimate of war in the near future between England and Japan. On December 6 he received from the FBI the transcript of the Mori telephone call. He was disturbed enough by the suspicious parts on the local flowers in bloom to insist on seeing Colonel Fielder and General Short late that afternoon. Fielder and Short were preparing to go out to dinner together and were evidently somewhat impatient at being detained. However, they took five minutes to look over the message, remarked that it was an accurate picture of conditions in Hawaii, and gave Bicknell the definite impression that they felt the message contained nothing alarming and that he was perhaps a little too "intelligence-conscious."

G-2 received two other signals independently of the Navy. One was sent from Washington by Brig. Gen. Sherman Miles, head of Washington G-2, to G-2 Hawaii on November 27, to ensure that the latter would take care of any sabotage in case war broke out with Japan (because, as Miles put it, that was G-2's "pigeon"). This message read:

> Japanese negotiations have come to practical stalemate stop Hostilities may ensue stop Subversive activities may be expected stop Inform commanding general and Chief of Staff only.[136]

The other message to G-2, sent on December 5, said:

> Contact Commander Rochefort immediately thru Commandant Fourteenth Naval District regarding broadcasts from Tokyo reference weather.[137]

This latter message was also signed by Miles. It was initiated in the office of Col. Rufus S. Bratton, head of the Far Eastern desk of G-2 in Washington, because he was not sure the Navy would pass on to the Army the information on the winds code.[138] As Lt. Col. C. Clyde Dusenbury,

---

[136] *Ibid.*, Part 14, p. 1329. Layton commented on this dispatch: "Please note this dispatch does *not* say to inform the Navy." (Interview, July 11, 1956.)

[137] *Hearings*, Part 14, p. 1334.

[138] Layton commented here: "G-2 was sure the Navy would not and could not, because of the Washington directive." (Interview, July 11, 1956.)

Bratton's assistant, put it: "there was believed to be lack of confidence by Edwin T. Layton, Navy Intelligence Officer as to Kendall J. Fielder, G-2, Hawaiian Department."[139] That this lack of confidence was justified is substantiated first by the fact that Fielder could not remember receiving the message (though all Signal Corps records indicate that it was sent and received), and second by the fact that it probably meant nothing to him, even if he did see it.

Fielder himself said to Clausen about this message: "I would in all probability have turned it over to Lt. Colonel Bicknell for action since he knew Commander Rochefort and had very close liaison with Captain Mayfield . . . particularly since the way the radio was worded it would not have seemed urgent or particularly important."[140] Bicknell testified before Clausen that he had seen the message on Fielder's desk, that he already knew about the winds code, that he had asked the local FCC to start monitoring for the execute signal (the local FCC denied this), and that when he saw the message he contacted Rochefort and was advised that he was also monitoring for the execute. (Rochefort had no recollection of this.) Bicknell said he also received the same information from the local FBI. Shivers of the FBI denied any knowledge of the exact form of the winds code. Mayfield had merely told him around December 1 that such a code existed. Even though Bicknell is reported by Clausen to have had this knowledge, it evidently did not figure in his estimate as to what the local destruction of Japanese codes signified. It seems unlikely that he had picked up more than a rumor about the winds code, since to Rochefort any such information would be classified as "ultra" and therefore he would not pass it on. If Bicknell had more than a rumor, it would certainly have been part of his job to inform Fielder, and if Fielder had been informed, he might be expected, even with very little intelligence experience, to have believed that something more than the weather was involved in the message from G-2 Headquarters, and to have some memory of it later.[141]

---

139 *Hearings*, Part 35, p. 25.

140 *Ibid.*, p. 88.

141 Before we leave this point, it might be noted that November 28 was the latest date possible for G-2 Washington to have received the information of the winds-code setup, since decoded intercepts were normally delivered on the day of translation. Why they waited until December 5 to inform G-2 Hawaii in this indirect manner of the existence of such a code is

What happened to this particular effort on the part of G-2 Washington to deliver a signal to G-2 Hawaii without affronting War Plans or Operations underlines one of the essential difficulties of security in intelligence. G-2 Washington did not know how much the G-2 Hawaiian Department knew, or how much it was learning locally, and except for some suspicions was utterly in the dark about the extent of Navy Intelligence in Hawaii, or what Navy Intelligence was authorized to give to G-2 Hawaii. Obviously the amount of accurate background information available determines to a large degree the interpretation of a signal. So when *A* reports a signal to *B*, this does not necessarily mean that *B* has received it if communication is attempted in a situation of tight security. To Fielder, a weather broadcast from Tokyo meant a weather broadcast, perhaps some interesting meteorological data, and that was that.

The list of signals available, then, to the best informed officer of G-2 Hawaii, Colonel Bicknell, was as follows:

> NOVEMBER 24 (PERHAPS)—Message to the Navy, "surprise aggressive movement in any direction."
>
> NOVEMBER 27—Warning message to the Army, "Negotiations with Japan appear to be terminated."
>
> NOVEMBER 27—Message to G-2, "hostilities may ensue."
>
> DECEMBER 2 OR 3—Dangerous buildup of Japanese forces in Indochina.
>
> DECEMBER 3 OR LATER—Unauthenticated rumors of Japanese code burning in different parts of the world.
>
> DECEMBER 5—Notice to contact Rochefort on Tokyo weather broadcasts.
>
> DECEMBER 6—FBI notice of local Japanese consulate's burning of secret papers.
>
> DECEMBER 6—Mori telephone call.

In Bicknell's mind, these signals added up to an aggressive move by Japan soon, against somebody, probably not directly against the United

---

unexplained. It suggests that an execute may have been received on the 4th or 5th, and that since G-2 could not send any action information to the theaters, it hoped to get it to the local unit through Rochefort, who conceivably might have intercepted the same or a parallel execute.

States, certainly not against Pearl Harbor, but maybe eventually involving the United States.

So far, research has uncovered no staff instructions detailing the theoretical function of G-2 Hawaii. The testimony of the local G-2 officers and a few hints in the Hawaiian Standing Operating Procedure seem to confirm Fielder's contention that the main task of G-2 was to spot sabotage. Its job of estimating enemy intentions fell under the heading of "combat intelligence" and therefore could only be performed in wartime. The idea that the local G-2 should have been responsible for warning of an enemy attack from without does not occur, except in the indignant questions of the investigators. They, like many an innocent layman, associated the word "intelligence" only with complete and mysterious penetration of all enemy secrets. Even at the headquarters of G-2 in Washington, as we shall see, the ability to anticipate attack from without was beyond the fondest dreams of its Chief of Staff, General Miles. While Bicknell's Contact Office was beginning on a very modest scale to deal with international summaries of events and estimates of intent, these were not its primary responsibility. And Bicknell, like all the other Army officers, was serene in the confidence that the Navy knew all, or at least enough to alert the Army at the proper moment, if there was danger of an attack by Japan.

In summing up this section on signals received in Hawaii during the period from November 1 to December 7, it is clear that Naval Intelligence was far better informed than G-2 and that consequently Navy officers in general stood a better chance of being alerted than Army officers. However, as it happened, communication within the Navy itself was almost as sluggish and ineffective as communication between the two services. Even with Layton and Rochefort on the job, and with Layton often exceeding the limits of his duties, the information available did not get translated into military action.

It is not the primary purpose of this chapter to trace the manner in which the signals delivered by Intelligence were in turn received and transmitted by the officers in charge of Operations. However, we shall set down briefly what happened to the major signals available to Short and Kimmel.

Admiral Kimmel had received from his Fleet Intelligence officer, Layton, all the Navy Intelligence signals that we have mentioned, with the possible exception of the order to authorize code destruction on the outlying islands. He also had received fairly detailed briefing letters from Admiral Stark. His estimate exactly paralleled Layton's on the movement into Southeast Asia. He did not make any changes in patrol or reconnaissance or alert conditions on November 27. His only action was to radio Admiral Pye, who was then at sea with the battleships, that there was danger of war and tell him to take all precautions. As far as Kimmel was concerned his fleet had been on a wartime footing for some time, with one quarter of the antiaircraft batteries manned at all times and ammunition ready for the remainder. He did *not* inform the following key officers of either the November 24 or the November 27 message: Rear Admiral Bellinger, his officer in charge of patrol planes; Capt. Arthur C. Davis, his air aide; or Rear Adm. John H. Newton, whom he sent on an expedition on December 5 with a task force of 3 carriers and 5 destroyers to deliver a squadron of aircraft to Midway. The officers he did inform were evidently in agreement with him and with his War Plans officer, Capt. C. H. McMorris, that there was no chance of a surprise air attack on Pearl Harbor at that particular time.[142]

Of the signals available to Army Intelligence, General Short had all but the rumors on code destruction and the notice to contact Rochefort. He had in addition two other messages urging precautions against sabotage, which he received after the November 27 message of general warning.

---

[142] On the advisability of conducting long-range air reconnaissance after receipt of the November 27 warning, Captain McMorris testified: "The matter was discussed . . . and various factors were weighed—the availability of patrol planes, the status of the training of those planes, the employment which they might be called upon to carry out, the offensive operations laid down in the War Plans, the importance of covering the surface ship training areas against submarine attack, the necessity for supplying personnel for new squadrons (etc.). . . . From time to time during the preceding year or two certain long-range searches had been made from Oahu, but always through narrow sectors because of the limited number of planes available, or of plane crews available. These sectors had been rotated from day to day. After due consideration, it was determined that the searches would not be initiated. It was my opinion that they would be largely token searches that would give only limited effectiveness, and that training would suffer heavily and that if we were called upon to conduct a war, that we would find a large proportion of our planes needing engine overhaul at the time we most required their services." (*Hearings*, Part 32, p. 570*f*.)

These were both sent from the War Department, Washington, on November 28.[143]

Short's impression of the November 27 Army warning was that "the avoidance of war was paramount and the greatest fear of the War Department was that some international incident might occur in Hawaii and be regarded by Japan as an overt act. . . . No mention was made of a probable attack on Hawaii since the alert message of June 17, 1940. . . . There was nothing in the message directing me to be prepared to meet an air raid or an all-out attack. 'Hostile action at any moment' meant to me that as far as Hawaii was concerned the War Department was predicting sabotage. Sabotage is a form of hostile action."

After a half-hour of deliberation with his Chief of Staff, Short replied to the November 27 message with the radiogram that was received and initialed but went unnoticed by Marshall, Stimson, and the heads of Army and Navy War Plans: "Report department alerted to prevent sabotage period Liaison with Navy reurad [in regard to your radiogram] four seven two twenty seventh."[144] On November 29 he replied to the Novem-

---

[143] The first read: "428 28th critical situation demands that all precautions be taken immediately against subversive activities within field of investigative responsibility of War Department paren see paragraph three . . . stop Also desired that you initiate forthwith all additional measures necessary to provide for protection of your establishments, property, and equipment against sabotage, protection of your personnel against subversive propaganda and protection of all activities against espionage stop This does not repeat not mean that any illegal measures are authorized stop Protective measures should be confined to those essential to security, avoiding unnecessary publicity and alarm stop To insure speed of transmission identical telegrams are being sent to all air stations but this does not repeat not affect your responsibility under existing instructions." (*Ibid.*, Part 14, p. 1330.)

The second said: "[484 28th] Attention Commanding General Hawaiian Air Force period That instructions substantially as follows be issued to all establishments and units under your control and command is desired colon against those subversive activities within the field of investigative responsibility of the War Department paren see paragraph three . . . the present critical situation demands that all precautions be taken at once period It is desired also that all additional measures necessary be initiated by you immediately to provide the following colon protection of your personnel against subversive propaganda comma protection of all activities against espionage comma and protection against sabotage of your equipment comma property and establishments period This does not repeat not authorize any illegal measures period Avoiding unnecessary alarm and publicity protective measures should be confined to those essential to security period Para it is also desired that on or before December five this year reports be submitted to the Chief Army Air Forces of all steps initiated by you to comply with these instructions period signed Arnold." (*Ibid.*)

[144] *Ibid.*

ber 28 message on sabotage with a list of the precautions taken against
subversive activities, and General Martin replied on December 4 to the
second sabotage message that had been directed to the attention of the
Commanding General of the Hawaiian Air Force (though Martin's message was not received in Washington until December 10).

Short passed on the November 27 warning to his Chief of Staff,
Colonel Phillips, to General Martin of the Air Force, to General Burgin
of Antiaircraft Artillery, to G-2, to the echelon commanders, and to two
division commanders. He informed no one else in the Army in view of
the directive in the November 27 message to "limit dissemination to
minimum essential officers." His dissemination, while not adequate from
the point of view of investigators after the event, was at least less spotty
than Kimmel's. Kimmel was, in fact, a rather important bottleneck.

Short did not have the benefit of detailed correspondence with General
Marshall to brief him on the progress of Japanese negotiations and other
current political events. He had none of Kimmel's signals from radio
intelligence except for the reassurance that the Navy was on the job, that
they believed the bulk of the carriers to be in home waters. He had no
notice of code destruction other than that available to his G-2. In brief,
he was about as well informed as his G-2, which is not saying much.

But no matter how poorly informed General Short was, he did have
some important signals in a time of extreme tension between Japan and
the United States—enough, it would seem, to translate into the action of
a full alert. The point to be made about Kimmel and Short is that they
simply were not tuned to the reception of danger signs. The only signal
that could and did spell "hostile action" to them was the bombing itself.
And they were certainly not alone. There is no testimony from any officer
in the Roberts Commission Report that expresses anything but complete
surprise; the noise of explosion was necessary before anyone identified the
aircraft as Japanese.

Yet as far back as 1936 war games and drills in the Hawaiian Islands
had been planned on the basis of a surprise attack on Pearl Harbor. In the
war plans under which Kimmel and Short were to operate, this contingency was defined as a surprise air raid by Japan (referred to as "Orange"
in the plans). The Martin-Bellinger report, as we have seen, had stated
that such a surprise might be achieved without any warning whatsoever.

In April a dispatch from Stark had warned all naval districts about the Axis propensity for week-end or holiday attacks and had directed Intelligence to take steps to see that "proper watches and precautions are in effect." However, even though surprise attack was the phrase in fashion, there seems to have been no realistic appraisal of what surprise would mean; no estimate of what such an attack could conceivably do to our fleet, air, and ground forces; and no calculation of probable damage to men and equipment—not even a tentative percentage figure. The Japanese had estimated roughly a one-third loss to themselves in the Pearl Harbor attack, perhaps because they *had* to plan realistically for such a risky venture. No comparable estimate was attempted by the side committed to receive the first overt blow.

We are constantly confronted by the paradox of pessimistic realism of phrase coupled with loose optimism in practice. What really determined reactions was the sort of belief that lay behind Admiral Pye's statement: "If we had ten minutes warning everybody would have been there [manning the guns], and we didn't anticipate that they could get in without ten minutes warning."[145] An even more complacent view was expressed in General Marshall's *aide-mémoire* of May, 1941, to the President:

> The Island of Oahu, due to its fortification, its garrison and its physical characteristics, is believed to be the strongest fortress in the world.
>
> . . . .
>
> With adequate air defense enemy carriers, naval escorts and transports will begin to come under air attack at a distance of approximately 750 miles. This attack will increase in intensity until within 200 miles of the objective the enemy forces will be subject to attack by all types of bombardment closely supported by our most modern pursuit.
>
> . . . Including the movement of aviation now in progress Hawaii will be defended by 35 of our most modern flying fortresses, 35 medium range bombers, 13 light bombers, 150 pursuit of which 105 are of our most modern type. In addition Hawaii is capable of reinforcement by heavy bombers from the mainland by air. With this force available a major attack against Oahu is considered impracticable.
>
> In point of sequence, sabotage is first to be expected. . . .[146]

[145] *Ibid.*, Part 22, p. 540.

[146] *Ibid.*, Part 15, p. 1635. In another memo to the President on September 22, 1941, reviewing ground forces in all U.S. possessions, Marshall had checked Hawaii "O.K., leave as is." He commented: "Presence of Fleet reduces threat of major attack. Reinforcements can be deferred as long as Fleet remains in the Pacific." (*Ibid.*, p. 1637.)

This estimate of the situation is the exact opposite of Martin and Bellinger's in its phrasing. The underlying attitude, however, was evidently the same.

Even under ideal circumstances of collection and evaluation, Intelligence can do no more than define a general level or area of tension. At the time of Pearl Harbor, the circumstances of collection in the sense of access to a huge variety of data were, at least in Washington, close to ideal. But War Plans and Operations, both there and in the theater, had taken unto themselves the major job of evaluation. (This split between collection and evaluation was especially evident in the Washington offices.) It is a truism that where responsibility ends, performance ends also, and on the limits of responsibility assigned to a job depends the prestige attached to it. The prestige attached to intelligence work was low, and reflected exactly the menial character of the job. Any Intelligence officer who stayed on the job long enough to become sensitive to signals was an exception, for he would automatically be regarded within the service as being of not very high caliber. The inference usually entertained was that nobody stayed in Intelligence who was capable of handling a command post. Those who remained were scarcely to be trusted with the delicate task of evaluation.

In fact, the job of collecting data is intimately bound up with the job of evaluating it. A sensitive collector knows what sounds to select out of a background of noise, and his presentation of the significant sounds is in itself a major first step in evaluation. For perception is an activity. Data are not given; they are taken. Moreover, the job of lifting signals out of a confusion of noise is an activity that is very much aided by hypotheses and by a background of knowledge much wider than the technical information we have considered so far. Such a background might have included awareness of the state of U.S. secret negotiations with the Japanese and of the actions that might be taken in response to Japanese moves. Theater Intelligence, however, was denied knowledge of both the negotiations and the diplomatic plans.

In the chapter to follow we shall see that this denial arose from a genuine need to protect the sources of the secret data and the security of official plans, but we shall also see how essential such knowledge was to a correct interpretation of the warning signals.

2 ▸ NOISE IN HONOLULU

Before December, 1941, there were three periods of extreme tension in American-Japanese relations that resulted in alerts in the Hawaiian Islands.[1] The first of these occurred in June, 1940; the second and third, in July and October, 1941. In June, 1940, and in October, 1941, there was disagreement between Army and Navy authorities in Washington as to the necessity for an alert, and consequently Army and Navy personnel in Hawaii were sent different directives and estimates. In July, 1941, they were sent one Joint Army-Navy directive and a series of differing estimates. In all three cases the Hawaiian services had different sets of signals before them and they arrived at conclusions varying from those of Washington and of each other.

There were many reasons why this sort of confusion could persist and the belief still prevail that the Army and Navy in Hawaii could function as a coordinated defense unit in an emergency. There was first of all the imperfect system of communication between the two services and between Washington and the overseas commands. The situation was not new, and attempts were being made to improve it. But the lack of communication helped to bolster Army illusions about the Navy's alertness and capabilities, and vice versa.

[1] There was a period of extreme tension in February, 1941, when a massing of Japanese naval forces at Saigon and Hainan seemed to threaten attack against Indochina, the Malay Peninsula, or the Netherlands East Indies. The forces were withdrawn in response to British protests. American policymakers, while alarmed, took no action, and made only a mild statement of disapproval. The Japanese, however, believed that American forces had been alerted.

Second, there was the difference in mission assigned to the Army and Navy with respect to Oahu. The Army was charged with defense of this island and its naval installations at all times, whether the fleet was in the harbor or not. For example, at the time of the first alert in June, 1940, the decision to keep the fleet based at Pearl Harbor had not yet been firmly made. Theoretically it was still a mobile unit, currently engaged in maneuvers, with its base at San Diego. It is to be expected therefore that in June, 1940, the Army might alert its defense forces in Hawaii more readily than the Navy, and that an Army alert might be instituted without a corresponding naval order.

Third, the criteria for a successful alert in peacetime had frequently been confused. In some cases an alert might be just a practice to increase efficiency and it was not important whether the enemy knew about it or not. In some cases, on the other hand, an alert might be intended to demonstrate readiness to meet an attack, and therefore to deter an attack, in which case it would be desirable that the enemy know about it. In still other cases, an alert might be part of a preparation for a surprise attack, and an attempt would be made to conceal it because such a preparation might be considered provocative. This last interpretation is especially true in a situation where the distinction between offensive and defensive weapons is not very strong. In Honolulu in 1941 many of our weapons, our submarines and aircraft, could have been used for reconnaissance and for defense against attack, but they were also quite adaptable for use in attacking Japanese forces. In Honolulu the alerts called were expected to meet all these needs: to make the services more efficient, to deter by maneuvering with a certain amount of publicity, and to take certain precautions in secret. Washington also considered an alert successful if in addition to meeting the above requirements, it did not interrupt the normal training program, disturb the morale of the men participating, or alarm the civilian population. The tendency in Hawaii was to ascribe success to all the alerts before November 27 as deterrent "demonstrations" simply because secrecy with a large Japanese population was impossible and because nothing actually did happen.[2]

[2]The ability to alert a command swiftly must give pause to the enemy and certainly must figure in the enemy's preparations. However, it is doubtful that these particular alerts functioned as deterrents since the Japanese had not prepared for such an attack much before December 7.

A fourth, and perhaps the most important, reason for differing esti-mates and directives was the immense difficulty of analyzing political alignments around the globe and of determining in these terms at what points of rising tension an alert should be called. This background during 1940 and 1941 was so complex and shifted so rapidly that even today, with the benefit of hindsight and the analyses of many historians, a number of unsolved and perhaps insoluble problems remain. This com-plexity made predictions about the actions of the U.S. government as difficult as those about foreign countries. For the theater commander and his staff the puzzles were necessarily greater than for the military chiefs and policymakers centered in Washington. Elementary security dictates keeping many of one's major decisions a secret from the enemy. If the enemy knows, for example, where one will draw the line in a war of nerves, this knowledge is equivalent to inviting him to press right up to that line. To keep the enemy guessing, Washington often has to keep its theater personnel guessing too. Our security policy explains in part why a theater commander's or a theater intelligence officer's view of an inter-national situation may be strikingly different from the view current in Washington policy circles. Add to this the fact that while some govern-ment decisions are deliberately hidden, in other cases the curtain of security may veil a state of indecision or a chaos of conflicting decisions, so that even well-informed quarters in the capital are at a loss to say precisely what our policy is or will be in the near future. This was certainly true of American policy on trade with Japan during 1940 and for the first six months of 1941 until the Embargo Act of July 25.

Turning to look at the three Hawaiian alerts in more detail, we may find it profitable to consider them in the same way that we have con-sidered the December 7 alert, i.e., in terms of the signals available to the officers who called the alert. It is worth repeating that by "signals" we mean signs indicating particular dangers. By "available" we mean recorded and communicated to certain key people. To say that a signal was available is not the same as saying that it was *perceived* in the sense that it was taken as evidence or as necessitating a specific course of action in response. Nor does it mean that sender and receiver perceived it as evidence of the same kind of danger. For example, it was not unusual for a signal to mean one kind of danger in Washington and another in the theater.

Washington advised General Short on November 27 to expect "hostile action" at any moment, by which it meant "attack on American possessions from without," but General Short understood this phrase to mean "sabotage." Washington was convinced that it had fully alerted the General and the General was quite as convinced that he was fully alert. And he was fully alert—to sabotage.

In examining these three alerts we shall ask: To what dangers were the Honolulu commanders alerted? To sabotage? To subversion? To a military attack by Japan against Russia? Against the Dutch? Against the British? Against American possessions? And what sorts of action were the commanders making ready in response to the danger signals as they perceived them? Were they preparing to prevent sabotage? To deter by demonstration? To go to the aid of an ally? To retaliate when struck? To strike first? The answers are not always clear because the questions were not always clearly posed at the time. However, a study of these alerts can teach us much about what questions to ask and how to frame them clearly today and in the future. We can also begin to understand the Hawaiian interpretation of the November alert messages from Washington when we see how the experience of these earlier alerts affected the perception of the local officers. The three alerts created a background of noise that obscured the warning notes of the final signals.

ALERT JUNE 17, 1940

The first of the three earlier Hawaiian alerts throws into sharp relief the need for better interservice communication. Intelligence played a very small part in this affair. Neither the Army nor the Navy Intelligence agencies recommended the alert; indeed it was definitely not within their province to do so.

The Office of Naval Intelligence in Washington did have a Foreign Intelligence branch that according to the printed record[3] was charged with collecting and evaluating information on the strength, disposition, and probable intentions of foreign naval forces. However, evaluation was actually under War Plans, and any action recommendations were decidedly outside the province of ONI.

[3] *Hearings*, Part 15, p. 1864.

Similarly, Army personnel in G-2 had their attention focused primarily on local subversive activities, and this was true of their Hawaiian unit as well as of the central office in Washington. While G-2 did participate in evaluating subversive domestic material, with respect to foreign powers it limited itself strictly to estimating capabilities rather than intentions. However, in May, 1940, consideration was given to the expansion of its foreign intelligence duties. General Marshall requested the maintenance of current estimates of predicted activity in the Caribbean area, the Latin and South American area, the Alaskan region, and the Far East. He also asked General Miles to look into the question of submitting periodic analyses of the lessons to be learned from the war in Europe.

Events in Europe were sparking activity in all branches of the military, and G-2, or MID (Military Intelligence Division) as it was then called, found its area somewhat enlarged. However, the estimating service requested by Marshall was probably not functioning by June 17,[4] and in general the techniques of discovery and communication of warning signals were much less advanced than they were by December, 1941. The Chief Signal Officer, Maj. Gen. Joseph O. Mauborgne, was especially interested in the art of decoding and was pushing this branch of activity. But the process of decoding messages and routing translations to key officers was much slower than it later became. Moreover, PURPLE, the top-priority Japanese diplomatic code that played so important a part in the United States–Japanese negotiations of 1941, was not broken until August of 1940.[5] Naval traffic analysis was neither so sophisticated nor so well

---

[4] No such periodic analysis as that requested by Marshall was found in the record before June 17.

[5] According to the testimony of Col. William F. Friedman, who broke the code. He claims that he had partially broken it before that date, but that the first complete message was read in August, 1940. Marshall's memory was, I believe, incorrect when he testified that MAGIC formed the basis for the alert order of June, 1940. MAGIC was the term coined by Admiral Anderson, Director of Naval Intelligence, to refer to any decrypted Japanese code message. PURPLE referred to Japanese *diplomatic* messages decrypted from a particularly complicated cipher. If we had had any relevant MAGIC at that time, we might have known that the Japanese were going to concentrate on getting concessions from the French rather than on entering into open hostilities with us. Marshall said he would produce the particular MAGIC messages, but the evidence he introduced as background does not contain them: They are nowhere in the published *Hearings*, and Mr. Mitchell, General Counsel, testified that he could locate nothing in the MAGIC file for 1940 that would have had a bearing on the alert. (See *Hearings*, Part 3, p. 1382.)

staffed. There were no radar stations in Hawaii, the Philippines, or Panama, and only a few ships were equipped with radar.

There were many other ways in which intelligence material and its communication were to be improved during 1941. For the June, 1940, alert, however, our Chiefs of Staff and our statesmen had to rely on reports from the various embassy staffs and on newspaper accounts as their primary sources. And since American officials and correspondents enjoyed no privileged glimpse into the policies of the Axis powers and the Japanese government, they had to do some complex estimating and they had to be sensitive to all kinds of indirect but open indications of possible shifts in Axis foreign policy. PURPLE later relieved them of this delicate task with respect to Japan and occasionally Germany. It may be that access to this privileged view during 1941 prevented American observers from making full use of publicly available signals.

Army and Navy Intelligence functioned on the sidelines then, but they were ready, as usual, to shoulder the responsibility for any military failure (the eternally convenient scapegoats). A few reports, however, filtered through G-2, and one report, prepared by ONI, played a part in the decision to call the June 17 alert.[6]

The first report to G-2 originated in the San Francisco Naval District and was directed to the Commandant.[7] It concerned a conversation on May 1, 1940, between a nameless German in Eureka, California, and the nameless friend of a soldier named Churchill in the San Francisco post. The German got drunk and told the friend of his plan to blow up the Panama Canal if American entry into war appeared imminent. A copy of this report went to the FBI, the ONI 12th District, and G-2, Ninth Corps Area. The report bore no date and there was apparently no follow-up.

The second report was shown to MID on June 13 by the State Department. It was a message for Capt. Ellis M. Zacharias dated June 10 and had originated with the commander of the Los Angeles section of the Coast Guard. It contained the information that members of a Brazilian crew had learned from members of a Japanese crew that "all Japanese

---

[6] Records gathered by Gen. George V. Strong, head of War Plans for General Marshall in 1940, for Marshall's appearance before the congressional committee.

[7] *Hearings*, Part 15, p. 1933.

ships have orders to scuttle if in the Panama Canal when USA declares mobilization."[8]

The third report came from Ambassador Joseph C. Grew in Tokyo to the Secretary of State. It was dated May 25, and paraphrased copies were sent to ONI and MID on May 28. The copy reprinted in the *Hearings* is illegible, so we reproduce below General Strong's summary:

> Mr. Grew discusses a flurry of official activity in Tokyo. Although he sees no reason to expect an attack on the Netherlands East Indies he acknowledges that preparations for such an attack would presumably be guarded with the utmost secrecy. (This, to our minds, did not exclude, but rather drew our attention to, the possibilities of attack or raids elsewhere.)[9]

A fourth report, dated June 3, was also from Ambassador Grew to the Secretary of State. There are no indications on the Secretary's copy of further circulation to ONI or MID. The report reviewed in detail three major schools of thought in Japan that were competing in a "state of political turmoil of unusual intensity."[10] All of them desired to bring about an early settlement of the China incident, the first by an alignment with Soviet Russia, the second by an alignment with Germany, the third by an alignment with the United States. Grew mentioned that the first group had been waning in influence lately, but that with events in Europe moving fast, "it is possible that Japan may feel that all her calculations are being upset, and that she may be tempted to resort to desperate courses."[11] The first group was made up of members of the reactionary societies and younger officers in the army. It proposed dividing China with Russia, favored seizure of the Netherlands East Indies, realized that economic reprisals by the United States would have to be faced, but discounted the possibility of war with the United States and believed "that in any case the Japanese fleet has nothing to fear from the use of force."[12] The other two groups were treated as equal in influence to one another provided each got support from the ally it favored, Germany on the one hand, and the United States on the other.

[8] *Ibid.*, p. 1927*f*.
[9] *Ibid.*, p. 1909.
[10] *Ibid.*, p. 1916.
[11] *Ibid.*, p. 1918.
[12] *Ibid.*, p. 1917.

General Strong, General Marshall's head of War Plans in 1940, summarized the dispatch of June 3 as follows:

> In surveying the Japanese situation, Mr. Grew states in diplomatic terms, that "a complacent view of the future would no longer be warranted." [There is no statement susceptible to such a paraphrase in the source document attached to General Strong's summary.] He cites the opinion of Japanese militarists that their fleet had nothing to fear from the use of force and expresses his own belief that Japan "may be tempted to resort to desperate courses."[13]

This summary gave to the report an alarmist tone that was lacking in the original, but Strong's selection from Grew's report is understandable if we recall the hypothesis of Soviet-Japanese accord held at this time by the War Plans Division.[14]

General Strong did not mention Ambassador Grew's report of June 10,[15] which contained Grew's opinion that the location of the U.S. Fleet at Hawaii was exercising a beneficial restraining influence on the more militaristic elements of the Japanese government (apparently referring to the first group described in the June 3 dispatch). This was not received as a countersignal by Strong simply because it did not fit into the framework of signals indicating the need for an alert. And at this moment in June the entire apparatus of the War Plans Division was sensitized to the receipt of danger signals to the United States not only from Europe, but from South America, the Caribbean, and the Far East.

The fifth report, also from Ambassador Grew to Secretary of State Hull, was dated June 17, 1940, and was shown to MID on that day. It read:

> Confidential reports have been coming to us from various sources of considerable concentration of Japanese military forces in Hainan, Formosa and Kyushu, but these reports are not subject to confirmation. Soviet and British attaches here are speculating with regard to a possible Japanese invasion of French Indo-China in the event of the capitulation of France in Europe.[16]

There are undoubtedly many other reports in the files of MID, but these are the five extracted for the hearings. In other words, these are the five

[13]*Ibid.*, p. 1909.
[14]See p. 86 concerning the Soviet-Japanese accord.
[15]Memo of conversation between Grew and Foreign Minister Hachiro Arita, June 10, 1940, in *Foreign Relations of the United States: Japan, 1931–1941*, Vol. II, pp. 67*ff.*
[16]*Hearings*, Part 15, p. 1932.

that looked significant after the fact to the officers who helped General Strong prepare his memorandum on the background of the June, 1940, alert. If we list these reports as signals, they appear as follows:

MAY 1—German sabotage of Panama Canal planned if American entry into war is imminent. (Source: Unidentified German in Eureka, California.)

MAY 25—Flurry of official activity in Tokyo, interpreted as possible secret preparations for attack on Netherlands East Indies. (Source: Ambassador Grew.)

JUNE 3—Japanese militarists are prepared for the Japanese Fleet to use force and are advocating seizure of Netherlands East Indies. (Source: Ambassador Grew.)

JUNE 13—Japanese ships have orders to scuttle if in Panama Canal when United States declares mobilization. (Source: Crew members of a Brazilian ship.)

JUNE 17—Japanese troop concentrations in Hainan, Formosa, and Kyushu interpreted as preparation for invasion of French Indochina when France falls. (Source: Ambassador Grew.)

This listing puts the worst possible interpretation on each of the signals and equates the reliability of the unofficial sources with that of Ambassador Grew. Even so, there are no signals here indicating a contemplated attack on a U.S. possession. An alert for the Panama Canal against sabotage is perhaps indicated, but even War Plans could not have predicted American policy in case of a direct attack by Japan on the Netherlands East Indies or on French Indochina. However, as General Strong states in his memorandum, these five reports cannot be considered in a vacuum. The developments that touched off the alert were not privileged information; knowledge of them was available to anyone who read the daily papers. They included Hitler's blitzkrieg advance across the Netherlands, the imminent collapse of France, and the prospect of the collapse of Great Britain—events that would leave Japan free for adventures in Southeast Asia. It was to this series of events that the ONI report preceding the June 17 alert was addressed.

This report of June 17 was issued as a result of a request from President Roosevelt four days earlier for an estimate of Great Britain's chances and an opinion on whether U.S. naval and air forces could prevent a German-

Italian victory in the Atlantic.[17] The ONI figures established that in the Atlantic the combined German, Italian, and French fleets would be about one-third greater than the British Fleet and greater also than the combined U.S. Atlantic and Pacific fleets. The report also expressed the opinion that Hitler might successfully invade England if he had the French Fleet at his disposal.[18] Army Intelligence had been asked for a similar expression of opinion and estimate of capabilities but its answer is not currently available.[19] We do know, however, that on June 17 both Army and Navy planners held a gloomy view of Allied prospects in the Atlantic.

Up until this moment the American public and some parts of the American government had relaxed in the belief that the British would and could carry on the battle of the Atlantic. Now this belief was challenged by the crucial question, Will the French Fleet fall intact into German hands? On June 17 the answer seemed to be, Yes.[20] If the French Fleet were lost to Germany, then how would the British Fleet survive? Our Pacific Fleet might very well have to be transferred to the Atlantic. But how would such a move affect the course of Japanese aggression in the Far East?

In the spring of 1940 the Pacific Fleet had been ordered to Hawaii on maneuvers with the idea that this demonstration of strength might give pause to the Japanese expansionists. Once there, it was allowed to stay

17 Langer and Gleason, *The Challenge to Isolation*, p. 549.

18 *Ibid.* See also *New York Herald Tribune*, June 23, 1940.

19 Mark S. Watson, *Chief of Staff: Prewar Plans and Preparations*, p. 109. Watson says that the request was referred to the War Plans Division; a considered reply was given to Marshall and Stark on June 26 by Colonel Clark and Captain C. J. Moore (Joint Planning Committee).

20 The U.S. government simply ignored the assurances of the French government that it would not allow the Germans to have the French Fleet, for it judged German intentions by German capabilities and their prior disregard for paper commitments, and French intentions by French capabilities. According to the evidence available today, it appears that Hitler did not intend to press France on the question of the fleet for fear that France would send it immediately to join the British Fleet. It appears also that France was determined not to surrender the fleet under any circumstances and that Admiral Darlan had given orders to scuttle the ships if necessary, even after the request for an armistice. However, on the evidence available on June 17, the prevailing estimate of the British and American governments was correct.

It is interesting that a year and a half later verbal assurances by Japan were not weighed so carefully in the balance against capabilities. The United States was much more chary of provoking an enemy in December, 1941, than of losing an ally in June, 1940. This problem of coordinating judgments of intention with capability is a delicate and difficult matter and one that will undoubtedly plague decisionmakers forever.

indefinitely, not as the result of a decision that it could function as a deterrent there better than anywhere else, but because Roosevelt feared that its withdrawal might be interpreted by the Japanese as an act of appeasement. Admiral James O. Richardson, who was in charge of this unit of the Navy, had originally been scheduled to return to San Diego on May 9. He was by no means comfortable about his assignment and on May 22 had written urgently to Admiral Stark who was Chief of Naval Operations at the time. He pointed out that training as well as other preparations for war could be carried on more efficiently from the west coast of the United States. Admiral Stark answered him on May 27:

Why are you in the Hawaiian area?

Answer: You are there because of the deterrent effect which it is thought your presence may have on the Japs going into the East Indies. In previous letters I have hooked this up with the Italians going into the war. The connection is that with Italy in, it is thought that the Japs might feel just that much freer to take independent action. We believe both the Germans and the Italians have told the Japs that so far as they are concerned she, Japan, has a free hand in the Dutch East Indies.

Your natural question may follow—well, how about Italy and the war? I can state that we have had Italy going into the war on 24 hours notice on several different occasions during the last two weeks from sources of information which looked authentic. Others have stated that it would occur within the next ten days. I have stated personally that cold logic would dictate her not going in for some time. It is anybody's guess. It may be decided by the time this reaches you. Events are moving fast in Northern France.

The above in itself shows you how indefinite the situation is.

Along the same line as the first question presented you would naturally ask—suppose the Japs do go into the East Indies? What are we going to do about it? My answer is I don't know and I think there is nobody on God's green earth who can tell you. I do know my own arguments with regard to this, both in the White House and in the State Department are in line with the thoughts contained in your recent letter.

I would point out one thing and this is that even if the decision here were for the United States to take no decisive action if the Japs should decide to go into the Dutch East Indies, we must not breathe it to a soul, as by so doing we would completely nullify the reason for your presence in the Hawaiian area. Just remember that the Japs don't know what we are going to do and so long as they don't know they may hesitate or be deterred. These thoughts I have kept very secret here.

The above I think will answer the question "why you are there." It does not answer the question as to how long you will probably stay. Rest assured that the minute I get this information I will communicate it to you. Nobody can answer it just now. Like you, I have asked the question, and also—like you—I have been unable to get the answer.[21]

If Stark's letter sounds today very indefinite and confused, it is because he was. The American policymakers kept themselves as well as the Japanese guessing. Roosevelt had the final say about the position of Richardson's fleet, as well as about the more vital question of U.S. action in case of a direct attack by Japan on the Dutch or the British. But he chose not to say. His explanation to Stark was certainly less diffuse than Stark's to Richardson. It was: "When I don't know how to move, I stay put."[22] So the fleet stayed on at Pearl Harbor for lack of a decision to withdraw it. On June 18 Stark, in a note to the President, had strongly urged its removal to the Atlantic. Six days later the President informed Stark: "Decision as to the return of the Fleet from Hawaii is to be taken later."[23]

From the pages of *The New York Times* for June, 1940, we can get a quick review of the publicly available signals of impending danger from the Far East. Attention was naturally centered on Europe: the entry of Italy into the war and the fall of France. Far Eastern news begins on page 7 or farther back. But it is reported in detail and it is not reassuring:[24]

> JUNE 1—Note from Germany to Japan, published in Japanese press May 27, giving Japan more or less carte blanche in the Dutch East Indies.
>
> FIRST 2 WEEKS OF JUNE—Frequent notices of large-scale bombings of Chungking, endangering American lives and property.

[21] *Hearings*, Part 14, p. 943.

[22] Langer and Gleason, *The Challenge to Isolation*, p. 597. The policy formulation of this form of indecision appears in Stanley Hornbeck's memo to Hull of May 24, 1940: "The situation in Europe being what it is, the situation in the Far East being what it is, and the limitations upon possible courses of action by this country being, within this country and at this moment, what they are, the most advisable course for this country to pursue for the present with regard to the Far East and the Pacific is to 'sit tight': make no new diplomatic move of major import, make no change in the disposal of the United States Battle Fleet, maintain the positions which we have taken, neither suggest nor assent to compromises, keep our hands free and our eyes and ears open." (*Ibid.*, p. 592.)

[23] *Ibid.*, p. 597.

[24] In the following list the event is usually one day earlier than the date of the paper in which it is described.

JUNE 10—Japan disavows responsibility for damage to foreign property in Chungking. Japan and the Soviet Union settle Manchukuo frontier dispute. Pact seen as a "boon to Japan," since it frees Tokyo's hand for adventures in the South Pacific.

JUNE 13—Hull protests bombings in Chungking, sends formal note to Japanese government.

JUNE 14—Tokyo disavows responsibility, requests all powers whose nationals are in Chungking to remove them. Japanese-sponsored regime in Nanking demands recall of troops and warships of Britain, France, and Italy from China.

JUNE 15—Japan disavows Nanking demand.

JUNE 16—Japan may attack Indochina.

JUNE 17—U.S. warship rocked by Japanese bomb. New air raid on Chungking by 113 aircraft, following Secretary Hull's denunciation.

JUNE 19[25]—Tokyo will oppose Indochina change. Report from China: Everyone is asking if Japan will take advantage of the French defeat to strike at Indochina.

On May 23, 1940, Roosevelt had said to the Business Advisory Council: "I cannot look very much—any more than any of us can—beyond four or five months."[26] We are fortunate in having a record dated June 13 of his look ahead for that period. It was considerably more optimistic than the ONI report and also more so than the views of his Joint Army-Navy War Plans staff. Roosevelt believed that the following situations would hold true in the fall and winter of 1940:

> Britain and the British Empire are still intact.
>
> France is occupied, but the French Government and the remainder of its forces are still resisting, perhaps in North Africa.
>
> The surviving forces of the British and French Navies, in conjunction with U.S. Navy are holding the Persian Gulf, Red Sea and the Atlantic from

[25] On June 19 it is interesting to read on page 1 of *The New York Times*: "Bill for two-ocean Navy [is] rushed to House, Stark's Navy plan startles capital." Under the continuation of this piece on p. 13 is a small item from Honolulu dated June 18: "Overtime Maneuvers Ordered. The Army ordered the 24,000 soldiers in its Hawaiian Department into overtime maneuvers today following Admiral James O. Richardson's announcement that scheduled visits of the U.S. Fleet to Pacific ports early next month had been cancelled. There was no explanation of either move."

[26] Langer and Gleason, *The Challenge to Isolation*, p. 472.

Morocco to Greenland. Allied fleets have probably been driven out of the Eastern Mediterranean, and are maintaining a precarious hold on Western Mediterranean.

Allied forces are maintaining their present hold in the Near East. Turkey maintains its present political relationship to the Allies.

Russia and Japan are inactive, taking no part in the war.

The U.S. active in the war, but with naval and air forces only. Plane production is progressing to its maximum. America is providing part of Allied pilots. Morocco and Britain are being used as bases of supplies shipped from the Western Hemisphere. American shipping is transporting supplies to the Allies. The U.S. Navy is providing most of the force for the Atlantic blockade (Morocco to Greenland).[27]

A juxtaposition of these views with those of the senior members of the Joint Planning Committee brings out several striking differences. The planners believed first of all that at the end of six months Great Britain, as distinct from the British Empire, would no longer be an active combatant in the war. The invasion of England by Germany was thought to be "within the range of possibility." France would not be able to put up much resistance from North Africa, since she would be cut off from her sources of supply.

The planners envisaged a strong possibility of concerted offensive action by Japan and the Soviet Union in the Far East. On American participation in the war as a belligerent, they argued in no uncertain terms that it would be quite "unreasonable" in the light of the "long-range national interests of the United States. Our unreadiness to meet such [totalitarian] aggression on its own scale is so great that, so long as the choice is left to us, we should avoid the contest until we can be adequately prepared."[28]

The two policies of the President that disturbed the planners most were the furnishing of munitions to the British at the expense of the American armed forces and the policy of making a show of strength in the Pacific. The War Department staff believed that such a show of strength as the stationing of the fleet at Hawaii might be taken by the Japanese government as a *casus belli*. It could act as a deterrent "only so long as other manifestations of government policy do not let it appear that the location

[27] Notes quoted by Matloff and Snell, *Strategic Planning for Coalition Warfare, 1941–1942*, p. 14.

[28] Report of June 26, 1940, "Views on Questions Propounded by President on War Situation," War Plans Division file number 4250–4253, quoted by Matloff and Snell, p. 15.

of the Fleet is only a bluff."[29] And apparently to the planners, it was a bluff. America, they believed, was totally unprepared to meet a hostile Japanese reaction. The President and the State Department, however, were favorably disposed to demonstrations of apparent strength.

By June 13, then, American officials were confronted by a series of competing hypotheses. And into the formation of these hypotheses, which would determine eventually whether an alert action would be called or not, there entered many personal and inexplicit assumptions about what actions would deter the Japanese enemy, as distinct from, say, the German. The delicate line between what would deter and what would provoke was evidently the subject of much discussion, little thought, and still less agreement among policymaking officials.[30]

In interpreting the signals for calling an alert in June, 1940, neither the State Department's nor President Roosevelt's hypotheses prevailed, but, rather, those of the Joint Army-Navy Board and its planning staff. Presumably the President and these agencies had the same sets of publicly available signals, and pretty much the same confidential sets. We can see what motivated Marshall and his Army staff by examining the minutes of his staff conference on the morning of June 17, 1940:

Subject: DEFENSE PROBLEMS

Present: General Marshall, General Strong, General Andrews, General Moore

The Chief of Staff remarked that in going over the various possibilities it seems that we may suddenly find Japan and Russia appear as a team operating to hold our ships in the Pacific. If the French navy goes to Germany and Italy, we will have a very serious situation in the South Atlantic. Germany may rush the South American situation to a head in a few weeks.

Are we not forced into a question of reframing our naval policy, that is, [into] purely defensive action in the Pacific, with a main effort on the Atlantic side. There is the possibility of raids with resultant public reaction. The main effort may be south of Trinidad, with any action north thereof purely on the basis of a diversion to prevent our sending material to South America. This seems to indicate that we are reaching a point where we should mobilize the National Guard.

[29] "Decisions as to National Action," quoted by Matloff and Snell, p. 16.
[30] The disagreements and discussions have been detailed by F. S. Dunn and B. C. Cohen in a private communication to the author entitled "Policy-planning for Deterrence: The American Experience with Demonstrations to Japan, 1939–1941."

General Strong stated that the Navy reports that they have definite information that the French fleet has already been turned over to and incorporated in the British fleet. (NOTE: Later information from the Navy Department indicates that this is questionable.) If this is so, and if the next move of the Germans, possibly through Ireland, results in the capitulation of Great Britain proper, the combined Atlantic fleets may move to the western hemisphere. In this case, they must operate from our ports, as there are no others adequate. From this point WPD and the Navy disagree on action. WPD believes in defensive operations only in the Pacific and concentrating everything in this hemisphere.

The Chief of Staff commented that if the British and French fleets come here the Navy point of view is O.K.; if not, it is all wrong. We have to be prepared to meet the worst situation that may develop, that is, if we do not have the Allied fleet in the Atlantic.[31]

Let us interrupt the transcript to note that two hypotheses that worsen the Atlantic situation were made explicit here:

1. Russia and Japan might form a team to hold our ships in the Pacific.
2. Germany might rush the South American situation to a head in a few weeks.

There was some evidence to support the first hypothesis. On June 10 Russia and Japan signed a treaty fixing the Manchukuo–Outer Mongolia border. This put an end to an undeclared border war that had been started by a unit of the Japanese Army without the sanction of the government in Tokyo and that had been costly to both sides in casualties as well as cash. General Strong also noted in his memorandum on the alert, drawn up for the congressional committee, that on June 12 Russia moved into Lithuania, and on June 16 demanded a change of government in Estonia and Latvia. Russia appeared to be cooperating with the Axis powers, and the inference from the border agreement was that Japan and Russia might be preparing to negotiate a neutrality pact. From these events Marshall had arrived at the conclusion that the *rapprochement* between Japan and Russia might be close enough to enable them to act as a team against the United States. (This may seem a little farfetched today, but in June of 1940 almost anything that would further Axis successes seemed plausible.)

[31] *Hearings*, Part 15, p. 1929f.

As for the second hypothesis, reports of Nazi infiltration in South America, especially in Brazil and Uruguay, where there were large German populations, seemed to point to the danger of a Nazi coup or series of coups. Since 1939 the Axis danger in South America had received attention from the Joint Army-Navy Board. Now in May and June, 1940, Ambassador Wilson's dispatches from Uruguay were causing much anxiety about possible Nazi political control in that country. On May 30, 1940, he telegraphed to the State Department that an armed uprising had been planned for May 25 or 26 and that only prompt action by the authorities had foiled it. He suggested that an imposing force of 40 to 50 American warships be sent to cruise off the east coast of South America, and that a powerful squadron remain at Montevideo for an indefinite period. The State Department submitted this proposal to Roosevelt, who promptly ordered the heavy cruiser *Quincy*, then off Cuba, to proceed to Rio de Janeiro and thence to Montevideo. Any large demonstration was out of the question. Admiral Stark was firmly opposed to withdrawing any ships from the Pacific and, on June 2, recommended sending only one other heavy cruiser, the *Wichita*, from the Atlantic Fleet. The President directed the *Wichita* to join the *Quincy*, and the demonstration ended there. On June 13 the local Nazi party was liquidated and its leaders arrested. Shortly thereafter they were released (with the *Quincy* still "demonstrating" offshore) and Wilson continued to send ominous reports of spreading Nazi power in South America.

On June 11, as the two American cruisers were nearing the coast of Uruguay, President Vargas of Brazil made an address that was interpreted by the American public to mean that he was following in the footsteps of Hitler and Mussolini. In this address he denounced "the sterile demogogy of political democracy."[32] Evidently President Roosevelt and the State Department realized that the Brazilian dictator's speech was for domestic consumption and was not intended as an answer to the President's Charlottesville address of June 10.[33] The U.S. War Department planners, however, may have read it as another danger signal, especially since on

[32] Langer and Gleason, *The Challenge to Isolation*, p. 618.

[33] Roosevelt's denunciation of Mussolini's declaration of war, and his first public statement of American policy to aid the Allies.

May 27 London had warned of an expedition of 6000 Nazis headed for Brazil on merchant ships and destined to be employed by the Nazi elements in Brazil to seize the government.[34] On June 14 Capt. Alan G. Kirk, U.S. naval attaché in London, advised his superior: "In my view, safety of United States would be definitely in jeopardy should British Empire fall, and would expect Italo-German combination to move swiftly in South America and Caribbean areas . . . safety of Canal seems paramount."[35]

The transcript of Marshall's staff conference of June 17 continued:

> Thinking out loud, should not Hawaii have some big bombers? We have 56. It is possible that opponents in the Pacific would be four-fifths of the way to Hawaii before we knew that they had moved. Would five or ten flying fortresses at Hawaii alter this picture?
>
> General Andrews stated that this small number would be overwhelmed by hostile pursuit. We are weak in pursuit and any small force would be destroyed. He believes we should not split our forces but should send more or none. He also believes that if we could get our reserves of ammunition, bombs, etc. to Hawaii, we could put big planes there in three days if necessary. The Chief of Staff remarked that three days might be fatal. General Strong thinks we would have less than 24 hours notice.
>
> We have a combined Army and Navy Air Force of 476 combat planes in Hawaii. Japan at present can hardly bring more than 400 because of the small size and number of her carriers. Merchant ships can be converted for launching planes, but the planes cannot again land on the ship.
>
> . . . .
>
> Both General Andrews and General Strong recommend ordering the National Guard into Federal Service. General Strong anticipates a desperate need within 60 days for troops in South America, (Brazil and Uruguay). The Chief of Staff thought that although we cannot at once send expeditions, we might be able to guarantee to some of the South American governments the occupation and holding of certain key ports.
>
> With respect to further equipment for the Allies as per the President's statement, we have scraped the bottom so far as the Army is concerned.
>
> . . . .
>
> The Chief of Staff directed consideration of all questions raised during this conference by the heads of staff divisions present.[36]

[34] Watson, *Chief of Staff: Prewar Plans and Preparations*, p. 95.
[35] Quoted in *ibid.*, p. 107.
[36] *Hearings*, Part 15, p. 1930f.

General Strong, according to his memorandum for the congressional committee, reasoned as follows:

> In looking to our own security I apprehended the most immediate threat to be a raid or major sabotage effort which would effectively close the Panama Canal. Evidence of sabotage plans existed: . . . in the event of a raid, a diversionary attack in the Hawaiian area could not be ruled out, since a large part of our fleet was based on Pearl Harbor. Accordingly, on 17 June 1940 I recommended placing these two Departments on an alert status. The documents directly bearing on my decision do not tell the story nearly so well as does a vivid recollection of Axis capabilities and American weakness at that time when the collapse of France was imminent and the fall of Britain by no means impossible.[37]

Marshall's reasoning is brought out in the draft of a letter composed on June 26 for the attention of General Herron, Commanding Officer in Honolulu. (The letter was not sent.)

> My dear Herron: You have no doubt wondered as to the alert instructions sent to you on the 17th. Briefly, the combination of information from a number of sources led to the deduction that recent Japanese-Russian agreement to compose their differences in the Far East was arrived at and so timed as to permit Japan to undertake a trans-Pacific raid against Oahu, following the departure of the U.S. fleet from Hawaii.
>
> Presumably such a raid would be in the interests of Germany and Italy, to force the United States to pull the Fleet back to Hawaii.
>
> Whether the information or deductions were correct I cannot say. Even if they were, the precautions you have taken may keep us from knowing they were, by discouraging any overt act.[38]

Strong assumed that a large part of the fleet was based at Hawaii. Marshall, on the other hand, assumed the imminent departure of the fleet from Oahu, in line with his knowledge of Stark's recommendation, which would go to the President the next day. The Japanese raid would then supposedly have been directed at the Navy and Army installations on the island. Marshall's reasoning was undoubtedly closer to the 1940 motivations for the alert. To Marshall the fleet was a deterrent; to Strong, a target. But this conception of the fleet as a convenient target was more

[37] *Ibid.*, p. 1908*f.*
[38] *Ibid.*, p. 1597.

acceptable after Pearl Harbor than before, and Strong's memorandum is based on recollections after the event.

To summarize now what seem to have been the available signals on June 17, 1940, we have the following items.

EUROPE: France collapsing. Germany may get French Fleet. Britain may fall. (ONI says, Yes; Joint Planning Committee says, Yes; Roosevelt says, Maybe.) We may then have to move our fleet to Atlantic. This means deterrent force in Hawaii withdrawn. Japan free to advance southward.

SOUTH AMERICA: Mounting danger signals of Nazi activity in Brazil and Uruguay. If Britain falls, South American and Caribbean coups may occur. June 14, U.S. naval attaché in London stresses that "safety of Panama Canal" is paramount if Britain falls and Nazis rush South American situation to a head. This warning reinforced by earlier threat of sabotage to Canal received in May.

FAR EAST: End of May, Germany gives Japan carte blanche in Dutch East Indies. First two weeks in June, large-scale bombings of Chungking, endangering American lives and property. Japan disavows responsibility, pays no attention to Hull's protest. June 10, Japan and Russia conclude border agreement. Japan, Russia, Germany, Italy may work together. Rumors rising of Japanese designs on Indochina if France falls. Grew dispatches indicate preparations for possible secret attack on Dutch East Indies and for attack on Indochina if France falls, and underline power of Japanese militaristic group that wants alignment with Russia in order to divide up China, favors attack on Dutch East Indies, and does not fear open break with United States.

This picture includes a lot of public information, a kind of intelligence omitted in the lists of signals for the December 7 attack given in Chapter 1 (see pages 48 and 53). There the generally known signals of rising war tension were taken for granted and the listing concentrated on additional confirmatory information coming in from highly confidential sources. These sources for the most part were not available for the 1940 alert. Instead, all published information on political developments affecting the Far East, South America, and Europe was painstakingly scanned to determine what Germany might do next and what new Axis alignments might be formed against the interests of the United States. The signals that resulted in the alert of June 17 were on the whole threats of aggression against the allies of the United States. None of these signals, and no combination of them, added up to an unequivocal forecast of sabotage in the Panama Canal on such-and-such a day, or an imminent trans-Pacific raid on Hawaii. The available information, however, did define an explosive atmosphere that made an alert a reasonable precaution.

At this moment in June most people were willing to credit the Axis with immense capabilities. The most daring and difficult move of a raid on Hawaii was believed to be probable, whereas a year later it was considered to be an extremely costly and unlikely gamble for the Japanese. Furthermore, the report of plans to sabotage the Canal, arriving in this tense atmosphere, was given ready credence, whereas the suspicious telephone call on December 6, 1941, from Honolulu to Japan was put down as just another bit of detail in the already very detailed Japanese espionage system for collecting information.

The alert order that the War Department sent to General Herron in Hawaii on June 17, 1940, was unambiguous. It read:

> Immediately alert complete defensive organization to deal with possible trans-Pacific raid comma to greatest extent possible without creating public hysteria or provoking undue curiosity of newspapers or alien agents. Suggest maneuver basis. Maintain alert until further orders. Instructions for secret communication direct with Chief of Staff will be furnished you shortly. Acknowledge.[39]

Herron had only one alert status, which was a full alert, and he instituted this full alert immediately. His reply to Marshall, sent June 17, was received at the War Department the next day:

> All anti-aircraft observation [posts manned] and detachments in position with live ammunition and orders to fire on foreign planes over restricted areas and in defense of any essential installations. Some local interest in ammunition issues but no excitement. Navy inshore and offshore air patrols in operations.[40]

On June 20 Herron received orders to modify the alert gradually. On July 16 the alert was for all practical purposes terminated, except that

[39] *Ibid.*, p. 1594.
[40] *Ibid.*, p. 1600.

precautions against sabotage were continued on the basis of instant readiness, and aerial patrol measures on a training basis. Marshall showed constant concern during this five-week period about the effect of the prolonged alert on the morale of the soldiers and on the maintenance of their equipment. Herron constantly reassured him, and his last statement on the subject on September 6 was as follows:

> My absolutely frank and honest opinion is that "the alert" as now carried on here does not dull the keen edge, or exhaust morale. . . .
>
> The presence of the fleet here and its frequent putting to sea with absolutely secret destinations and periods naturally eases the situation very much. As things now are, I feel that you need not have this place on your mind at all.[41]

General Herron was never informed of the foreign policy estimates that had prompted the alert. Since he had an unambiguous order, this did not matter too much. General Marshall had planned to inform him briefly, but on General Strong's recommendation the letter was not sent. General Strong felt that the background of the alert was obvious from press reports, and that it would endanger our security to send such a message. He wrote to Marshall:

> I am inclined to think that developments of the last ten days, as reflected in the press, have given both [General Van Voorhis in Panama and General Herron] all the background necessary.
>
> Another point to be considered is that air mail may be tampered with, any reference . . . [to] the matter covered in your secret code [the encoded alert order of June 17] might jeopardize that code.
>
> However, if you think that you should write them, I suggest that the communication go by registered mail. . . .[42]

This policy of withholding information from subordinate officers and of using extreme caution about sending messages in code would have been sound if Washington had assumed the entire responsibility for instituting alerts in the theaters and if its orders had been clear-cut and open to only one interpretation. Neither of these conditions prevailed in December, 1941.

In 1940, according to Herron's later testimony, he received no information whatsoever on the international situation from the War Department.

---

[41] *Ibid.*
[42] *Ibid.*, p. 1597.

He had received one message in 1939 informing him that Germany had marched into Poland. In answer to the question, "Did you feel that it was necessary for you to have a fairly intimate picture of things happening in the Pacific and in the Far East in order for you to accomplish your mission?" he replied, "I felt that it would be a great help, but that I was condemned to go along in the dark as to that. I assumed the War Department had much more knowledge than I had, but I also assumed that what they had could not be very vital or they would tell me something."[43]

Herron responded with alacrity to the alert order. Whether it seemed to him an order that was "obviously" necessary to meet the international situation we do not know. The Honolulu newspapers at this time certainly did not provide as accurate or detailed a guide to the international scene as did the press of Washington, D.C., and of New York City. As Herron testified, "I had no evidence. I had only a War Department order." And he answered "No" to the question, "You did not know whether it was based on an impending threat or not?"[44] It is easy to fall into the fallacy of believing that the international scene looks the same from the theaters as it does from Washington. But nothing could be farther from the truth. In December, 1941, a crisis that seemed painfully obvious to Washington officials[45] was regarded in Honolulu as being on exactly the same level as many other critical situations during the year.

While Army authorities in Washington alerted their Panamanian and Hawaiian Commands, the Navy took another kind of action. Admiral Stark ordered Admiral Richardson to take the fleet out óf Pearl Harbor and proceed on a two-day excursion in the direction of the Canal. Richardson was to arrange for a leak on his fleet movements in order to test the hypothesis that sabotage in the Canal Zone was probable under these conditions. The order was apparently sent on June 19, 1940,[46] and read:

> Reliable sources persistently report any movement in force by major Fleet units toward Atlantic will occasion extensive sabotage in Canal. Army there informed and in alert status. I desire you make test on or about June 24 by

[43] *Ibid.,* Part 27, p. 127.

[44] *Ibid.*

[45] So obvious that Stark withheld some information from Kimmel for fear of "crying wolf."

[46] The dispatch is not dated, but by its position on the microfilm roll and the numerals contained in the time group number, it is presumed to have originated on June 19, 1940. (*Hearings,* Part 3, p. 1409.)

having a major portion of Fleet in company put to sea without previous announcement but you arranging for leak to effect that probable destination is Canal, and this not denied by authorities. Proceed toward Canal for approximately two days when return Hawaiian ports. Maintain radio silence exercising at your discretion. Anticipate ordering you to Washington for conference on your return.

On the copy of the message made available to the congressional committee, there appears below in handwriting: "20 June shown to General Marshall. He sent warning meg [message] to Canal. Fleet may proceed to Atlantic. . . ."[47] Admiral Stark did not alert naval officers in Hawaii on June 17 or at any time later in that month, with respect to a raid on Hawaii. "I was not impressed," he testified, "so far as the Navy was concerned, with any particular gravity at that time. That is the reason that I did not initially send Admiral Richardson anything in regard to it, and . . . I assume I looked on it largely as an Army affair."[48] Stark had previously explained: "That was a War Department dispatch at that time, and I cannot recall on what specific information it was founded, and certainly we were not perturbed and we were not looking for war at that time, and we have been able to find nothing to justify it."[49] He did recall the June 19 order to Richardson: "I remember very distinctly telling Joe to take the fleet out and to provide for a leak . . . and I also recall extending his time 2 days. . . . But that it happened at the same time as this alert is, in my opinion, just a coincidence."[50]

At this time the American Navy's point of view was influenced by its unusually good relationship with the Japanese Navy. Many of the Japanese naval leaders had been trained in American schools, and were personal friends of American naval officers. In spite of the fact that both American and Japanese war plans assumed Japan and America to be hypothetical opponents in the Far East, the two services were so friendly that within Japan the Japanese Navy was accused of being pro-American. And until the American embargo of July, 1941, it held out against Japanese Army pressure for war with the United States. The Japanese Army obviously had no such relationship with the American Army.

The disagreement in Washington about the necessity of alerting Hawaii had some repercussions in the theater that would have been serious if an

47 *Ibid.*
49 *Ibid.*, p. 2378.
48 *Ibid.*, Part 5, p. 2453.
50 *Ibid.*, p. 2453.

attack had actually occurred. General Herron, on receipt of the alert order, immediately informed Admiral Bloch, Commandant of the 14th Naval District, and requested cooperation in the form of a daylight air patrol. Bloch later gave the following account of their discussion:

> Sometime in the summer of 1940, the date I cannot recall, General Herron ... came to my office and stated that he had just received a dispatch from the Chief of Staff of the Army to the effect that an overseas raid was impending and that he was to go on the full alert at once. He told me that he had received this dispatch, that it was a bolt from the blue, that he knew nothing about it, but he had gone on the alert and came down to see me and wanted to know if I had received a similar dispatch. I told him, no; I knew nothing about it. He then said that he was very much disturbed about this, he didn't know the nature of the raid, didn't know what it was going to be, what it was about, but he wanted my advice. And I said, "Well, I'm not the senior officer present in the Fleet ... there is a superior officer here, Vice Admiral Andrews, and I think you had better show him the dispatch." We went aboard the flagship and told Admiral Andrews about this, and after conference, it was decided by Admiral Andrews that we would have morning and dusk reconnaissance patrols, and patrols were then ordered to be sent out. The Commander-in-Chief was Admiral Richardson, but he was not present. Admiral Andrews sent him a dispatch telling him of the condition. Admiral Richardson flew in and as he had never heard of the warning, he sent a dispatch to the Chief of Operations and it was my recollection that he never received a reply to it. Now this alert continued for some two or three weeks. When the Army had this alert, had been warned of an overseas raid, they were not told it was an exercise or drill. ... The Navy was in a position of knowing nothing about it. I think, subsequently, the Commander-in-Chief got information about it here in Washington, but so far as I know, we got nothing there.[51]

We reproduce this account in full because it gives some sense of the time consumed in communicating a danger signal. All of these steps— the discussion between Herron and Bloch, and their discussion with Andrews, the ordering of the air patrols, the dispatch to Richardson— took time, more time than would have been necessary if the Navy had also been alerted. It was not until June 18 that Andrews communicated with Richardson, explaining the patrol plan and requesting confirmation. Richardson wired Bloch in reply later that day: "Would like to know whether request of Commanding General Hawaiian Department for addi-

---

[51] *Ibid.*, Part 36, p. 367.

tional air patrol is a part of Army exercise or is it based upon information from the War Department."[52] On June 19, Richardson received Bloch's reply: "Request of Commanding General was based upon a directive from the War Department. He has no information as to whether or not it is an exercise."[53] Bloch followed this with a letter to Richardson on June 20, describing the dispatch received by Herron and continuing:

> I have no idea of how long this situation will exist, nor as to the gravity thereof; for two days I had out the Fleet Marine force and their anti-aircraft guns with ammunition. I called them in yesterday inasmuch as it was necessary to keep their ammunition under tarpaulins in the vicinity of the guns and this did not look like a very safe practice inasmuch as they were deployed in the heart of the navy yard.[54]

Richardson finally flew back to Pearl Harbor on June 21. On June 22 he wired Stark for information. On this same day Stark evidently dictated the following reply to his request: "War Department directive concerning alert issued as precautionary measure after consultation with Navy and State Department. Request you continue cooperation."[55]

Neither Andrews nor Bloch remembered this wire. Richardson recalled only that he had talked to Marshall and Stark in Washington much later about the alert and that they had referred to it as an Army exercise, put into action by a simulated war warning whose realism was designed to elicit an efficient response. Later Richardson wrote to the congressional committee:

> This dispatch was received by me after 5:00 P.M. Honolulu time on Saturday, 22 June, when my mind was fully occupied with secret sortie of the major portion of the fleet which was to take place early Monday morning and since the reply left me in doubt as to the reality of the warning, the fact that I received any reply escaped my mind.[56]

On June 22, Richardson also wrote a letter to Stark informing him that he had flown to Pearl Harbor "to clarify the situation." He described the main measures taken by the Army and reported that "The Navy increased their distant plane patrol from 180 miles to 300 miles and enlarged the sector being covered to include from 180 degrees to 360 degrees, as well

[52] *Ibid.*, Part 14, p. 950.   [53] *Ibid.*
[54] *Ibid.*, p. 951.   [55] *Ibid.*, Part 3, p. 1055.
[56] *Ibid.*, p. 1056.

as establishing a 30 mile inner patrol." He went on to describe his dilemma:

> The Army "alert" and action taken caused me some concern though I felt positive that any Army intelligence bearing on the above would be available to and evaluated by the Navy, with information to me. Of course, anything of this character tends to aggravate the tenseness of the situation and to interrupt training, as the Fleet is operating from Lahaina and Pearl by single ships and groups and without the full screening and scouting which a more serious situation would necessitate.
>
> As a similar situation may arise again, I believe a remedy would be to insure that where possible, when joint action is involved, even in drills, that the Commanders of the Army and Navy be jointly informed, with definite information to me as to whether the alarm is real or simulated for purposes of training.[57]

If naval officers were bewildered by the absence of information from the Navy Department in Washington, they were not alone. General Herron seems to have been considerably disturbed upon learning that the Navy was not alerted. Finally, on the afternoon of June 21, he wired the War Department:

> In interpreting your cable consideration is given to the fact that Navy here has nothing from Navy Department regarding Alert. Navy now turning over to Army inshore aerial patrol in accordance with existing local joint agreement. Will not modify Army Air and Antiair Alert before Monday except on further advice from you.[58]

He received the following reply, sent from Washington on June 22:

> In view of present uncertainty instructions for the Navy other than local Naval Forces have not been determined. Continue your Alert in accordance with modifications directed. . . .[59]

Much later, in his testimony before the Army Pearl Harbor Board, Herron explained how he had reacted to the Army order as if it were the real thing, but after a day or two he concluded it must be a drill: "when the Navy did not get any orders, like ours, it was a fair conclusion that it was a drill and not based on an international situation."[60]

In other words, Washington's failure to coordinate Army and Navy alert orders meant not only that more time (time that might have been

[57] *Ibid.*, Part 14, p. 948.   [58] *Ibid.*, Part 15, p. 1595.
[59] *Ibid.*   [60] *Ibid.*, Part 27, p. 127.

precious) was consumed in communication in the theater, but also that
the significance of the Army alert order itself was put in question. While
Admiral Andrews was cooperating with General Herron in furnishing an
air patrol, neither he nor Bloch considered it necessary to put their ships
on a full alert because of an Army order. Furthermore, no one in the
Navy informed Herron of the fleet's order to proceed to the Canal on
June 24. Conceivably, Herron and Bloch, had they put their two orders
together, might have wondered if a raid were expected on Hawaii, and
if the object of the raid were to destroy a major part of the fleet, then
why should the fleet leak its position and destination at that particular
time.[61] Certainly no better service could be performed for the enemy
raiders. But the habit of infrequent and reluctant communication between
the services prevented any such comparison or further speculation.

Of course, neither Marshall nor Stark nor, fortunately, the Japanese
had a raid on the Pacific Fleet in mind. Marshall envisaged an attack on
the Army and Navy installations at Oahu, aimed at bringing the fleet
back to the Pacific, so that Germany and Italy could have a free hand in
the Atlantic. Stark envisaged possible sabotage of the Panama Canal, but
no danger in the Pacific. The Japanese were concentrating on Indochina.
But not all these hypotheses were available to the theater commanders.
And in the absence of documents, Stark's reasoning in particular remains
a mystery.

ALERT JULY 25, 1941

A little more than a year later—on July 25, 1941—a Joint Army-Navy
dispatch alerted both services in the Hawaiian Islands. The diplomatic and
historical background for this particular moment of tension has been told
many times. The first major event was a Japanese ultimatum served on

---

[61] In the Panama Canal Zone the Army and the Navy were explicitly at odds. When General Van Voorhis sent the Naval District Commander a directive for implementing the alert
of June 17, he received the following communication:

1. The Fifteenth Naval District not being part of the command of the Panama
Canal, and orders emanating from that source having no authority in said District,
enclosed order is returned herewith.

2. If it becomes necessary to communicate important information to the Commandant of the Fifteenth Naval District he may be found through telephone 2-2661 or
2-2662.

(Watson, *Chief of Staff: Prewar Plans and Preparations*, p. 461.)

the Vichy government demanding the use of air and naval bases in French Indochina, followed by Japanese occupation of those bases on July 21. The second was the announcement by the U.S. government on July 26 of an embargo on the export of petroleum and cotton products to Japan, in retaliation for the Japanese move. Only a month earlier Nazi Germany had invaded the Soviet Union and there was great fear among the Allies of a firm Japanese-Axis alignment. The Japanese move into Indochina was seen by many policymakers as an index of successful German pressure on Vichy in an effort to get Japan's wholehearted cooperation. Once more a high point in Far Eastern tension seemed dangerously connected with the Atlantic and European areas.

As seen in Washington from the vantage of the White House, the State Department, Army and Navy Intelligence, and the Army and Navy Chiefs, the information on the unfolding of this crisis was extremely full and accurate. The steps that Japan contemplated in this part of her program of aggression were clear. They were announced in advance with details as to time and place in MAGIC messages to her various consulates, and the Intelligence services in Washington were able to intercept and decode these messages with time to spare. What was not clear was the attitude or action that the United States was going to take—whether preventive, or retaliatory, or both. There was great conflict of opinion on the wisdom of imposing an embargo on Japan; the conflict continued after July 26 and was reflected in the elastic wording of the Embargo Act itself. Calculations about what the Japanese might do if and when the United States imposed an embargo varied between two extremes: from the belief that they would thereby be deterred from further aggression to the belief that they would retaliate by an immediate attack on U.S. possessions. There was enough agreement, however, among the military heads in Washington for them to send a joint dispatch to the Hawaiian commanders in order to give them advance notice of the embargo decision. In other words, the military feared that this act of the U.S. government might provoke some form of retaliatory action. From the point of view of signals for ordering an alert, it is important to note that an official move *by the U.S. government* inspired the message of July, 1941. In June, 1940, the motivation had been a general state of alarm and suspicion about certain actions *on the part of the potential enemy*. As the year 1941 drew to its close, the interaction of Japanese and American moves became more and more complicated, until finally it was impossible to distinguish stimulus from response.

Although Washington was fully informed about this crisis, it is difficult to say how much the local Hawaiian commanders knew or what their personal reactions were to the information they received during July. The documentation from Honolulu records is slight. As was the case in the following December, however, the Army authorities had less to go on than their Navy opposites. In both commands the crisis caused little more than a ripple in the calm of business-as-usual, and it lived in memory only hazily. For example, Admiral Bloch recalled:

> In 1941, possibly July or August, some tense situation arose and I cannot recall how we received information of it, whether it was by letter to the Commander-in-Chief or the radio. At any rate, Admiral Kimmel had a conference on the subject and I suggested to him the advisability of sending out reconnaissance patrol planes with the median line of the sector pointing to Jaluit. I think the sector was 15 to 20 degrees. And we sent planes out every morning to 500 miles. He adopted the suggestion and sent planes out a few days and it was discontinued.[62]

Major General Philip Hayes, who was Chief of Staff to General Short, remembered an all-out alert sometime in July of 1941:

> ... we were notified by the State Department, with a 6-hour advance notice, that they were going to freeze the assets of the Japanese, and he [General Short] went into alert 3,[63] with all the troops out in position. The order came out, there was no disturbance of any kind, and he left them as I remember in maneuvers then for the purpose of ... showing that it was [not] an alert ... but that they were just out training, and they stayed out there for several days; then he called maneuvers off.[64]

At the time of Hayes' testimony before the Army Pearl Harbor Board an effort was made to locate the records on this alert, but General Russell testified that he could find no records whatsoever in the War Department on this subject. Whether the Hawaiian files were ever consulted is not indicated. However, we do have a record in the exhibits of the final

---

[62] *Hearings*, Part 36, p. 408.
[63] See the Appendix for General Short's alert procedures.
[64] *Hearings*, Part 27, p. 138.

congressional hearings of the messages that went from the War and Navy Departments to the local commanders during July, 1941.

Signals to the Army in Hawaii

On July 8 General Short, who had succeeded General Herron, was sent the following message:

> Nine two four seventh AGMC for your information deduction from information from numerous sources is that Japanese Govt has determined upon its future policy which is supported by all principal Japanese political and military groups period This policy is at present one of watchful waiting involving probable aggressive action against maritime provinces of Russia if and when Siberian Garrison has been materially reduced in strength and it becomes evident that Germany will win a decisive victory in European Russia period Opinion is that Jap activity in the south will be for the present confined to seizure and development of naval army and air bases in Indo-China although an advance against the British and Dutch cannot be entirely ruled out period Neutrality pact with Russia may be abrogated period They have ordered all Jap vessels in U.S. Atlantic ports to be west of Panama Canal by first August period Movement of Jap shipping from Japan has been suspended and additional merchant vessels are being requisitioned.[65]

This message was sent in naval code and therefore went first to Kimmel. According to Short's testimony, it made a definite impression on his memory because it contained a "rather definite prediction." It "was the only prediction that the War Department ever made direct to me. . . . No message of the Army after July 8 pointed anywhere."[66] The prediction that Short had in mind was that of probable Japanese aggression against Russia. It was a favorite hypothesis in Washington, and was held right up to the week of the Pearl Harbor attack by the President and many of his advisers. Short received no notice of any change in the views of the July 8 message, and he was correct in assuming that this hypothesis was still entertained in December, though not as an exclusive alternative to the southeastern drive.

There is no record of any answer by Short either to the message of July 8 or to the one that he received on July 25. The July 25 message was

[65] *Ibid.*, Part 14, p. 1326.
[66] *Ibid.*, Part 7, p. 3180.

also sent in naval code and went first to Admiral Kimmel. It was marked "priority" for immediate processing and delivery:

> This is a joint dispatch from the CNO and the Chief of Staff U.S. Army X Appropriate adees [addressees] deliver copies to Commanding Generals Hawaii, Philippines and Caribbean Defense Command and to General Chaney in London XX You are advised that at 1400 GCT July twenty-sixth United States will impose economic sanctions against Japan X It is expected these sanctions will embargo all trade between Japan and the United States subject to modification through a licensing system for certain material X It is anticipated that export licenses will be granted for certain grades of petroleum products cotton and possibly some other materials and that import licenses may be granted for raw silk X Japanese assets and fund[s] in the United States will be frozen except that they may be moved if licenses are granted for such movement X It is not repeat not expected that Japanese merchant vessels in United States ports will be seized at this time X United States flag merchant vessels will not at present be ordered to depart from or not to enter ports controlled by Japan X CNO and COS do not anticipate immediate hostile reaction by Japan through the use of military means but you are furnished this information in order that you may take appropriate precautionary measures against possible eventualities X Action being initiated by the United States Army to call the Philippine Army into active service at an early date XX This despatch is to be kept secret except from immediate Army and Navy subordinates X SPENAVO [Special Naval Observer] inform CNS but warn him against disclosure X Action adees this dis[trict] are Cincpac Cinclant Cincaf Com Fifteen Spenavo London XX[67]

As far as we know, in the absence of records, Short's G-2 had no further information to give him on the July crisis. What G-2 in Washington sent to G-2 in the theaters was known as "static information."[68] This consisted of digests of military intelligence on the countries of the world "of statistical and informative character, with little evaluation material contained therein."[69] These digests contained political and economic sections as well as sections dealing with combat, civil aviation, and military aviation, and they were "voluminous." They were revised yearly, by the forwarding of looseleaves for inclusion in the material already collected, and "whenever this information became more than information per se and became in any

[67] *Ibid.*, Part 14, p. 1327.

[68] For a full discussion of the assignment of "static" rather than "active" information to Intelligence, see Chap. 5.

[69] *Hearings*, Part 2, p. 783.

sense a directive or suggestion of the War Department, then that information . . . was transmitted through command channels."[70] Short's G-2 knew nothing about the "situation estimates" produced by Washington G-2 for the Chief of Staff. These included information on the Indochina crisis, which had led to the imposition of economic sanctions, but local G-2's were left to their own devices for picking up information about immediate military threats beyond the yearly postings of the size and location of various foreign armies.

During the first twelve days of May, 1941, General Short had conducted maneuvers simulating a full alert. He reported to Marshall in a letter dated May 29, 1941:

> The maneuver was divided into three phases. The first phase consisted of the air action and the actual issue of one day's fire and of Engineer Supplies for Field Fortifications and of Engineer Tools. During the air phase our bombers acted under Navy command in cooperation with the Naval Patrol Squadrons and actually located and bombed airplane carriers 250 miles out at sea. The movement of the carrier was entirely free so that the Navy patrol planes had the mission of locating the ship and notifying our bombers and they then made the attack. Pursuit attacked enemy bombers represented by Naval planes and our own bombers when they came in to attack ground defenses. Upon receipt of the warning for this phase our bombers were sent to fields on outlying islands and pursuit planes were dispersed. The Navy cooperated very fully during this phase and I believe we learned more about the coordination of the Army Air Force, Navy Air Force and antiaircraft than we had during any previous exercise.
>
> Ammunition and engineer supplies had never been actually issued before and we got considerable data in regard to the time and transportation required to complete the issue.[71]

Here we get the impression of lively and active cooperation between the Army and the Navy in drills, and this is borne out by Short's testimony.[72] Kimmel also had reported to Stark on air drills in a memorandum dated June 4, 1941:

[70] *Ibid.*, p. 782.
[71] *Ibid.*, Part 15, p. 1622.
[72] *Ibid.*, Part 7, p. 3074f. Admiral G. A. Rood characterized all the drills before Pearl Harbor as "tin soldier exercises." (Interview, July 19, 1958.) Rood was in command of the cruiser *St. Louis* at the time of the attack, and successfully maneuvered his ship out of Pearl Harbor during the attack.

The liaison betwixt the Army and Navy Air Corps in Hawaii is very satisfactory and weekly drills in air raid alarms with the two services acting in
unison are held. These drills have developed many weaknesses but the conditions are steadily improving and it is felt they are in much better shape
now than they were a few months ago. The conditions will continue to be
unsatisfactory until certain equipment has been supplied and the personnel
drilled in its use.[73]

Again, the impression received in Washington was somewhat misleading. Short had written Marshall: "Ammunition and engineer supplies had
never been actually issued before and we got considerable data in regard
to the time and transportation required to complete the issue." These data
we do not have today, but during Mr. Murphy's questioning of General
Short, it appeared that during this entire twelve-day period, no live ammunition had been issued, and no shots had been fired.[74] The boxes of ammunition had been delivered to the proper batteries, but none of them had
been opened. In fact, before December 7 Short held no drill or alert in
which the boxes of ammunition were opened. His concern for keeping
his supplies "clean" brought considerable criticism after the attack from
the Army Pearl Harbor Board. However, under this so-called full alert
he was still better prepared for an enemy attack in July than he was later
in December on an alert for sabotage only.

The signals available to General Short on July 25 or early July 26 may
be summarized as follows:

1. The United States will impose economic sanctions on Japan
on July 26 at 2 P.M. Greenwich time: "immediate hostile reaction" not anticipated, but "appropriate precautionary measures" advisable.

2. The United States will call the Philippine Army into active
service at an early date.

3. Japan will attack Russian maritime provinces provided Germany wins decisive victory in European Russia.

4. Japan has seized and will seek to develop naval, army, and
air bases in Indochina. (The seizure of these bases occurred on
July 21, and it was assumed that Short knew this from public or
naval sources of information.)

[73] *Ibid.*, Part 16, p. 2173.
[74] *Ibid.*, Part 7, p. 3087.

5. The Japanese may advance southward against British and Dutch.

6. Japan has ordered all her merchant vessels in U.S. Atlantic ports to be west of Panama Canal by August 1. Japanese shipping from Japan suspended.

We have no way of knowing why General Short decided to call a full alert. Perhaps one of the reasons behind his action was the fact that his signals included notice of two unfriendly acts[75] initiated by the government of the United States and directed against Japan: (1) the embargo and (2) the mobilization of the Philippine Army (which went into effect on July 26).

Signals to the Navy in Hawaii

While General Short had enough information available to call a full alert, the Navy in Hawaii had much more. Neither Admiral Kimmel nor Admiral Bloch nor anyone in Naval Intelligence mentioned passing on his information to, or consulting with, the Army about the alert instituted on July 25. Since there was not much communication between the two services in Hawaii during November and December, 1941, it is probably fair to assume that there was also very little in July, and that only the Navy had the benefit of the MAGIC messages forwarded from Washington.

Besides getting more information, the Navy in Hawaii also received it earlier. The message of July 8 to the Army about future Japanese policy and movements had been sent to Admiral Kimmel on July 3.[76] It was worded much more strongly by the naval drafters than the Army one. This was a characteristic of naval messages that played an important part in the reactions to the final alert messages of November 27. The naval version characterized the "deduction" about Japanese policy as "unmistakeable" and stated that it "probably involved war *in the near future*," that "the neutrality pact *will* be abrogated" (where the Army had said "*may* be abrogated"), and that the "major military effort *will be* against their [the Russian] maritime provinces which will probably be toward

[75] The War Plans Division had consistently held that Philippine mobilization might stimulate Japan to action. Cf. minutes of Joint Board meeting, July 12, 1941, cited by Watson, *Chief of Staff: Prewar Plans and Preparations*, p. 495.

[76] *Hearings*, Part 14, p. 1396.

the end of July though attack may be deferred until after collapse of European Russia [author's italics]." The dispatch to Kimmel contained the order "using utmost secrecy, inform principal Army commanders," but Short did not remember receiving this information before the arrival of the Army dispatch on July 8. Since the Army in Washington had access to the same MAGIC information on which the naval message was based, one cannot help but wonder why the Army, if it was going to send a separate message, delayed five days before doing so.

The July 3 dispatch to Kimmel was followed by another sent a few minutes later:

> Definite information has been received that between July 16 and 22 the Japanese Government has issued orders for 7 of the 11 Nip vessels now in the North Atlantic and Caribbean area to pass through the Panama Canal to the Pacific. Under routine schedules three of the remaining ships will move to the Pacific during the same period. The one remaining ship, under routine movement, can be clear by July 22. Briefly, all Nipponese merchant vessels will be clear of the Caribbean and North Atlantic areas by July 22. In Jap business communities strong rumors are current that Russia will be attacked by Japan on July 20. From unusually reliable Chinese sources it is stated that, within two weeks Japan will abrogate neutrality treaty with Russia and attack. The present strength and deployment of Nip Army in Manchuria is defensive and the present distribution of Jap Fleet appears normal and that it is capable of movement either north or south. That a definite move by the Japanese may be expected during the period July 20 dash August 1 is indicated by the foregoing.[77]

The dispatch was correct in that the Japanese did make a definite move on July 21, but into Indochina; the prediction about a move against Russia was incorrect. The detail and definiteness of this dispatch, even though partly wrong, should be kept in mind when we review again the wording of the dispatches to the Army and Navy in Hawaii that were regarded as constituting the final alert messages.

On July 7 two sets of messages[78] based on translations of MAGIC were forwarded to Kimmel. These were part of the important evidence for the Navy dispatches of July 3:

[77] *Ibid.*, p. 1397.
[78] *Ibid.*, p. 1397f.

7 July 1941

FROM: Opnav

ACTION: Cincaf

INFO: Cincpac

Tokyo to Washington 1 *July* 329:

Japan directs eight Marus[79] on East Coast United States rush cargo handling and proceed Colon Pass through Canal to Pacific between 16 and 22 July on following schedule: 16th, Tokai; 17th, Amagisan; 18th, Awajisan; 19th, Tosan; 20th, Kiyosume; 21st, Kirishima; 22nd, Norfolk and Asuka X.

Tokyo to Berlin 2 *July* 585 (English text note to Ribbentrop in part):

"Japan is preparing for all possible eventualities regarding Soviet in order join forces with Germany in actively combatting Communist and destroying Communist system in eastern Siberia X at same time Japan cannot and will not relax efforts in south to restrain Britain and United States X new Indo-China bases will intensify restraint and be vital contribution to Axis victory."

Berlin to Tokyo 2 *July* 825:

Oshima delivers above note and tells Ribbentrop in part, "Matsuoka will soon submit a decision X if you Germans had only let us know you were going to fight Russia so soon we might have been ready X we were planning to settle South Seas questions and China incident hence decision cannot be reached immediately, but Japan will not sit on fence while Germany fights Russia."

The second group of messages was based on translations dating back to the middle of June.

7 July 1941

FROM: Opnav

ACTION: Cincaf

INFO: Cincpac

Tokyo to Berlin and Vichy 16 *June* 519:

Matsuoka requests Ribbentrop's aid in demand on French for following naval bases: "Saigon and Camranh"; and following air bases in southern French Indo-China: "Saigon, Bienhoa, Phnompenh, Kompontrach, Nhatrang, Soctrang, Touraine, Simreap" X Japan determined acquire above quickly, diplomatically if possible or by force if necessary in order expand and strengthen them X Chief reason given is to prevent British moving in.

[79] Japanese merchant vessels with regular round-trip schedules.

Berlin to Tokyo 21 *June* 739:

Ribbentrop reluctant to force issue now.

Tokyo to Berlin and Vichy 22 *June* 549 *and* 246, *respectively*:

Matsuoka will negotiate directly with French X Repeats determination get bases soon.

Tokyo to Vichy 28 *June* 258:

French Indo-China base question this date receives Imperial sanction.

Tokyo to Vichy 30 *June* 252:

Japan now considers it absolutely essential to force France accede to demands for above bases.

There followed dispatches to Kimmel on July 15, 17, 19, and 20 setting forth accurately and in detail all the steps planned and subsequently carried out by the Japanese in their campaign to obtain bases in Indochina. On July 15 Kimmel was informed that

Japan will propose in name of mutual defense taking over southern French Indo-China naval and air bases outlined [in July 7 message] ... X At same time Japan will attempt to station necessary army navy air forces in that area peacefully with French agreement if possible X If French object Japan has decided to use force X Japan does not intend move further south or interfere with colonial government X ... Tokyo wishes avoid friction with Britain and particularly the United States if possible but risk is necessary.[80]

On July 17 a dispatch to Kimmel outlined the six terms of the Japanese ultimatum to Vichy, which was to be answered by July 20. The MAGIC message quoted in this dispatch had been sent by Tokyo to Vichy on July 12, and read:

Japan will send necessary army navy air forces to southern French Indo-China X French turn over naval and air bases listed ... X expeditionary force to have right to maneuver and move about freely X French withdraw forces at landing points to avoid possible clashes X Vichy authorize French Indo-China military to arrange details with Japanese either before or after landing X colony to pay Japan twenty-three million piastres annually to meet cost of occupation.

The dispatch included another MAGIC message sent from Tokyo to Vichy on July 14: "army now planning advance on about twenty July X" and a third from Tokyo to Hanoi and Saigon on July 16: "Japan intends carry out plans by force if opposed or if British or United States interferes: X Kanju Maru being held at Saigon to evacuate all Japanese there sailing early dawn 24 July X burn codes X Japanese in northern areas evacuate or move into Hanoi."[81]

Still another MAGIC dispatch intercepted on July 14 on the Canton-Tokyo circuit was forwarded to Kimmel five days later and gave information from military officials in Canton. It bristled with angry expressions against Anglo-American interference with Japan's "natural expansion," and provided the following details:

> . . . immediate object will be to attempt peaceful French Indo-China occupation but will crush resistance if offered and set up martial law X secondly our purpose is to launch therefrom a rapid attack when the international situation is suitable X after occupation next on our schedule is sending ultimatum to Netherlands Indies X in the seizing of Singapore the Navy will play the principal part X Army will need only one division to seize Singapore and two divisions to seize Netherlands Indies X with air forces based on Canton, Spratley, Palau, Singora in Thailand, Portuguese Timor and Indo-China and with submarine fleet in Mandates, Hainan, and Indo-China we will crush British American military power and ability to assist in schemes against us X three X occupying force will be reorganized as twenty fifth Army corps of four divisions and also thirtieth Army corps consisting of South China forces to be assigned special duty with airplanes, tanks and howitzers . . . X

The Office of Naval Operations, where the message to Kimmel originated, appended a comment that "above is not a directive but appears to express thinking and opinions of Canton orange military."[82]

Another dispatch on the same day from the Combat Intelligence unit of the 16th District (Com 16) gave Kimmel the information, which Tokyo was sending to all its consulates, that "although cabinet has changed there will of course be no departure from the principle that tripartite pact forms keystone of Japans national policy and new cabinet will also pursue policy of former cabinet in all other matters."[83] The cabinet change referred to was a slight reshuffle on July 16 that dropped Matsuoka as Foreign Minister and substituted Adm. Teijiro Toyoda in his place. Critics of the Roosevelt administration interpret this action as a Japanese concession

[81] *Ibid.*
[82] *Ibid.*, p. 1399.
[83] *Ibid.*

to American public opinion, since Matsuoka was very outspoken in espousing Axis recommendations and in expressing disapproval of America's resistance to Japanese expansion. Prince Konoye in his *Memoirs* has added to their ammunition by lamenting the fact that this cabinet change did not, as he had expected, facilitate Japanese-American negotiations. As Washington knew from the dispatch just quoted, however, the change was only skin deep. Toyoda had privately assured the German ambassador: "As successor of former Foreign Minister Matsuoka, I intend to continue his foreign policy and to strengthen even more the close unity of Japan, Germany, and Italy and march forward in the common spirit."[84]

The last dispatch to the Navy in Hawaii before the July 25 message on the embargo decision went on July 20 from Com 16 to Kimmel and to Com 14. It gave MAGIC information transmitted from Tokyo to Vichy the day before: "army has all preparations made XX have decided to advance on twenty-fourth regardless of whether demands accepted or not X orders for advance will be issued on July twenty-third Japanese time X remainder of message contains instructions to ambassador regarding exchange of official documents in case of acceptance X instructions regarding notifying Tokyo of France's reply et cetera."[85] This dispatch was sent "routine" to Kimmel and "priority" to the Office of Naval Operations. The speed with which a dispatch is sent is the first crude index to the importance assigned the dispatch by the sender. Evidently Indochina was not considered by Com 16 to have a very direct bearing on any action that Kimmel might take. However, it is significant that Kimmel in July was receiving information directly from Com 16 that did not duplicate information sent him from Washington. Com 16 was the command that included the MAGIC intercepting and decoding station at Cavite. Kimmel was not informed in August that for security reasons he would cease to receive this information, not only from Cavite, but also from Washington. He was equally unaware, as we have seen, of the special character of the source: MAGIC, and in particular, PURPLE, interception and decoding. In July, however, he could not complain. He was getting plenty of information.

[84] "Tokyo War Crime Documents," No. 4052 F, quoted in Langer and Gleason, *The Undeclared War, 1940–1941*, p. 640. Reported in *The New York Times*, July 22, 1941, in somewhat weaker form.
[85] *Hearings*, Part 14, p. 1399.

In addition to MAGIC, Kimmel's traffic analysis unit at Honolulu had a good deal of information on the position of the various Japanese Fleet units. During July, as later in November and December of 1941, a good portion of the Japanese Fleet was "lost" in the sense that 'the ships were not communicating with each other by means that our traffic unit could intercept. Layton therefore assumed that the ships were in home waters, and he was correct. But in July, unlike November and December, the call signals had not recently been changed, and there was also visual confirmation for Layton's interpretation of the radio silence. On July 8, for example, Tokyo correspondent Otto Tolischus, in an article in *The New York Times* headed "EMPEROR CONSULTS ON JAPAN'S COURSE," reported that what appeared to be the major part of the Japanese Fleet had steamed into the harbor of Yokohama and anchored right in front of all the foreign consulates and business establishments "without any attempt at secrecy." He also commented on the large number of shore leaves for the crew. Whether Layton had this visual confirmation we do not know. But it was certainly there for U.S. consular agents to get and to pass on.

The final piece of information on the Indochina crisis that was made available to Kimmel was the Joint Army-Navy dispatch of July 25 that gave notice of the U.S. embargo. There is no record of Kimmel's response to this or to any previous message received during July, and no reply was requested by Washington. In a letter dated July 3, received by Kimmel six days later, Stark alluded to one of the July 3 dispatches in a significant postscript: "It looks to us at the moment as you will judge by a dispatch you will receive ere this as though the Germans had persuaded the Japs to attack Russia within the next month. It is anybody's guess and only time will tell."[86] The letter itself was brief and concerned the American-Dutch-British Report,[87] but this postscript must have reinforced in Kimmel's mind the emphasis on an impending Russo-Japanese conflict.

There was, it is true, some inconsistency in the information that Kimmel had before him by July 25. On the one hand, statements from Tokyo indicated a desire to avoid friction with the United States, but, on the

[86] *Ibid.*, Part 16, p. 2171.

[87] Usually referred to as "ADB," this is a report of staff conversations at Singapore in April, 1941, between military and naval representatives of the United States, Great Britain, and the Netherlands. The purpose of the meeting was to draft a plan for joint conduct of operations in the Far East in the event of war.

other, these were coupled with statements supporting Axis policies and a campaign to invade Indochina and then expand further to the south. There was no signal indicating an intent to attack any U.S. possession directly, though there were ominous remarks about crushing Anglo-American resistance to Japanese occupation of Indochina and about the necessity of taking risks. In terms of source reliability all the signals were of a high grade and practically all on the same level. In the face of the information available, Kimmel's concern seems to have been quite properly for America's allies. He was worried about what action the United States would take if Japan directly attacked the British, the Dutch, or the Russians. And, like Admiral Stark, he was primarily interested in speculating on the prospect of a Russo-Japanese conflict. Unfortunately we do not have his on-the-spot reactions during the first three weeks in July, since the selection of his correspondence with Stark that was later presented in evidence omitted the period from June 4 to July 26.

On July 24 Admiral Stark had forwarded to Kimmel a copy of a letter addressed by him to Admiral Hart, who was in command of the Asiatic Fleet and consequently much more closely concerned than Kimmel with the latest Japanese move. Kimmel did not receive this letter until July 29, so it cannot be included properly here as part of the information available to him at the time of calling an alert. However, it represents substantially what Stark was thinking during that month of July and what he may have communicated to Kimmel in letters to which we do not have access. This letter of July 24 described a conversation that Stark had just had with Nomura, the Japanese ambassador. Stark wrote in part:

> We have had very plain talk. I like him, and as you know, he has many friends in our Navy. Nomura dwelt at length on his country's need for the rice and minerals of Indo-China. My guess is that with the establishment of bases in Indo-China, they will stop for the time being, consolidate their positions, and await world reaction to their latest move. No doubt they will use their Indo-China bases from which to take early action against the Burma Road. Of course, there is the possibility that they will strike at Borneo. I doubt that this will be done in the near future, *unless* we embargo oil shipments to them.[88]

[88] *Hearings*, Part 16, p. 2173.

Stark had made his position on embargoes clear long before this. Once more in this letter he reiterated:

> This question of embargo has been up many times and I have consistently opposed it just as strongly as I could. My further thought is that they will do nothing in regard to the Maritime provinces until the outcome of the German-Russian war on the continent is more certain. If the Russians are well beaten down, I think it highly probable that they will move into Siberia. Meanwhile, they are merrily going their way and just where it will all end I do not know.[89]

Kimmel in the meantime wrote a letter to Admiral Stark on July 26.[90] He made no comment on the Indochinese situation, nor did he indicate that he had received the dispatch of July 25. He was apparently quite relaxed on the subject of a U.S.-Japanese conflict, but very much concerned about American commitments should Britain, the Netherlands, or Russia tangle with Japan first. It is significant that he stressed his need to know American attitudes and probable moves. The need was very real, even though security considerations necessarily limit the knowledge of a theater commander about his government's intentions.

Kimmel's letter of July 26 read, in part:

> Dear Betty: When the proposed visit of the Under Secretary was announced my staff prepared a list of topics which might be of interest for discussion while Mr. Forrestal and his party are here. Not knowing the purpose of Mr. Forrestal's visit or whether he is informed concerning the general nature of our war plans and our problems I decided it better to combine these notes into a letter to you and believe quicker action can be obtained in that way. Following are the principal items of which I have been thinking.
>
> 1. The importance of keeping the Commander-in-Chief advised of Department policies and decisions and the changes in policies and decisions to meet changes in the international situation.
>
>   a. We have as yet received no official information as to the U.S. attitude towards Russian participation in the war, particularly as to the degree of cooperation, if any, in the Pacific, between the U.S. and Russia if and when we become active participants. Present plans do not include Russia and do not provide for coordinated action, joint use of bases, joint communica-

[89] *Ibid.*
[90] Received by Stark on August 2. Stark's reply was dictated on August 19.

tion systems and the like. The new situation opens up possibilities for us which should be fully explored and full advantage taken of any opportunities for mutual support. Pertinent questions are:

(1) Will England declare war on Japan if Japanese attack Maritime Provinces?

(2) If answer to (1) is in the affirmative, will we actively assist, as tentatively provided in case of attack on N.E.I. or Singapore?

(3) If answer to (2) is in the affirmative, are plans being prepared for joint action, mutual support, etc?

(4) If answer to (1) is negative, what will England's attitude be? What will ours be?

(5) If England declares war on Japan, but we do not, what is attitude in regard to Japanese shipping, patrol of Pacific waters, commerce raiders, etc?

b. Depending upon the progress of hostilities the Russian situation appears to offer an opportunity for strengthening of our Far Eastern defenses, particularly Guam and the Philippines. Certainly, no matter how the fighting goes, Japan's attention will be partially diverted from the China and Southern adventures by either (1) diversion of forces for attack on Russia or (2) necessity for providing for Russian attack on her. It is conceivable that the greater the German success on the Eastern front, the more Russia will be pushed toward Asia, with consequent increased danger to Japan's "New Order" for that area. In my opinion we should push our development of Guam and accelerate our bolstering of the Philippines. The Russo-Axis war may give us more time.[91]

The questions confronting Kimmel were of course among those that were disturbing the planners in Washington, and the answers were not easy to come by. To Kimmel, as to many others, the prospect of an attack by Japan on Russia or vice versa held out the hope of more time to prepare for war in the Pacific. This prospect, while certainly not desirable for Russia or for those concentrating on Axis defeat in European Russia, naturally appealed to American commanders in the Pacific. The likelihood of a Japanese attack on Russia, however, was not supported by enough evidence at this moment to eliminate the need for a Hawaiian alert. Kimmel was undoubtedly also influenced by Stark's disapproval of embargoes on Japanese trade and by Stark's view of the gravity with

[91] *Hearings*, Part 16, p. 2239. When Stark was a plebe at Annapolis, his classmates gave him the name of the wife of Gen. John Stark, a Revolutionary War hero, for his christening. Whenever he met an upperclassman, he had to declaim, "Beat them, or Betty Stark will sleep in widowhood tonight."

which Japan would view their imposition. In consultation with Bloch, therefore, Kimmel called an alert. He had in effect the same signals as General Short, but with more documentation and evidence. For example, he had details from Layton on the location of the Japanese Fleet, from ONI on the withdrawal of Japanese merchant ships from the Atlantic, and from CNO on the Japanese ultimatum to Vichy; the specific location and names of the Indochinese bases to be occupied by Japan; Japanese business rumors about an impending Japanese attack on Russia; Admiral Stark's hunches in his letters about such an attack; and some Japanese expressions of determination to resist Anglo-American interference.

The following list summarizes the signals available to Admiral Kimmel from confidential sources:

DURING JULY—Major part of Japanese Fleet "lost," believed in home waters for covering action in case of Anglo-American resistance to Indochina base seizure. (Source: Naval radio traffic analysis, Com 14 and Com 16.)

JULY 3—Japan will abrogate neutrality treaty with Russia and will attack her during period July 20 to August 1. Japan's action in Southeast Asia will be confined to seizing and developing Indochina bases. However, an attack against British and Dutch holdings cannot be ruled out. Japanese Fleet capable of movement north or south. All Japanese merchant vessels ordered to be clear of the Caribbean and North Atlantic by July 22. (Source: Two dispatches from CNO.)

JULY 7—Tokyo on June 16 asked Germany for help in getting bases in Indochina by putting pressure on Vichy government. List of bases given. Ribbentrop reluctant. June 28 Imperial sanction given to demands on Indochina. June 30 Tokyo declares she will use force if diplomacy fails with Vichy government. Tokyo to Berlin July 2: Tokyo says she is preparing to join forces with Germany in fighting Communism in Eastern Siberia, but will not relax efforts in Southeast Asia to restrain United States and Britain. (Source: Dispatches from CNO relaying MAGIC.)

JULY 9—Japan may attack Russia within the month. (Source: Letter from Admiral Stark.)

JULY 15—Japan repeats determination to use force to get Indochina bases. (Source: CNO relaying MAGIC.)

JULY 17—Terms of ultimatum to Vichy government. Japanese Army will advance into Indochina on July 20. (Source: CNO relaying MAGIC.)

JULY 19—Japanese military in Canton say next targets are Netherlands Indies and Singapore: "We will crush British-American military power and ability to assist in schemes against us." (Source: CNO. Evaluation: not a directive, but merely opinion of Japanese military.)

JULY 20—Japanese Army will advance on July 24 whether Vichy accepts demands or not. (Source: Com 16 relaying MAGIC.)

JULY 25—United States will embargo oil and cotton products on July 26: "Immediate hostile reaction" not anticipated but "appropriate precautionary measures" advisable. United States will call Philippine Army into active service in near future. (Source: Joint Army-Navy directive.)

The most important signals indicating the need for an alert were the same for Admiral Kimmel as for General Short. These were the notice of reprisals taken by the United States in response to the Indochina invasion: the Embargo Act and the mobilization of the Philippine Army. The only reported measure that Admiral Kimmel took was to increase his reconnaissance patrol for a few days to 500 miles on a 15- to 20-degree sector.

Apparently neither the Army nor the Navy in Honolulu reported its alert action to Washington. Both maintained the alert measures for only a few days. In the Army's case, what Short characterized as a "half alert against sabotage" was maintained permanently after July 25 "because the community was extremely uneasy at that time; it [the embargo] affected their pocketbooks, it closed up businesses operated by Japanese."[92] Admiral Kimmel regarded his fleet as being on a wartime footing for the whole of 1941.

[92] *Ibid.*, Part 7, p. 3130.

Views of the Crisis

In Washington, at the offices of the CNO and the Chief of Staff, the action taken in Honolulu as a result of the July 25 dispatch was evidently of little moment. Rear Admiral R. K. Turner, who drafted the dispatch for the Navy, did not expect Admiral Kimmel to take any action because, while he anticipated a hostile reaction to the American moves, he did not anticipate it in the immediate future. General Marshall, whose memory of the economic and political situation of 1941 was understandably dim by 1945, testified that the only alert prior to November 28, 1941, was that of June, 1940. "I don't think they were alerts," he said of the July and October messages. "They were information bearing on the increasing and critical situation. Just what they were on the specific dates I am not prepared to testify."[93]

This vagueness may be partly explained by Marshall's general reticence as a witness. But it can also be laid to the Army's traditional lack of interest in economic or diplomatic events and their implications for foreign policy. These areas were left to the State Department and the White House. Marshall, for example, when questioned as to how he felt in 1941 about the effect of embargoes on American-Japanese relations, said he could add no comment to the wording in the joint dispatch of July 25.[94] He did remark, however, that during this period "our state of mind . . . I am referring now to both Stark and myself—was to do all in our power here at home, with the State Department or otherwise, to try to delay this break to the last moment, because of our state of unpreparedness, and because of our involvement in other parts of the world."[95] It is probable that in sending the joint dispatch Marshall simply went along with the Navy, perhaps in response to the urgency with which the latter viewed the situation, perhaps for the sake of interservice unity. Whatever the case, he made no recorded objection to the Embargo Act. Herbert Feis in his book *The Road to Pearl Harbor* concludes that Marshall "either thought the freezing action outside his province or that it would not cause a break."[96] The Army is on record pleading for delay many times during 1941. But its overriding interest was in the materiel available for local

[93] *Ibid.*, Part 3, p. 1298. [94] *Ibid.*, p. 1079.
[95] *Ibid.*, Part 32, p. 560. [96] Feis, *The Road to Pearl Harbor*, p. 240.

defense; how best to distribute the limited amounts among the various commands; and how best to make their great needs known to Congress so as to increase the quality, quantity, and speed of delivery.

In the official account of WPD thinking during World War II, written by Mark Watson, the same emphasis prevails. Watson's account of the Far East during the July crisis and the summer of 1941 attends only to the problem of increasing the defensive capabilities of the Philippines. He speculates on exactly what stimulated American interest in the Philippines; he rejects as a cause the new Japanese threats that we have described; he does not mention the issue of trade embargoes; and he finally concludes:

> ... one may reasonably suspect that America's great burst of activity in the Philippines came about not so much from alarms over the new threats as from a sudden awareness that in the newly developed B-17 heavy bombers America at last had a weapon with which the Philippines could actually and effectively and for the first time be armed against threats.[97]

If this was typical of Army thinking as late as 1950, when Watson's book was published and when the full record was available, it seems probable that in 1941 the technology of weapons and availability of materiel also weighed more heavily than other considerations in the Army's foreign-policy estimates. Beginning in July the defense of the Philippines was certainly given more urgent attention than the defense of the Hawaiian Islands and therefore was remembered more clearly by the officers concerned. Honolulu at this time had been supplied with more equipment than any other American outpost and was generally regarded as being impregnable.

In contrast to the Army, the Navy had taken a strong and articulate stand against the imposition of sanctions. Reticence on the subject did not characterize naval witnesses at the congressional inquiry. Admiral Turner, for example, testified to his disapproval of an embargo:

> I believed it would make war certain between the U.S. and Japan.
>
> . . . .
>
> I think it made sure the fall of the third Konoye Cabinet, which had begun in the middle of July, and I think that it made sure the going in of the militaristic Cabinet. It undermined the Konoye Cabinet which I believe

[97] Watson, *Chief of Staff: Prewar Plans and Preparations*, p. 440.

was trying to keep from war with the United States, but not trying to keep out of war with Britain and the Dutch.[98]

Admiral Stark, too, has left a long record of pronouncements on the subject of embargoes. Before President Roosevelt made his final decision to embargo trade with Japan, he had consulted Admiral Stark, who in turn requested Admiral Turner to make a study. Turner's study was completed on July 19 and forwarded to the President with a covering letter giving Stark's approval. His main conclusion read:

> An embargo would probably result in a fairly early attack by Japan on Malaya and the Netherlands East Indies, and possibly would involve the United States in early war in the Pacific. If war in the Pacific is to be accepted by the United States, actions leading up to it should, if practicable, be postponed until Japan is engaged in a war in Siberia. It may well be that Japan has decided against an early attack on the British and Dutch, but has decided to occupy Indo-China and to strengthen her position there, also to attack the Russians in Siberia. Should this prove to be the case, it seems probable that the United States could engage in war in the Atlantic, and that Japan would not intervene for the time being, even against the British.[99]

He recommended that "trade with Japan not be embargoed at this time."

This conflict of policy between the Army and Navy naturally led to differing estimates of the signals available, though perhaps "conflict" is too strong a word. More accurately, the Navy had a policy; the Army was indifferent. This discrepancy accounts for the calmer tone of the Army dispatch of July 8 and perhaps for the five-day delay in sending it to Hawaii. It also partly accounts for the interpretations of the signals by Army Intelligence and the War Plans Division.

How G-2 Interpreted the Signals

At this point in time we link WPD and G-2 because their evaluations were very similar. The War Plans Division of the Army was the organization closest to the Chief of Staff and in the best position to influence his judgment, for in 1941 it had already assumed a leading role in guiding and coordinating the various G's in the War Department.[100] No WPD

[98]*Hearings*, Part 4, p. 1945.
[99]*Ibid.*, Part 5, p. 2384.
[100]WPD was G-5. The other divisions were G-1 (Personnel), G-2 (Intelligence), G-3 (Mobilization and Training), and G-4 (Supply), all of which were primarily concerned with Zone of Interior problems.

strategic estimates of the July crisis were released for the hearings, but we know that this organization and G-2 were exchanging information. General L. T. Gerow, who helped to draft the joint dispatch of July 25, was head of WPD for this period and was responsible for all operational orders to the theaters. He testified that he depended on G-2 for "evaluation of all enemy intelligence."[101] Unfortunately he was not questioned by anyone about the July and October messages of 1941. But we do have a selection of the G-2 strategic estimates for this period.

These G-2 estimates appeared for the most part over the signature of the Intelligence Chief, Sherman Miles. They followed pretty closely the content of the MAGIC dispatches quoted above. The hypotheses elaborated also paralleled the ones that we have mentioned: speculation on the probability of a northern rather than a southern move by Japan, and Japanese attitudes toward open conflict with the United States. Reproduced below are the main hypotheses and predictions from the G-2 memoranda presented in evidence at the congressional hearings.

> JULY 7—*From memo for Chief of Staff on eastern Siberian situation*: "the Japanese are unlikely to take aggressive action against Eastern Siberian land forces ... [because of] reluctance to change from their present southern orientation to a northern one. This ... does not preclude increasing Japanese pressures through Outer Mongolia, towards Verkhneudinsk, of naval blockades of the entrances to the Sea of Japan, the Sea of Okhotsk and possibly Bering Sea."[102]

> JULY 11—*From memo for Assistant Chief of Staff, WPD*: "the naval authorities, and business interests will exert every effort to avoid a conflict with the United States regardless of the latter's participation in the European War. . . .
>
> ". . . Japan will probably continue to assemble, by gradual withdrawals from China, a field force for possible employment either in Southeastern Asia or against Russia. Her hopes of empire are bound up with an Axis victory and she is subject to strong German pressure to attack Russia at once; nevertheless it is believed that she will avoid precipitate action and will continue her policy of avoiding war with Russia on the one hand and with the United States and Great Britain on the other. If forced, or if selecting to choose between action against Russia or to the Southwest, she will be influenced by Ger-

---

[101] *Hearings*, Part 3, p. 1039.
[102] *Ibid.*, Part 14, p. 1335.

many's success against Russia, ... and by America's action, particularly as regards the distribution of United States' naval strength, and as regards attempts to send supplies to Russia through Vladivostok. Should the choice be the southward advance, it will probably consist of a containment of Hong Kong and the Philippine Islands while attacking British Malaya via Thailand and Indo-China."[103]

JULY 17—*From memo for Chief of Staff on Japanese movement into French Indochina* (*this memo gives the details of the Japanese ultimatum to the Vichy government and the announcement of the Japanese Cabinet's resignation on July 16*): "One fact seems evident ... and that is that Vichy will be given a breathing spell and the expedition to Indo-China may be deferred or even abandoned."[104]

JULY 17—*From memo for Chief of Staff on the mobilization of additional Japanese manpower*: "In the opinion of this Division the first aggressive move if made, will be into Indo-China to deny this region to a DeGaulist, Pro-British, Pro-American faction steadily growing in power there. Japan, while building up her strength in Manchoukuo, will then await the outcome of the German-Soviet war. If and when Germany crushes European Russia and the Siberian Garrison deteriorates in strength or morale, Japan will probably move in to seize the long desired Maritime Provinces of Siberia."[105]

JULY 18—*Memo for Chief of Staff on new Japanese Cabinet*: "The new Cabinet may be regarded as strongly nationalistic, and while probably more moderate and conservative than would have been the case had an Army Officer been given the portfolio as Foreign Minister, it may be that added impulse will be given to Japan's Southward Advance.... Admiral Toyoda has just completed a tour as Minister of Commerce and Industry, and is fully aware of the deplorable conditions of Japan's foreign trade and internal economy."[106]

JULY 25—*From memo for Chief of Staff on sanctions against Japan, which includes penciled note*, "Written prior to receipt of information regarding embargo decision": "For some time, the policy of our government has been based upon a desire to restrain Japan by moral embargoes and export control, neither of which were stringent enough to drive Japan into further aggressive action toward Malaysia and the Netherlands Indies.... Japan has now burst through these mild restraints ... and is now embarked upon new aggression which endangers the safety of all the areas in the Southwestern Pacific,

[103] *Ibid.*, p. 1337f.   [104] *Ibid.*, p. 1342.
[105] *Ibid.*   [106] *Ibid.*, p. 1343.

including the Philippine Islands ... the last reason for withholding effective sanctions against Japan has been brushed aside. ...

. . . .

" ... Effective economic sanctions against Japan imposed by us today, would not, in the opinion of this Division, force Japan to take any steps in the way of aggressive action which she does not plan to take anyway, when a favorable opportunity arises, nor would they precipitate a declaration of war on us by Japan. Such action on our part need not and should not distract our attention from the main theater of operations. On the contrary, by adopting such a policy we will be able to conserve for Britain and for ourselves supplies which, from the viewpoint of our national defense, are being worse than wasted when we place them in Japanese hands."[107]

If we attend to the dates of these particular memos, and compare them with the dates at which MAGIC on the one hand, and public news sources on the other hand, revealed the information, we see that in timing, the G-2 estimates were about even with the public news sources. In content they were a little less knowledgeable. For example, no one writing for *The New York Times* jumped to the conclusion that the Japanese Cabinet change of July 16 meant a breathing spell for the Vichy government.

A quick glance at the main Far Eastern articles from *The New York Times* for July, 1941, confirms this impression. For example, in a July 4 dispatch from Shanghai we read: "Japan, presumably in a deal with Germany ... is preparing to move southward within two weeks against French Indo-China and perhaps Thailand"; she hopes to avoid conflict with the United States and Britain until she can get naval and military bases from which to attack the Netherlands East Indies. Reports of the same date from Tokyo announced the withdrawal of Japanese ships from the Atlantic, and the cancelation of two shipments of chrome ore to the United States. Dispatches from July 1 to July 17 speculated on what policy the Japanese Cabinet would adopt toward the Russo-German war. A July 11 notice by Otto Tolischus reported Konoye as having said that Japan must go her own way and rely on her own powers. The Japanese press, Tolischus continued, was maintaining an icy neutrality on the Russo-German war, and attacking the United States and Britain for helping

[107] *Ibid.*, p. 1344f.

Chungking. A July 14 dispatch enumerated new war strictures, including censorship of cable and telephone messages to England and the United States. The growing restraints on communications had important consequences for intelligence, yet there is no mention of them in available G-2 or ONI files for July.

On July 15 Japanese news moved up to the front page, with an Associated Press dispatch headed "JAPANESE ATTACK IN SOUTH HELD NEAR—INDO-CHINA AND THAILAND SEEN AS TARGETS—CLOSING OF KOBE EMBARKATION PORT TO FOREIGNERS FOR TEN DAYS." Japanese military and naval authorities in Shanghai appeared to be spreading reports that Japan intended to attack Russia in Siberia, either "on the day Moscow falls" or on August 15. Foreign military men, however, were convinced that this was at once a war of nerves on Russia and a smoke screen to cover Japan's real intentions. They said that Indochina would be the next objective, but that Japan might risk attacking Siberia if European Russia collapsed.

On July 16 Douglas Robertson reported from Shanghai a division in the Japanese Cabinet about the course of the projected war in the Far East. Matsuoka, the Foreign Minister, favored a southward drive; Shigemitsu urged an attack on Siberia. An item of the same date listed the demands presented by Tokyo to Adm. Jean Decoux, Governor General of French Indochina. The *Times* of July 17 carried news of the resignation of the Japanese Cabinet, and notice of a troop shift from China, which might portend a drive on Siberia. Dispatches of July 18 and 19 concerned the new cabinet and Toyoda's succession to the post of Foreign Minister. A column from Washington by Hallett Abend saw the cabinet shift as an excuse to clear Japan of ties with Russia and the Axis and leave her to the unhampered pursuit of self-interest. On July 22, however, Toyoda was reported to have reassured the Axis ambassadors that the Triple Alliance stood firm. News about Indochina continued to emphasize troop concentrations near the border, departures to the south of Japanese warships, and alleged insults by the British and French in Indochina that would justify Japanese occupation of the country.

On July 23 a front-page headline over an article by John H. Crider in Washington, D.C., announced that "U.S. PLANS ECONOMIC CURBS ON JAPAN TO COUNTER ANY INDO-CHINA INVASION." The United States would freeze Japanese assets, prohibit the export of petroleum products to Japan, and stop Japanese gold purchases. On the following day the news came that Vichy had yielded to Japan's demands for bases in southern French Indochina and that the United States had cut off conversations with Japan. On July 25, it was reported that Roosevelt had hinted at an oil embargo, and Sumner Welles condemned Japanese "aggression." A dispatch from Saigon reported that Japanese warships had reached Indochina. The President explained informally to members of the Volunteer Participation Committee why he had so far refrained from imposing sanctions on Japan. The July 26 issue carried the front-page headline: "U.S. AND BRITAIN FREEZE JAPANESE ASSETS." Tolischus commented from Tokyo that Japan was bitter over the U.S. stand. A small announcement read: "Alert status in Hawaii. U.S. Army order, Honolulu, July 25, announces precautionary training. Army officials declined to comment on reports that the order came because of increasing tension between the U.S. and Japan." The July 27 headline proclaimed: "ROOSEVELT PUTS FILIPINO FORCES IN U.S. ARMY AS JAPAN FREEZES AMERICAN-BRITISH FUNDS."

The foregoing is an extremely condensed summary of the Far Eastern news for the period from July 1 to July 27 as reported in *The New York Times*, but it is enough to suggest that G-2's estimates might just as well have been based on publicly available material as on MAGIC. The first mention of Indochina in the selection of G-2 estimates (see page 121) occurred on July 11, but in a rather vague context: "Should the choice be the southward advance, it will probably consist of a containment of Hong Kong and the Philippine Islands while attacking British Malaya via Thailand and Indo-China."[108] Anyone with access to MAGIC, such as G-2's Far Eastern team, should have known by this date that Japan had already decided on a specific program for Indochina. The G-2 memorandum of July 17 mentioned that the Chief of Staff had been informed on July 15 of the ultimatum presented to the Vichy government by Japan; the details were available in *The New York Times* of July 16. The cabinet resignation reported in the *Times* of July 17 was the subject of a G-2 memorandum on July 18. The recommendation of sanctions appeared in the *Times* of July 23 and in a G-2 memorandum on July 25.

[108] This was a word-for-word repetition of a judgment made in the May 24, 1941, estimate. (*Ibid.*, Part 21, p. 4759.)

On the first notice of the Japanese Cabinet's resignation, G-2 analysts had concluded that "the expedition to Indo-China may be deferred or even abandoned." By the next day (July 18), with knowledge of the new cabinet's composition, they believed an "added impulse will be given to Japan's Southward Advance." These two statements were among their few definite short-range predictions; unfortunately they contradicted each other. The G-2 memorandum of July 7 was in distinct disagreement with the dispatch sent to the Army in Honolulu on July 8. It said: "The Japanese are unlikely to take aggressive action against Eastern Siberian land forces. . . ." Here was another fairly definite prediction, and it was correct. However, it ran counter to all the thinking being done at the time by Army and Navy planners, and it soon disappeared, to be replaced in the memorandum of July 17 by the more popular view: "If and when Germany crushes European Russia and the Siberian Garrison deteriorates in strength or morale, Japan will probably move in to seize the long-desired Maritime Provinces of Siberia." The two contrary predictions would very likely not have been made if the MAGIC dispatches and the dispatches to the theater had been available to the writer and understood by him. If these dispatches actually were available, then the only conclusion possible is that G-2 was less informed and less equipped to estimate the situation than a good news agency, and even more cautious.

The predictions of G-2 consisted primarily of a careful listing of alternatives, preceded by such phrases as "it may be" or "it seems." General Miles, who headed G-2, refused to weigh the evidence on the issue of a move north or south. But he did take a clear stand in favor of embargoes, in contrast to the Navy. We may assume that in this particular case Miles was reflecting, rather than guiding, WPD opinion, particularly since he recorded his approval so late (i.e., on July 25, just before the embargo went into effect). Indeed, he already had headlines in *The New York Times* to tell him that it was safe to voice his approval. As we have seen, news of the impending Embargo Act leaked to the press on July 22 and was printed the following day. The position taken by G-2, and perhaps also by the War Department, that imposition of sanctions would not increase the probability of war between the United States and Japan, may partly account for the fact that the embargo and the alert of July 25 dropped from the memory of Army officials in Washington.

More Washington Signals

To be fair to G-2, however, we must remember that even the Japanese Cabinet was divided on the subject of whether to move north or south and that the U.S. administration was divided on the embargo issue. Secretaries Stimson, Morgenthau, and Ickes had urgently and frequently recommended to the President an embargo on oil exports. Evidently the President had been holding off because he shared the naval view that this act might be the final stimulus to drive Japan to attack either Russia or the Dutch East Indies. As he wrote to Harold Ickes on July 1, 1941:

> I think it will interest you to know that the Japs are having a real drag-down and knock-out fight among themselves and have been for the past week—trying to decide which way they are going to jump—attack Russia, attack the South Seas (thus throwing in their lot definitely with Germany) or whether they will sit on the fence and be more friendly with us. No one knows what the decision will be but, as you know, it is terribly important for the control of the Atlantic for us to help keep peace in the Pacific. I simply have not got enough Navy to go round—and every little episode in the Pacific means fewer ships in the Atlantic.[109]

By July 8 a Japanese MAGIC message to Berlin, intercepted on July 2, had been translated and distributed. It described the decisions of the cabinet to abide by the Tripartite Pact, to press on with its program of southern expansion, and to prepare for eventual war with the United States and Britain. In the face of this information, Roosevelt and Hull evidently changed their view of an embargo as a provocation and came to see it as a deterrent. By July 21 Roosevelt was counting on the threat of a complete embargo to bring the Japanese into line. This view, coupled with administrative indecision, explains the loose phrasing of the Embargo Act, so that in Roosevelt's words, the "policy . . . might change any day and from there on we would refuse any and all licenses."[110] In a cablegram to Harry Hopkins in London on July 26 Roosevelt expressed satisfaction with the results of the Anglo-American action freezing Japanese assets:

> I hear their Government much upset and no conclusive future policy has been determined on. Tell him [Churchill] also in great confidence that I have

[109] *F.D.R.: His Personal Letters: 1928–1945*, ed. Elliott Roosevelt and Joseph P. Lash, Vol. II, p. 1174. Hereafter cited as *Letters*.

[110] Notes on cabinet meeting of July 24, 1941, quoted by Langer and Gleason, *The Undeclared War, 1940–1941*, p. 649.

suggested to Nomura that Indo-China be neutralized by Britain, Dutch, Chinese, Japan and ourselves, placing Indo-China somewhat in status of Switzerland. Japan to get rice and fertilizer but all on condition that Japan withdraw armed forces from Indo-China in toto. I have had no answer yet. When it comes it will probably be unfavorable but we have at least made one more effort to avoid Japanese expansion to South Pacific.[111]

The MAGIC message of July 2 (translated July 8) was available to G-2 and ONI, but was not forwarded to Kimmel. G-2 does not seem to have made any immediate use of it. We have no way of knowing what the Office of Naval Intelligence did with it, since the only strategic estimate submitted in evidence for this period was a memorandum of July 2, 1941, written by Comdr. A. H. McCollum, head of ONI's Far Eastern Division, and entitled "Possibility of Early Aggressive Action by Japan." This memorandum gives the substance of the information forwarded in the second naval dispatch of July 3 to Kimmel:

1. The Commandant of the 3rd Naval District reports that a reliable informant close to Japanese industrial interests has stated that these interests expect Japan to make an aggressive move against Russia on July 20th. Too much credence should not be placed in this report as in the past the Japanese industrial and business community in New York has *not* proved to be a very reliable barometer of Japanese government action [author's italics]. Nevertheless the following factors would seem to indicate that some sort of action probably distasteful to the United States may be planned, namely:

a) Since about June 25th, there has been an absence of sailings from Japan of merchant vessels bound for United States East coast and gulf ports and if this trend continues, in about two weeks there will be no Japanese merchant ships in the Atlantic.

b) Simultaneous recognition by the Axis powers of the Japanese-sponsored Wang Ching-wei government of China may have been procured by Japan's promise to take aggressive action against the non-Axis powers.

c) The announcement today that the Japanese government had decided on its policy in regard to the Russo-German war, coupled with the fact that publication of any policy whatsoever or comment on any such policy had been deferred, suggest the possibility that the policy may be other than the often publicised southward advance policy.

d) Japan has for many years coveted the pre-Amur provinces of Siberian Russia, both as a security measure and for the natural resources of these areas.

[111] *Letters*, Vol. II, p. 1189*f*.

2. The present disposition of the Japanese armed forces would seem to preclude the possibility of any sudden thrust against Russia. Their disposition and composition appear to be such that if any sudden aggressive action at all is planned, such action would be in the direction of further minor action against the South China coast or possibly directed towards seizure of additional bases in French Indo-China. Nevertheless the naval forces in particular may be reoriented in a very short interval of time and the situation is such that the possibility of Japanese action against Russia, though still considered unlikely, cannot be ruled out entirely.[112]

It is interesting to notice that the ONI evaluation of information coming from Japanese businessmen as "not . . . very reliable" was omitted from the dispatch to Honolulu reporting the rumor that Japan would attack Russia on July 20.

Other information available to G-2 and ONI through the State Department confirmed reports that Japan was about to seize military control of Indochina and Siam so as to threaten the Burma Road, Singapore, and the Netherlands Indies: a telegram from Ambassador Winant in London on July 4, 1941; a memorandum to Hull from his Far Eastern adviser Maxwell Hamilton on July 5; a State Department summary of Far Eastern developments dated July 10; and a message from Chiang Kai-shek to the President on July 8. The message from Chiang Kai-shek read:

> From most reliable sources originating from Japan it is learned that a secret agreement has been concluded and signed between Germany, Italy and Japan on the 6th of July, covering on the one hand recognition of Japanese spheres of interest, and on the other Japanese undertaking to advance southward and against Siberia. Please communicate the news to the President immediately.[113]

A telegram on the same day from Chiang Kai-shek's Minister of Communications had reported "definite information" of a Japanese decision "to move southward against Singapore and the Dutch East Indies first before coping with the Siberian problem."[114] The Minister had forwarded a telegram originating in Berlin on July 4 which reported that

> although understanding was reached as to the respective spheres of interests and responsibilities the three Axis partners were unable to agree on the tempo of action. Germany and Italy desired immediate Japanese advance

112 *Hearings*, Part 15, p. 1852.
113 *Ibid.*, Part 19, p. 3496.
114 *Ibid.*, p. 3497.

southward to which Matsuoka would not agree owing to the then prevailing situation. I now learn that since the outbreak of the Russo-German conflict complete agreement has been reached which calls for early action against Vladivostok by Japan, simultaneous with consolidation of Japanese bases in Indo-China and Thailand preparatory to an advance southward against the British and the Dutch.[115]

During July Ambassador Grew and his staff were also forwarding communications to the State Department on the internal division in the Japanese Cabinet, on probable lines of action with respect to the Axis, on Japanese press reports, and on rumors of the impending Indochina invasion. Grew urged that the United States privately inform the Japanese government of its intention to impose sanctions should Japan attack Indochina, so that the embargo could serve as a bargaining point before the event rather than as punishment for a *fait accompli*. Grew was not on the list of those receiving MAGIC information. Indeed the information reaching him from Washington was so sparse at this time that he cabled on July 10 complaining that he was obliged to go to his British colleague to learn the progress of the current State Department conversations with the Japanese ambassador in Washington.[116] This meant that while Grew was an expert interpreter of Japanese political activities and his dispatches to Washington were full of sound information, they lacked the sure confirmation available in the capital. This particular denial of information raises once more the delicate question of the value of secrecy at this level. It also occasions some speculation about what Washington expected an ambassador to accomplish by diplomatic conversations in the dark.

In addition to MAGIC, then, Washington had confirmatory signals from a large number of sources: public news media of a very high caliber, the embassy in Tokyo, Chiang Kai-shek's government, Far Eastern experts in the State Department, and the Navy's traffic analysis unit. (The information coming out of G-2 added nothing new to the picture, and ONI interpretations were sparse.) These signals did not point clearly to an impending Japanese movement to the south or to the north in Asia. At the same time, none of them announced a direct attack on the United States, any more than did the signals for June, 1940. There was implicit danger in Japan's threat to use force against any "resistance" by the British

[115] *Ibid.*, p. 3498.
[116] Langer and Gleason, *The Undeclared War, 1940–1941*, p. 637.

or the Americans to Japanese expansion into Indochina. As in 1940, however, no one could safely predict what U.S. policy would be, beyond the expression of moral disapproval, whether Japan moved north or south.

Rumors about a possible embargo were in the air, however, and had come up for discussion in the preceding months often enough for Ambassador Grew to urge private disclosure to the Japanese government of our intentions, and for Admiral Stark to predict war with Japan as a sure result, and for Secretary Ickes to threaten to resign unless an embargo were put into effect. The timing of the decision, after months of debate, came as a surprise to many people within our own government, as well as to the Japanese. That the embargo might be interpreted as Anglo-American "resistance" was something that Washington decided to risk. The military in Washington interpreted it as a provocative rather than a deterrent action, and made this clear in the joint dispatch. The obvious conclusion is that the primary signal for the alert of July 25 was the action taken by Washington, rather than the Japanese move to the south.

It is by now also apparent that Washington military officials, in both Intelligence and Operations, as well as State Department and White House officials, were in receipt of many more signals than the overseas commands. They were in fact bombarded with conflicting messages about Japan's next aggressive moves and with divergent interpretations of conversations with Nomura and public statements by Japanese officials. They were also tossed in a storm of policy discussion about what would and what would not effectively deter Japan. The theater commands received a distillation of this profusion of material outlining the main moves of both Japan and the United States for the immediate future. Fortunately, with MAGIC as a sure guide, most of what the theaters received was correct, the major exception being the prediction of a move against Siberia. The messages were also worded in such a way as to alert both services, whether or not Washington intended them to go on an alert.

If anything emerges clearly from a study of this alert, it is the soundness of having a center for evaluating a mass of conflicting signals from specialized or partisan sources. It would have created endless confusion if Washington had tried to relay all available signals to the overseas commands. It is also clear that the evaluating center must be equipped with trained interpreters of international news, since special access to secret information is neither necessary nor sufficient for anticipating the course of events. The real uncertainties in political prediction arise from the great complexity of the international interests involved, and consequently the knowledgeability of a good news reporter is more helpful than access to a few top-secret cables. A reporter will usually have available a multiplicity of public evidences of the secrets contained in the cables themselves, since it is only in the last days of crisis that a government will attempt total censorship.

To expect a good reporter's interpretative ability from a theater commander would be unrealistic. His focus is necessarily on his own local problems. To expect it from G-2 and ONI, however, would not seem to be asking too much.

ALERT OCTOBER 16, 1941

From July to October, American-Japanese relations deteriorated even further. From the Japanese point of view, the American oil embargo figured prominently in this deterioration. While negotiations proceeded in terms of polite generalities between Ambassador Nomura and Secretary Hull, on the economic level the Japanese program of military training and territorial expansion was beginning to feel the pinch. The Japanese made several suggestions for releasing oil and scrap iron—by payments in Latin America, for example, or in return for gold shipments. But the officials in the State, Treasury, and Justice Departments who handled these requests evaded the issue. They were acting under Hull's instructions that "a direct answer be delayed as long as possible."[117] Consequently no oil or scrap was released, and by October 1 the American press was carrying news of a bitter Japanese press campaign against America's double-dealing: soft words and hostile acts.

It was also reported publicly that pressure was being put on the moderate Konoye government to get some concessions from the United States or resign. The Japanese military had in fact given Prince Konoye until October 15 to accomplish some *rapprochement* with the United States that

---

[117] Morgenthau Diaries, manuscript, Vol. 447, pp. 128*ff.*, quoted in Langer and Gleason, *The Undeclared War, 1940–1941*, p. 709.

would enable Japan to settle the China incident and proceed with her program for a "Greater East Asia Co-Prosperity Sphere." What Japan was willing to cede in return for a relaxation of the embargo was quite as narrow and rigid as what the United States was prepared to countenance in the way of further Japanese aggression. However, even at this late date Konoye set great store by a conference between leaders of the two countries, and there is some evidence that Roosevelt and the State Department seriously considered his suggestion. But in spite of Konoye's frantic communications to Nomura and in spite of Ambassador Grew's recommendations, no meeting was arranged and the Konoye Cabinet fell on October 15.

This was one deadline that the MAGIC cables had not explicitly revealed in advance, and Konoye's resignation, while expected, was not expected quite so soon. When news of the resignation reached Washington, President Roosevelt canceled his regular cabinet meeting and spent the afternoon of October 16 in conference with Secretaries Hull, Stimson, and Knox, General Marshall, Admiral Stark, and Harry Hopkins. Out of this meeting came a dispatch from Admiral Stark to the Atlantic, Pacific, and Asiatic fleets. It was sent the same evening in the most secure naval code, and in Honolulu was received first by Admiral Kimmel and forwarded immediately to General Short.

Signals to the Army in Hawaii

The dispatch that General Short received read as follows:

FROM: CNO
ACTION: CINCLANT CINCPAC CINCAF (Acknowledge)
1622Ø3

The resignation of the Japanese Cabinet has created a grave situation X If a new Cabinet is formed it will probably be strongly nationalistic and anti-American X If the Konoye Cabinet remains the effect will be that it will operate under a new mandate which will not include rapprochement with the U.S. X In either case hostilities between Japan and Russia are a strong possibility X Since the U.S. and Britain are held responsible by Japan for her present desperate situation there is also a possibility that Japan may attack these two powers X In view of these possibilities you will take due precautions including such preparatory deployments as will not disclose strategic

intention nor constitute provocative actions against Japan X Second and third
Adees inform appropriate Army and Naval District authorities X Acknowledge XX[118]

There is no record of communication from General Short to the War
Department concerning this cable. However, he testified before the Naval
Court of Inquiry that the impression he received from this message was
that "there was a very strong possibility of war between Russia and
Japan. . . . That weakened, as far as I was concerned, the probability of
immediate war between the U.S. and Japan, because apparently they had
considered the strongest possibility was between Russia and Japan."[119] In
other words this message simply reinforced the central prediction made in
the dispatch of July 8, which Short had characterized as "the only definite
prediction the War Department ever made to me."[120]

The ordering of contingencies in the October dispatch from "strongly
possible" to "possible" raises the question of what precautions a commander is supposed to take to meet a hostile situation that is not probable
but that still has a fair chance of occurring. In Washington the designa-
tions "possible," "strongly possible," and "probable" were carefully
weighed before the first two were selected for the dispatch of October 16.
The dispatch reached General Short in Honolulu at a time when the
Hawaiian Command was concerned about the presence of a large local
Japanese population and about the need for precautions against sabotage
and subversion. In this atmosphere the threat of a Japanese attack on
Russia or on British possessions in the Pacific would have underlined the
necessity for precautions against sabotage. Only the probability of a direct
attack on the United States or its possessions would have occasioned a full
alert. Pearl Harbor, however, was not on the American list of most-
probable Japanese targets. For General Short the characterization of a
Russo-Japanese war as "strongly possible" eliminated the probability of a
Japanese attack on Great Britain or America in the near future, and his
attention remained focused on dangers from local sabotage. He did not
remember any specific actions taken in response to the dispatch of October
16. As he testified, "we had tightened up all our guards against sabotage,

[118]*Hearings*, Part 14, p. 1402.
[119]*Ibid.*, Part 32, p. 191.
[120]*Ibid.*, Part 7, p. 3180.

and . . . against subversive measures . . . at the time of the freezing of the Japanese assets, and we had never taken off a great part of those; and I figured when I got that message that we were all right . . . and I was probably just a little more watchful."[121] As far as the published record indicates, General Short did not report to the War Department either the July or the October measures that he took to prevent sabotage and subversion.

On October 20 General Short received another dispatch that was also sent to the Commanding General, U.S. Army Forces in the Far East, and the Commanding General, Western Defense Command:

> Following War Department estimate of Japanese situation for your information. Tension between United States and Japan remains strained but no repeat no abrupt change in Japanese foreign policy appears imminent.[122]

There is no indication that General Short passed this information on to Admiral Kimmel. As far as Short was concerned, it definitely confirmed his belief that the dispatch of October 16 did not call for any alert measures from the Army beyond those already in force.

In addition to these two dispatches, General Short received two G-2 estimates of the Japanese situation from his local G-2 Contact Office, which was headed by Colonel Bicknell. The first of these, dated October 17, was written before the composition of the new Japanese Cabinet was known. It described the situation as "extremely critical" and "uncertain," and estimated that "Japan will, in the near future, take military action in new areas in the Far East."[123] Future Japanese moves were listed in the order of decreasing probability:

1. Attack Russia from the east.
2. Pressure French Indo-China and Thailand for concessions in the way of military, naval, and air bases, and guarantees of economic cooperation.
3. Attack British possessions in the Far East.
4. Defend against an American attack in support of the British.
5. Attack simultaneously the ABCD block at whichever points might promise her greatest tactical, strategic, and economic advantages.[124]

Bicknell isolated five reasons why the Japanese would attack Russia: (1) to extend their first line of defense as far to the west as possible as

121 *Ibid.*, Part 32, p. 191.   122 *Ibid.*, Part 14, p. 1389.
123 *Ibid.*, Part 18, p. 3196.   124 *Ibid.*, p. 3197.

insurance against aerial attacks on Japan proper, (2) to set up a buffer state between themselves and Germany, (3) to get raw materials from Siberia, (4) to stamp out communism, and (5) to continue their aggressions without risking active military intervention by the United States or Britain. Pressure on Indochina or Thailand, Bicknell argued, might either "precede or follow or occur simultaneously with an attack on Russia."[125] As for attacking the British, he believed that

> Japan, if faced with certain British military resistance to her plans, will unhesitatingly attack the British; and do so without a simultaneous attack on American possessions, because of no known binding agreement between the British and Americans for joint military action against Japan, and that the American public is not yet fully prepared to support such action. However, it must be evident to the Japanese that in case of such an attack on the British, they would most certainly have to fight the United States within a relatively short time.[126]

A simultaneous attack on the ABCD powers could not in Bicknell's view be entirely ruled out if Japan thought that war with the United States would be an inevitable consequence of her actions against Russia. If this were so, then Japan would strike at the most opportune time.

Bicknell's estimate of October 17 is remarkable primarily for its explicit statement that the Japanese would not attack American possessions directly. Knowing that they would have to fight America soon after they attacked the British, the Japanese nevertheless would initiate hostilities against the British, thereby surrendering the advantages of a surprise attack on America. Although in 1941 the advantages of the initial attack were not nearly so great as they are today, it is still striking that Bicknell should attribute to the Japanese such a low estimate of these advantages.

Bicknell wrote another memorandum on October 25, in which he pointed out that the Japanese Cabinet had fallen because of the unsuccessful negotiations with America and that the new cabinet had announced its intentions of working closely with the Axis powers. This announcement, Bicknell believed, "definitely places Japan in a camp hostile to the United States and other democracies; makes all protestations of peaceful intentions a sham . . . and forces America into a state of constant vigi-

[125] *Ibid.*, p. 3198.
[126] *Ibid.*

lance."[127] It is difficult to say today whether these words reflected Bicknell's personal alarm and indignation or whether they were a stereotype of current American statements about Japan's foreign policy, and therefore charged with a more general emotionalism. Bicknell's conclusion suggests that his alarm of October 17 had abated at least somewhat: "it seems logical to believe that no major move will be made before the latter part of November—in any direction—with a chance that the great break, if it comes, will not occur before spring."[128] He brought in support of this conclusion several pieces of evidence. The American government had taken two steps to avoid an incident. The first was the naval order to American vessels to avoid Asiatic ports in the North Pacific, including Shanghai; the other was the decision to use Archangel rather than Vladivostok as a port of entry for war supplies to Russia. Also three Japanese actions indicated a desire for delay. Premier Hideki Tojo had expressed his interest in continuing negotiations; Nomura announced that he would return to Japan for consultation with the new cabinet; and three Japanese vessels visited American ports to transport stranded Americans and Japanese to their respective homelands.

These two estimates from Bicknell are, unfortunately, the only products of Honolulu G-2 in the record. They suggest that Bicknell was at least an interested newspaper reader, for the evidence in his memorandum of October 25 was all public information. The Navy dispatch rerouting American vessels, for example, was published in the press and only in this way became available to the Army in Honolulu.

Bicknell's most startling beliefs—that Japan would not attack America directly and that America would enter the war at a pace of its own choosing in order to aid the British—were quite familiar in the United States at this time. They operated to color the perception of last-minute signals in Washington as well as in Honolulu: indications of danger to the United States were interpreted as signs of Japanese delay or of an impending attack *elsewhere*. Bicknell's reasoning was not corrected by Washington, because it was established policy for Washington G-2 not to communicate on such subjects with any theater G-2.[129] Therefore G-2 in Washington

127 *Ibid.*, p. 3202.
128 *Ibid.*
129 For a full discussion of Washington G-2, see Chap. 5.

had no way of correcting any misinterpretations that Bicknell might be making, or even of knowing what his interpretations were. In this case, it is doubtful that the central office would have found anything to correct, since its reasoning was fairly close to Bicknell's. (General Short was not influenced for the worse, since he had little contact with his Intelligence officers and gave the estimates only passing consideration.)

Bicknell's predictions followed closely the leads given in the dispatches of October 16 from the Chief of Naval Operations, and October 20 from the War Department. The timing and sequence of attacks "in the near future" described in his October 17 memorandum reflected the urgency of the October 16 CNO dispatch. A week later he moved the date of these attacks forward from the "near future" to the end of November or the following spring as a result of the reassuring tone of the October 20 dispatch. Though his estimate of October 25 warned that Japanese policy was forcing America "into a state of constant vigilance," there was no sign of such vigilance in the Hawaiian Department of the Army after receipt of the October 20 dispatch.

This message of October 20 was drafted in Washington on the 18th by General Gerow, head of Army War Plans, and was approved by General Marshall for dispatch to the theaters. Gerow's accompanying memorandum to Marshall stated briefly: "Our G-2 does not concur in the situation pictured by the Navy. War Plans Division agrees with G-2. Navy dispositions may require adjustment and a special alert. This is not true for the Army."[130] The difference of opinion between the Navy and the Army in Washington had repercussions in the Hawaiian Department of the Army, not at this moment, but later. Short remembered the alarmist wording of the Navy dispatch of October 16 and the restraining tone of the Army dispatch of the 20th. On November 27, therefore, when he read the message to the Navy, "This is a war warning," it made no great impression on him—"no more so than the fact that they [CNO] had said before that the Japs would probably attack."[131] When Short later testified to this, Mr. Kaufman, Associate General Counsel for the Joint Congressional Committee, questioned indignantly: "Do you mean to say, General, that with information of that kind, you were justified in not going on an

---

[130] *Hearings*, Part 14, p. 1389.
[131] *Ibid.*, Part 7, p. 2983.

all-out alert?" Short replied: "I think very definitely that I was. The fact that the War Department did not even inquire or give me any direct information [serves] to justify it."[132] Kaufman questioned: "Had you ever in your experience seen a message to a field commander using the words, 'This is a war warning'?" Short answered:

> No, sir; but I knew that the Navy messages were habitually rather more aggressive than the Army [ones]. On October 16 we had a message in which they said Japan would attack. On October 20 I had one from the War Department saying they didn't expect any. My message [of November 27] said nothing about a war warning and his [Kimmel's] did; I think the Navy messages were inclined to be more positive, possibly you might say more alarming, in the context.[133]

General Short's estimate of the Navy's language was correct for the July and October dispatches that we have examined. He was also influenced by their content. When he received the final alert message in November, his mind was still on a Russo-Japanese conflict, and he continued to believe that the targets for Japanese aggression were first Russia, then Southeast Asia, or possibly a simultaneous attack on both areas. Since he had received no information to the contrary from the War Department, he assumed that the basic hypotheses of the July and October dispatches were still in effect. This was not an unnatural assumption for him to make. For it is only in the context of Washington's more complete knowledge that the final warning messages of November 27 unambiguously signaled the danger of imminent war between the United States and Japan. Only after the event could they be interpreted as a warning to prepare for an attack on Pearl Harbor from without. In Honolulu before the attack the Army warning message seemed to call for an alert against sabotage and for preparation to support the British, if necessary.

It cannot be emphasized too strongly that a warning to a field commander is always read in the specific local context. The messages of November 24 and 27 left a great deal to the interpretation and discretion of the local commander without taking into account the effect of prior messages on the local interpretation. To measure this effect was probably an impossible job, considering the distance between Washington and the overseas commands, the infrequency of communication, and the differ-

[132] *Ibid.*, p. 2977.
[133] *Ibid.*, p. 2983.

ences between local and national interests. Nevertheless when the basis for an alert was something other than a local phenomenon, Washington was probably better equipped to determine the time and type of alert than was the local commander. Any specification would naturally have been subject to local constraints, but when Washington initiated an alert action, it appears that it should have taken full responsibility for ordering the exact degree of alert and making sure that the order was put into effect in the manner intended.

Signals to the Navy in Hawaii

Again in October, Admiral Kimmel had more information than General Short. For this crisis Kimmel did not have the benefit of relayed MAGIC dispatches, and neither he nor his Intelligence officers knew that this source was now closed to the theaters. He had, however, several dispatches from the Office of the Chief of Naval Operations that were an index to the increasing tension in U.S.-Japanese relations. One of these, forwarded to Kimmel on October 16, was a warning sent to all merchant vessels: "There is a possibility of hostile action by Japan against U.S. shipping." All ships in the western Pacific were ordered into friendly ports.[134] This information also appeared in the press and was therefore available to General Short and Colonel Bicknell.

A dispatch of October 17 to the Asiatic Fleet, with a copy to Kimmel for information, rerouted all trans-Pacific shipping to and from the Far East through the Torres Straits between Australia and New Guinea and well clear of the Japanese Mandates.[135] This clearing of the sea lanes to the

[134]"There is a possibility of hostile action by Japan against U.S. shipping. United States merchant ships at sea in the Pacific proceed now as follows: In Chinese waters, China Sea or Dutch Indies waters, proceed immediately to Manila, Singapore or a North Australian port. In North Pacific westbound, except those bound to Vladivostok, proceed to Honolulu unless close to the Philippines, in the latter case proceed there. Ships bound for Vladivostok, proceed on voyage. If Honolulu bound continue voyage. If in North Pacific eastbound, continue voyage. If in South Pacific continue voyage. Vessels operating coastwise off of South America or between the United States and the west coast of South America, continue voyage. All coastwise shipping eastern Pacific, continue voyage. Usual trade routes should be avoided." (*Ibid.*, Part 14, p. 1402.)

[135]"Effective immediately route all trans-Pacific U.S. flag shipping to and from the following areas Far East area plus Shanghai and India and East India area as defined in WPL 46 thru Torres Straits keeping to the southward and well clear of Orange mandates taking maximum advantage of Dutch and Australian patrolled areas. Make arrangements with Australian naval board for Torres Straits pilots." (*Ibid.*, p. 1403.)

north and northwest of Oahu was one reason why the Japanese task force could approach Pearl Harbor without being observed by American ships. Another dispatch on the same day ordered Kimmel to "take all practicable precautions for the safety of the airfields at Wake and Midway."[136] These two islands were important steppingstones on the trans-Pacific route of the long-range bombers being sent to reinforce the Philippines. Kimmel issued a preparatory order on November 10 to implement this directive. His plan was to put twelve marine fighters on Wake, eighteen on Midway, and prepare facilities for basing PBY patrol planes. He interpreted "precautions" as measures against attack, not against sabotage. Finally, on October 23 Kimmel received notice that all transports with reinforcements for the Philippines were to proceed only in convoy or under naval escort.[137]

In addition to these dispatches, Admiral Kimmel had received a number of letters from Admiral Stark. Stark was extremely modest about his information and frequently professed confusion or ignorance. But in reality he had much to offer. For example, on July 31 he wrote to Capt. Charles M. Cooke, Commander of the *Pennsylvania*, who forwarded the letter to Kimmel:

> Some of the things that you have asked, and some of the things which Kimmel has recently asked, and which I will answer as soon as I can, are things for which I have been striving to get answers in Washington. The press on many of these points really gives you as much information as I have.[138]

[136] "Because of the great importance of continuing to reenforce the Philippines with long range Army bombers you are requested to take all practicable precautions for the safety of the airfields at Wake and Midway." (*Ibid.*)

[137] "Until further orders all army and navy transpacific troop transports, ammunition ships and such others with sufficiently important military cargo will be escorted both ways between Honolulu and Manila. Authorized route slow vessels in above categories which would unduly prolong voyage via Torres Straits without escort. To insure minimum demands for escort from Pacific fleet schedules must be arranged so that these ships proceed in company. CINCAF should take over escort when and where practicable as arranged between CINCPAC and CINCAF. General escorting other transpacific American flag shipping not considered warranted at this time in view of routing prescribed in my 162258. Where cargo in merchant bottoms for Guam is involved normal routing is authorized.

"Cargo for Guam should be so assembled and loaded that a minimum number of ships be required to make that port...." (*Ibid.*)

[138] *Ibid.*, Part 16, p. 2175.

Despite this unpromising beginning, Stark went on to give an informative summary of the Navy's thinking on Japan:

> As you probably know from our despatches, and from my letters, we have felt that the Maritime Provinces are now definitely Japanese objectives. Turner thinks Japan will go up there in August. He may be right. He usually is. My thought has been that while Japan would ultimately go to Siberia, she would delay going until she had the Indo-China-Thailand situation more or less to her liking and until there is some clarification of the Russian-German clash. Also she may concentrate on the China "incident." Of course, embargoes or near embargoes may cause any old kind of an upset and make a reestimate of the situation necessary.[139]

Admiral Stark evidently believed that Kimmel's press information in Honolulu was quite as good as that in Washington, D.C. For example, after the *Kearny* was torpedoed, Stark wrote to Kimmel on October 17 that he was still waiting for news of the number of casualties and other details and added: "I will release everything to the press as soon as I can, so you should know almost as soon as I do." This belief in the speed and efficiency of Honolulu's international news service[140] was shared by Admiral Turner, head of Navy War Plans, and it led to a bitter exchange between Turner and Kimmel before the Naval Court of Inquiry.[141] Turner claimed that Kimmel could have been adequately prepared for the December 7 attack on the basis of an intelligent reading of the Honolulu newspapers.

Actually Admiral Stark's opinions were frequently at odds with the press reports. For example, in a letter of September 22 to Admiral Hart, Commander of the Asiatic Fleet, he wrote:

> The press is making much at the moment of the way the Far Eastern situation has apparently quieted down. One cannot help being impressed with the optimistic note of the editorial writers and columnists in this regard. For my own part, I feel that false hopes are being raised. While on the surface the Japanese appear to be making *some* effort at reaching a satisfactory solution, I cannot disregard the possibility that they are merely stalling for time and waiting until the situation in Europe becomes more

[139] *Ibid.*, p. 2176.

[140] Air editions of the east coast newspapers, if there had been any subscriptions, would have arrived five to seven days late.

[141] *Hearings*, Part 32, p. 612.

stabilized. If Russia falls, Japan is not going to be easily pried away from her Axis associations. She will no doubt grab any opportunity that presents itself to improve her position in Siberia. If Russia can hold out (which, at the moment, hardly appears possible), I feel that there might be more hope of some sort of an agreement with Japan.[142]

The central preoccupation of naval thinking in Washington was still the projected Japanese campaign against Siberia.

Kimmel received a copy of this letter to Hart along with Stark's reply of September 23 to some of his questions about shooting orders for the Pacific. Stark closed his letter with a despairing postscript, indicating that there was little time before the outbreak of open war with Japan. But at the same time he enjoined extreme caution on Admiral Kimmel to avoid any action that might provoke an incident:

> At the present time the President has issued shooting orders only for the Atlantic and Southeast Pacific sub-area.
> The situation in the Pacific generally is far different from what it is in the Atlantic. The operations of raiders in the Pacific at present are not very widespread or very effective. Most of the merchantmen in the Pacific are of United States or Panamanian flag registry. Instituting any steps towards eliminating raiders outside of waters close to the continents of North and South America might have unfavorable repercussions, which would not be worth the cost to the United States in the long run. The longer we can keep the situation in the Pacific in status quo, the better for all concerned.
>
> . . . .
>
> . . . we have no definite information that Japanese submarines have ever operated in close vicinity to the Hawaiian Islands, Alaska or our Pacific Coast. They may have been near Wake recently. The existing orders, that is not to bomb suspected submarines except in the defensive sea areas, are appropriate. *If conclusive, and I repeat conclusive, evidence is obtained that Japanese submarines are actually in or near United States territory, then a strong warning and a threat of hostile action against such submarines would appear to be our next step.* Keep us informed [author's italics].[143]

It may be that Stark's emphasis on maintaining the status quo in the Pacific, the need for "conclusive" evidence, and the dictated response of a warning or threat of hostile action rather than hostile action itself were important factors in Kimmel's interpretation of the final signals before the Pearl Harbor attack. The letter went on to echo some of the Army's

142 *Ibid.*, Part 16, p. 2210.
143 *Ibid.*, p. 2212.

optimism about reinforcing the Philippines and about increases in British and Dutch strength in the Pacific, concluding that these measures "should make Japan think twice before taking action."[144]

However, Stark's postscript to this letter of September 23 again switched to a pessimistic note:

> P.S. I have held this letter up pending a talk with Mr. Hull who asked me to hold it very secret. I may sum it up by saying *that conversations with the Japs have practically reached an impasse.* As I see it we can get nowhere towards a settlement and peace in the Far East until and unless there is some agreement between Japan and China—and just now that seems remote. Whether or not their inability to come to any sort of an understanding just now *is*—or *is not*—a good thing—I hesitate to say [Stark's italics].[145]

This came very close in wording to the final Army alert message, which was to read:

> Negotiations with Japan appear to be terminated to all practical purposes with only the barest possibilities that the Japanese Government might come back and offer to continue. Japanese future action unpredictable. . . .[146]

On September 29 Stark added a second postscript:

> P.S. 2 Admiral Nomura came in to see me this morning. We talked for about an hour. He usually comes in when he begins to feel near the end of his rope; there is not much to spare at the end now. I have helped before but whether I can this time or not I do not know. Conversations without results cannot last forever. . . .[147]

Even though Stark's personal opinions carried less weight with Kimmel than a directive from Stark's office, it is hard to see how Kimmel could have avoided being affected by the succession of gloomy predictions in these letters. They read very much like the final warning messages.

Kimmel reacted promptly to the CNO dispatch of October 16. He outlined the measures he had taken in the following letter to Admiral Stark dated October 22. (These measures did not include additional air reconnaissance from the Hawaiian Islands.)

> Dear Betty: On receipt of your despatches following the change in the Japanese cabinet, we made the following dispositions:
> Continued to maintain the patrol of two Submarines at Midway.
> Despatched twelve patrol planes to Midway.

144 *Ibid.*   145 *Ibid.*, p. 2213.
146 *Ibid.*, Part 14, p. 1328.   147 *Ibid.*, Part 16, p. 2213f.

Despatched two submarines to Wake. They will arrive there on 23 October.

Despatched the CASTOR and two destroyers to Johnston and Wake with additional marines, ammunition and stores.

The CURTISS arrives at Wake on 21 October with gas, lube oil and bombs.

Prepared to send six patrol planes from Midway to Wake, replacing the six at Midway from Pearl Harbor.

Despatched additional marines to Palmyra.

Placed Admiral Pye, with the ships making a health cruise, on twelve hours notice after 20 October.

Had six submarines prepared to depart for Japan on short notice.

Put some additional security measures in effect in the operating areas outside Pearl Harbor.

Delayed the sailing of the WEST VIRGINIA until about 17 November when she is due to go for an overhaul to Puget Sound and deferred final decision until that time.

With minor changes I propose to continue the health cruises to the Pacific Coast until something more definite develops. The despatch in regard to the submarines for Manila went forward to you today.[148]

Stark's acknowledgment was dictated on November 7 and arrived in Honolulu on November 14. Almost a month had passed since the October 16 dispatch, and about three weeks since Kimmel's announcement of measures taken.[149] Stark approved everything Kimmel had done: "OK," he wrote, "on the disposition which you made in connection with the recent change in the Japanese Cabinet. The big question is—What next?!"[150] If the disposition had not been "OK," presumably Kimmel would have been informed by radio immediately, although the CNO has always respected the independent judgment of his local commanders.

Kimmel had sent his letter of October 22 before he received a letter of October 17 from Stark, which followed up the October 16 dispatch with a detailed background. By October 18 alarm in Washington naval circles over the fall of the Japanese Cabinet had been somewhat allayed by the translation of a MAGIC intercept of the 16th from Tokyo, indicating Tojo's desire to continue negotiations with the United States. But even before receipt of this information, Admiral Stark had apparently been less

---

148 *Ibid.*, p. 2249.

149 The clipper service to Honolulu was limited to one flight per week in 1941, and the time between writing and receipt of a letter varied from five to seven days.

150 *Hearings*, Part 16, p. 2219.

alarmed than his War Plans staff. On the 17th he had requested and received an estimate of the situation from Capt. R. E. Schuirmann, the Navy's liaison officer with the State Department. Schuirmann believed that the new cabinet would be "no better and no worse" than the previous one, and that the Japanese military should be watched, rather than the changing composition of successive cabinets. Stark enclosed this estimate in his letter to Kimmel, noting that it "sums up my thoughts better than I have been able to set them down."[151]

Schuirmann's estimate read in part:

> I believe we are inclined to overestimate the importance of changes in the Japanese Cabinet as indicative of great changes in Japan's political thought or action.
>
> The plain fact is that Japanese politics has been ultimately controlled for years by the military. . . .
>
> . . . . : . . . . . .
>
> The most that can be claimed for the last Konoye Cabinet is that it may have restrained the extremists among the military, not that it has opposed Japan's program of expansion by force. When opportunities arise, during the coming months, which seem favorable to the military for further advance, they will be seized.
>
> At the present time the influence of the extremists goes up and down depending on the course of the war in Russia. . . .
>
> . . . .
>
> Present reports are that the new cabinet to be formed will be no better and no worse than the one which has just fallen. Japan may attack Russia, or may move southward, but in the final analysis this will be determined by the military on the basis of opportunity, and what they can get away with, not by what cabinet is in power.[152]

Schuirmann took a point of view, associated with a policy line of "deeds, not words," that Americans like to think of as "getting tough." He was reflecting the beliefs of the strongest faction in the State Department, which favored aid to China and supported "firmness" toward Japan in the form of cutting off all trade.[153] Stark, on the contrary, feared the results of the increasing pressure exerted by our existing embargoes on the Japanese. But in terms of signals, he evidently thought a cabinet

[151] *Ibid.*, p. 2215.
[152] *Ibid.*, p. 2215*f.*
[153] See Chap. 4.

change in Japan was not particularly significant. As he says in his letter
of October 17:

Dear Kimmel: Things have been popping here for the last twenty-four
hours but from our despatches you know about all that we do.

Personally I do not believe the Japs are going to sail into us and the
message I sent you merely stated the "possibility"; in fact I tempered the
message handed to me considerably. Perhaps I am wrong, but I hope not.
In any case after long pow-wows in the White House it was felt we should
be on guard, at least until something indicates the trend.

If I recall correctly I wrote you or Tommie Hart a forecast of the fall of
the Japanese Cabinet a couple of weeks ago after my long conference with
Nomura and gave the dope as I saw it.

You will also recall in an earlier letter when War Plans was forecasting
a Japanese attack on Siberia in August, I said my own judgment was that
they would make no move in that direction until the Russian situation showed
a definite trend. I think this whole thing works up together.

With regard to merchant shipping it seemed an appropriate time to get
the reins in our hands and get our routing of them going. In other words,
take the rap now from the Hill and the Press and all the knockers, so that
if and when it becomes an actual necessity to do it, it will be working
smoothly.

We shall continue to strive to maintain the status quo in the Pacific.
How long it can be kept going I don't know, but the President and Mr. Hull
are working on it.

The stumbling block, of course, is the Chinese incident and personally
without going into all its ramifications and face-saving and Japanese Army
attitude, civil attitude and Navy attitude I hardly see any way around it. I
think we could settle with Nomura in five minutes but the Japanese Army
is the stumbling block. Incidentally, the Chinese also think that they will lick
Japan before they get through and are all for keeping going rather than
giving way anywhere. A nice setup for not sounding the gong. . . .

. . . .

Off hand without going into the "ins" and "outs" I see no reason for
your stopping your normal visits to the Coast. The ships concerned constitute self-contained task forces. We have left it up to you and I am just
giving you my reaction. . . .

. . . .

I know how you and Admiral Hart must be pleased with the Army increased air in the Philippines. The Island of Wake is a vital link in this
connection. If it is put out of commission it stops Army air reinforcements.
I hope we can maintain the integrity of these Island bases and push as fast

as possible their completion. You have all the dope that I have on this and know the studies that are being made for alternate routes.[154]

The second paragraph in this letter—"Personally I do not believe the Japs are going to sail into us . . ."—was quoted many times in the course of the hearings as a possible explanation for Kimmel's failure to respond to the message of November 27. But it is clear from the context that Stark's remark referred only to the situation on October 16. As we have seen from previous quotations, Stark's tone on the subject of U.S.-Japanese relations had been considerably more pessimistic, and it was to be so again. His letter of November 7, in which he approved Kimmel's fleet dispositions, once more sounded an ominous note:

> Things seem to be moving steadily towards a crisis in the Pacific. Just when it will break, no one can tell. The principal reaction I have to it all is what I have written you before; it continually gets "worser and worser"! A month may see, literally, most anything. Two irreconcilable policies can not go on forever—particularly if one party cannot live with the set up. It doesn't look good.[155]

There is no mention in the record of information made available to Kimmel by naval radio traffic analysis, by ONI, or by British intelligence. Kimmel's signals, as we know them today, came primarily from the CNO dispatches, from Admiral Stark's letters, and from the Honolulu press.

The following list summarizes and compares the signals available to Admiral Kimmel and to General Short between August 8 and October 25, 1941[156]:

	Admiral Kimmel	*General Short*
August 8:	Stark writes that he believes Russia to be a definite Japanese objective.	
August 8 and October 4:	Stark mentions Turner's prediction of an imminent Japanese attack on Siberia. But Stark believes that Japan will clear up Southeast Asian situation first and stall until European situation is stabilized.	

[154]*Hearings*, Part 16, p. 2214*f.*   [155]*Ibid.*, p. 2220.

[156]Dates for letters from Admiral Stark indicate day of arrival in Honolulu, rather than day of dictation.

	Admiral Kimmel	*General Short*
October 4:	Stark explains that shooting orders do not apply to Kimmel's Pacific area. Orders are to bomb submarines in defensive sea areas. If conclusive evidence is obtained of Japanese submarines in or near U.S. territory, next step is U.S. threat of action. American policy is to keep status quo in Pacific. Stark believes the arming of Philippines and the British reinforcements in Pacific should make Japan think twice before taking action.	
October 16:	CNO dispatch to Kimmel: Resignation of Konoye Cabinet has created a "grave situation," since new cabinet will probably be anti-American.	CNO dispatch forwarded by Kimmel to Short: Same.
	A war between Japan and Russia is a "strong possibility."	Same.
	An attack by Japan on the United States and Britain is "a possibility."	Same.
	Pacific Fleet is ordered to take precautions including "preparatory deployments." Strategic intentions *not* to be disclosed. "Provocative" measures *not* to be taken.	Same.
October 17:	CNO dispatch warns of possibility of hostile action by Japan against U.S. merchant shipping. All vessels in western Pacific ordered into friendly ports.	Estimate from G-2 Hawaii states that Japanese situation is "extremely critical." "In the near future" Japan will attack Russia, press French Indochina for new concessions, and attack British possessions in Far East, but will not attack American possessions.

Admiral Kimmel	*General Short*

CNO dispatch warns Kimmel to "take all practicable precautions" for safety of airfields at Wake and Midway (stepping-stones on trans-Pacific route to Philippines).

CNO dispatch orders all trans-Pacific U.S. flagshipping to and from Far East to be routed through Torres Straits, keeping well clear of Japanese Mandates.

October 20:

War Department dispatch to General Short explains that U.S.-Japanese relations are strained but no abrupt change in Japanese foreign policy is imminent.

October 23: CNO dispatch orders all transports with reinforcements for Philippines to proceed only in convoy and under escort.

Letter from Stark clarifies the October 16 dispatch. Stark believes that a Japanese attack on the United States is merely a possibility: "Personally I do not believe the Japs are going to sail into us."

Schuirmann, Navy liaison officer with the State Department, estimates that Japan may attack Russia or may move southward, but this will be determined by military expediency, not by the particular cabinet composition.

October 25:

Estimate from G-2 Hawaii states that new Japanese Cabinet is pro-Axis and promilitary. Next major move will be delayed until latter part of Novem-

ber or following spring, based
on the following signals: (1)
Tojo has expressed desire to continue negotiations with the
United States; (2) three Japanese vessels will continue to
American ports to transport nationals to homeland; (3) Nomura has announced intention to
return to Japan for consultation
with cabinet; (4) Navy Department has ordered American merchant vessels to avoid Asiatic
ports; and (5) American government will abandon Vladivostok as port of entry for war
supplies to Russia.

The background information provided by Admiral Stark's letters is
difficult to distill into the abbreviated form of signals because they contain
so much complex and delicate weighing of evidence and so many con-
fessions of uncertainty and qualifications to the absolute statements. In
the main Stark supported the hypothesis of an eventual Japanese attack on
the Maritime Provinces after consolidation of their position in Southeast
Asia, and he cautioned that everything possible be done to maintain the
status quo in the Pacific without taking "provocative" measures. The advice in the letters, however, cannot be put in the balance with the CNO
dispatches. As signals the dispatches carried much more weight. The dispatch of October 16, estimating the cabinet change as "grave" and an
attack by Japan on the United States and Britain as a "possibility," represented a consensus and was not meant to be superseded or canceled by
the statement in the letter received by Kimmel on October 23, "Personally
I do not believe the Japs are going to sail into us. . . ." The October 16
dispatch, however, may have been weakened by emphasis on the "stronger
possibility" of a Japanese attack on Russia, or by the directive to take
preparatory deployments. For these preparatory deployments directed
Kimmel to put his ships in a position to move against the Marshalls
rather than to deploy them in the most satisfactory way to meet an attack.

Admiral Kimmel's signals therefore certainly added up to a more serious situation than did General Short's. The two dispatches that General Short had received convinced him of a Russian-Japanese war in the near future and the necessity for continued vigilance against sabotage at Pearl Harbor. His only direct communication from the War Department said in effect to take it easy. Admiral Kimmel's October dispatches from the CNO also stressed Japanese ambitions in Siberia, but they did more. They pointed up the dangers to American merchant shipping in the Pacific and to American reinforcements bound for the Philippines. Admiral Kimmel evidently interpreted these dangers to be primarily those of submarine attack in the waters near the islands of Wake, Midway, Johnston, and perhaps Hawaii. He also anticipated possible air attacks on the airfields at Wake and Midway, and therefore began to increase the number of patrol planes and submarines there. He had six submarines prepared to depart for Japan on short notice, an implementation in part of our war plans for the Pacific to be set in motion if the Japanese attacked an ally or an American possession in the Pacific. Even after Kimmel had received Stark's calming interpretation of the October 16 dispatch, he still had some direct authoritative signals of U.S. steps that were being taken to avoid any precipitate clash. These steps meant in turn that America seriously feared an incident in the Pacific—not a major incident such as an attack on Pearl Harbor, but a minor one that might give the Japanese an excuse to go to war with the United States.

Notice that none of the signals mentioned so far for the October alert has included code burning by the Japanese. According to testimony from Admiral Kimmel, General Short, and several of their subordinates, they did receive messages about code burning in Honolulu from time to time during 1941. The first time they were alarmed, but thereafter they took it in stride, and they did not react to the news of paper burning at the Japanese consulate in Honolulu in the first week of December. It would be helpful to know at what particular points in time they received the earlier code-burning signals. If they received them during the first weeks of July or October, then the importance of code burning in Honolulu as a short-term danger signal in a context of other danger signals would certainly have been lowered in the minds of the commanders—since nothing happened. Unfortunately there is nothing in the published record beyond personal testimony on this subject, and until G-2 and ONI open their 1941 files, there is no way to evaluate either the testimony or the signal.

As for code burning by the Japanese in other parts of the world, we have seen one MAGIC intercept of July 16 from Tokyo to Hanoi and Saigon (see pages 108–109) containing the directive "burn codes." Kimmel received a copy of this message. The directive was limited to Hanoi and Saigon, but it may have suggested to Kimmel that the Japanese would take care to destroy codes at points where the British or the Dutch or the Americans might conceivably seize all embassy and consular documents in retaliation for Japanese aggression elsewhere. At least he used this sort of reasoning at the hearings to explain his reaction to the December MAGIC directive to destroy all but one code in the major Japanese embassies. As we saw in Chapter 1, Navy officials testified at that time that Tokyo's orders to destroy codes were clear signals of Japan's intent to attack all countries where such orders were received. To Kimmel the destruction order was merely a measure to protect Japanese codes. General Short, who did not receive the information on code destruction, felt certain that he would have viewed this signal with alarm and would have instituted a full alert. But of course both commanders were reasoning after the event.

The Picture in Washington

The Army. There is more information on the background of Army thinking with respect to the October 16 crisis than is the case with the other two alerts. A communication from General Gerow to Secretary Stimson on October 8, entitled "Strategic Concept of the Philippine Islands," was forwarded by General Marshall to General MacArthur on October 18 with the notation that it represented "present War Department thought on this subject."[157] It pointed out that Japan's ambitions in the Siberian Maritime Provinces, China, and Malaya were being retarded by (1) Russia's unexpectedly long resistance to Germany, (2) China's resistance to Japan, (3) the economic embargoes, and (4) Japanese uncertainty about the outcome of a new war. It underlined the importance of keeping

[157] War Plans Division file number 3251–3260, quoted in Watson, *Chief of Staff: Prewar Plans and Preparations*, p. 445.

Japan nonbelligerent so that the Allies could concentrate their resources against Germany; and to further this goal, it recommended continuing the existing deterrent measures and providing strong offensive air forces that would be clearly visible to the Japanese and therefore clearly intimidating. It was further suggested that the Philippines in particular be strengthened with offensive air power and integrated with anti-Axis nations in the Far East.

The report concluded on a note of high optimism:

> Consideration of Japan's forces and her capabilities leads to the conclusion that the [American] air and ground units now available or scheduled for dispatch to the Philippine Islands in the immediate future have changed the entire picture in the Asiatic Area. The action taken by the War Dept. may well be the determining factor in Japan's eventual decision and, consequently, have a vital bearing on the course of the war as a whole.[158]

This optimism about the deterrent effect of our embargoes and our offensive power naturally affected G-2 and its interpretations. On the one hand it influenced G-2 to recommend a "tough" policy in response to Japanese overtures or attempts to negotiate. On the other hand it seems also to have bathed in a rosy haze the Japanese signals of hostile intent against the United States. What the Navy tended to view with alarm, G-2 greeted with indifference or with hopeful predictions of peace in the Pacific.

The "tough" policy was worded in the following way by G-2:

> ... this Division believes that forceful diplomacy vis-à-vis Japan, including the application of ever increasing military and economic pressure on our part, offers the best chance of gaining time, the best possibility of preventing the spread of hostilities in the Pacific area and of the eventual disruption of the Tripartite Pact. The exercise of increasingly strong "power diplomacy" by the United States is clearly indicated.[159]

This formulation first appeared in an August 16 memorandum for the Chief of Staff entitled "Developments in the Far Eastern Situation." It was predicated on the comforting belief that Japan would "resort to every means available to keep the United States out of the war,"[160] and that any relaxation of American pressure would be viewed as appeasement. Hono-

158 *Ibid.*
159 *Hearings*, Part 14, p. 1347.
160 *Ibid.*, p. 1346.

lulu G-2, as we have seen, shared this belief, and it was also current in Washington G-2 throughout the month of October. For example, in the "Brief Periodic Estimate of the World Situation," for September 3–December 1, 1941, General Miles, head of Washington G-2, reaffirmed: "In the maelstrom of Japanese indecision, one thing stands out clearly—that is, that the Japanese do not want the United States to become involved in the war. . . ."[161]

Confidence in our immunity from Japanese aggression was also partly bolstered by the belief that Japan was preparing for an all-out attack on Siberia, to be timed with the collapse of European Russia. Japanese agitation for a conference of leaders was therefore viewed as a cover for the Siberian preparations, and in this connection the formula for forceful diplomacy was repeated word for word in the G-2 memoranda to the Chief of Staff on September 23 and again on October 2. To the formula was also added the following sentence: "The United States can and should judge only by the acts and not by the words of that government."[162]

The memorandum of October 2, signed by Col. Hayes A. Kroner, elaborated:

> This Division is of the opinion that neither a conference of leaders nor economic concessions at this time would be of any material advantage to the United States unless a definite commitment to withdraw from the Axis were obtained from Japan prior to the conference. The immediate objective of the United States is to weaken Hitler in every way possible. A Japanese guarantee not to attack Russia in Siberia would free Russia, psychologically and militarily, for stronger opposition to Hitler. With this in mind, a definite condition precedent to such a proposed conference should be a complete withdrawal by Japan from the Axis and a guarantee, backed by substantial evidence of sincerity, not to attack Russia in Siberia."[163]

The next paragraph began: "Since it is highly improbable that this condition can be met by the Japanese Government at the present time our course lies straight before us."[164] There followed immediately the recommendation for increasingly strong "power diplomacy."

In this atmosphere the October cabinet change caused much less consternation than the one of July 16 and evidently occasioned no re-estimate of the probable direction and timing of Japan's next move. A G-2 memo-

---

[161] *Ibid.*, p. 1353.
[163] *Ibid.*, p. 1358.
[162] *Ibid.*, p. 1357.
[164] *Ibid.*

randum of October 16 on the fall of the Konoye Cabinet stated that it was "the logical result of Foreign Minister Toyoda's failure to secure a relaxation of the economic pressure on Japan by the U.S. Government,"[165] and that it was also a result of "nationalistic pressure for termination of Japanese-American peace negotiations."[166] In other words, G-2 understood that the fall of the cabinet was directly related to America's economic acts, but it made no connection between America's threatening role and any possible danger to America. The focus was still on Siberia:

> It is highly probable . . . that the trend will be toward the Axis, with the Army, rather than the Navy, exercising the controlling influence. This Army element will not be slow to take advantage of any weakening of the Siberian Army brought about by Russian reverses in Europe.[167]

Apparently G-2 did not find worthy of mention the October 16 press item on Capt. Hideo Hiraide, Director of Naval Intelligence for Japan. Captain Hiraide publicly attacked America's naval expansion and said that "the Imperial Navy is itching for action" against America. This item was noted by Admiral Stark, Sumner Welles, and Secretary Stimson. Stimson commented in his diary: "The Japanese Navy is beginning to talk almost as radically as the Japanese Army, and so we face the delicate question of the diplomatic fencing to be done so as to be sure that Japan was [*sic*] put in the wrong and made the first bad move—overt move!"[168]

With knowledge of the selection of General Tojo as Prime Minister on October 17, G-2 commented: "Any cabinet selected by General Tojo may be expected to have Axis leanings, but will be otherwise anti-foreign and highly nationalistic."[169] By October 18, G-2 and War Plans had gotten together on the dispatch to Short and MacArthur to assure them that this cabinet composition held no particular menace for the United States. On October 21, G-2 was once more concentrating on Russo-Japanese developments. It submitted a report on the relative strength of the Kwantung and Siberian armies, pointing out that

> If and when the Kwantung Army feels that it has a combat superiority over the Siberian Army of 2 to 1, it is highly probable that it will take the

[165] *Ibid.*, p. 1359.
[166] *Ibid.*
[167] *Ibid.*
[168] Quoted in Langer and Gleason, *The Undeclared War, 1940–1941*, p. 730.
[169] *Hearings*, Part 14, p. 1360.

offensive regardless of the policy and intentions of the Tokyo Government. When this ratio rises to 3 to 1 or better the probability will become a certainty.[170]

The report concluded:

> ... it is very much to our interest ... to take whatever steps may be possible to maintain the present Russian equality in combat strength vis-à-vis the Kwantung Army.[171]

In other words, during this month of October, G-2 kept its attention focused primarily on a Japanese-Russian conflict. Furthermore, its recommendations and predictions were determined by this preoccupation and by the background of optimism already mentioned rather than by the specific information and rather realistic analyses available to its personnel. Perhaps the high point in optimism was reached on September 11 after receipt of a United Press dispatch from Tokyo stating that Emperor Hirohito had that day taken direct command of Japanese Army Headquarters and had moved to assure close Army collaboration with Premier Konoye's government. Miles not only sent his memorandum on this news item to General Marshall but gave the original copy to General Watson to convey personally to the President. "A proper evaluation of the news," Miles cautioned, "is impracticable at this early date but a definite trend seems indicated— a trend away from the Axis and toward better relations with the United States and Great Britain. The new system is interpreted as an effort to strengthen the civilian government, check militaristic domination of Imperial policy, and erect a barrier to possible dissatisfaction among the militarists with the future course of events."[172] The final sentence then compressed all the wishful thinking of that time: "It is probable that Japan will find a peaceful way out of one of the greatest crises in her history and seek a means to realign her foreign policy in an anti-Axis direction."[173]

In contrast to the note of hope and confidence struck by G-2's evaluation of current events is the body of the estimates in which are presented some rather closely considered and hardheaded reasonings about the Japanese political and economic situation. For example, the "Brief Periodic

[170]*Ibid.*, p. 1361.   [171]*Ibid.*
[172]*Ibid.*, p. 1354.   [173]*Ibid.*

Estimate of the World Situation," for September 3–December 1, 1941, took a very serious view of the effects of the embargo:

> Because of the ever-increasing stringency of the embargo placed on Japan by the United States, Great Britain and the Netherlands East Indies, the economic situation in Japan is slowly but surely becoming worse. The Japanese have always lacked war materials, adequate foreign exchange and sufficient foreign trade; the embargo has served to increase the deficiencies in these categories. These deficiencies are serious but are not likely to become dangerous before December 1, 1941.
>
> . . . .
>
> The stoppage of trade is reducing Japan's raw materials drastically— raw materials which are vital to the organic well-being of Japan and to her ability to wage war successfully. No other country even approaches the United States in importance to Japan's economic welfare, both as a source of raw materials and as a market for the exports of Japan.[174]

Admiral Stark, with this information before him, reasoned that if Japan could not get her materials in the usual way of trade, she would strike out and get them by force. G-2 from the same set of data reasoned that the "Co-Prosperity Sphere . . . is about to fall apart," and "Japan finds herself in a very poor bargaining position."[175]

This wave of optimism about Japan, which was expressed most naïvely in G-2, swept over the highest policy circles. President Roosevelt wrote to Churchill on October 15: "The Jap situation is definitely worse, and I think they are headed North—however in spite of this you and I have two months of respite in the Far East."[176] Churchill himself believed that Japan would not move against the Pacific powers until Russia was firmly defeated, and that Japan would prefer not to attack the United States until the British Empire had been defeated.[177] Roosevelt evidently gave Churchill's opinion a good deal of weight in making his own appraisals of American chances for delaying war with Japan. The British intelligence office in London was also forwarding information to the War Depart-

---

[174] *Ibid.*, p. 1353.

[175] *Ibid.*

[176] *Letters*, Vol. II, p. 1223.

[177] Report of July staff conference in London, attended by Hopkins, in Sherwood, *Roosevelt and Hopkins: An Intimate History*, p. 316. (Cf. Churchill's telegram of October 1 in *The Grand Alliance*, p. 590.)

ment in Washington that tended to bear out Churchill's views. During the October crisis the London office cabled the War Department as follows:

> It is thought that Japan will not advance southward, except possibly into Thailand, because of the danger of becoming embroiled with the U.S. and Britain, especially in view of the firm stand taken by the U.S.
>
> Agreement among all previously divergent opinions in the Army and Navy in order to make certain of their assistance in any future projects launched is one aim of the new cabinet, which is unquestionably geared for war. The new Premier is wholly pro-German. It is believed that the Japs will advance on Vladivostok and the Maritime Provinces the minute Soviet disintegration appears imminent. . . . Speeches by the new cabinet should be viewed as obscuring their real intent. The Russians are still believed stronger in Siberia in spite of possible transfers of troops to the other theaters, but the Maritimes and Vladivostok unquestionably could be captured by the Japs.[178]

The picture coming in from the American embassy in Japan also reinforced the belief in Japanese orientation toward the north and tended to allay any fears about policy changes under the new Japanese Cabinet. Ambassador Grew fervently hoped for a continuation of the negotiations and looked eagerly for good signs in spite of his earlier dire predictions about a cabinet change. According to his information, it was the Emperor who had insisted on the policy of continued negotiation with America, and who had insisted on Tojo's commitment to this policy.[179] Our military attaché in Tokyo reflected Grew's hopes in a cable to the War Department on October 20:

> Since the make-up of the new Cabinet appears to be essentially conservative in character, the resignation of the old Cabinet is not regarded as indicating any drastic change in Japan's policy in the immediate future, at least. . . . While General Tojo is first of all a thoroughgoing Japanese, with the national ambitions and welfare inherent in his make-up, he is believed to have a breadth of vision which would seem to preclude the possibility of his taking extreme radical actions.[180]

On October 21 Secretary Stimson, in a letter to the President, expressed Army hopes in most enthusiastic terms:

> . . . A strategic opportunity of the utmost importance has suddenly arisen in the southwestern Pacific. Our whole strategic possibilities of the past twenty

[178] *Hearings*, Part 16, p. 2140.
[179] *Foreign Relations of the United States: Japan, 1931–1941*, Vol. II, pp. 697–699.
[180] Quoted in Sherwood, *Roosevelt and Hopkins: An Intimate History*, p. 419.

years have been revolutionized by the events in the world in the past six months. From being impotent to influence events in that area, we suddenly find ourselves vested with the possibility of great effective power. Indeed we hardly yet realize our opportunities in that respect. We are rushing planes and other preparations to the Philippines from a base in the United States which has not yet in existence the number of the planes necessary for our immediate minimum requirements in that southwestern Pacific theatre. This is a result of our deferments to the British of last year. From nowhere but the United States can come the needed planes, the crews, the equipment, and the training. *Yet even this imperfect threat, if not promptly called by the Japanese, bids fair to stop Japan's march to the south and secure the safety of Singapore, with all the revolutionary consequences of such action.* As you well know, however, the final success of the operation lies on the knees of the gods and we cannot tell what explosion may momentarily come from Japan. If we had the reserve necessary in the United States, we should not be in this present period of uncertainty.

Simultaneously with this southwestern Pacific opportunity, another such chance is opening in the northwestern Pacific. Vladivostok is one of three gateways to Russia. The Archangel gate may be closed at any moment. The Persian Gulf gate is insignificant in capacity. The propinquity of Alaska to Siberia and the Kamchatka Peninsula and the facilities which we believe (although we have not yet had opportunity for testing them) exist in that neighborhood, present us with the opportunity for another use of these bombers supplementary to the one I have just described in the south. That locality can possibly form the base of a northern pincer movement of American influence and power, this time not only to protect against aggression of Japan but to preserve the defensive power of Russia in Europe. Its operation would fit into and supplement the operation from the south by permitting a circular sweep of these bombers which would greatly increase their safety by permitting those in the south, after passing over Japan and stopping at Vladivostok to proceed to safety in the north in a way similar to the sweeps which Germany is now employing through the North Atlantic from Norway to France. The power of such a completed north and south operation can hardly be over-estimated. The control over the western Pacific which it would open could hardly fail to have immense powers of warning to Japan as well as of assurance to Russia. It might well remove Japan from the Axis powers [author's italics].[181]

In addition to these estimates from American policymakers, embassy observers, Army Intelligence officers, and Army planners, another guide

[181] *Hearings,* Part 20, p. 4443.

to Japanese intentions was the MAGIC intercept translated on October 18:

> ... regardless of the make-up of the new Cabinet, negotiations with the
> United States shall be continued along the lines already formulated. There
> shall be no changes in this respect.[182]

MAGIC continued to carry such reassuring messages, replying, for example,
to Nomura's offer of resignation:

> ... the outcome of those negotiations ... [has] a great bearing upon the
> decision as to which road the Imperial Government will pursue. ... We are
> placing all of our reliance on your Excellency's reports for our information
> on this matter.
>
> For the above reason, we express our hope that you will see fit to sacrifice
> all of your own personal wishes, and remain at your post.[183]

These intercepts seemed to indicate that hostile action against the United
States would not be immediate.

The Navy. As we have seen, the naval estimate of the American em-
bargo policy pointed to serious consequences: war at an early date between
Japan and Britain, if not a direct attack on the United States. Admiral
Stark was somewhat infected by the Army's optimism on the subject of
the Philippines and by the dispatch of British reinforcements to the
Pacific. He did not personally take a very grave view of the fall of the
Konoye Cabinet. But he thought highly of his War Plans officer, Admiral
Turner, and approved his dispatch of October 16, after toning down some
of the more alarming phrases. And Admiral Turner was evidently alarmed.

According to Turner's later testimony, he

> was convinced then [on October 16] that if Japan attacked Britain in the
> Far East ... the United States would immediately enter the war against
> Japan. The Japanese for some years before 1941 had apparently determined
> that they were going to drive Britain out of the Far East. I believe that a
> certain section of the Japanese hierarchy were very anxious to keep the
> United States out of the war, that is keep the United States from assisting
> Great Britain, but many of the moves that had been made against Japan
> during 1940 and 1941 were made by the United States. The whole political
> situation, their interest in the Philippines, convinced me that war would be
> not far off and that it would be against the United States and Great Britain.[184]

182 *Ibid.*, Part 12, p. 76.
183 *Ibid.*, p. 82.
184 *Ibid.*, Part 32, p. 604.

Mr. Mitchell, the first General Counsel for the Joint Congressional Committee, inquired: "Was it your judgment at the time that you wrote that [October 16] dispatch . . . that the conditions you had spoken of might result in war in a very short time?" Turner answered:

> No sir; not a short time. That is relatively. The new Cabinet would have to be formed. It took a certain amount of time to do that, to make their pronouncement, get the approval of the Emperor, and to issue orders to deploy their forces and to load their ships. So at that time, so far as the United States and the British and Dutch were concerned, I did not believe that there would be any possibility of war for at least a month.
>
> It was somewhat different with respect to the Russians, because there they were close to the Russians. They already had an army in Manchuria, deployed or not, we did not know. They had a great part of the Navy in her home waters, so that action against Russia could have been taken at an earlier date possibly.[185]

Turner, as Stark wrote to Kimmel, had been predicting as early as August that Japan would attack Russia. In the October 16 dispatch, Stark persuaded him to change the prediction from a "probability" to a "possibility." It is likely that in October Turner foresaw war between Japan and Russia within a matter of days or weeks rather than in a month. He had in mind certain precautions and certain fleet dispositions that were not conveyed in detail to Kimmel but that Kimmel actually put into effect by October 22. As Turner testified, preparatory deployments were

> . . . intended to include sending submarines out to the westward along approximately the 180th meridian . . . just east of the Marshalls, to have the Fleet at sea, or part of it, a considerable part of the time to the westward of Hawaii and up generally in a supporting position for Midway and Wake and covering positions for Palmyra and Johnston, and it was expected that they would be in a position from previous deployments so that we could get warning of any attack that was coming so that they could take measures against any Japanese force that came in.[186]

Although Turner represented these deployments at the hearings as being reconnaissance measures, they were actually means of implementing the war plan for attacking the Marshalls, should war break out between Japan and the United States. Kimmel had been alerted for months to the requirements of this plan.

[185] *Ibid.*, Part 4, p. 1945f.
[186] *Ibid.*, Part 32, p. 606.

In referring to Japan's "desperate situation" in his dispatch of October 16, Turner had in mind "the fact that through our action, her trade had been cut off not only with the U.S., but with the British possessions and the Dutch [and that] . . . in a comparatively short time her own large stocks [of petroleum] . . . would be exhausted."[187] In short, Japan's economic situation was desperate. Turner took full responsibility for the directive in the October 16 dispatch to take such precautions as would not constitute provocative action. Looking back in 1945, he explained:

> The State Department and the Navy Department, I think, were in accord that we should get as much time as we ourselves could to prepare in a material way for the war. . . . Now . . . there were conversations going on constantly with the Japanese which appeared on the surface to be possibly a solution so that there wouldn't be any war and that was the desire of the government, that we not get into war with Japan at that time. Therefore, we did not want our Fleet, for example, to cruise over near the Marshalls and assume a threatening attitude. We didn't want them to arrest all the known disloyal elements in Hawaii and we didn't want them to send any submarines out near the Japanese Islands. It was an attempt to retain the peace as long as possible and to make sure that when war came that it would be initiated by Japan and not by the U.S.[188]

The Office of Naval Intelligence was not supposed to predict enemy intentions or to evaluate intelligence material. However, the information that it had seemed to support Turner's hypotheses. Its memorandum on the October 16 cabinet change underlined Japan's renewed collaboration with the Axis powers and pointed out that Japan had "the position and strength to attack Siberia." It also suggested cautiously that, since the Japanese Army clearly intended to dominate the new government, "positive action detrimental to United States interests may be expected."[189] The strain on the Japanese economy was detailed and clearly attributed to the U.S. embargo policy. Japan, it was pointed out, had to have access to overseas markets or open up an overland supply route to Europe through Russia.

Here again the plausible hypothesis of a Siberian campaign occupied the center of naval attention. There is none of the optimism of G-2 in this

[187] *Ibid.*, Part 4, p. 1945.
[188] *Ibid.*, Part 32, p. 606.
[189] *Ibid.*, Part 15, p. 1845.

memorandum, perhaps because Naval Intelligence analysts were not permitted to express any attitudes that would suggest evaluation. In any case the information and estimates of the Navy Department were considerably more sober than those emanating from the War Department. It was the Navy Department that was responsible for alerting Honolulu on this particular occasion, and its series of dispatches to Kimmel indicated the danger of attack perhaps as close as Wake and Midway, perhaps on American merchant shipping, requiring of Kimmel the deployments preparatory to attacking the Marshalls.

The Press. Besides privileged information, Washington policymakers had the benefit of excellent press coverage on Japanese news during this period. For the first two weeks of October the main articles on Japanese internal politics in *The New York Times* pointed to an approaching cabinet crisis in Tokyo. On October 1, for example, Hallett Abend reported from Manila that another cabinet overturn was expected, with the re-emergence of extremists such as Matsuoka. On October 7 Otto Tolischus wrote that the ultra-nationalists were pressuring the government to obtain some relaxation of the embargoes. Japan, they claimed, was "choking." For two months she had had "not a drop of gasoline or a piece of scrap-iron," while America and Britain were growing steadily stronger in the Pacific.

On October 16 the front page carried Tolischus' report of the speech by Capt. Hideo Hiraide, Japan's Director of Naval Intelligence. Hiraide warned that relations between Japan and the United States were "now approaching the final parting of the ways." He predicated his warning on rumors that the United States might extend its convoy system from Iceland to the British Isles and might seek Siberian bases in return for aid to Russia. Hiraide's speech continued:

> America, feeling her insecurity in this situation, is carrying out naval expansion on a large scale. But at present America is unable to carry out naval operations in both the Atlantic and Pacific simultaneously. The Imperial navy is prepared for the worst and has completed all necessary preparations. In fact, the Imperial navy is itching for action, when needed.

The New York Times also quoted the Japanese newspaper *Asahi*'s comment that Hiraide's statement was significant because it was the "first clarification of the naval attitude of determination" relative to American-

Japanese relations. And the Domei News Agency, on the authority of "well-informed quarters," declared that American double-dealing was intolerable: America was conducting diplomatic negotiations with Japan and maintaining a hostile posture at the same time.

The main headline for this same issue of *The New York Times* ran: "U.S. STUDIES TENSION IN FAR EAST. WASHINGTON UNEASY OVER ORIENT IN CASE MOSCOW FALLS." On page 5, Hallett Abend contributed an interesting item on a new Japanese commercial airline that had just started running between Palau Island and Portuguese Timor. The airline did not appear to be justified by any increase in trade, and Darwin, Australia, just 452 miles away, was "alarmed." Abend commented:

> Just when all eyes in the Far East have been directed to the north expectantly watching for Japan to make a military move against Siberia ... Japan has announced this surprise move by which she gains a foothold on the Portuguese or eastern end of Timor Island.

On October 17 the news of the fall of the Konoye Cabinet dominated the front page. The paper speculated that the new cabinet would be pro-Nazi under General Tojo's premiership. Tolischus quoted the *Japan Times Advertiser* as laying the blame for the current crisis at the door of the American people. America, this newspaper complained, was giving weapons, technical assistance, and military advice to the Chinese fighting Japan: "Japan in no wise has interfered with America's sphere of influence or living area, whereas the United States has leaped an ocean to intrude into the affairs of the Far East." Roosevelt's conference with his military aides was reported in this issue of *The New York Times* but nothing was given on the decisions reached at the conference. Another column, however, reported the subsequent Navy Department order to American merchant ships in the Asiatic area to come into port for "instructions."

On the following day, Tojo's appointment as Premier was said to be definite. Tolischus reported that the new cabinet would be largely military in composition, but that negotiations would not be cut off and might even be facilitated, since now the United States would be negotiating directly with the Japanese Army. The new government's foreign policy, however, would remain unchanged: to settle the China incident and get on with the program of the Greater East Asia Co-Prosperity Sphere.

Hanson Baldwin commented on the cabinet change: "Whether or not Japan will move north toward Siberia or south toward Thailand or elsewhere is another question; what is clear is that an overthrow of the Konoye cabinet . . . was a necessary prelude to any move." China's Foreign Minister predicted an attack on Russia as Japan's next move. Hallett Abend also foresaw an invasion of Siberia as a prelude to a southern expedition in the spring. Japan, he believed, was confident that the United States would not take active steps to oppose her. News reports emanating from Shanghai and Singapore continued to emphasize a movement against Siberia.

Japanese news disappeared from the front page after the new Premier's statement on October 19 that his government's policy was unchanged and that he intended "to promote amicable relations with friendly powers." Tolischus reported on October 21 and 22 that Tojo was talking of "world peace," and other "vague formulas." Meanwhile, all news interpretations in Japan seem to have agreed that Japan's policies were "immutable" and that although she desired to bring the Washington negotiations to a successful conclusion, she required first that Washington change its attitude.

On October 22 a column carried this heading: "PHILIPPINE FORCES ARE KEPT ON THE ALERT." The report read: "The armed forces have been doubly alert during the crisis, with most of the U.S Asiatic Fleet gathered in Manila Bay, planes on constant patrol, and Army forces held in readiness." However, "Informed sources believe present tension is relaxing. . . . The U.S. Navy's order sending American ships into port has been relaxed to the point of allowing two vessels to depart from Manila. . . ."

On October 23 the main headline concerned the rerouting of aid for Russia through Archangel instead of Vladivostok. The *Times* attributed this change to the American government's desire to avoid an incident with Tokyo. The White House indignantly denied this the following day. The news was received very favorably in Tokyo, according to Tolischus' report of the 24th. The Tokyo press, however, renewed its charges that the United States was seeking Siberian bases for use against Japan, and Tolischus interpreted a practice blackout in Tokyo as one more step toward all-out war preparations.

In short, the press, like many other sources of information, stressed the hypothesis of an attack by Japan on Siberia. It reflected accurately the official alarm over the cabinet change and the sudden relaxation of tension that followed Tojo's announced intention to continue negotiations. But in addition, it reported that the Japanese press was consistently hostile to the United States and Britain and linked this hostility directly to America's stranglehold on the Japanese economy and to America's desire for Siberian bases from which to attack Japan.

The events of October are interesting primarily for the explicit conflict between Army and Navy estimates in Washington and their dispatches to Honolulu, and for the effect of this conflict on the interpretation in Hawaii of the final November alert messages. They also illustrate very clearly how a basic attitude, such as optimism about our capabilities in the Philippines, can color the perception of danger signals. The Navy was aware of danger in the Japanese Cabinet change only insofar as it was alert to the dangers inherent in the American embargo of Japanese trade, and only insofar as it was skeptical about the deterrent effect of our preparations in the Philippines.

SUMMARY

Of the three alerts described in this chapter, the first, in June, 1940, was touched off by a general atmosphere of alarm created by the fall of France and the possibility of fascist aggression in South America. In this atmosphere danger of an attack on Pearl Harbor was read into bits of information that a year later would have commanded only the most cursory attention from a collection agency.

The second alert, in July, 1941, was inspired by two American measures directed against Japan—the imposition of embargoes and the activation of the Philippine Army—plus the fear that Japan might retaliate. There was no reason to expect an attack on Pearl Harbor, or even sabotage, to be part of the Japanese plan for seizing bases in Indochina. At most the Japanese might have attacked the British. But American military leaders anticipated that the Japanese reaction to an American embargo might be unfriendly and might even lead to active hostilities.

The third alert, in October, 1941, was occasioned by a Japanese event: the fall of the moderate Konoye Cabinet and its replacement by the militaristic Tojo Cabinet. On examination, the fall of the moderates is seen to be clearly associated with Konoye's inability to soften the American embargo policy; this signal, therefore, is not unambiguously a Japanese event, but more accurately an event in Japan directly occasioned by an American action. From this event in turn American military officers anticipated a rapidly decreasing probability of peace in the Pacific.

By the time of the third alert, the distinction between stimulus and response in describing our relations with Japan had become increasingly difficult to make. In July, 1941, it was easy to see the Japanese action in Indochina as the final stimulus to our decision to impose embargoes. But from this time on, the maze of diplomatic notes and protested incidents grew denser and deeper. The effects of the embargo were multiple and mounting, but the rate of pressure was not easy to calculate. And, finally, in order to interpret a signal of danger to us—i.e., a specific military or diplomatic move by Japan—it was absolutely essential to know the latest American move, and to know it within a matter of hours. The problem of communicating with the theaters during these last hours, therefore, became a matter of primary importance.

Communication lies at the center of the confusion in these earlier alerts. For all three alerts, information was more complete in Washington than in the theater. Press coverage on the east coast of the United States was also much more extensive and more reliable than in Honolulu. But even in Washington the services were usually in disagreement about (1) what information to send to the theaters, (2) how to word that information, (3) what situation dictated an alert order, and (4) precisely what kind of an alert was indicated. Sometimes the disagreements were explicit; sometimes the policies were too vague to be sharply opposed. The Office of Naval Operations sent more information and evaluations to Honolulu than did the Army and almost invariably worded its messages in a way that the Army would have considered somewhat alarmist. The Army messages were infrequent and very cautiously worded. However, both services used a type of phrasing that left a great deal to the discretion of the local commander, both as to his interpretation of the intent of the message and the possible actions that he might put into effect as a result. The same message was sometimes intended as an alert order for one service, but not for the other.

Except for the alert order of June 17, 1940, none of these messages used the word "alert." They said in effect, "Something is brewing," or "A month may see literally anything," or "Get ready for a surprise move in any direction—maybe." Phrases characterizing contingencies as "possible" or "barely possible" or "strongly possible" or saying that they "cannot be entirely ruled out" or are "unpredictable" do not guide decision with a very sure hand. To say, for example, in the Army warning of November 27, 1941, that Japanese future action was unpredictable added nothing at all to the knowledge or judgment of General Short or Admiral Kimmel. Local pressures being what they were, General Short read a danger of sabotage into his final messages from Washington, while Admiral Kimmel read danger of attack by Japan on an ally or even on an American possession somewhere near the Hawaiian Islands.

Communication between Washington and the theater in 1941 was at such a rudimentary level that local interpretations were not subject to check. There was no standard procedure for acknowledgment or follow-up. Most top officials in Washington had only the haziest idea of what information was sent as a matter of course to the theaters, and since intentions were excellent, everybody assumed, much as we do today, that all essential or critical items of information were being sent out quickly. Admiral Turner, for example, was unaware that Kimmel did not have his own MAGIC decoding unit at Pearl Harbor. He also believed, like Admiral Stark and other Navy leaders, that the top-secret information received by both services in Honolulu was identical, that Short and Kimmel exchanged immediately whatever information they received, that there was a good press coverage in Honolulu, and that all the key officers read the daily papers with good judgment. As we have seen, none of these beliefs was justified.

When an alarm was raised by Washington on the basis of signals available only to Washington, leaving the type of alert to the discretion of the local commander seems to have been a questionable procedure. Naturally our security dictated the denial of certain kinds of information to the theater, especially critical information about our own future moves that we wanted to conceal from the enemy, or information that might disclose to the enemy our access to his secrets—thus endangering that access. And quite apart from security, common sense dictated a process of selection, the sending of only those items considered relevant and accurate by our Intelligence agencies in Washington. But precisely because of this limitation of information, it was important not to leave any latitude of interpretation to the local commander about *Washington's intent.* If Washington had the complete picture, it appears that Washington should also have taken the complete responsibility for specifying the date and degree of alert required and for following up the order to see that it had been put into effect. On the other hand, specific local tensions and local signals of broader threats might have provoked a local alert directly.

During the months treated in this chapter, the Army, both in Washington and in Hawaii, was less interested in and less informed about foreign policy than was the Navy; consequently the Army's judgment, especially that of its Intelligence branch, was sometimes less sound than the Navy's. G-2 predictions varied from safe tautologies—such as "The Japanese move into Thailand will either precede or follow or occur simultaneously with a move into Indochina"—to rashly exact short-term predictions that might be negated the following day or week—such as the forecast that the July 16 Japanese Cabinet change would bring about a relaxation of pressure on Vichy and French Indochina. The Office of Naval Intelligence had no opportunity to display good or bad judgment, since prediction of enemy intentions was not one of its duties.

The only markedly effective branch of Intelligence during 1941 was cryptanalysis. The messages decoded and translated from MAGIC provided vital data for predicting Japanese moves. However, though top Intelligence officers in Washington had access to this material, their use of it in general lagged behind that of the highest operational commanders. As we remarked earlier, to make good use of secret signals, the recipient must first be able to observe and analyze public information. Indeed, in comparing the top-secret Intelligence evaluations of enemy intentions with estimates in the contemporary press, one is struck by the relative soundness of the less privileged judgments. It is hard not to conclude that general knowledgeability in the world of international affairs, and close observation of overt developments, are the most useful ingredients in making such estimates.

Even MAGIC was not magical in its properties; its interpretation required subtlety and political good sense. Yet seeing MAGIC in this realistic perspective does not deny its critical importance. We turn now to an account of its nature and use.

3 ▸ MAGIC

To the layman, by far the best-known and most fascinating intelligence work done just before Pearl Harbor is the detective activity that resulted from mastery of the Japanese codes and ciphers known as MAGIC.[1] For dramatic suspense the last-minute signals revealed by the officers in charge of this top-secret source have no equal. The ability to read these codes gave the United States a remarkable advantage over the enemy—an advantage not likely to be repeated. America's military and government leaders had the privilege of seeing every day the most private communications between the Japanese government and its ambassadors in Washington, Berlin, Rome, Berne, Ankara, and other major Japanese embassies throughout the world. They saw the reports of Japanese military attachés and secret agents in Honolulu, Panama, the Philippines, and the major ports of the Americas. They knew in advance the diplomatic moves that Japan was contemplating and the sorts of information that her agents were collecting on American defense preparedness. Yet even this advantage—alone or in combination with information from other sources, such as British intelligence,[2] aerial reconnaissance, naval radio traffic

---

[1] In this chapter, code and cipher systems are not distinguished, partly because our primary interest is in the content of the messages, and partly because the distinction was not made in the testimony offered at the various Pearl Harbor hearings. The exact disguises that the Japanese used in secret communication were either deliberately obscured or not printed for security reasons. While PURPLE was a cipher system, it is usually called the PURPLE "code" by laymen.

[2] Admiral McCollum has pointed out that British knowledge of political and naval matters in the Far East was "surprisingly deficient and vastly inferior to our own in 1941." (Interview, September, 1956.)

analysis, radar, and the American embassy in Japan—was not enough to prevent the United States from being surprised.

What did MAGIC say during 1941? How much did it tell? And to whom in the American government was it able to speak? These are the questions that we want to answer. For this purpose we shall treat MAGIC first as an isolated signal source, looking simply at the raw material. Later we shall look at the preconceptions that determined its use in 1941 and see how it fitted into the total signal picture in Washington.

ARMY AND NAVY MAGIC

Both the Army and the Navy had special sections to handle the decoding of Japanese intercepts, but there was very little duplication of effort and no evidence of interservice rivalry. In the Navy Department the section that handled MAGIC was known as the Communications Security unit. During 1941 this unit had a total staff of about 300; it was under the supervision of Comdr. Laurence F. Safford. He had charge of all U.S. naval ciphers and codes as well as all interception and decoding of secret foreign-language communications for the Navy. For the latter purpose the Navy had intercept stations at Bainbridge Island, Washington; at Jupiter, Florida; at Winter Harbor, Maine; at Cheltenham, Maryland; at Cavite in the Philippines; and at several other places in the United States and the Pacific. All intercepts were forwarded from these stations to Safford's unit for processing.

A special section of Naval Intelligence that worked closely with Commander Safford was Lt. Comdr. A. D. Kramer's translation unit, which handled the translating of the Japanese diplomatic intercepts once they were decrypted. Kramer had a staff of one officer, two yeomen, and six translators.[3] Three of the translators were still in training and could not yet be trusted with material from the more important Berlin and Washington circuits. Kramer himself was a skilled Japanese linguist, but a good deal of his time was taken up with the supervision and distribution of the intercepts. He hand-carried the translated material to the list of approved recipients for the Navy.

[3] *Hearings*, Part 9, p. 4168.

Safford's Communications Security unit was one part of the Navy Communications Division. This Division was a kind of Western Union for the Navy and toward the end of 1941 it was handling a daily average of 4000 messages.[4] Rear Admiral Leigh Noyes was its chief from August, 1939, to February, 1942. Formally his office was on a par with both War Plans and Naval Intelligence, and Noyes testified that he functioned closely with both Rear Admiral Turner of War Plans and Capt. T. S. Wilkinson of ONI. The Office of Naval Intelligence, for example, determined what messages of MAGIC were important enough for our policy-makers and chief military men to see. Admiral Noyes had nothing to do with this. Lieutenant Commander Kramer of Naval Intelligence would make the first selection and would then review the material with his chief, Commander McCollum, who headed the Far Eastern desk of ONI. McCollum in turn would get Wilkinson's formal approval. Since Wilkinson disclaimed any knowledge of diplomatic language, we may assume that Kramer and McCollum therefore had rather complete determination of what was selected. Their judgment, as is evident from all the testimony, was highly regarded.[5]

In the Army the job of intercepting foreign coded messages was handled by the Signal Corps in a special section known as the Signal Intelligence Service, or SIS. Colonel Otis K. Sadtler was head of the military branch of the Signal Corps and acted as supervisor of SIS as well as of all the communication services, the Army pictorial work, and the signal schools. "In general," he said, "my position was one of operations only . . . we were concerned primarily with the collection of data that came to our attention through various intercept means, and we were not concerned with the evaluation or the analysis of the content of those messages."[6] Evaluation was the job of Col. Rufus S. Bratton, head of Far Eastern Intelligence, G-2, who selected MAGIC for distribution. During the period in which we are interested, Lt. Col. Rex W. Minckler headed the Signal Intelligence Service. The principal cryptanalyst, Col. William F. Friedman, was responsible for cracking the top-priority Japanese diplo-

---

[4] *Ibid.*, Part 23, p. 915. Rear Admiral Joseph R. Redman, Assistant Director of Navy Communications in 1941, estimated that his office handled a daily average of 26 incoming MAGIC messages during November.

[5] *Ibid.*, Part 10, p. 4750.

[6] *Ibid.*, Part 29, p. 2428.

matic code known as PURPLE. He had made his first completely de-
ciphered text in August, 1940, after working on the problem for some
eighteen to twenty months.[7]

The Army had seven intercept stations in the United States and its
possessions for picking up encoded diplomatic material.[8] All intercepts
from these stations were forwarded to SIS for processing.

Decryption of PURPLE, the top-priority MAGIC code, seems to have
involved first finding the key, which depended on getting a certain amount
of traffic in that key, and then decoding by machine. The PURPLE
machines were intricate, and they had to be made slowly and laboriously
by hand. In 1941 there were only four of them in existence. The Army
and Navy each had one machine in Washington; one had been sent to
Cavite in the Philippines and was manned by Fleet Intelligence officers
from the 16th Naval District, and a fourth had been sent to Great Britain
in return for the keys and machines necessary to decode German codes and
ciphers. A fifth one, destined for Pearl Harbor, was in production. With
the aid of these machines it was sometimes possible for American officials
to have information from Tokyo more rapidly than the Japanese themselves. Captain Safford testified that in most cases there was some delay
in finding the key, but "there were very few purple keys which we failed
to solve, maybe two or three per cent."[9] Army and Navy decoding units
cooperated in the effort to solve the keys.

One of the recurring questions in the congressional investigation concerned the length of time it took to process certain coded intercepts. Some
were available in a smooth translation on the same day that they were
intercepted; others did not appear in smooth form until a month later.
The longest time interval in the published record was a Honolulu to
Tokyo intercept that took fifty-nine days to process.

The main lag in processing MAGIC occurred between the date of interception at the radio station and the arrival of the intercept in Washington.
Airmail was the means most frequently used for forwarding the intercepts,
but sometimes only train or ship mail was available. For example, inter-

[7] *Ibid.*, Part 36, p. 312.
[8] These stations were located at Ft. Hancock in New York Harbor; San Francisco, California; San Antonio, Texas; Panama; Honolulu; Manila; and Ft. Hunt, Virginia.
[9] *Hearings*, Part 36, p. 319.

cepts were sent from Honolulu by air clipper, which departed for the mainland approximately once a week in good weather. When bad weather delayed the clipper for more than several days, the intercepts would go by ship. This time interval alone could amount to two weeks or more. In 1941 teletype was being installed in some of the intercept stations, but as of December 7, 1941, the Army's San Francisco station and the Navy's Bainbridge Island station were evidently the only ones that had it. Army and Navy radio facilities were also sometimes used, though according to Friedman's testimony, "we didn't have the radio circuits and facilities adequate to be able to forward all of the intercepted material by radio."[10]

Another major bottleneck was in the translation from Japanese to English. As we have mentioned, the Navy unit under Kramer had six translators, only three of them experienced enough to work independently. They were all civilians drawn from Civil Service personnel; they were not eligible for overtime pay, though they consistently worked overtime. There are no figures given for the number of translators in the Army unit, but it seems unlikely that the number was higher than six. From the evidence available, some of them were apparently civilians, since Bratton complained that the "Manchu Laws" limited strictly the Army personnel available for duty in Washington.[11] Most of the Army's trained Japanese specialists were in the field serving with the troops.

The entire SIS organization on December 7 consisted of 44 officers and 180 soldiers and civilians in Washington, and 150 personnel in the field at monitoring stations.[12] By contrast, at the end of the war, SIS had 666 officers and a total of 10,000 individuals in Washington alone. The Navy had 6000 people in its Communications Security unit in Washington.

Because of the shortage of translators the Army and Navy divided the task of translating Japanese material. At first the Navy took all messages originating in Tokyo on odd days, while the Army took all messages originating there on even days. Each service took the messages coming from its own intercept stations, and after determining the date of origin, which required some preliminary deciphering, they kept it or sent it to the other service. Later, as the press of work became very intense, the Army

---

[10] *Ibid.*, p. 311.

[11] *Ibid.*, Part 9, p. 4563. These laws required an officer to serve with the troops for two years running out of every six.

[12] *Ibid.*, Part 3, p. 1146.

simply took messages arriving in their office on even days and the Navy took those arriving in their office on odd days. In emergencies, even this system broke down, and whatever personnel were on hand in either section were used.

Naturally the Japanese used more than one code for sending diplomatic messages, and neither the Army nor the Navy cryptanalytic unit had enough personnel to process immediately all the intercepts for which each was responsible; so there was almost always a backlog of undecoded and untranslated material. Each unit therefore had set up a priority for decoding following as closely as possible the priority used by the Japanese. All intercepts coming over in PURPLE were worked on first; then J-19 and others in the J-series (such as J-17 K6, J-18 K8, and J-22); then PA-K2; and finally LA. PA-K2 seems to have been regarded by the cryptanalysts as relatively simple to solve, involving anywhere from twelve hours to five days, depending on the amount of traffic. Friedman described it as a "rather good form of enciphered code," which is "a high grade code involving keyed columnar [transposition] of code text."[13] J-19 was somewhat more difficult and Safford estimated that they failed to recover about 10 to 15 per cent of the keys. Code analysts were also trying to crack some of the major Japanese military and naval codes, but they testified that before December 7, 1941, they had not succeeded. During the last week before Pearl Harbor the Japanese located in American or Allied embassies and consulates received instructions to destroy all their codes except PURPLE: as a result there was very little traffic in either J-19 or PA-K2, and finding the keys became extremely difficult during that period.

The personnel in Army SIS and the Naval Communications Security unit worked under tremendous pressure. They knew that time was precious in decoding secret material because with too long a delay the material might have no value whatsoever. Furthermore both of these units were understaffed to the point where Commander Kramer usually had to work a 16-hour day in order to act as messenger boy as well as to exercise his own particular skills of translating and evaluating. Evaluation was just as important as translation, since any message that did not seem after rough translation to have political or military value had to be laid aside or discarded so that adequate time could be given to smooth

[13] *Ibid.*, Part 36, p. 310.

translation of the important intercepts. The pressure on the men who were trying to break the codes was of course just as great. Colonel Friedman suffered a nervous breakdown in December, 1940, after his constant work with Japanese codes. He was not working on Japanese material at the time of the Pearl Harbor attack.

SECURITY

The fact that we could read MAGIC was a closely guarded secret. Only a very few government officials were privileged to see these communications. According to an agreement drawn up by G-2 and ONI on January 23, 1941, distribution in Washington was limited as follows: within the War Department to the Secretary of War, the Chief of Staff, and the Director of Military Intelligence; within the Navy to the Secretary of the Navy, the Chief of Naval Operations, the Chief of the War Plans Division, and the Director of Naval Intelligence. The only other recipients were the Secretary of State and the President's military aide, who gave the material to the President. The intercepts selected for distribution after translation into smooth English were collected into folders; the folders were placed in locked pouches and personally delivered to the recipients, each of whom had a key to his pouch. The Army was responsible for distributing one set of pouches daily (or more often when necessary) to the War and State Departments; the Navy for distributing another set of pouches at the same time to the Navy Department and the White House.[14] Commander Kramer delivered for the Navy; Colonel Bratton and occasionally his assistant, Colonel Dusenbury, delivered for the Army. During a good part of 1941, Commander Kramer included a gist sheet with the translations. This gave a brief paraphrase of all the messages so that the reader could get a rapid idea of the entire contents of the pouch. Kramer also used a system of asterisks to call attention to some messages: one asterisk indicated an interesting message and two asterisks an important or urgent message. Because of the press of work, he

---

[14] Captain Kramer's testimony, *ibid.*, Part 33, pp. 850*ff.* Admiral Noyes believed that there was only one folder for the Army and one for the Navy. Originally the Army and the Navy alternated in delivering to the White House and the State Department. After May, 1941, G-2 refused to deliver to the White House because the President's aide had mislaid a folder. (*Hearings*, Part 11, p. 5475*f.*)

had to abandon the gist sheet in the fall of 1941 and give his evaluations orally to the recipients when he felt it necessary or when they had questions. Colonel Bratton delivered a gist or evaluation with his pouch until August 5, 1941, after which, on orders from General Marshall, he delivered only the raw material.[15] He then used a system of red check marks for important messages.

There were good reasons for guarding our mastery of MAGIC. Its value to the United States lay precisely in the fact that the Japanese did not know that their messages were being read and therefore continued to entrust crucial information to this channel. As Marshall explained in a letter to Gov. Thomas E. Dewey, written during the course of the war:

> ... our main basis of information regarding Hitler's intentions in Europe is obtained from Baron Oshima's messages from Berlin reporting his interviews with Hitler and other officials. . . . These are still in the codes involved in the Pearl Harbor events.
>
> ... the battle of the Coral Sea was based on deciphered messages and therefore our few ships were in the right place at the right time. Further, we were able to concentrate our limited forces to meet their naval advance on Midway when otherwise we almost certainly would have been some 3,000 miles out of the way. . . .
>
> Operations in the Pacific are largely guided by the information we obtain of Japanese deployments. We know their strength in various garrisons, the rations and other stores continuing available to them, and what is of vast importance, we check their fleet movements and the movements of their convoys. The heavy losses reported from time to time which they sustain by reason of our submarine action, largely result from the fact that we know the sailing dates and routes of their convoys and can notify our submarines to lie in wait at the proper points.
>
> . . . .
>
> As a further example of the delicacy of the situation, some of Donovan's people (the OSS) without telling us, instituted a secret search of the Japanese Embassy offices in Portugal. As a result the entire military attaché Japanese code all over the world was changed, and though this occurred over a year ago, we have not yet been able to break the new code, and have thus lost this invaluable source of information, particularly regarding the European situation.[16]

15 *Ibid.*, Part 9, p. 4584.
16 *Ibid.*, Part 3, p. 1129.

With so much at stake, great care had to be taken not to reveal to the Japanese our ability to read MAGIC, and one obvious method was to limit its distribution. For Washington did have moments of alarm. In April and May of 1941, the intercept stations picked up a series of messages indicating that the Japanese suspected the Americans of reading their codes.[17] Several messages between Berlin and Tokyo in April pointed to two auxiliary codes and PA-K2 as possibly broken by American crypt-analysts and definitely broken by the Germans. On May 3, a German agent called on Japan's Ambassador Oshima in Berlin, to tell him that the German Intelligence Agency in the United States had reliable information that the U.S. government was reading Ambassador Nomura's messages to Tokyo. Foreign Minister Matsuoka wired Nomura two days later:

> According to a fairly reliable source of information it appears almost certain that the United States Government is reading your code messages.
> Please let me know whether you have any suspicion of the above [Navy translation, May 5, 1941].[18]

Nomura replied on the same day:

> For our part, the most stringent precautions are taken by all custodians of codes and ciphers, as well as of other documents.
> On this particular matter I have nothing in mind, but pending investigation please wire any concrete instances or details which may turn up [Navy translation, May 6, 1941].[19]

There followed a series of frantic wires instituting greater precautionary measures in the use of codes. Then on May 20 Nomura wired:

> Though I do not know which ones I have discovered the United States is reading some of our codes.
> As for how I got the intelligence, I will inform you by courier or another safe way [Army translation, May 21, 1941].[20]

These communications were all carried on in PURPLE; so it might be argued that the Japanese felt that this system was still secure. There is no record of a further wire by Nomura specifying which codes he suspected of being broken. However, this background is referred to in the course of the hearings either as one of the main reasons for not sending to the

[17] *Ibid.*, Part 4, pp. 1860–1863, and Part 5, p. 2069*f*.
[18] *Ibid.*, Part 4, p. 1861.
[19] *Ibid.*, p. 1862.
[20] *Ibid.*, p. 1863.

theaters information based on MAGIC after that date, or to justify a general policy of not sending it to the theaters.

The question of why and when MAGIC was confined to a few recipients in Washington is the subject of much confused and conflicting testimony. Many people at the policy level denied that there was ever a change in policy; they claimed that there had, on the contrary, always been a policy not to send MAGIC to the theaters because of the necessity of guarding the secret. General Miles, for example, took this position, and in addition claimed that he never knew of any suspicions on the part of the Japanese that we were breaking their codes.[21] It was only Senator Ferguson's sharp insistence at the hearings that finally produced the messages just quoted, and Miles did not remember them. Admiral Noyes, head of Naval Communications, also testified that there had been no change in policy. Colonel Bratton of G-2, however, remembered being ordered by General Miles in August, 1941, to limit MAGIC distribution to Washington.

It is difficult to get at the truth behind these conflicting statements. If this particular series of wires in April and May did form the basis for a further restriction in the distribution of MAGIC, we would expect the change to have taken place in May or at the latest in June. (Army and Navy translation of this material was extremely prompt. Most of the messages were translated within 24 hours of the date of intercept, some of them on the same day that they were intercepted.) However, a good deal of MAGIC material was sent out to Admiral Kimmel by the Navy in July and most of it actually gave the Tokyo serial number and mentioned the source as PURPLE, both of which references seem indiscreet in view of Tokyo's suspicions.

It is also true that after the alert of July, 1941, neither Opnav nor Com 16 sent any MAGIC material to Kimmel until the first week in December, and then the material was much more abbreviated than it had been previously. The difference in the amount of information does suggest a policy change within the Navy, though the late dating of the change remains a mystery.

Evidently the major justification for the policy of confining MAGIC to Washington was a sound one: fear that transmission to the theaters conceivably might be intercepted by the Japanese. This was bolstered by the

[21] *Ibid.*, Part 3, p. 1369.

belief that Washington was the prime evaluating center, and by the fact that any attempt to encipher and send the information in any quantity would have overtaxed the communication facilities.

However, the fact that MAGIC was so closely guarded also had its disadvantages. It meant that no one ever had a chance to sit down and analyze the messages over a period of time, to check trends, to make quantitative estimates and comparisons. Each of the separately distributed copies was destroyed as soon as it was returned to the translating unit, and only one master copy was kept in each service. Most readers scanned the messages rapidly while the officer in charge of delivery stood by to take the copy back again. General Gerow, head of Army War Plans, for example, did not attempt to evaluate, but merely to keep "informed as to the general situation."[22] General Marshall testified: "If I am supposed to have [had] the final responsibility of the reading of all MAGIC, I would have ceased to be Chief of Staff in practically every other respect. . . . It was very difficult for me to read MAGIC sufficiently, even as it was."[23] Gerow and Marshall never discussed MAGIC because each knew the other had seen it.

The use of this top-secret material in 1941, then, had to be impressionistic. Its readers got a blow-by-blow, day-by-day view of diplomatic maneuverings. Only certain experts in the Far Eastern offices of ONI and G-2 had a proper view of the range and significance of this type of indicator, but their judgments unfortunately did not carry much weight outside of their own divisions.

Another consequence of the careful guarding of MAGIC was the prevalence of rumors about its character as a secret weapon, what it was, what it could do, who could get it, the size of the organization handling it, etc. Those least informed in the services thought that we could read Japanese naval and military codes as well as the diplomatic ones. Those who were better informed believed that we could read only the Japanese diplomatic codes, but they were also convinced that the Army and Navy shared in this knowledge equally in Washington and in the theaters.

The fact of the matter was that the Army did intercept at Manila, but it forwarded its intercepts for processing to the Navy at Cavite and to

[22] *Ibid.*, Part 4, p. 1601.
[23] *Ibid.*, Part 3, p. 1515.

Washington. The only PURPLE decoding machine in the Philippines was at Cavite and it was handled entirely by the Navy. Naval officers there determined what part of the traffic that they had read was to go locally to Admiral Hart and General MacArthur and what should be sent to Admiral Kimmel. In addition they forwarded all intercepts in the raw to the Washington naval unit.

At Pearl Harbor neither the Army nor the Navy had facilities for reading diplomatic traffic. The Army could and did intercept PURPLE, J-19, and other diplomatic codes, but forwarded the messages unchanged to Washington SIS for processing. Rochefort's naval traffic analysis unit was not supposed to intercept diplomatic traffic and did not attempt to do so.

General MacArthur could not recall having seen any of the MAGIC translations presented in evidence at the hearings.[24] He may have received some of this information orally, however, by way of Admiral Hart. Admiral Kimmel had received some MAGIC material from Washington and Cavite during the first part of 1941, but the policy of sending this to his command had been discontinued after the July crisis. What Kimmel did receive as "information" rather than as an "action" directive was not passed on to General Short.[25]

In Washington the following beliefs about MAGIC were current: Within the Navy some of the major officials believed that in Pearl Harbor Admiral Kimmel was reading MAGIC. Admiral Noyes knew that this was

[24] See Maj. Gen. C. A. Willoughby's protest on naval monopoly of MAGIC (*ibid.*, Part 35, p. 87) in an affidavit of May 8, 1945: "In an otherwise meritorious desire for security (though every modern nation knows that crypto-analysis is going on), the Navy has shrouded the whole enterprise in mystery, excluding other services, and rigidly centralizing the whole enterprise. At this date, for example, this same system is still in vogue: as far as SWPA is concerned, the crypto-analysis is made in Melbourne, forwarded via 7th Fleet D.N.I.; the Melbourne station is under direct orders of Washington, is not bound by any local responsibilities, forwards what they select, and when it suits them. The possibility of erroneous or incomplete selection is as evident now as it was in 1941. The only excuse the Navy has is that its field is primarily naval intercepts, but there is a lot of Army traffic or other incidental traffic. This collateral traffic is not always understood or correctly interpreted by the Navy, in my opinion.

"The solution to this vexing and dangerous problem is a completely joint, interlocking intercept and crypto-analytical service, on the highest level, with the freest interchange of messages and interpretation."

[25] Admiral Layton claims that Kimmel was under orders from Washington *not* to pass on information except when so directed, and he cites as his written authority regulation RIP3.

not true and so did the key personnel of his Communications Security unit.
However, Admiral Stark, the Chief of Naval Operations, testified: "I
inquired on two or three occasions as to whether or not Kimmel could
read certain dispatches when they came up and which we were interpreting
. . . and I was told that he could." He added: "that did not influence me
in the slightest regarding what I sent."[26]

Admiral Stark named his Chief of War Plans, Admiral Turner, as his
source of information that the Navy had a cryptanalytic unit at Pearl
Harbor. Admiral Turner explained at some length:

> On three occasions, I think all three times at Admiral Stark's initiative, I
> asked Admiral Noyes as to whether or not Admiral Kimmel and Admiral
> Hart were receiving the same decrypted information that we were receiving
> here. I do not know that I specified diplomatic intercepts.
>
> On each occasion Admiral Noyes assured me that since these dispatches
> were being intercepted by both Admiral Hart and Admiral Kimmel, that
> those officers had the same information that we had.
>
> Now, in the testimony before the Naval Court of Inquiry, Admiral Noyes
> states that he knew that the particular codes that we were using for the
> decryption of the diplomatic messages were not in the possession of either
> Admiral Hart or Admiral Kimmel and in his testimony he said that he could
> not understand how he could have given me such information.
>
> The only conclusion that I can arrive at is that I did not make my ques-
> tion to Admiral Noyes clear and that he misunderstood what I was trying
> to get at.[27]

If communication about MAGIC between the head of War Plans and the
head of Communications within the same service, in the same city, was
thus beset with difficulties, then we need not be surprised if communication about MAGIC between Washington and the theaters was similarly
complicated.

The source of the confusion here may lie in the use of the word
"intercept." To Admiral Noyes, as to other experts in Communications,
an "intercept" would have meant the Japanese message as our radio
station picked it up in its encoded form—a series of nonsense syllables
until it was decoded and translated. In the layman's usage, and conceivably
in Admiral Stark's and Admiral Turner's, the word "intercept" would
have referred not to the encoded message, but to the decoded and trans-

[26]*Hearings*, Part 5, p. 2175.
[27]*Ibid.*, Part 4, p. 1975*f*.

lated end product, or the "clear" as it is known in cryptanalytic parlance. (The word is sometimes used in both senses at once by the layman.) So if Admiral Turner asked Admiral Noyes, for example, "Is Honolulu getting these intercepts?" Admiral Noyes could certainly answer, "Yes," since Honolulu's Army radio station was picking up the encoded Japanese diplomatic messages. On the other hand, it never saw any of these messages in the clear.

Within the Army the same sort of misunderstanding occurred. General Marshall at first made out an affidavit for Colonel Clausen, dated August 28, 1945, in which he described "the intercepts of Japanese radio diplomatic messages" and went on to say: "Concerning intercepts of the character mentioned, it was my understanding in the period preceding 7 December 1941 that the Commanding General of the Hawaiian Department was aware of and was receiving some of this information from facilities available in his command."[28]

Now General Marshall may have been talking only about raw intercepts, i.e., encoded messages. At any rate, at the congressional investigation he changed his testimony. He said that the intercepts he was talking about were not the MAGIC ones, but rather those concerning the location of Japanese vessels at sea—in other words, the intercepts made by the naval traffic analysis unit under Rochefort. These were encoded, of course, and never broken. But they were naval intercepts and *not* diplomatic ones; so he was talking about intercepts in an entirely different code.

According to Marshall the diplomatic material was passed from the Signal Corps to Army G-2, and circulation from that point on was entirely under the direction of G-2. Marshall had never issued any specific instructions that he could recall to furnish or not to furnish these intercepts to Hawaii.[29] However, as General Miles testified, "there was a general policy laid down by the Chief of Staff that these messages and the fact of the existence of these messages or our ability to decode them should be confined to the least number of persons; no distribution should be made outside of Washington."[30] It is clear that Miles and Marshall and also Gerow of Army War Plans knew that the Army was not sending any MAGIC in-

[28] *Ibid.*, Part 35, p. 104.
[29] *Ibid.*, Part 3, p. 1210*f.*
[30] *Ibid.*, Part 2, p. 791.

formation to the theaters except very occasionally in paraphrased form in the body of a directive. However, it is not clear what they believed the Navy in Honolulu to possess in the way of cryptanalytic facilities. Marshall's Clausen affidavit implies that he believed the Navy in Honolulu to be receiving everything, both encoded and decoded, but passing only some of it to General Short. It is certainly likely that if both Stark and Turner thought that Kimmel had information, Marshall would think so too. His communications with Stark and Turner were much more frequent than with Noyes.

General Miles' affidavit for Clausen was unambiguous:

> ... it was my belief that in the period preceding 7 December 1941, that the Navy was intercepting, decrypting, decoding and translating this material, consisting of Japanese diplomatic and consular messages, at Hawaii, for use in connection with the fleet. I was given so to understand by Naval sources, but I do not recall who told me.[31]

Within Army Intelligence Lt. Col. Moses Pettigrew, executive officer of G-2 from August to December 7, 1941, testified in the third person to his belief that

> the Hawaiian Department was in possession of the same information he had received in Washington; that he reached this conclusion by statements. . . of Naval personnel, whom he does not now recall, to the effect that Hawaii had everything in the way of information that Washington had; and, that the Navy had a cryptoanalytic unit in Hawaii under Commander Rochefort which was monitoring and receiving these intercepts and breaking and translating the codes, as well as Washington, in the interest of saving time, utilizing personnel there available, and a subsequent exchange of intercept translations as a check one against the other.[32]

Colonel Clyde Dusenbury, assistant to Colonel Bratton of Army Far Eastern Intelligence who delivered MAGIC to its Washington recipients, believed that Commander Rochefort had access to MAGIC in Honolulu, either intercepted directly at Honolulu or received from the Navy Department in Washington. "I understood," he said, "the Navy had about four or five hundred Naval personnel in Hawaii doing monitoring, breaking, and translating of the Japanese diplomatic codes."[33]

[31] *Ibid.*, Part 35, p. 102.
[32] *Ibid.*, p. 23*f*.
[33] *Ibid.*, p. 25.

For Army personnel to believe that the Navy in Honolulu had all the privileged information that Washington had was one thing. It was another thing to go one step further and believe that Navy Intelligence in Honolulu would pass everything on to Army Intelligence there, or that top Navy officials would pass everything to the top Army officials. This optimistic view tended to be the dominant one, especially among top military officials in Washington. Marshall, for example, believed that the results of Rochefort's analysis went directly to Hawaiian G-2, and that any message of military importance going out in naval code would automatically get to General Short. For the Army never used its own codes to send messages to the theaters; it preferred a naval code that both services regarded as "most secure." General Miles also testified a number of times that "we had every reason to believe, thought we had, that a message sent by Navy code would always be transmitted by them to their opposite number in the Army command."[34] It was his understanding that "the information that the Navy was sending prior to July was information which would be passed on to the Army representatives at Hawaii."[35] He saw no reason after July, 1941, to inform the Army in Hawaii that this sort of information would no longer be sent: "The Navy was giving them the essence of certain information we received from MAGIC, but I do not remember that they had been informed of the source, nor was there any reason, therefore, to tell them we were discontinuing that particular source."[36]

Miles had a letter, dated September 6, 1941, and received by him on September 17, that would seem to support his view. This letter from Colonel Fielder, head of G-2 Hawaii, requested Miles to discontinue sending intelligence summaries, since they were already being supplied by the local ONI. The letter stated emphatically that "cooperation and contact between Office Naval Intelligence, Federal Bureau of Investigation, and the Military Intelligence Division in this Department, is most complete and all such data is received simultaneous with the dispatch of information to the respective Washington offices."[37] In short, according to Miles, "there was a long-standing agreement or policy of complete interchange

[34] *Ibid.*, Part 2, p. 811.   [35] *Ibid.*, p. 812.
[36] *Ibid.*   [37] *Ibid.*, p. 846.

of information between the Army and Navy (both in Hawaii and other places where we operated together)."[38]

On the other hand, some of the lower-ranking officers in G-2 had a more realistic view. Colonel Dusenbury, for example, was skeptical about the relationship between Kimmel's Intelligence officer, Commander Layton, and the head of G-2 Hawaii, Colonel Fielder. Colonel Dusenbury and Colonel Bratton drafted this message to G-2 Hawaii on December 5:

> Contact Commander Rochefort immediately thru Commandant Fourteen Naval District regarding broadcasts from Tokyo reference weather. [signed] Miles

If liaison had been automatic, there would have been no special reason for sending this cablegram, which Miles approved and signed. As we have seen in Chapter 1, nothing that Washington sent to the Navy was ever passed to the Army unless it carried the explicit directive to do so.

In sum, the zealous guarding of MAGIC had the following results: First, very few people were privileged to see MAGIC at all. Those who saw it had it in hand only momentarily, and the brevity of their examination naturally limited their analysis and inference. They were also generally wrong in their assumptions about who else saw it, and this was particularly critical in their estimate as to what would be redundant or unnecessary in a warning message to the theater or in communication with other policymakers in Washington. Those who did not see MAGIC were generally wrong in their assumptions about who did see it and how much information it contained. And all the wrong assumptions erred on the side of optimism.

DIPLOMATIC MESSAGES

One of the most frequent complaints of Admiral Kimmel and General Short is that they were denied the use of MAGIC either in the raw, or paraphrased, or with evaluation.[39] In view of the extreme difficulties put in their way when they tried to get access to MAGIC files in order to prepare

---

[38] *Ibid.*, p. 986. According to Admiral McCollum, General Miles and Colonel Fielder in their reference to Naval Intelligence and the Navy were speaking only of an agreement between the local G-2 and the Intelligence officer of the 14th Naval District, and not at all about either Layton or Rochefort. If this is so, the distinction was certainly not clear to the congressional committee, and it may not have been clear to General Miles.

[39] Kimmel, *Admiral Kimmel's Story, passim,* and General Short's testimony in *Hearings,* Part 5, *passim.*

their defense, it is evident that top Washington officials were certainly reluctant to have the issue publicized. Washington's reluctance arose, however, not from their policy of keeping that information from the theaters, which was undoubtedly sound, but rather from their apparent failure to evaluate it properly at the time. After the event MAGIC seemed to contain some very obvious clues to a direct Japanese attack on the United States, and Washington's inability to predict such an attack can easily be made to look like gross stupidity or negligence or a conspiracy to conceal vital information. Before the event, however, the clues in MAGIC were by no means so obvious.

In Chapter 1 we have already listed some signals based on MAGIC that went to Honolulu during the last crucial days. These included the following:

NOVEMBER 28—Order to Rochefort to monitor for winds-code execute.

DECEMBER 1—MAGIC message on Japanese intrigue in Thailand to provoke British invasion.

DECEMBER 3.—Two messages based on MAGIC of code-machine and secret-paper destruction by Japanese in major embassies.

Both Admiral Kimmel and General Short have insisted that there were several sorts of signals contained in MAGIC in addition to these, which, had they received them, would have radically affected their estimates of the situation and therefore their alert actions. They mentioned first the series of "deadline messages." This was a group of six messages from Tokyo to the Japanese embassy in Washington, the first intercepted and translated on November 5, 1941, the last intercepted and translated on November 24, 1941.[40] Taken together, without the intervening messages, they register a crescendo of tension. However, they were never seen as a group by any recipient of MAGIC before December 7, 1941. The message of November 5 read in its entirety:

#736

(Of utmost secrecy)

Because of various circumstances, it is absolutely necessary that all arrangements for the signing of this agreement [the last Japanese diplomatic pro-

[40] There are actually two other references to the deadline—one on November 19 and one on November 25—reproduced (p. 196) in the listing of messages emphasizing speed.

posals before the outbreak of hostilities, known as Proposals A and B] be completed by the 25th of this month. I realize that this is a difficult order, but under the circumstances it is an unavoidable one. Please understand this thoroughly and tackle the problem of saving the Japanese-U.S. relations from falling into a chaotic condition. Do so with great determination and with unstinted effort, I beg of you.

This information is to be kept strictly to yourself only.[41]

Another message, intercepted on November 11, and translated on November 12, emphasized the need for speed, and repeated that November 25 was an "absolutely immovable" deadline:

Judging from the progress of the conversations, there seem to be indications that the United States is still not fully aware of the exceedingly [sic] criticalness of the situation here. The fact remains that the date set forth in my message #736 is absolutely immovable under present conditions. It is a definite dead line and therefore it is essential that a settlement be reached by about that time. The session of Parliament opens on the 15th (work will start on (the following day?)) according to the schedule. The government must have a clear picture of things to come, in presenting its case at the session. You can see, therefore, that the situation is nearing a climax, and that time is indeed becoming short.

I appreciate the fact that you are making strenuous efforts, but in view of the above-mentioned situation, will you redouble them. When talking to the Secretary of State and others, drive the points home to them. Do everything in your power to get a clear picture of the U.S. attitude in the minimum amount of time. At the same time do everything in your power to have them give their speedy approval to our final proposal.

We would appreciate being advised of your opinions on whether or not they will accept our final proposal A.[42]

In a message intercepted and translated on November 15, Tokyo again referred to the deadline:

It is true that the United States may try to say that since we made no particular mention of the changed status of the talks, they were under the impression that they were still of a preliminary nature.

Whatever the case may be, the fact remains that the date set forth in my message #736 is an absolutely immovable one. Please, therefore, make the United States see the light, so as to make possible the signing of the agreement by that date.[43]

[41] *Hearings*, Part 12, p. 100.
[42] *Ibid.*, p. 116f.
[43] *Ibid.*, p. 130.

Next, to a plea from Ambassador Nomura in Washington that Japan be patient for one or two months, Tokyo sent the following reply on November 16:

I have read your #1090, and you may be sure that you have all my gratitude for the efforts you have put forth, but the fate of our Empire hangs by the slender thread of a few days, so please fight harder than you ever did before.

What you say in the last paragraph of your message is, of course, so and I have given it already the fullest consideration, but I have only to refer you to the fundamental policy laid down in my #725. Will you please try to realize what that means. In your opinion we ought to wait and see what turn the war takes and remain patient. However, I am awfully sorry to say that the situation renders this out of the question. I set the deadline for the solution of these negotiations in my #736, and there will be no change. Please try to understand that. You see how short the time is; therefore, do not allow the United States to sidetrack us and delay the negotiations any further. Press them for a solution on the basis of our proposals, and do your best to bring about an immediate solution [translated November 17].[44]

Again on November 19 the Washington negotiators pleaded for time. They reported that they assumed November 25 to be an absolutely unalterable date and that they were pressing the United States for some definite reply within ten days. But they asked permission not to announce at the moment that they were "having ships, with all the accompanying dark implications, leave on or about the 25th or 26th." (The ships referred to here were for the evacuation of Japanese nationals from the United States and Panama.) They felt that such a step would not be in keeping with their attempts to get an early settlement.[45] In the reply of November 22 (intercepted and translated on the same day), Tokyo extended the deadline four days:

To both you Ambassadors [Nomura and Kurusu].

It is awfully hard for us to consider changing the date we set in my #736. You should know this, however, I know you are working hard. Stick to our fixed policy and do your very best. Spare no efforts and try to bring about the solution we desire. There are reasons beyond your ability to guess why we wanted to settle Japanese-American relations by the 25th, but if within the next three or four days you can finish your conversations with the Americans;

[44] *Ibid.*, p. 137*f*.
[45] *Ibid.*, p. 159.

if the signing can be completed by the 29th, (let me write it out for you—
twenty ninth); if the pertinent notes can be exchanged; if we can get an
understanding with Great Britain and the Netherlands; and in short if everything can be finished, we have decided to wait until that date. This time we
mean it, that the deadline absolutely cannot be changed. After that things are
automatically going to happen. Please take this into your careful consideration
and work harder than you ever have before. This, for the present, is for the
information of you two Ambassadors alone.[46]

On November 24, in the last of the deadline messages, Tokyo reminded
both ambassadors that the time limit set in their message of November 22
was in Tokyo time.

Before we accept these messages at their face value, we must ask
whether or not—at other periods of crisis in U.S.-Japanese relations—such
a phenomenon has occurred. Was there this insistence on speed or a
specific deadline set for terminating a negotiation in any private, encoded
messages between Tokyo and Washington at an earlier date? Or does this
series constitute a unique signal in itself?

The only places that we can look for an answer are in the published
intercepts for July to November, 1941. These are not complete, but they
are vouched for as a selection of the intercepts significant for U.S.-
Japanese relations. There are no signs of alarm in this selection until
rumors of the Embargo Act were confirmed in the American press. And
then the alarm is entirely on the part of the Japanese ambassadors in
Washington; they are worried—not about Japan—but about the United
States' setting off some sudden explosion. For the sudden retaliatory move
by the United States was a surprise to the Japanese. Some of the phrasing
in the messages sent by the ambassadors is familiar:

> AUGUST 7—*Washington to Tokyo*: U.S.-Japanese relations have
> now reached an extremely critical stage. . . .[47]

> AUGUST 16—*Washington to Tokyo*: As I have successively reported
> to you, Japanese-American relations have today reached a stage in which
> anything might happen at any moment, and they are likely to grow
> worse suddenly as soon as Japan makes her next move. . . .[48]

[46] *Ibid.*, p. 165.
[47] *Ibid.*, p. 13.
[48] *Ibid.*, p. 17.

At the time of imposing the embargo, the United States had called off its conversations with the Japanese, and the ambassadors were understandably worried about getting back in touch. Then on August 26, a dispatch from Tokyo was intercepted that read like some of the late-November messages:

> Now the international situation as well as our internal situation is strained in the extreme and we have reached the point where we will pin our last hopes on an interview between the Premier and the President.[49]

However, the instructions and attitude were primarily conciliatory. For example, on September 3, Tokyo cabled:

> ... we would like to make all arrangements for the meeting around the middle of September, with all possible speed, and issue a very simple statement to that effect as soon as possible. (If the middle of September is not convenient, any early date would meet with our approval.)[50]

On that same day the Japanese press somehow got hold of the news that a meeting between Premier Konoye and the President was pending, and this leak evidently had some unfortunate repercussions. On September 4, Tokyo reported that because of the leak it was "urgent to hold the conference as soon as possible." October 15, we must remember, was the date set by the military for the Konoye Cabinet to reach some agreement with the United States. However, the tone of the messages from Tokyo remained restrained. Tokyo did send on the suggestion that no hint should be given to the United States that Japan was really finding the embargo very damaging, but the ambassadors were to report at least that Japanese public opinion was provoked by the sending of petroleum supplies by way of Vladivostok to Russia when Japan was being denied these supplies, and that the United States might do well to send them by another route. Finally on October 13 the cables from Tokyo became more frequent and more insistent:

> The situation at home is fast approaching a crisis and it is becoming absolutely essential that the two leaders meet if any adjustment of Japanese-U.S. relations is to be accomplished. I cannot go into details now, but please bear this fact in mind.[51]

[49] *Ibid.*, p. 20.
[50] *Ibid.*, p. 25.
[51] *Ibid.*, p. 64.

There was also a message setting up a code for a telephone conversation at noon, Japanese time, on October 14 between the Chief of the American Bureau of the Tokyo Foreign Office and Minister Wakasugi in Washington. The code had six terms to cover the following contingencies:

> U.S. attitude is reasonable.
> U.S. attitude is unreasonable.
> General outlook of the negotiations.
> The Four Principles.
> Will they stick to it?
> Is there some way through it?[52]

Another message sent out a bit later on the 13th repeated that

> circumstances do not permit even an instant's delay. Please, therefore, submit a report on the rough outline and the general tone of the conference between Wakasugi and Welles immediately, and dispatch a cable giving the details, subsequently.[53]

In these messages just before the fall of the Konoye Cabinet, there were definite expressions of the need for speed—not "an instant's delay," "immediately," "fast approaching a crisis"—and they were combined with phrases characterizing U.S.-Japanese relations as "strained" and "extremely critical." Furthermore, these expressions were coming from Tokyo rather than from Washington; therefore they bore some relation to the November deadline messages. But notice that the only specific date mentioned at any time was the middle of September, "or any early date." And this was not referred to again except in a vague way, whereas in the deadline messages there were eight precise references to November 25 and then an extension to November 29. In terms of quantity also (we have reproduced all the October references to speed), the variety of ways of saying "hurry" and the frequency of such expressions were much greater from November 2 on than at any time preceding either the July or the October crisis.

On November 2, for example, Tokyo wired Washington:

> The Government has for a number of days since the forming of the new Cabinet been holding meetings with the Imperial headquarters. We have carefully considered a fundamental policy for improving relations between Japan and America, but we expect to reach a final decision in a meeting on the

52 *Ibid.*, p. 65.
53 *Ibid.*, p. 66.

morning of the 5th and will let you know the result at once. *This will be our Government's last effort to improve diplomatic relations.* The situation is very grave. When we resume negotiations, the situation makes it urgent that we reach a decision at once. This is at present only for your information. When we take up these negotiations once more, we trust you will handle everything with the greatest of care [author's italics].[54]

This sort of phrasing—"our Government's last effort"—was repeated in much more urgent fashion in a three-part cable dated November 4 and translated by us on the same day. This was cable No. 725, referred to in one of the deadline messages as outlining the fundamental policy making a deadline imperative. It began:

Well, relations between Japan and the United States have reached the edge, and our people are losing confidence in the possibility of ever adjusting them. . . .

The second paragraph elaborated:

Conditions both within and without our Empire are so tense that no longer is procrastination possible, yet in our sincerity to maintain pacific relationships between the Empire of Japan and the United States of America, we have decided, as a result of these deliberations, to gamble once more on the continuance of the parleys, but *this is our last effort*. Both in name and spirit this counter-proposal of ours is, indeed, *the last*. I want you to know that. If through it we do not reach a quick accord, I am sorry to say *the talks will certainly be ruptured*. Then, indeed, will *relations between our two nations be on the brink of chaos*. I mean that the success or failure of the pending discussions will have an immense effect on the destiny of the Empire of Japan. In fact, we gambled the fate of our land on *the throw of this die* [author's italics].[55]

The next part of the cable underlined how long the negotiations had dragged out, pointed to the patience and sincerity of the Japanese and the stubborn, unyielding character of the American government, and continued:

. . . our temperance, I can tell you, has not come from weakness, and naturally there is an end to our long-suffering. Nay, when it comes to a question of our existence and our honor, when the time comes we will defend them without recking the cost. If the United States takes an attitude that overlooks or shuns this position of ours, there is not a whit of use in ever broaching the

---

[54] *Ibid.*, p. 90.
[55] *Ibid.*, p. 92f.

talks. This time we are showing the limit of our friendship; this time *we are making our last possible bargain*, and I hope that we can thus settle all our troubles with the United States peaceably [author's italics].[56]

The final part of the cable said that as soon as the conference was over, the Japanese ambassador would be informed and he should go immediately to Roosevelt and Hull and "tell them how determined we are and try to get them to foster a speedy understanding." The cable emphasized that instructions should be followed to the letter, that the policy outlined represented the unanimous opinion of the government and the military high command, and ended with the words, "there will be no room for personal interpretation."

There is no doubt about the meaning of this cable. It said that the Japanese government was making its last effort to come to an agreement with the United States, that speed was essential, and that if this effort failed, relations would be broken off. The manner of saying this—"a throw of the die," "the brink of chaos,"—was also dramatically urgent, even if somewhat alien to the American mode of speech.

From November 2 to November 26 there was scarcely a message from Tokyo that did not reiterate the need for speed and the fact that this was the last chance. The following is a brief listing, without reference to the specific context of the messages, and not including any parts of the deadline series. With one exception, these are messages originating in Tokyo; the italics have been supplied:

> NOVEMBER 2—I said [to the American Ambassador in Japan], "I am very sorry that Japanese-American relations have lately been growing *worse* and *worse*. If this continues, I fear that *unfortunate* results will ensue. For six months, negotiations have been dragging along, and our people are growing *impatient*. Therefore, I hope that a *speedy* settlement will be reached.[57]
>
> NOVEMBER 2—I saw him [the British ambassador] again (yesterday?) and endeavored to impart to him the impression that the situation is waxing *more and more acute and will not permit of procrastination.*[58]
>
> NOVEMBER 4—I earnestly hope and pray that you can *quickly* bring about an understanding [transmitting Proposal A].[59]

[56] *Ibid.*, p. 93.   [57] Tokyo to Washington. (*Ibid.*, p. 90.)
[58] *Ibid.*, p. 91.   [59] *Ibid.*, p. 96.

NOVEMBER 4—since the situation *does not permit of delays*, it will be necessary to put forward some substitute plan. Therefore, our second formula is advanced with the idea of making *a last effort to prevent something happening* [transmitting Proposal B].[60]

NOVEMBER 4—In view of the *gravity* of the present negotiations . . . Ambassador Kurusu is leaving—on the 7th by clipper to assist you.[61]

NOVEMBER 5—at the *earliest possible moment*. Under present conditions, *speed is an absolutely essential factor*.[62]

NOVEMBER 5—As stated in my previous message, this is the Imperial Government's *final step*. Time is becoming *exceedingly short* and the situation *very critical*. *Absolutely no delays* can be permitted. Please bear this in mind and do your best. I wish to stress this point over and over.[63]

NOVEMBER 6—now that we are on the *last lap* of these negotiations. . . .[64]

NOVEMBER 11—The Imperial Government has made the maximum concessions she can in drawing up its *final proposal*, I explained [to the British ambassador]. . . . Our domestic political situation will permit *no further delays* . . . it is absolutely impossible that there be any further delays . . . [I suggested that his country] cooperate in bringing about an *early* agreement.

. . . I pointed out the *criticalness* of the situation. The Ambassador listened to what I said very attentively, giving indications that he was realizing for the first time how critical the situation was . . . he himself would do his best to bring about a *speedy* settlement.

. . . there are indications that the United States Government is still under the impression that the negotiations are in the preliminary stages. . . .

That the United States takes this lazy and easy going attitude in spite of the fact that as far as we are concerned, this is the *final* phase, is exceedingly unfortunate.[65]

NOVEMBER 13—Judging from the tone of these talks, the United States is apparently still assuming that they are of a preliminary nature. We pleaded with the U.S. Ambassador again on the 12th to try and see the *seriousness* of the situation. Will you, too, do everything in your power. . . .[66]

NOVEMBER 15—Please be aware of the fact that the "B" suggestion was taken up because we thought it might be a *short cut* to settle-

[60] *Ibid.*, p. 96f.   [61] *Ibid.*, p. 97.   [62] *Ibid.*, p. 98.
[63] *Ibid.*, p. 99.   [64] *Ibid.*, p. 101.   [65] *Ibid.*, p. 118f.
[66] *Ibid.*, p. 123.

ment . . . we thought it would *speed* up the procedure. We do not wish to give it even a chance to further complicate and prolong matters.[67]

NOVEMBER 15—describe our determinations . . . cooperate with him in an unsparing effort to guide the negotiations to any *early* settlement. . . .[68]

. . . In view of the fact that the *crisis is fast approaching,* no subsidiary complications can be countenanced even when considering the *time element alone.* Such an eventuality would make impossible the surmounting of the crisis.

. . . do everything in your power to make the United States come to the realization that it is indeed a *critical* situation.[69]

NOVEMBER 19—if we were to go into a discussion of each of these particulars, we would have to give up hopes of the possibility of reaching a settlement *in a short time,* (see my #736 [the deadline message]). Now that matters have progressed this far, we think the only way to reach a full solution is to conclude an agreement now on a few absolutely essential items in order to prevent matters from going from bad to worse by long-view political adjustments, thus first of all avoiding the danger of an outbreak of war.

. . . the transfer of troops from southern French Indo-China to the northern part, is an important concession we would venture to make *for the sake of speeding the agreement* . . . in order to save the situation and with President Roosevelt's *immediate* (this should mean within one week) approval, have it ready for signatures of both countries.[70]

NOVEMBER 19—Article 2 . . . is an important concession we venture to make *for the sake of speeding* the conclusion of the agreement.[71]

NOVEMBER 24—We here in Japan, in view of the extremely critical situation, only hope most earnestly for a *speedy* settlement.[72]

NOVEMBER 25—As the *time limit* is near please have them (defer?) for a while.[73]

NOVEMBER 25—We are advised by the military that we are to have a reply from the United States on the 25th.[74]

NOVEMBER 26—In view of the fact that *time is getting short* with but *few days left* this month, I would like to have you *at once* contact the United States authorities again.[75]

NOVEMBER 26—The situation is momentarily becoming *more tense* and telegrams take *too long.* [There follow instructions for a telephone code.][76]

[67] *Ibid.,* p. 129.   [68] *Ibid.,* p. 130*f.*   [69] *Ibid.,* p. 131.
[70] *Ibid.,* p. 156.   [71] *Ibid.,* p. 157.   [72] *Ibid.,* p. 172.
[73] Tokyo to Nanking. (*Ibid.,* p. 173.)   [74] Hanoi to Tokyo. (*Ibid.,* p. 174.)
[75] Tokyo to Washington. (*Ibid.,* p. 176.)   [76] *Ibid.,* p. 178.

Listed together in this way, the insistence on speed seems to have been repeated *ad nauseam*. Combined with the deadline series, the repetitions give an impression of extreme urgency. And combined further with other clues available in MAGIC, they indicate that something impressively big is going to happen. But we must remember that no decisionmaker ever looked at these messages for an entire month in the way that we are doing now.

Nor did any such reader ever have the time or the opportunity to read the Tokyo messages alone, to see how they differed in tone from the messages coming out of the Japanese embassy in Washington. To an interpreter of MAGIC the expressions of hope and earnest effort coming from Nomura and Kurusu would function primarily as "noise." The two ambassadors were working pretty much in the dark themselves, but they were negotiating in good faith. They caught at such straws as a sympathetic expression on Hull's face, or his informal suggestion that the United States act as mediator in the Sino-Japanese conflict. The tone of their messages—earnest, patient, optimistic—contrasts with the menacing urgency of Tokyo's exhortations.

So far it has been unnecessary to mention the actual content of the negotiations, and there are still some other ways of considering MAGIC that do not require exercising diplomatic or military judgment. If any one person had been in a position at the time to reflect on it, the recurrence of certain phrases might have been regarded as significant parts of the signal picture. For example, in the way that we collected references to speed, we could ask: How many times did the Japanese Foreign Ministry state in intercepts available to Washington before December 7 that "Negotiations will be ruptured unless . . . "? How many times after November 25 did it report that "Negotiations are ruptured"? How many contingencies did it prepare for "in the event that war breaks out" or more precisely "in the event that war breaks out with England and the United States"? And was this phrase ever used interchangeably with "in the event that negotiations are ruptured"? Among these contingencies were there some that seemed to indicate preparations for war more clearly than others? Was there any clue as to whether these preparations were for an attack by Japan on the United States, or for an attack by the United States on Japan?

A count based on the published intercepts will give us only an approximate answer. For example, Sadtler testified that Washington intercepted sixteen "Haruna" messages before December 6.[77] "Haruna" was the code word sent to Tokyo to indicate that the embassy had destroyed its codes. None of these "Haruna" messages was reproduced in the selection of intercepts for the congressional hearings.[78] Yet the code-destruction order was consistently viewed in Washington as an extremely significant time-warning signal. There are very probably similar gaps for other types of messages, either because we were never able to intercept all the messages sent out from Tokyo in MAGIC, or because the inclusion of certain intercepts may have been regarded as unnecessary because they were repetitive. However, it is well to bear in mind that nobody in Washington before the event had the time to make even an approximate count.

There were nine messages in which Tokyo expressed fear or threatened that negotiations would be ruptured:

> NOVEMBER 2—*Tokyo to Washington*: The attitude of the United States is entirely too theoretical, and if this continues there will be scant chance of a settlement. . . . If the negotiations turn out to be a failure, cannot tell but what a lamentable situation will occur [translated November 3].[79]
>
> NOVEMBER 4—*Tokyo to Washington*: If through it [Proposals A and B] we do not reach a quick accord, I am sorry to say the talks will certainly be ruptured [translated November 4].[80]
>
> NOVEMBER 11—*Toyko to Washington, reporting a conversation with the British ambassador*: The Imperial Government has made the maximum concessions she can in drawing up its final proposal, I explained. . . . If, unfortunately, the United States refuses to accept those terms, it would be useless to continue the negotiations [translated November 12].[81]
>
> NOVEMBER 14—*Tokyo to Hong Kong*: Though the Imperial Government hopes for great things from the Japan-American negotiations, they do not permit optimism for the future. Should the negotiations

[77] *Ibid.*, Part 10, p. 4630.

[78] The *Hearings* contain a reprint of a Signal Corps memo indicating that only nine of these messages were intercepted before December 7. (*Ibid.*, Part 5, p. 2077.)

[79] *Ibid.*, Part 12, p. 91.

[80] *Ibid.*, p. 92.

[81] *Ibid.*, p. 118.

collapse, the international situation in which the Empire will find herself will be one of tremendous crisis [translated November 26].[82]

NOVEMBER 19—*Tokyo to Washington, instructing the ambassador to present Proposal B*: If the U.S. consent to this cannot be secured, the negotiations will have to be broken off; therefore, with the above well in mind put forth your very best efforts [translated November 20].[83]

NOVEMBER 20—*Tokyo to Ankara*: In the light of the trend of past negotiations there is considerable doubt as to whether a settlement of the negotiations will be reached . . . the situation not permitting any further conciliation by us, an optimistic view for the future is not permitted. In the event that negotiations are broken off, we expect that the situation in which Japan will find herself will be extremely critical [to be relayed to Switzerland, Turkey and Moscow, France, Spain, Portugal, Sweden, Finland, South Africa, Roumania, Bulgaria, and Hungary] [translated November 28].[84]

NOVEMBER 26—*Telephone conversation between Washington and Tokyo*: Kurusu says, "I have made all efforts, but they will not yield. . . . I rather imagine you had expected this outcome." Yamamoto replies, "Yes, I had expected it, but wished to exert every effort up to the final moment in the hope that something might be accomplished" [translated November 26].[85]

NOVEMBER 28—*Tokyo to Hanoi*: Even though the worst possible situation developed, and it will in all likelihood, the Imperial Government has made no decisions with regard to changing the position of the French Indo-Chinese Government [translated December 1].[86]

NOVEMBER 29—*Berlin to Tokyo, reporting Ribbentrop as saying*: We have received advice to the effect that there is practically no hope of the Japanese-U.S. negotiations being concluded successfully, because of the fact that the United States is putting up a stiff front.

If this is indeed the fact of the case, and if Japan reaches a decision to fight Britain and the United States, I am confident that that will not only be to the interest of Germany and Japan jointly, but would bring about favorable results for Japan herself. [The Japanese ambassador then replies that he is "not aware of any concrete intentions of Japan."] [translated December 1].[87]

There were two messages in which Tokyo announced that negotiations with the United States were about to be ruptured, and one in

---

[82] *Ibid.*, p. 126. [83] *Ibid.*, p. 155. [84] *Ibid.*, p. 160.
[85] *Ibid.*, p. 179*f*. [86] *Ibid.*, p. 196. [87] *Ibid.*, p. 200.

which she informed Berlin that the conversations "now stand ruptured":

> NOVEMBER 28—*Tokyo to Washington*: with a report of the views
> of the Imperial Government on this American proposal which I will
> send you in two or three days, the negotiations *will be de facto
> ruptured* [author's italics] [translated November 28].[88]
>
> NOVEMBER 30—*Tokyo to Berlin*: it has only been in the negotia-
> tions of the last few days that it has become . . . clear that the Imperial
> Government *could no longer continue negotiations* with the United
> States [author's italics] [translated December 1].[89]
>
> NOVEMBER 30—*Tokyo to Berlin*: The conversations begun between
> Tokyo and Washington last April . . . *now stand ruptured* [author's
> italics] [translated December 1].[90]

Another set of signals mentioned by Kimmel and Short indicates
Japanese duplicity about the negotiations after the deadline date. The first
message that they brought in evidence was that of November 28, No. 844,
which said:

> Well, you two Ambassadors have exerted superhuman efforts but, in
> spite of this, the United States has gone ahead and presented this humiliating
> proposal. This was quite unexpected and extremely regrettable. The Imperial
> Government can by no means use it as a basis for negotiations. Therefore,
> with a report of the views of the Imperial Government on this American
> proposal which I will send you in two or three days, *the negotiations will
> be de facto ruptured.* This is inevitable. *However, I do not wish you to
> give the impression that the negotiations are broken off. Merely say to them
> that you are awaiting instructions* and that, although the opinions of your
> Government are not yet clear to you, to your own way of thinking the
> Imperial Government has always made just claims and has borne great
> sacrifices for the sake of peace in the Pacific. Say that we have always
> demonstrated a long-suffering and conciliatory attitude, but that, on the other
> hand, the United States has been unbending, making it impossible for Japan
> to establish negotiations [author's italics]. . . .[91]

There were several earlier dispatches that also suggested careful con-
cealment of a plan, but Admiral Kimmel and General Short did not make
use of them in their defense. On November 5, a message reporting the
Imperial Council's approval of Proposals A and B said:

> We wish to avoid giving them the impression that there is a time limit
> or that this proposal is to be taken as an ultimatum [Proposals A and B are

88 *Ibid.*, p. 195.   89 *Ibid.*, p. 205.
90 *Ibid.*, p. 204.   91 *Ibid.*, p. 195.

consistently referred to as ultimatums in Tokyo MAGIC]. In a friendly manner, show them that we are very anxious to have them accept our proposal.[92]

Nomura's reply to this point stated that two important Japanese newspapers had published a notice of a November 15 deadline for completion of the negotiations:

> There is danger that America will see through our condition. If we have really made up our minds to a final course of action it would be the part of wisdom to keep still about it.[93]

On November 6, in explaining the mission of Ambassador Kurusu, Tokyo wired:

> I wish him . . . to communicate to you at first hand . . . the exact situation here in Japan, and now that we are on the last lap of these negotiations, I do hope that he can help you in unraveling this bewildering maze and through cooperation lead to a solution, and that right soon. To make it sound good, we are telling the public that he is coming to help you quickly compose the unhappy relations between the two nations.[94]

Kimmel and Short mentioned also an intercepted dispatch of November 29, instructing the ambassadors to make "one more attempt verbally," but ending with the caution: "please be careful that this does not lead to anything like a breaking off of negotiations."[95] They also added a dispatch intercepted on December 1 in which Tokyo noted that the deadline of November 29 had come and gone, and

> the situation continues to be increasingly critical. However, to prevent the United States from becoming unduly suspicious we have been advising the press and others that though there are some wide differences between Japan and the United States, the negotiations are continuing. (The above is for only your information.)[96]

In a code telephone conversation between Yamamoto in Tokyo and Kurusu in Washington on November 27, Kurusu was instructed to carry on negotiations. He was reported as saying, "Oh! My!" and then with a resigned laugh, "Well, I'll do what I can." And later, "But without anything,—they want to keep on negotiating. In the meantime we have a

---

[92] *Ibid.*, p. 99.
[94] *Ibid.*
[96] *Ibid.*, p. 208.

[93] *Ibid.*, p. 101.
[95] *Ibid.*, p. 199.

crisis on hand and the [Japanese] army is champing at the bit. You know the army."[97]

On November 30 the two men talked again together on the telephone, Kurusu protesting about the bad effect that the Premier's speech of November 30 was having in America. (This was the speech in which the Premier promised to "purge" East Asia "with a vengeance" of hostile British and U.S. influences.[98]) Here again Kurusu was told to continue negotiations, and he replied:

> You were very urgent about them before, weren't you; but now you want them to stretch out. We will need your help. Both the Premier and the Foreign Minister will need to change the tone of their speeches!!!! Do you understand? Please all use more discretion. . . .
> . . . .
> Actually the real problem we are up against is the effects of happenings in the South [notices in the press of further Japanese troop movements into southern Indochina]. You understand, don't you?[99]

Of this set of dispatches and telephone conversations it has been argued that the fraudulent character of the negotiations could be deduced only after the event. There is a good deal of sense in this argument because the evidence indicates that the Japanese ambassadors themselves did not know the true intent of their government. Furthermore, only a very few people in Japan outside the military knew about the Pearl Harbor attack plan, so it could also be argued that not only the ambassadors but even the foreign minister who sent out the messages may have been in the dark[100] and may have seriously entertained the hope that a miracle could happen at the last moment. The Pearl Harbor task force was under orders to return up to 24 hours before D-day if anything favorable developed in the U.S.-Japanese negotiations. Moreover, since diplomatic negotiations are always a matter of fencing, with endless variations of slight retreat and slight advance, it is very difficult (and perhaps not worth much at any time) to

[97] *Ibid.*, p. 191.

[98] Langer and Gleason, *The Undeclared War, 1940–1941*, p. 909. See Chap. 4, p. 271*n*, for a more exact translation of the quoted phrases.

[99] *Hearings*, Part 12, p. 207.

[100] Grew, *Ten Years in Japan*, p. 498. Grew believed that "His Imperial Majesty's Minister for Foreign Affairs had no prior knowledge that an act of war was to be committed by the Japanese forces [against America]."

say what is sincere and what is fraudulent, how much is real and how much is bluff.

However, anyone responsible for evaluating decoded enemy material would be expected to keep constantly in mind the question of how far Tokyo was trusting her own representatives. (The United States did not keep Ambassador Grew fully informed, though in the case of America this was negligence rather than a conscious policy.) Unless this question of trust is kept in mind, along with the other danger signals available to our decisionmakers, there is not enough evidence of fraud in the dispatches alone to arouse suspicion. Tokyo did trust her two ambassadors to the extent of revealing her urgency, though not the detailed reasons for it, and at the same time asking them to try for a quick settlement without revealing to the United States that there was a deadline. Kurusu—as the translator noted—really acted surprised when he was told over the telephone on November 27 that "a crisis does appear imminent" between Japan and the United States. He evidently had had some hope until that date of postponing or averting the crisis. Afterward he simply went through the motions of negotiating, complaining to Tokyo that they gave him nothing to offer the United States and that the whole business seemed farcical to him in view of the open Japanese moves into the South. He feared some bold U.S. reprisal in response to the Japanese moves. Hopes and fears of this sort, which the two ambassadors expressed at length to Tokyo, served to blur the lines of Tokyo's policy. But U.S. Intelligence, we must remember, had more evidence of Tokyo's intent than the Japanese ambassadors. In MAGIC alone there were available messages to other Japanese embassies —Berlin, Berne, Ankara, Bangkok—that never reached the Washington embassy. America should have been less trusting than Kurusu and Nomura.

Beginning on November 14 Tokyo prepared for a number of contingencies "in the event of war" or "tremendous crisis," or "in the case of a sudden change in the international relations." These phrases were sometimes used alone and sometimes in conjunction with "if the negotiations are ruptured" or "should the negotiations not end in success." The latter phrases dropped out, naturally, after November 26. The first message of this sort from Tokyo to Hong Kong outlined the Empire's foreign policy toward China "should the negotiations collapse" and began with the statement: "We will completely destroy British and American power in China."[101]

A set of dispatches between Tokyo and Bangkok outlined Tokyo's policy toward Thailand in the event of an attack on Burma and Malaya, and also sketched an intrigue for provoking a British attack on Thailand. (Notice of this intrigue had been sent to Admiral Kimmel's Fleet Intelligence officer in Honolulu.) Another set of dispatches between Hsingking and Tokyo reported detailed measures and policies for treatment of American and British nationals in Manchukuo "in the event that war breaks out with England and the U.S.," and announced that it would be Japan's policy to have Manchukuo participate actively in the war. Several dispatches between Tokyo and Washington concerned the return of Japanese officials and company employees to Japan. Tokyo at the same time requested the embassy to "secretly" advise the consuls: "a) to help our citizens who remain behind to work together for the common good; b) to destroy immediately such secret documents and so forth as are in the possession of Japanese companies and chambers of commerce," and promised to wire next a plan for reducing the members of staffs.[102]

By far the most frequent and detailed set of instructions, however, dealt with the destruction of existing codes and the substitution of new emergency codes. On November 15 a naval station intercepted the first of these directives, which gave three paragraphs of directions on the order and methods of destroying code machines "in the event of an emergency."[103] On November 19 two messages setting up the winds code were intercepted.[104] This code was to be used "in case of emergency (danger of cutting off our diplomatic relations)" when the usual means of international communication were cut off. The code had only three terms, which referred to U.S.-Japanese relations, Russo-Japanese relations, and British-Japanese relations. The terms set up for the code in the two messages were not exactly equivalent, but if any one term was broadcast in the manner prescribed, the recipient was told in one message to recognize the broadcast as a warning, and in the other he was told in addition to destroy "all code

---

[101] *Hearings*, Part 12, p. 126.
[102] *Ibid.*, p. 153.
[103] *Ibid.*, p. 137.
[104] We have already reproduced these messages on pp. 51–52. See also pp. 214–215.

papers, etc." Tokyo sent out both of these messages in the J-19 code, and they were therefore not processed until November 26 and November 28.

On November 26 Tokyo sent to Washington a 28-term telephone code, with the explanation that "the situation is momentarily becoming more tense and telegrams take too long. Therefore, will you cut down the substance of your reports of negotiations to the minimum and, on occasion, call up Chief Yamamoto of the American Bureau on the telephone and make your report to him."[105]

On November 27 Tokyo sent out another code known as the "hidden word code." This message, translated on December 2, began: "With international relations becoming more strained, the following emergency system of despatches, using 'INGO DENPO' (hidden word, or misleading language telegrams) is placed in effect."[106] There were 54 terms to this code, and the English word STOP was used at the end of each sentence as an indicator, rather than the Japanese equivalent. Among the terms were such expressions as the following:

EDOGUTI— Prepare for evacuation.

HATAKEYAMA—Relations between Japan and———have been severed.

HATTORI— Relations between Japan and———are not in accordance with expectation.[107]

HIZIKATA— Japan's and———military forces have clashed.

HOSINO— Japan and———are entering a full-fledged general war.

KODAMA— Japan.

KOYANAGI— England.

KUBOTA— USSR.

MINAMI— USA.

[105] *Hearings*, Part 12, p. 178.
[106] *Ibid.*, p. 186*f.*
[107] The correct translation, discovered after the Pearl Harbor attack, was "are on the brink of catastrophe."

At this time there began a whole series of messages on destruction of existing codes.[108] Starting on November 30 there were communications between Tokyo and Manila, London, Havana, and Washington, with orders to relay to the Japanese embassies all over the world. First London, Hong Kong, Singapore, and Manila were ordered to destroy their code machines; Batavia's machine was to be sent back to Japan. The first detailed instruction to Washington was a December 2 message to burn all the telegraphic codes except

> . . . those now used with the machine and one copy each of "O" code (Oite) and abbreviating code (L). (Burn also the various other codes which you have in your custody.)
>
> Stop at once using one code machine unit and destroy it completely.
>
> When you have finished this, wire me back the one word "haruna."
>
> At the time and in the manner you deem most proper dispose of all files of messages coming and going and all other secret documents.
>
> Burn all the codes which Telegraphic Official Kosaka brought you [translated December 3; corrected December 4]. . . .[109]

A similar message went to Havana, Ottawa, Vancouver, Panama, Los Angeles, Honolulu, Seattle, and Portland. This message added the precaution:

> Be especially careful not to arouse the suspicion of those on the outside. Confidential documents are all to be given the same handling.
>
> The above is preparatory to an emergency situation and is for your information alone. Remain calm.[110]

Other instructions intercepted from Tokyo asked the recipients to retain until the last moment the "hidden meaning" codes and the codes to be used in conjunction with radio broadcasts. A special instruction to Washington on December 4, translated on the same day, asked that the codes brought by Kosaka be taught to all the telegraphic staff before burning, and if the keying had not yet been burned to keep it until the last moment and then have some suitable courier take it by air to the ministry in Mexico.[111]

[108] Tokyo serial numbers 809, 2436, 2444, 2443, 867, 2445, 2447, 2461, 92, 881, 367, and 897, reproduced in this order in *Hearings*, Part 12, pp. 208*ff*.

[109] *Ibid.*, p. 215.

[110] *Ibid.*

[111] *Ibid.*, p. 231.

On December 2 the Japanese embassy in Rio de Janeiro sent a detailed substitute code to Santiago, to be relayed to Salvador, Lima, São Paulo, Mexico City, Washington, Panama, Caracas, and Bogota. Unlike the other codes, the terms were primarily the names of cities and minerals and shipping regulations. Other code instructions relevant to the signal picture were not translated until after December 7.

Beginning on November 30 messages were also intercepted informing Tokyo that code destruction had been completed. Most of those presented in Exhibit No. 1 for the congressional hearings were translated after December 7. One message from Washington on December 5, translated on December 6, informed Tokyo that codes had been destroyed with the exception of one machine that they needed "since the U.S. Japanese negotiations are still continuing."[112] (This is a good example of a statement from the Japanese embassy in Washington indicating that the ambassadors were still trying at the last moment to continue negotiations; it is easy to see how their persistence could have served to allay American suspicions about Japanese intent.) Tokyo replied on December 6 that one machine might be retained.

There are a few other messages involving shifts in personnel that seem to have indicated preparations for war. One from Berlin to Tokyo on December 4 read: "In case of evacuation by the members of our Embassy in London, I would like to arrange to have Secretary Matsui of that office and three others ... from among the higher officials and two other officials ... stay here."[113] Tokyo instructed Washington on December 5 to have Terasaki and several others from the Embassy leave by air "within the next couple of days."[114] Terasaki—as Kramer noted in pencil on his distributed copies—was head of Japanese espionage for the western hemisphere and was being sent to South America. Kurusu replied on the same day:

I feel confident that you are fully aware of the importance of the intelligence set-up in view of the present condition of the Japanese-U.S. negotiations. I would like very much to have Terasaki, who would be extremely difficult to suddenly replace ... remain here until we are definitely enlightened as to

112 *Ibid.*, p. 236.
113 *Ibid.*, p. 234.
114 *Ibid.*

the end of the negotiations. I beg of you as a personal favor to me to make an effort along these lines.[115]

(Note that Kurusu here again was acting as a negotiator in good faith.)

There were also several messages to embassies other than Washington referring to Tokyo's intent. Most detailed and most significant after the event was the statement in one of the late messages to Berlin (November 30) following the announcement that the negotiations had ended:

> The conversations begun between Tokyo and Washington last April during the administration of the former cabinet ... now stand ruptured— broken. . . . In the face of this, our Empire faces a grave situation and must act with determination. Will Your Honor, therefore, immediately interview Chancellor HITLER and Foreign Minister RIBBENTROP and confidentially communicate to them a summary of the developments. Say to them that lately England and the United States have taken a provocative attitude, both of them. Say that they are planning to move military forces into various places in East Asia and that we will inevitably have to counter by also moving troops. Say very secretly to them that there is extreme danger that war may suddenly break out between the Anglo-Saxon nations and Japan through some clash of arms and add that the time of the breaking out of this war may come quicker than anyone dreams.
>
> If, when you tell them this, the Germans and Italians question you about our attitude toward the Soviet, say that we have already clarified our attitude toward the Russians in our statement of last July. Say that by our present moves southward we do not mean to relax our pressure against the Soviet and that if Russia joins hands tighter with England and the United States and resists us with hostilities, we are ready to turn upon her with all our might; however, right now, it is to our advantage to stress the south and for the time being we would prefer to refrain from any direct moves in the north.
>
> This message is important from a strategic point of view and must under all circumstances be held in the most absolute secrecy [translated December 1]. . . .[116]

An earlier message indicating Tokyo's intentions was a cryptic note on November 25 to naval authorities in Nanking:

> We are now in the midst of very serious negotiations and have not reached an agreement as yet. As the time limit is near please have them (defer?) for a while [Navy translation, November 27].[117]

115 *Ibid.*, Part 9, p. 4202.
116 *Ibid.*, Part 12, p. 204.
117 *Ibid.*, p. 173.

A message from Hanoi to Tokyo on November 25, translated on November 26, began:

> We are advised by the military that we are to have a reply from the United States on the 25th. If this is true, no doubt the Cabinet will make a decision between peace and war within the next day or two. . . .
>
> Should . . . the negotiations not end in a success, since practically all preparations for the campaign have been completed, our forces shall be able to move within the day.[118]

Hanoi, though ready to go, nevertheless requested information as to the outcome of the negotiations and complained: "We feel as if we, a Foreign Office organ, alone have been left out of the picture."[119]

Captain Kramer introduced some additional intercepts from the Berlin-Tokyo circuit that add to the evidence of Tokyo's intent and lead one to suspect the existence of a mass of relevant material from this circuit that was not presented in the exhibit of the diplomatic intercepts compiled for the congressional investigation. For example, Kramer quoted in full a message of December 3, translated and delivered on December 6, recounting a conversation between Ribbentrop and the Japanese ambassador to Berlin, in which the ambassador was trying to obtain some sort of commitment from Hitler, who could not, unfortunately, be reached until December 5. Ribbentrop said: "As I have told you before, we cannot make an official reply until the Fuehrer has given his approval. . . . " And the Japanese ambassador commented on the whole conversation:

> I told him that the situation is more critical than is imagined and therefore we are very anxious to have a formal reply as soon as is possible. From my previous experience with Ribbentrop I feel fairly confident when I say that you will not be mistaken if you assume there will be no objections. Arrangements have been made for a direct telephone connection between Ribbentrop at the general headquarters and here. However he said that whenever possible he would come back here and contact me.[120]

To sum up the signals so far from MAGIC alone, in addition to those already mentioned as going to Hawaii, we have the following:

NOVEMBER 4–29—Eight messages stating doubts that negotiations will be successful.

[118]*Ibid.*, p. 174.
[119]*Ibid.*, p. 175.
[120]*Ibid.*, Part 9, p. 4200.

NOVEMBER 5—Announcement of a November 25 deadline date for success in negotiations.

NOVEMBER 5–25—Seven repetitions of deadline date.

NOVEMBER 14—Outlining of Japanese policy toward China in the event of war with Britain and the United States.

NOVEMBER 14–29—Outlining of Japanese policy toward Thailand in the event of war with Britain.

AFTER NOVEMBER 14—Many preparations "in the event of an emergency or of war."

NOVEMBER 15–DECEMBER 4—Orders to destroy codes in major embassies, not including Rome or Berlin.

NOVEMBER 18—Return of Japanese nationals from the United States.

NOVEMBER 26–DECEMBER 2—Delivery of new emergency codes to Washington, D.C.

NOVEMBER 26–DECEMBER 6—Messages to Japanese embassies (particularly Berlin) indicating anticipation of sudden outbreak of war with Anglo-Saxon nations.

NOVEMBER 28—Japanese policy for interning American and British nationals in Manchukuo.

AFTER NOVEMBER 28—Two messages announcing that negotiations are to be ruptured (one message to Berlin, the other to Washington). Another message announcing actual rupture.

NOVEMBER 30–DECEMBER 6—At least nine notices of code destruction completed in major Japanese embassies.

DECEMBER 5–6—Shifts in espionage personnel from Washington to South America and from London to Berlin embassy.

DECEMBER 6—All but one code machine destroyed in Japanese embassy in Washington.

It should be noted here that no signals such as these had occurred in either the July or the October crisis. In October we had received a few expressions of the need for speed, and one simple telephonic code. In quantity and in type the November–December signals were all new. They seem so obviously explicable today, in terms of the Japanese attack that we now know was to take place, that it is incredible in retrospect that they were not so interpreted. It is hard to keep in mind the fact that there were many plausible alternative hypotheses that might also have explained this set of signals. Most of the partisan reviews of the Pearl Harbor material forget these alternative explanations.

Not one of these signals was an unambiguous indication of Japanese intent to attack the United States. The United States was also returning citizens to the homeland, destroying its codes in Southeastern Asiatic embassies, indicating pessimism about the outcome of the negotiations, and announcing publicly that it would not tolerate further Asiatic aggression. It is clear enough that Japan was preparing for an all-out war with England and America, but it is nowhere clear whether she intended to make the first move by attacking either power directly, or whether she was preparing to meet a sudden blow from England or America. The dispatches to Berlin, for example, would seem to indicate preparations for a counterattack by the United States in response to further Japanese moves to the south. The deadline might have applied only to this southern advance. However, even if the MAGIC signals were not unambiguous, they were at least good enough to provide a basis for decision. They indicated quite clearly a level of tension where an accident on either side could open a full-scale war.

ESPIONAGE MESSAGES

In addition to the diplomatic messages from the Japanese embassy in Washington, there was a series of espionage messages between Tokyo and Hawaii, the Panama Canal, the Philippines, Southeast Asia, the Netherlands East Indies, and the West Coast (San Francisco, Seattle, San Diego, Vancouver, etc.). These messages were sent from Tokyo in codes other than PURPLE, usually in the simpler J-19 or PA-K2; and they were therefore processed after PURPLE. However, once a smooth translation had been achieved, it was included in the folders for delivery by Kramer and Bratton. Several messages between Honolulu and Tokyo were singled out during the congressional investigation as important signals—if only they had been noticed—and they were also mentioned by Admiral Kimmel and General Short as significant signals denied to them.

The most frequently mentioned message was one that was intercepted on September 24 and translated by the Army on October 9, 1941, request-

ing the Japanese agent in Honolulu in making his reports to divide the
waters of Pearl Harbor into five subareas:

Area A.   Waters between Ford Island and the Arsenal.
Area B.   Waters adjacent to the Island south and west of Ford Island. . . .
Area C.   East Loch.
Area D.   Middle Loch.
Area E.   West Loch and the communicating water routes.

The message continued:

> With regard to warships and aircraft carriers, we would like to have you
> report on those at anchor (these are not so important), tied up at wharves,
> buoys and in docks. (Designate types and classes briefly. If possible, we
> would like to have you make mention of the fact when there are two or more
> vessels along side the same wharf.)[121]

This message was delivered by Commander Kramer with a mark
indicating that it was interesting and with a gist reading: "Tokyo
directs special reports on ships in Pearl Harbor which is divided into five
areas for the purpose of showing exact locations." The Navy file copy
was also stamped as going to Cincaf, but not to Cincpac. Kramer testified
that anything sent to Cincaf was automatically forwarded for information
to Cincpac.[122] However, with this particular dispatch, the procedure was
evidently not followed.

After the event this message was referred to as the "bomb-plot" message. Another significant message translated before December 7 was a
Tokyo to Honolulu dispatch intercepted on November 15 and translated
on December 3:

> As relations between Japan and the United States are most critical, make
> your "ships in harbor report" irregular, but at a rate of twice a week.
> Although you already are no doubt aware, please take extra care to maintain
> secrecy.[123]

Then, on November 20 there was a request from Tokyo to "Please in-
vestigate comprehensively the fleet [unreadable] bases in the neighborhood of the Hawaiian military reservation."[124] This was translated on

---

[121] *Ibid.*, Part 12, p. 261.
[122] Admiral Layton says that this was not the case, though Kramer may have believed it to
be. Cf. *ibid.*, Part 9, pp. 4193*ff*.
[123] *Ibid.*, Part 12, p. 262.
[124] *Ibid.*, p. 263.

December 4, and on the following day another message, which had been intercepted on November 29, instructed the agent that "We have been receiving reports from you on ship movements, but in future will you also report even when there are no movements."[125]

At the time it was received, the September 24 message was regarded primarily as an effort to cut down on the length of espionage communications and to get the proper sort of detail of interest to the Japanese Navy. According to Commander McCollum, consular reports were often more voluble than the Japanese Navy wished, and there were frequent requests to cut down on traffic.[126] Captain Wilkinson interpreted the messages as "an evidence of the nicety of their intelligence."[127] Furthermore he pointed out that far from indicating a bomb plot, the berthing plan could have been equally valuable as an indication of the facility with which the U.S. Fleet was prepared to sortie. Commander Kramer tried to recall his conversations with the recipients of MAGIC: "I do not believe it was interpreted by any of those persons as being materially different than other messages concerning ship movements being reported by the Japanese diplomatic service."[128] Rather, he thought, it was considered "an attempt on the part of the Japanese diplomatic service to simplify communications."[129] Admiral Stark could not recall having seen the message. "I can only say," he testified, "that it went through our people, it went through the Army, who were likewise vitally interested in the defense of Pearl Harbor, and I do not recollect anyone having pointed it out. There was literally a mass of material coming in. We knew the Japanese appetite was almost insatiable for detail in all respects. The dispatch might have been put down as just another example of their great attention to detail."[130]

These interpretations were understandable at the time. The intercepts picked up between Tokyo and Honolulu formed only a small fraction of a large number of requests for similar information from other important ports in the United States and from the Philippines and the Panama Canal. If the September 24 message was actually a bomb plot, then certainly enough information was being forwarded to Tokyo for the Japanese to prepare attacks on Manila, the Canal, Seattle, San Diego, etc. It is true

[125] *Ibid.*   [126] *Ibid.*, Part 8, p. 3405.   [127] *Ibid.*, Part 4, p. 1748.

[128] *Ibid.*, Part 9, p. 4177.   [129] *Ibid.*   [130] *Ibid.*, Part 5, p. 2174f.

that they collected a vast amount of detail that could not be put to immediate use. But Wilkinson's argument that the Japanese wanted this information in order to determine how fast the Pacific Fleet could sortie to prevent, or retaliate against, Japanese aggression in Southeast Asia would seem to have provided sufficient reason for informing Admiral Kimmel of the message. It was important for Kimmel to know exactly what information the enemy was keeping current on his fleet capabilities and movements. To give that information some perspective, Washington might have mentioned other ports, cities, and installations where the enemy was seeking identical data.

No reader of the espionage messages in Washington, however, had had time to put them together and determine whether the requests from Tokyo were changing in any significant way for different probable target areas. Perception was limited to the observation that Tokyo was collecting a large mass of useful, as well as useless, information on American ships and ports throughout the world. In fact, the requests from Tokyo to Manila and Pearl Harbor increased during November and the first week of December and were more specific than at any earlier date.

EAST WIND RAIN

Before turning to the last-minute signals of December 6 and 7, let us look for a moment at the controversial question of the winds-code execute. As mentioned in Chapter 1, it is impossible with the evidence available to establish whether or not an authentic execute of the winds code was received, and in any case it is not essential to do so for the general points that need to be made about the signal picture. American Intelligence intercepted two messages establishing a winds code, neither of them worded in such a way as to make plausible the interpretation of the code as an advance announcement of Tokyo's war decision. One message, as translated by the Navy, said:

> Regarding the broadcast of a special message in an emergency.
>
> In case of emergency (danger of cutting off our diplomatic relations), and the cutting off of international communications, the following warning will be added in the middle of the daily Japanese language short wave news broadcast.
>
> (1) In case of a Japan-U. S. relations in danger: HIGASHI NO KAZEAME [east wind rain].

(2) Japan-U. S. S. R. relations: KITANOKAZE KUMORI [north wind cloudy].

(3) Japan-British relations: NISHI NO KAZE HARE [west wind clear].

This signal will be given in the middle and at the end as a weather forecast and each sentence will be repeated twice. When this is heard please destroy all code papers, etc. This is as yet to be a completely secret arrangement.

Forward as urgent intelligence.[131]

The other message was worded as follows:

When our diplomatic relations are becoming dangerous, we will add the following at the beginning and end of our general intelligence broadcasts:

(1) If it is Japan-U. S. relations, "HIGASHI."

(2) Japan-Russia relations, "KITA."

(3) Japan-British relations, (including Thai, Malaya and N. E. I.), "NISHI."

The above will be repeated five times and included at beginning and end.

Relay to Rio de Janeiro, Buenos Aires, Mexico City, San Francisco.[132]

These messages have received so much publicity that it is worth going beyond the translations made at the time to the Japanese words as they emerged from the American decoding process. We do not have copies of the Japanese originals as they left the War Ministry in Tokyo. They may in fact have been destroyed before the Imperial rescript of August 14, 1945. The American intercepts were decoded as follows:

Circular 2353. Kanchoo fugoo atsukai kokusai jigyoo no hippaku no kekka itsu saiaku no jitai ni tachi itaru kamo hakararezaru tokoro kakaru baai wagahoo to aitekoku tono tsuushin wa tadachi ni teishi serarubeki wo motte wagahoo no gaikoo kankei kiken ni hinsuru baai ni wa waga kaigai hoosoo no kakuchi muke nihohoo news no chuukan oyobi saigo ni oite tenki yohoo to shite. 1. Nichibei kankei no baai ni wa "higashi no kaze ame." 2. Nichiso kankei no baai ni wa "kita no kaze kumori." 3. Nichiei kankei no baai ("tai" shinchuu "maree" Netherlands E. I. kooryoku oboe fukumu ("nishi no kaze hare." 02 do zutsu kurikaeshi hoosoo seshimeru koto to seru wo motte migi ni yori angoo, shorui too tekitoo shobun aritashi. Nao migi wa gen ni gokuhi atsukai to seraretashi.

Circular 2354: Gokuhi. Wagahoo no gaikoo kankai kiken ni hinsen to suru baai ni wa ippah joohoo hoosoo no bootoo oyobi matsubi ni: 1. Nichibei

[131] *Ibid.*, Part 12, p. 154. The Japanese expressions have been reproduced exactly as they appear in the *Hearings.*

[132] *Ibid.*, p. 155.

kankei hippaku no baai ni wa "higashi." 2. Nichiso kankei no baai niwa "kita." 3. Nichei kankei ("tai" shin chuu "maree" Netherlands E. I. kooryoku oboe fukumu (no baai mi wa "nishi." Narugo 05 do ate soonyuu subeki ni tsuki goryoochi aritashi.[133]

For the Japanese specialist[134] it is evident that there has been some garbling in the process of transmission. There are indeed problems of information loss at each successive stage from the Japanese originator of the message to the American decisionmaker reading the translation of an intercept. Even the ungarbled Japanese original would be open to several interpretations, for the Japanese language permits large ambiguities. The word "hippaku," which may be variously translated "grave crisis" or "critical situation," suggests the possibility of a rupture of negotiations—perhaps even war. Some interpreters might take the phrase "wagahoo no gaikoo kankei kiken" (repeated in both messages) to mean "in case of war," literally "in case our foreign relations reach a danger point." But the uncertain reference of the Japanese language leaves in doubt who is the actor in the role of responsibility for the opening act of war or danger. The words " 'tai' shinchuu" (literally "Thai advance" or "Thai invasion") tease the imagination today because they seem to put Japan in the role of invader, since no other country was planning to invade Thailand.

On the other hand the significant words in the code are "east," "north," and "west." While "rain," "cloudy," and "clear" have contrasting literal meanings, in the code they all stand for danger and are simply fillers to simulate a weather warning. However, it is interesting that bad weather is linked with the United States. The source of the trouble must be understood from the geographical position of Tokyo: winds coming out of the north from Russia, winds coming out of the west from Great Britain, and winds coming from the west coast of the United States, which is of course to the east of Japan. This interpretation does not necessarily imply, but would be consistent with, a Japanese anticipation of action by one or another of these countries requiring code destruction to protect the security of the Japanese codes.

[133] *Ibid.*, Part 18, p. 3307*f*.

[134] Professor Paul Langer of the University of Southern California has provided me with new translations of the decodes as well as comments on their structure and meaning. I have used these in the text.

A close examination of the translations of MAGIC might shed some light on remaining puzzles, although the Japanese specialist Robert Butow suggests that the majority of errors in the selection he examined do not do violence to the basic content of the messages.[135] Yet the problem of possible error and information loss at each step of sending, intercepting, decoding, and translating illustrates some of the vicissitudes of warning. It is not only the weather code that has the fickleness of Japanese weather.

Our decisionmakers were dependent on the translations with which they were presented, and the present analysis will be confined to the signals in that form. The first of the winds messages provided for a signal to destroy codes after regular commercial channels had been cut off, and this provision is significant in itself. It is on the same level as the other directions for code destruction listed earlier. Any execute of this code intercepted after December 1 would have been merely confirmatory of the December 1 order to major Japanese embassies to destroy their codes. It would not be a new signal containing new information about when or where to expect a Japanese attack. Either message could mean at the most an expected break in relations with whatever countries were mentioned, possibly even war, but expected by Japan, not necessarily initiated by Japan.

From the moment that these messages were translated they received special attention from both Army and Navy sections. The Navy distributed a set of cards to its MAGIC recipients inscribed with the formulas:

> East wind rain: Japan-U.S.
> North wind cloudy: Japan-USSR
> West wind clear: Japan-British

This was to make it possible for the watch officers monitoring the teletype to telephone the information immediately without going through the regular channels for distribution, and it was an absolutely novel procedure. In the Army Colonel Bratton, Colonel Dusenbury, and General Miles carried similar cards with them.[136] Both the Army and the Navy also put several stations on 24-hour monitoring schedules for the regular Japanese

---

[135] Robert J. C. Butow, *Tojo and the Coming of the War*, p. 335.
[136] *Ibid.*, Part 10, p. 4624.

news and intelligence broadcasts. As a result normal teletype traffic increased from 3 or 4 feet per week to 200 feet per day.

There were naturally a good many weather broadcasts, but none that fitted the code exactly until December 8—at least none that have survived in the record. However, Commander Safford was convinced at the time that an authentic execute was received on December 4 or 5 that said "Japan-British, Japan-U.S., but not Japan-Russia." According to Safford's testimony, Kramer showed him the piece of teletype paper, saying, "This is it." Safford telephoned the information to Noyes, who called the MAGIC recipients.

Kramer was convinced in 1941 that he had seen an authentic execute, though he remembered at first that it said "Japan-British, Japan-U.S." and did not mention Russia. Later he changed his testimony to limit the execute to "Japan-British." Still later he testified that he was no longer convinced that the execute was authentic because of evidence provided by the MacArthur interrogation of Japanese prisoners, where the Japanese denied ever sending out a winds-code execute. (As Senator Ferguson pointed out, in these same interrogations the Japanese also denied setting up a winds code in the first place; so the word of those questioned is not worth much.) On the whole Kramer's frequent changes in testimony are hard to understand; and one cannot help harboring some doubts about a luncheon at the home of Admiral Stark in September, 1945, where, Kramer reported, his memory was "refreshed." Safford held to his original account, even under considerable pressure. However, there seems to be no basis for his belief that the execute was directed as a war signal to the Japanese Navy and to the London embassy, which had already destroyed its code machines.

Of the MAGIC recipients who were supposed to have received a copy or notice of this execute, only Rear Adm. R. E. Ingersoll, Stark's assistant CNO, and Rear Admirals Turner and Noyes remembered it. Turner and Ingersoll gave it only cursory attention because they had already seen the earlier Japanese code-destruction order, and their reaction would seem to have been a likely one at the time, and one that would have been shared by the other recipients. Admiral Noyes testified that he had decided at the time that the execute was not authentic. This reaction was unusual. For customarily Noyes allowed Safford and Kramer the last word on decisions regarding decoded material. Kramer was the man he trusted completely to weed out and distribute the important MAGIC messages. If Kramer believed in 1941 that an authentic execute had been received, and persisted in believing so until 1945, then that is very good evidence that it was authentic. Noyes would scarcely have wished to take the responsibility for deciding the reverse.

The original piece of teletype and any copies that may have been made have now disappeared and so have the cards distributed by the Navy and Army. Much has been made of their disappearance by those who wish to establish that a handful of U.S. conspirators provoked the Japanese attack, knew when and where the attack would occur, and destroyed the evidence of their knowledge. The absence of documents, the many changes in sworn testimony, and the special handling given the winds code from the beginning all contribute to the atmosphere of political intrigue.[137] However, all the conspiratorial accounts assume that the winds code was a means of announcing Tokyo's decision to attack the United States. This is not the case. An authentic execute would have told Washington nothing that it did not already know on December 4.

LAST-MINUTE MAGIC

There were four main last-minute MAGIC signals. These have become known as the pilot message; the 14-part message; the 1 o'clock, or time-of-delivery, message; and the final code-destruction message. At the congressional hearings these were regarded by everyone—the technical staff of SIS and Navy Communications, Army and Navy Intelligence, Army and Navy Operations, the State Department, the President's advisers, and

---

[137] On the matter of disappearing documents, the routine procedure was to destroy immediately any teletype material that was a false execute. So the fact that the document no longer exists would certainly support Admiral Noyes' contention that he had found it false, were it not for the fact that he was not in the habit of exercising this sort of judgment. An authentic execute would not normally have been filed with the MAGIC files, since it was not to be distributed in the usual manner. In view of the confusion that occurred in 1945 in the testimony concerning the winds code on the subject of "a false Tokyo weather broadcast," it is easy to imagine this teletype being destroyed by mistake. A "false Tokyo weather broadcast" could mean either of two things: (1) an authentic execute of an authentic code that was itself a false weather broadcast or (2) a false execute of an authentic code that was a true weather broadcast. An authentic execute may have been destroyed because it was referred to as "false," and that word was understood in the second sense, rather than in the first.

the President himself—as being the crucial tip-off signals. Even the congressional investigators proceeded on this assumption; so it became an essential part of their inquiry to determine at what hour precisely the privileged list of recipients looked at these messages and what decision, if any, they came to as a result. For this purpose it is not so important to fix the day of translation as to fix the time of distribution to the relevant decisionmakers. Some intercepts marked as translated on December 6 were not delivered until December 7. One half-hour's delay in processing time on December 6 could mean the difference between delivery on the evening of December 6 or during the mid-morning of December 7.

At this point, however, the historian encounters some major obstacles. Who saw what MAGIC and who gave what to whom on the evening of December 6 is a very touchy subject. The reams of testimony are loaded with contradictions. Accounts in the fall of 1945 almost invariably conflicted with accounts presented to earlier investigating bodies. In 1945 documents were withheld or had disappeared and memories had been "refreshed" or had totally blanked out, so that in some cases the main response to the insistent questioning makes a dull refrain: "I don't remember." Even senators intent on making political capital of the investigation got tired and let the matter drop.

One clue in tracing the course of a message from interception to delivery is, of course, the filing system used. However, one discovers that gremlins have been at work here. The numbers have been "doodled" on in some cases so that they are illegible, and no other copies have been located. (The explanation to the congressional committee was that someone was doing research and got bored—bored with this politically explosive subject in 1945!) Some numbers are missing, but this is not astonishing in view of the fact that only about one-third of the intercepts processed daily were judged consequential enough for delivery. However, the main source of chaos for the historian is the order in which the intercepts were presented for the congressional hearings, an order that apparently had no relation to either the Army or the Navy filing system.

The filing system, as far as can be inferred, was something like this: The intercepting stations marked the original messages with the Tokyo serial number, the Tokyo time of filing, and the Washington time of interception. When the message reached the Navy processing unit it was

given a time stamp and a 20-G file number[138] and was filed in chronological order according to the date received. With the original message
in the 20-G file there were also filed the work sheets and a copy of the
completed translation. A duplicate of this translation was given a JD
number,[139] determined by the order in which it was received by the
translator, and then was filed in a separate JD file in the order of completion. The JD file contained only translations, and included any translations sent over from the Army unit. Army messages in the Navy file were
assigned a JD number in addition to the SIS number and were filed in
chronological order according to the date that they were received from
the Army, which was usually the same day on which the translation was
completed. The sequence of the messages in the 20-G file and in the JD
file was therefore quite different. The Army SIS numbers are in a different order in the Army file. A fourth order is presented by the selection
made for Exhibit 1 of the congressional hearings, perhaps because it was
compiled from both Army and Navy files. A typical juxtaposition in this
exhibit is JD 1:7053 intercepted on December 3, next to JD 1:7848, also
intercepted on December 3 but evidently some 800 messages away in terms
of the date of translation.

Such juxtaposition would be no problem if the original files were
available. But in Exhibit 1 the JD number is very often omitted and in
some cases this number is decisive in determining the date of delivery.
None of the testimony by witnesses from the Communications section
fills in this sort of gap.

Since there is no way to speak precisely in the absence of these files, we
shall present here only the messages themselves. In the chapters following,
with evidence from other sources, we shall follow the main steps in their
distribution and reception in Washington.

The first of the four messages, known as the pilot message (Tokyo No.
901), announced that the Japanese government was sending a reply to the
American proposal of November 26:

> This separate message is a very long one. I will send it in fourteen parts
> and I imagine you will receive it tomorrow. However, I am not sure. The

[138] 20-G was the number assigned to the Communications Security unit in the Navy's
organization.
[139] JD stood for "Japanese Diplomatic."

situation is extremely delicate, and when you receive it I want you to please
keep it secret for the time being.

Concerning the time of presenting this memorandum to the United States,
I will wire you in a separate message. However, I want you in the meantime
to put it in nicely drafted form and make every preparation to present it to
the Americans just as soon as you receive instructions.[140]

This was the reply for which the Japanese ambassadors had been
waiting; they had been warned on November 28 that with this reply to
the American proposal, "the negotiations will be de facto ruptured."[141]
The Japanese obviously regarded their answer and its timing as extremely
important, and the length of the message—requiring 14 parts—was also
unprecedented. The pilot message announcing the arrival of the 14-part
message was intercepted by the Navy at 7:20 A.M. on December 6 and
was received by the Army translating unit at noon on that day. SIS and the
Navy's Communications Security unit alerted all their stations for receipt
of the 14-part message to come, as well as for a notice regarding the time
of presentation.

In spite of this buildup, when the 14-part message (Tokyo No. 902)
began to come in, it turned out to be a long-winded presentation of
Japanese views about their earnest efforts for peace in Asia and the
obstructions of the United States and Great Britain. These views had been
stated in the same manner many times before. The fourteenth part alone
contained some new information. It was the declaration by Japan that she
was formally closing negotiations, ending with the following statement:

> Thus, the earnest hope of the Japanese Government to adjust Japanese-
> American relations and to preserve and promote the peace of the Pacific
> through cooperation with the American Government has finally been lost.
>
> The Japanese Government regrets to have to notify hereby the American
> Government that in view of the attitude of the American Government it
> cannot but consider that it is impossible to reach an agreement through
> further negotiations.[142]

The Navy station on Bainbridge Island (in Puget Sound, opposite
Seattle) started intercepting this long message on the morning of December 6; the first thirteen parts came in approximately in order all through

[140] *Hearings*, Part 12, p. 238f.
[141] *Ibid.*, p. 195.
[142] *Ibid.*, p. 245.

that morning, and were forwarded to Washington, D.C., by teletype just before noon and during the early afternoon.[143] Part 14, however, was not intercepted by the Bainbridge Island Navy station until 3 A.M., Washington, D.C., time, on the morning of December 7. All of these parts were decoded by the Navy and no translation was necessary, since the clear came out in English.

The so-called 1 o'clock message, Tokyo No. 907, said briefly:

> Will the Ambassador please submit to the United States Government (if possible to the Secretary of State) our reply to the United States at 1:00 p.m. on the 7th, your time.[144]

This message was intercepted at 4:30 A.M., Washington, D.C., time, on December 7 by the Bainbridge Island Navy station and was sent to the Army SIS for translation. The final code-destruction message (Tokyo No. 910) read:

> After deciphering part 14 of my #902, and also #907, #908, and #909, please destroy at once the remaining cipher machine and all machine codes. Dispose in like manner also secret documents.[145]

Tokyo Nos. 908 and 909 were messages to the ambassadors, thanking them for their efforts, and to the commercial attaché and his staff, commending their efforts on behalf of Japan and praying that they continue in good health. Tokyo No. 910 was intercepted by the Navy station at 5 A.M. on December 7, decoded by the Navy, and sent over to the Army for translation.

It might be interesting to recall at this point that on November 28 Tokyo had announced that an unfavorable reply acknowledging the rupture of negotiations would be sent "in a few days," a sort of advance pilot message. Receipt of the later pilot message and receipt of the 14-part note were therefore anticipated, and anything except an unfavorable reply was regarded in Washington as extremely unlikely, except perhaps by Kurusu and Nomura. The thirteenth part of the Tokyo reply in fact even used some of the same vocabulary as one of the notices on November 30

[143] Parts 1–4 were received on December 6 at 11:49 A.M., Washington, D.C., time. Parts 9 and 10 were received sometime between 11:49 A.M. and 14:51 P.M., and Parts 5–8 and 11–13 at 14:51 P.M., Washington, D.C., time. (*Ibid.*, Part 33, p. 764.)

[144] *Ibid.*, Part 12, p. 248.

[145] *Ibid.*, p. 249.

to the Japanese embassy in Berlin on the closing of negotiations. The Berlin notice had referred to "one insulting clause" stipulating that "in case the United States entered the European war at any time the Japanese Empire will not be allowed to give assistance to Germany and Italy." This clause alone, Tokyo claimed, "makes it impossible to find any basis in the American proposal for negotiations."[146]

Since the contents of the note were anticipated, the time of this signal should have been the moment that it started coming over the wires on Saturday morning, not the moment that Marshall and Stark read the fourteenth part, sometime after 9:30 on Sunday morning. On the basis of MAGIC alone, a rupture of negotiations was expected. MAGIC, combined with other signals such as Japanese Fleet and armament movements, should have made that rupture and its date almost certain. If we believe in signals at all, we have to do at least this much anticipating.

For it is extremely unlikely that the unequivocal final signal—in code or in some other form—will be sent, or if sent, that it will be intercepted, or if intercepted, that it will be properly interpreted in time to act on it. The time for action is before that final signal is on the air.

To take another example from Pearl Harbor, a final tip-off signal might have been a message sent out by the Japanese in the "hidden word," or "INGO DENPO," code, which was intercepted and translated by the Navy on the morning of December 7 and included in the pouch that went to Stark on Kramer's second delivery Sunday morning. It may have reached Marshall on the Army's first Sunday delivery. It read: "Relations between Japan and England are not in accordance with expectation."[147] This information was not new; indeed it was a magnificent understatement. Unfortunately what it said had little relation to the Japanese original. Colonel Friedman testified that he re-examined the intercept a few days after Pearl Harbor and the translation aroused his suspicions because "any fool would realize that on December 7 Tokyo was not going to send a message out saying 'relations between Japan and England are not in accordance with expectations' when the die had already been cast."[148]

---

[146] Cf. Part 13 of the 14-part message: "Therefore, viewed in its entirety, the Japanese government regrets that it cannot accept the proposal as a basis of negotiation." (*Ibid.*, p. 244.)

[147] *Ibid.*, p. 251.

[148] *Ibid.*, Part 36, p. 308.

He discovered two errors. The original Navy translation of the code had been too mild; it should have read "are on the brink of catastrophe." Second, in the press of work that morning, the code word meaning "the United States" had been omitted by the translator. The message should have read: "Relations between Japan and England and the United States are on the brink of catastrophe."[149] In Japanese this was serious, for as Kramer repeatedly testified, Japanese custom tended to polite restraint in describing desperate situations. However, this warning was missed and it should not be surprising that it was missed.

Regarding all these last-minute messages it is less important to determine the exact hour on Saturday or Sunday that the decisionmakers received them than to determine *the way they handled the evidence available before that time.* If a rupture of negotiations was going to be taken by them as equivalent to a declaration of Japanese intent to go to war with the United States, then the evidence was already in. The only possible exception is the 1 o'clock delivery message, which we now read as setting the time for attack, even if it did not mention the place. To many top officials the significance of this message was apparent, however, only after the event. And in spite of the prevalent assumption about the criticality of these last-minute signals, they did not function as such before the attack. No one really believed—in the sense of belief implying a course of action—that a diplomatic rupture firmly announced by Japan would mean immediate war initiated directly against the United States. There was absolutely nothing in MAGIC that established such a Japanese intent clearly and firmly. And even if there had been, there would still have been doubt as to whether Pearl Harbor was to be included in the Japanese plan of attack.

We have, of course, to make a systematic distinction between signals of a coming event—first, as seen after the event, and second, as seen before the event. Afterward, when we know the actual physical links between the signals and the event, it seems almost impossible that we could have ignored the now-obvious connection. We forget how matters looked at the time the signal appeared in the midst of thousands of competing indications, the signal itself compatible not only with a single catastrophe, but also with many other possible outcomes.

149 *Ibid.*

It is only to be expected that the exemplary acuity of everybody's hindsight should affect the disputes still raging about responsibility for the Pearl Harbor disaster. A most typical feature of these arguments is that each commander stresses the ambiguity of the signals he did receive and the unequivocal precision of the signals he did *not* receive. Each commander argues in his own behalf the vagueness of the intelligence and the Delphic straddling of the war warnings that Washington sent to him. Each demonstrates how much like previous alarms these warnings were, and asks just what was expected of the local commanders that they failed to do. Each is sure that he would have prepared for attack if only he had had such clear indications of the attack as the winds-code setup and the execute message.

But Washington is correct in stating that the winds code concerned unambiguously only the existence of tension between the countries mentioned, and the necessity for code destruction. Washington is wrong in maintaining the clarity of its warnings to the theaters. They were not clear warnings because Washington did not clearly anticipate the Pearl Harbor attack, and it is doubtful that the local commanders would have been further enlightened if they had had the pieces of the puzzle that were denied them.

The point is that the puzzle is never complete. The signals that the local commanders later argued were muffled and fraught with uncertainty are the ones they viewed before the event. The signals that seem to stand out and scream of the impending catastrophe are the ones learned about only after the event, when they appear stripped of other possible meanings.

All decisions are made in the face of uncertainty, even those that depend simply on an understanding of natural phenomena. But decisions based on reading the intentions of others, and in particular, the intentions of an enemy, are especially difficult. These intentions are complicated and shifting, and subject to change between the time the intent is signalized and the time of the intended act. Sometimes they are also deliberately obscured, or invented to mislead, as in the case of bluffing. At least in reading natural phenomena, we have Albert Einstein's famous assurance that God is subtle but not plain mean. The same cannot be said for the enemy.

In spite of these deliberate and accidental ambiguities, however, intelligence can do a great deal to diminish the uncertainty of military decision. MAGIC did have a lot to say, even if it did not tell all. It did not say, "Air raid on Pearl Harbor," but it did support the hypothesis of hostile action by the Japanese in Southeast Asia breaking over the week end of November 30 or close to that date, involving the British and the Dutch, if not the Americans. It is important to point out that the Pearl Harbor air attack was the only part of the Japanese war plan that took Washington unawares. Washington was surprised that the Japanese chose Pearl Harbor in the first place, and then that they chose an air raid rather than sabotage. The attack on the outlying islands and the Philippines had been entertained as one of many plausible hypotheses by some of our policymakers, beginning on November 26. But no one could be sure. All of the signals were ambiguous. And perhaps one of the important lessons to learn from Pearl Harbor is that intelligence will always have to deal with shifting signals. Its evidence will never be more than partial, and inference from its data will always be hazardous.

4 ▸ SIGNALS AND NOISE AT HOME

MAGIC was the most important single device for listening in on secret Japanese communications and was therefore one of the key guides to detection of Japanese intentions. But American policymakers had many other guides at their disposal. The signals sent to Honolulu, which we examined in Chapter 1, came from a wide variety of sources and represented a very condensed selection of the information available in Washington.

Let us look now at this wider background in Washington for the last three weeks before the attack. We shall review briefly the diplomatic maneuvers that MAGIC was recording—last-minute feints and delaying devices—and we shall try to filter out the main signals that motivated the dispatch of warnings to all Far Eastern Army and Navy commands. In tracing the way in which the signals sent to Honolulu were selected in November, 1941, one thing at least becomes clear: it was a sound policy, and perhaps the only practicable one, for the military to select rather than to send all of their information to the theaters. For while it is true that the Washington agencies together had a much greater pool of information than the theaters, they also had a large number of conflicting signals. There was as much noise as there were significant sounds.

The job of separating the signals from the noise was an extremely delicate and difficult task, one that a local theater commander could not be expected to add to his list of duties. Furthermore, the apparatus for reception and communication of this mass of signals was infinitely more complicated in Washington than in Honolulu. We have seen what happened to one top-secret source, MAGIC, and the multiple barriers to its interpretation even in the course of a rather short and simple path of communication. The imagination staggers at the spectacle of the blocks in the way of information that had to travel a longer or more tortuous and less protected path. Inevitably in the din of jurisdictional battle, interoffice and interdepartmental memos, opposing estimates of the situation, and rival views of the value of risk, the essential item was sometimes lost. The large number of particles of information that penetrated all barriers to arrive at those "who need to know," the decisionmakers, is not only something of a miracle, but also bears testimony to the still greater number that started on the journey and never arrived. For there was no single person or agency in Washington that had all the signals available at any one time.

A particularly complicating feature of the Washington signal picture was the fact that not only were signals from foreign countries collected and interpreted there, but Washington itself was an important originator of signals. The moves of American government agencies were the main content of the enemy's intelligence on the United States, and they naturally formed an important part of the total American signal picture. But the meaning or motivation of America's own moves was sometimes more difficult for Americans to define or predict than that of the enemy.

In 1941, unfortunately, it was customary for most people in the government, even in Washington, to have a more current and less confused picture of Japan's policy toward the United States and her important moves in Southeast Asia than they had about American policy toward Japan and American activities in the Pacific. In other words they had bits of one half (the Japanese half) of the current critical signal picture. One explanation of this ignorance of U.S. policy is the natural tendency to take one's own position for granted, as self-evident or obvious. But a more likely explanation is that it was not easy then (nor is it now) to put American Far Eastern policy into a few, simple, clear sentences. Instead, to approximate a statement of that policy, one had to ask what each of President Roosevelt's advisers wanted, what the President himself wanted, how strong an influence was exerted by the isolationist sector of public opinion, how strong an influence was exerted by the China lobby, etc., and then out of this welter of conflicting interests extract what would seem to be a probable direction. The difficulties of charting this direction were enhanced by Roosevelt's familiar method of preserving conflicting pressures by successively agreeing with opposing sides.[1]

For our purpose it is enough to sketch this conflicting pull of interests for the few weeks before the Pearl Harbor attack. The main outlines of our government's hypotheses and hopes, decisions and indecisions, can be determined from existing documents in the State, War, and Navy Departments and from published diaries and memoirs. But history leaves us with many puzzles. It is hard to discover exactly when or how the decision was reached to warn the theaters or to say precisely what targets and what sort of attack were expected at the time the warning messages were drafted.

The most important single thing to note about our government in the last weeks before Pearl Harbor is the enormous absorption of almost everyone in the Atlantic and European battle areas.[2] President Roosevelt was so deeply interested in the European situation that he left Far Eastern matters almost entirely to Secretary Hull. Interest in Europe rather than the Far East also characterized the general public, as evidenced in the contemporary press, newsreels, and public opinion polls.

To put the Far Eastern crisis in perspective then, we must keep constantly in mind this overriding interest in the European front and events in the Western Hemisphere. Otherwise an understandable lack of attention may be interpreted as deliberate deafness or conspiratorial silence, and a genuine attempt to deter aggression may appear as an invitation to attack. The ease with which the historian today charts the direction and intensity of the Japanese crisis is quite misleading. In the fall of 1941 Japanese aggression was a constant threat, of course, demanding careful diplomatic attention to prevent war on two fronts; but compared to Germany's war machine, the menace of Japan seemed more remote and manageable.

There were, for example, a good many policymakers in Washington, including the President himself, who had become accustomed to thinking

---

[1] Herman Kahn, Director of the Franklin D. Roosevelt Library, points out that it would be more accurate to say that the Roosevelt technique was "to permit each opposing side to believe that he agreed with it."

[2] This emphasis is documented in detail in Conn and Fairchild, *The Framework of Hemisphere Defense.*

of the U.S. Pacific Fleet as a deterrent rather than a target. This belief not only bolstered the hopes of those who were busily pushing reinforcement of the Philippines; it also served to justify concentration on the Atlantic battle. And it was part of a general attitude that projected American psychology onto the Japanese government. Ambassador Grew had discerned this tendency and fought it as well as he could from the distance of Tokyo. In one of his last reports (November 3), he had vigorously warned Secretary Hull against "any possible misconception of the capacity of Japan to rush headlong into a suicidal conflict with the United States. National sanity would dictate against such an event, but Japanese sanity cannot be measured by our own standards of logic."[3] But Grew's warning gathered meaning in Washington only after the event.

During this month before Pearl Harbor, the War and Navy Departments in Washington expressed a clearly defined position. Admiral Stark and General Marshall, solidly backed by their War Plans Divisions, sounded the plea for more time, more men, more equipment. Their memos to the President were all directed at soft-peddling any State Department efforts toward a "firm stand" with Japan.

The State Department presented a fairly definite image at the top in the person of Secretary Hull, who personally conducted the negotiations with the Japanese ambassadors. By November, Hull was—more than anything else—weary. Again and again the private accounts from government circles describe him with this adjective. He had gone, in his own words, "around and around the same circle" for so long that he no longer hoped for a peaceful settlement with Japan or the imposition of some kind of restraint on her military aggressions. He could only use his remaining energy to try to gain more time for the U.S. military, and this meant a constant balance between severity and patience with the Japanese delegates, being careful not to be so severe as to cause a break in relations and not so kind as to offend China or Britain or the Netherlands. But minimum and maximum concessions for each side had been pretty rigidly defined by then, and the possibilities of diplomatic maneuvering were consequently restricted. Even within these confines, Hull persisted in his efforts to maintain peace in the Pacific and to keep the President firmly persuaded of this goal. For the President had other advisers, such as

[3] *Hearings*, Part 14, p. 1056.

Ickes and Stimson, who were sometimes violent in their denunciation of the appeasing line of the State Department. Even within his own Department, Hull had two factions to keep in balance: the pro-China faction and the pro-Japan faction, and on December 1 he professed himself tired of having everybody in the government telling him how to run the State Department: "They all come at me with knives and hatchets,"[4] he complained to his assistant Adolf A. Berle.

This sense of being assailed by conflicting opinions and advice, all aggressively and persuasively expressed, may also have characterized the President's state of mind in these last weeks. At any rate, this state of mind (combined with his absorption in European affairs) makes more understandable the absence from the record of his personal reactions to the Far Eastern situation. In reading the memoirs of the men surrounding the President, one finds a constant preoccupation with the puzzle of what was going on in the President's mind. What did that smile or that raised eyebrow or that grim look actually betoken? A few of these advisers complained that they could not get a straight deal from the President, but most of them watched and waited patiently, as if the President were pregnant with decisions, and only God knew the moment at which the birth was due. Take, for example, this entry in Ickes' diary for Friday, November 21:

> The President remarked to me that he wished he knew whether Japan was playing poker or not. He was not sure whether or not Japan had a gun up its sleeve. My reply was that I had no doubt that sooner or later, depending upon the progress of Germany, Japan would be at our throats; as for me, when I knew that I was going to be attacked, I preferred to choose my own time and occasion. I asked the President whether he had any doubt that Japan would attack Siberia if the Germans overcame the Russians. He said that he hadn't. I felt that by going to war with Japan now we would soon be in a position where a large part of our Navy, as well as of the British Navy and of the Dutch East Indies Navy, could be released for service in the Atlantic. The President's feeling was that Japan would draw herself in and that she was too far away to be attacked. It seemed to me that the President had not yet reached the state of mind where he is willing to be aggressive as to Japan.[5]

This comment of Ickes illustrates one of a number of important and conflicting views being pressed on Roosevelt (the view that Japan could

[4] Berle, "Diaries."
[5] Ickes, *The Lowering Clouds*, p. 649*f*.

and should be quickly disposed of to release American resources for the Atlantic war), as well as the anxious observation of Roosevelt's developing state of mind. Again, as in the debate on whether to continue basing the fleet at Pearl Harbor, the President did not know which way to move; so he stayed put. It was a matter of fencing and waiting, with no real hope anywhere in top Washington circles that the fencing could stave off for very long the Japanese blow in the Pacific against the British or the Dutch or maybe even the Americans. But the hectic days of November 25, 26, and 27 did bring decision, and from then until December 7 the President and his advisers waited for the blow to fall.

DIPLOMATIC FENCING: NOVEMBER 20–26

On November 20 the Japanese ambassadors had presented a *modus vivendi*, referred to in MAGIC as Proposal B or Plan B. This they characterized in MAGIC as their last possible attempt to bargain with the United States. The presentation was coincidental with Secretary Morgenthau's submittal to the State Department of a plan written up by Harry Dexter White that also envisaged a *modus vivendi*. This plan went through many discussions and drafts in connection with the Japanese proposals. The details of these drafts and discussions have been collected in the twenty-seventh chapter of Langer and Gleason's *The Undeclared War, 1940–1941*. For our purpose, it is enough to compare the Japanese Plan B with the form of the State Department *modus vivendi* submitted for approval to the British, Dutch, and Chinese representatives.

The Japanese Plan B proposed:

(1) Both the Governments of Japan and the United States undertake not to make any armed advancement into any of the regions in the Southeastern Asia and the Southern Pacific area excepting the part of French Indo-China where the Japanese troops are stationed at present.

(2) The Japanese Government undertakes to withdraw its troops now stationed in French Indo-China upon either the restoration of peace between Japan and China or the establishment of an equitable peace in the Pacific area.

In the meantime the Government of Japan declares that it is prepared to remove its troops now stationed in the southern part of French Indo-China to the northern part of the said territory upon the conclusion of the present arrangement which shall later be embodied in the final agreement.

(3) The Government of Japan and the United States shall cooperate with a view to securing the acquisition of those goods and commodities which the two countries need in Netherlands East Indies.

(4) The Governments of Japan and the United States mutually undertake to restore their commercial relations to those prevailing prior to the freezing of the assets.

The Government of the United States shall supply Japan a required quantity of oil.

(5) The Government of the United States undertakes to refrain from such measures and actions as will be prejudicial to the endeavors for the restoration of general peace between Japan and China.[6]

These proposals were rather general but could be considered as a possible basis for a preliminary agreement. State Department officers were discussing two of the points mentioned in connection with their own draft: (1) rescinding the freezing order and (2) suspending aid to China during negotiations between China and Japan. In his reception of the two Japanese ambassadors, however, Secretary Hull was quite short-tempered about the suggestion of suspending aid to China as long as Japan remained a party to the Tripartite Pact, and from the extremity of his denunciation of Plan B, one would never have guessed that such a proposal was currently being debated in his own Department. Hull was interested in gaining time for the Army and Navy, and as a device for gaining time, there were some things to be said in favor of Plan B; but Hull characterized it later as "of so preposterous a character that no responsible American official could ever have dreamed of accepting."[7]

President Roosevelt in reporting Plan B to Churchill had a much milder reaction. On November 24 he gave Churchill the outline of the American counterproposal for a three-month *modus vivendi*, commenting: "This seems to me a fair proposition for the Japanese but its acceptance or rejection is really a matter of internal Japanese politics. I am not very hopeful and we must all be prepared for real trouble, possibly soon."[8]

The final text of this American *modus vivendi* read as follows:

(1) The Government of the United States and the Government of Japan, both being solicitous for the peace of the Pacific, affirm that their national policies are directed toward lasting and extensive peace throughout

[6] *Foreign Relations of the United States: Japan, 1931–1941,* Vol. II, p. 755f.
[7] Hull, *The Memoirs of Cordell Hull,* Vol. II, p. 1070.
[8] *Letters,* Vol. II, p. 1246.

the Pacific area and that they have no territorial designs therein. They undertake reciprocally not to make by force or threat of force, unless they are attacked, any advancement, from points at which they have military establishments, across any international border in the Pacific area.

(2) The Japanese Government undertakes forthwith to withdraw its armed forces now stationed in southern French Indochina, not to engage in any further military activities there, including the construction of military facilities, and to limit Japanese military forces in northern French Indochina to the number there on July 26, 1941, which number in any case would not exceed 25,000 and which number would not be subject to replacement.

(3) The Government of the United States undertakes forthwith to remove the freezing restrictions which were placed on Japanese assets in the United States on July 26 and the Japanese Government agrees simultaneously to remove the freezing measures which it imposed in regard to American assets in Japan. Exports from each country would thereafter remain subject to the respective export control measures which each country may have in effect for reasons of national defense.

(4) The Government of the United States undertakes forthwith to approach the British and the Dutch Governments with a view to those Governments' taking, on a basis of reciprocity with Japan, measures similar to those provided for in paragraph three above.

(5) The Government of the United States would not look with disfavor upon the inauguration of conversations between the Government of China and the Government of Japan directed toward a peaceful settlement of their differences nor would the Government of the United States look with disfavor upon an armistice during the period of any such discussions. The fundamental interest of the Government of the United States in reference to any such discussion is simply that they be based upon and exemplify the fundamental principles of peace which constitute the central spirit of the current conversations between the Government of Japan and the Government of the United States.

In case any such discussions are entered into between the Government of Japan and the Government of China, the Government of the United States is agreeable to such discussions taking place in the Philippine Islands, if so desired by both China and Japan.

(6) It is understood that this *modus vivendi* is of a temporary nature and shall not remain in effect for a period longer than three months unless renewed by common agreement.[9]

To this text there was attached another document, the Ten Point Note, listing America's position under ten headings. The third and fourth points,

[9] *Hearings*, Part 14, pp. 1113–1115.

demanding evacuation of China and Indochina and Japanese recognition of the government of Chiang Kai-shek, together with point 9, which required Japan's withdrawal from the Tripartite Pact, made the document a most extreme and uncompromising statement of American terms. Its severity was somewhat tempered, however, by the fact that it was put forward as a basis for long-term discussions of Japanese-American differences, to be undertaken only after acceptance of the *modus vivendi.* The text of the Ten Point Note follows:

(1) The Government of the United States and the Government of Japan will endeavor to conclude a multilateral non-aggression pact among the British Empire, China, Japan, the Netherlands, the Soviet Union, Thailand and the United States.

(2) Both Governments will endeavor to conclude among the American, British, Chinese, Japanese, the Netherlands and Thai Governments an agreement whereunder each of the Governments would pledge itself to respect the territorial integrity of French Indochina and, in the event that there should develop a threat to the territorial integrity of Indochina, to enter into immediate consultation with a view to taking such measures as may be deemed necessary and advisable to meet the threat in question. Such agreement would provide also that each of the Governments party to the agreement would not seek or accept preferential treatment in its trade or economic relations with Indochina and would use its influence to obtain for each of the signatories equality of treatment in trade and commerce with French Indochina.

(3) The Government of Japan will withdraw all military, naval, air and police forces from China and from Indochina.

(4) The Government of the United States and the Government of Japan will not support—militarily, politically, economically—any government or regime in China other than the National Government of the Republic of China with capital temporarily at Chungking.

(5) Both Governments will give up all extraterritorial rights in China, including rights and interests in and with regard to international settlements and concessions, and rights under the Boxer Protocol of 1901.

Both Governments will endeavor to obtain the agreement of the British and other governments to give up extraterritorial rights in China, including rights in international settlements and in concessions and under the Boxer Protocol of 1901.

(6) The Government of the United States and the Government of Japan will enter into negotiations for the conclusion between the United States and Japan of a trade agreement, based upon reciprocal most-favored-nation

treatment and reduction of trade barriers by both countries, including an undertaking by the United States to bind raw silk on the free list.

(7) The Government of the United States and the Government of Japan will, respectively, remove the freezing restrictions on Japanese funds in the United States and on the American funds in Japan.

(8) Both Governments will agree upon a plan for the stabilization of the dollar-yen rate, with the allocation of funds adequate for this purpose, half to be supplied by Japan and half by the United States.

(9) Both Governments will agree that no agreement which either has concluded with any third power or powers shall be interpreted by it in such a way as to conflict with the fundamental purpose of this agreement, the establishment and preservation of peace throughout the Pacific area.

(10) Both Governments will use their influence to cause other governments to adhere to and to give practical application to the basic political and economic principles set forth in this agreement.[10]

On November 21 Secretary Hull showed a preliminary version of the American *modus vivendi* [11] to Admiral Stark and General Gerow (General Marshall being out of town). They agreed that "in general the document was satisfactory from a military standpoint."[12] Gerow underlined his approval by sending in the written comment:

The adoption of its provisions would attain one of our present major objectives—the avoidance of war with Japan. Even a temporary peace in the Pacific, would permit us to complete defensive preparations in the Philippines and at the same time insure continuance of material assistance to the British—both of which are highly important.

The foregoing should not be construed as suggesting strict adherence to all the conditions outlined in the proposed agreement. War Plans Division wishes to emphasize it is of grave importance to the success of our war effort in Europe that we reach a modus vivendi with Japan.[13]

Hull next consulted with the British and Chinese ambassadors and the Australian and Netherlands ministers on November 22, presenting to them both Proposal B and the version of the American *modus vivendi* quoted above. The first reaction was evidently favorable: "Each of the gentlemen present seemed to be well pleased . . . except the Chinese Ambassador, who

---

[10]*Foreign Relations of the United States*: *Japan, 1931–1941*, Vol. II, p. 769f.

[11]This preliminary version of the *modus vivendi* was closer to the Morgenthau-White original and somewhat more favorable to Japan than the version quoted here, though it also included some of the American demands later put into the separate Ten Point Note.

[12]*Hearings*, Part 14, p. 1103.

[13]*Ibid.*, p. 1106.

was somewhat disturbed, as he always is when any question concerning China arises not entirely to his way of thinking."[14] However, he did not show "serious concern, in view of the provision in our proposed *modus vivendi* which would block a Japanese attack on China in order to destroy the Burma Road." The American substitute was regarded by all as preferable to a "specific reply to the Japanese proposal, section for section."[15] Hull concluded the conference by saying that there was "probably not one chance in three that they [the Japanese] would accept our reply."[16]

According to Langer and Gleason,[17] the reception on November 22 of the translated MAGIC intercept postponing the deadline to the 29th and announcing that after that date "things are automatically going to happen," had a heavy influence in determining the subsequent course of American policy in the Far East. Admiral Stark, with this intercept in mind, dispatched his first theater warning on November 24. But it is hard to understand why this postponement of the deadline should have stimulated a more pessimistic sense of fatality than any of the other indications. MAGIC had been whispering in Secretary Hull's ear all month that this was his last chance. Why he was now so gloomy and so short-tempered seems more easily explainable by the months of delicate negotiating combined with the news of actual Japanese military advances. The Secretary seems also to have been deeply impressed with the moral superiority of the Chinese position and consequently very sensitive to criticisms that he was letting China down. His second meeting on November 24 with the Chinese, British, and Dutch representatives precipitated a chain of such criticisms.

At this meeting the Chinese ambassador first objected to having more than 5000 Japanese troops stationed in Indochina. The Secretary

> again stated that General Marshall had a few minutes before expressed . . . his opinion that 25,000 troops would be no menace and that, while this Government did not recognize the right of Japan to keep a single soldier in Indochina, we were striving to reach this proposed temporary agreement primarily because the heads of our Army and Navy often emphasize to me that time is the all-important question for them, and that it is necessary to be

[14] *Ibid.*, p. 1123.
[15] *Ibid.*
[16] *Ibid.*
[17] *The Undeclared War, 1940–1941*, p. 884.

more fully prepared to deal effectively with the situation in the Pacific area in case of an outbreak by Japan.[18]

During the course of the conversation it became apparent that none of the representatives except the Dutch had received any instructions from their governments about the *modus vivendi*. Hull made clear his disappointment and commented bitterly that "each of their Governments was more interested in the defense of that area of the world than this country, and at the same time they expected this country, in case of a Japanese outbreak, to be ready to move in a military way and take the lead in defending the entire area."[19] He closed the meeting by saying he was not sure that he would present the American proposal to the Japanese ambassador "without knowing anything about the views and attitude of their Governments."[20]

Early the next morning, Tuesday, November 25, Hull met with Secretary of War Stimson and Secretary of the Navy Knox. In spite of his irritation with the British and Chinese representatives, Hull was continuing work on the *modus vivendi*. He showed Stimson and Knox the latest draft. Stimson felt that "it adequately safeguarded all our interests" but believed there was little chance of the Japanese accepting it. We were asking them "to at once evacuate and at once to stop all preparations or threats of action, and to take no aggressive action against any of her neighbors, etc." and in return "we were to give them open trade in sufficient quantities only for their civilian population."[21]

The November 25 meeting of Hull, Stimson, and Knox was one of a series of regular meetings held every Tuesday morning for review of the international situation. This particular Tuesday turned out to be a very busy day. At noon the three men met again with General Marshall, Admiral Stark, and the President at the weekly session of the War Council. Stimson's diary gives the gist of the discussion. The President "brought up entirely the relations with the Japanese" and the fact that "we were likely to be attacked perhaps (as soon as) next Monday, for the Japanese

[18] *Hearings*, Part 14, p. 1143*f*.
[19] *Ibid.*, p. 1145.
[20] *Ibid.*, p. 1146.
[21] Stimson diary, in *ibid.*, Part 11, p. 5433.

are notorious for making an attack without warning." There follows a passage that has been the center of much controversy:

> The question was how we should maneuver them into the position of firing the first shot without allowing too much danger to ourselves. It was a difficult proposition. Hull laid out his general broad propositions on which the thing should be rested—the freedom of the seas and the fact that Japan was in alliance with Hitler and was carrying out his policy of world aggression. The others brought out the fact that any such expedition to the South as the Japanese were likely to take would be an encirclement of our interests in the Philippines and cutting into our vital supplies of rubber from Malaysia. I pointed out to the President that he had already taken the first steps towards an ultimatum in notifying Japan way back last summer that if she crossed the border into Thailand she was violating our safety and that therefore he had only to point out (to Japan) that to follow any such expedition was a violation of a warning we had already given. So Hull is to go to work on preparing that.[22]

Stimson's diary is unambiguous in indicating his belief in the inevitability of war and in our own unwillingness to fire the first shot. It also clearly implies his hope that whatever the incident, it would not result in "too much danger to ourselves." Both sides, American and Japanese, were maneuvering now to clear the record for history and world opinion. However, Stimson's wording of the first sentence in the passage just quoted was later translated into the Army warning: "If hostilities cannot, repeat cannot, be avoided, the United States desires that Japan commit the first overt act." The substance of the two sentences is almost the same, but the warning has always been criticized for weakening our alert by instructing our commanders to let the Japanese strike first, whereas Stimson has been criticized for his provocative intentions. It was Stimson, acting for Roosevelt, who saw to it that the Army warning was revised to contain this provision that Japan should commit the first overt act. And the warning, in contrast to the diary passage, does imply some doubt about the certainty of war.

The political controversy that is the mainspring of such arguments is outside the scope of this study, except where it touches on the subject of Stimson's and Roosevelt's estimate of Japanese intentions. We *are* interested in how much our policymakers knew. Hostile critics of Roosevelt's

[22] *Ibid.*

administration take this passage not only as evidence of a plot to involve the United States in war but also as evidence of Stimson's foreknowledge of the attack. They confuse his frank recognition of the *desirability* of an incident with *knowledge* of the Pearl Harbor attack. But why hope and scheme for a mere incident, a "first shot," when a full-scale attack is under way? Neither Stimson nor Roosevelt had any occult knowledge beyond the rest of the people who were scanning the sets of indications for clues. And contemporary intelligence experts can draw scant comfort from the history of those last hours. A deluge of general indications of war in the Pacific and risks of many possible incidents had the administration straining to see specifics. But no specific pointing at Pearl Harbor was understood.

According to Langer and Gleason, who have seen the full Stimson diary, the consensus in the War Council on November 25 was that the Japanese attack would fall on Siam, Malaya, or the Dutch East Indies rather than the Philippines. This is consistent with all the published material. Concern was therefore how to justify American intervention under such circumstances and how to present the case to Congress.[23] For the members of the War Council believed that the Japanese, like themselves, realized that an attack on an ally would embarrass the United States far more than a direct attack on a U.S. possession.

After the War Council meeting, Hull returned to the Department of State to find the response of the British government to the *modus vivendi*. Lord Halifax politely expressed the usual British sentiment that Washington should make the final decision but recommended that the U.S. government pitch its demands high and its offering price low, and suggested that the United States demand total withdrawal not only of Japanese troops but also of naval and air forces from Indochina and the prohibition of further military advances against China or any other region.

At this same time, violent objections to the *modus vivendi* were coming from China. Chiang Kai-shek appealed to his political adviser, Owen Lattimore, to make clear his strong opposition; instructed the Chinese ambassador Hu Shih to the same effect; sent a message of protest to Churchill; and even appealed directly to Secretaries Stimson and Knox through his brother-in-law. "Chinese national trust in America," he

[23] *The Undeclared War, 1940–1941*, p. 887.

proclaimed, "would be undermined by reports of Japan's escaping military defeat by diplomatic victory."[24] Hu Shih visited Secretary Hull on the evening of November 25 to report the Generalissimo's opposition, and Hull once more patiently went over the reasons for the *modus vivendi* and America's need for time, reminding Hu Shih that "very recently the Generalissimo and Madame Chiang Kai-shek almost flooded Washington with strong and lengthy cables telling us how extremely dangerous the Japanese threat is to attack the Burma Road through Indochina."[25] Now the *modus vivendi* would take care of this threat, he went on to say, but Chiang Kai-shek ignores this fact and brings up another danger about releasing certain commodities to Japan. Hull continued:

> He also overlooks the fact that our proposal would relieve the menace of Japan in Indochina to the whole South Pacific area, including Singapore, the Netherlands East Indies, Australia and also the United States, with the Philippines and the rubber and tin trade routes. All of this relief from menace . . . would continue for ninety days. One of our leading admirals stated to me recently that the limited amount of more or less inferior oil products that we might let Japan have during that period would not to any appreciable extent increase Japanese war and naval preparations. I said that, of course, we can cancel this proposal, but it must be with the understanding that we are not to be charged with failure to send our fleet into the area near Indochina and into Japanese waters, if by any chance Japan makes a military drive southward.[26]

In spite of the firm and reproachful tone that he took with Hu Shih, Hull was shaken by both the British and the Chinese opposition. He consulted once more with his colleagues, and sometime during the evening of the 25th or early in the morning of the 26th he decided, with Roosevelt's approval, to abandon the *modus vivendi*. His decision was evidently precipitated by Roosevelt's reaction to a message from Churchill characterizing the *modus vivendi* as "a very thin diet" for Chiang Kai-shek, and by news from G-2 on Japanese troop movements. The Churchill message and the G-2 report intensified the general atmosphere of pessimism already provided by MAGIC and by accusations of "appeasement" in the public press.

24 *Hearings*, Part 20, p. 4473.
25 *Ibid.*, Part 14, p. 1168.
26 *Ibid.*, p. 1169.

The news from G-2 was the sighting of Japanese transports off the coast of Formosa. (This actually was Admiral Ozawa's expeditionary force against the Malay Peninsula.) Stimson had received this news as soon as he got back to the office after the November 25 War Council meeting. His diary reports that "five divisions have come down from Shantung and Shansi to Shanghai and there they had embarked on ships— 30, 40, or 50 ships—and have been sighted south of Formosa. I at once called up Hull and told him about it and sent copies to him and to the President of the message from G-2."[27]

This information had come from British intelligence. It had been cabled to London on November 21 and from there to Washington G-2. Early in the morning on November 25, G-2 received the same information from ONI. ONI's source was a Shanghai report of the 21st. The same information went to Honolulu from the British representative in Manila and may have gone some time around December 3 from the British representative in Honolulu to Army G-2 at Pearl Harbor. Washington G-2's comment on the information had been that it represented a "normal" movement, i.e., nothing beyond what the Japanese had announced that they were going to do.[28] The British comment revealed serious concern and was coupled with an estimate indicating that the British expected "early" involvement of Japan in a war with England and the United States. Hull received notice by telephone from Stimson. The President evidently did not receive his copy of the G-2 report, because on the morning of November 26 Stimson asked the President over the telephone

> whether he had received the paper which I had sent him over last night about the Japanese having started a new expedition from Shanghai down toward Indochina. He fairly blew up—jumped up into the air, so to speak, and said he hadn't seen it and that that changed the whole situation because it was an evidence of bad faith on the part of the Japanese that while they were negotiating for an entire truce—an entire withdrawal ... —they should be sending this expedition down there to Indochina. I told him that it was a fact that had come to me through G-2 and through the Navy Secret Service and I at once got another copy of the paper I had sent last night and sent it over to him by special messenger.[29]

[27] *Ibid.*, Part 11, p. 5433*f*.
[28] *Ibid.*, Part 20, p. 4476.
[29] *Ibid.*, Part 11, p. 5434.

The location of these troopships off the coast of Formosa was evidently decisive for President Roosevelt in estimating Japanese intentions and in determining his approval of Hull's decision to abandon the *modus vivendi*. It played some part too in Hull's decision, though Chinese objections seem to have weighed more heavily on Hull. Stimson had spoken to the Secretary of State on the telephone before he spoke to the President on the morning of November 26 and learned that Hull "had about made up his mind not to give ... the proposition ... to the Japanese but to kick the whole thing over—to tell them that he has no other proposition at all. The Chinese have objected to that proposition ... because it involves giving to the Japanese the small modicum of oil for civilian use during the interval of the truce of the 3 months."[30]

Stimson, Hull, and especially President Roosevelt viewed the troopship movement with alarm. The reaction of these policymakers was sharply different from that of G-2, where the news became transformed into a "normal movement." It is interesting to observe here that this decisive Japanese signal had taken five days (from November 21 to the morning of November 26, reporting movements beginning on November 17) to reach the chief policymaker, and it seems somewhat accidental that it should have turned out to be decisive. Tempers had been frayed, and reactions close to the edge for some days, and the G-2 news was, of course, decisive only in this context and in combination with the pressures from China and Great Britain.

The telephone conversation between Hull and Stimson about "kicking the whole thing over" took place about 10 A.M. on the morning of November 26. Before that time Hull had had a conference with Roosevelt on the Japanese-American negotiations. His decision to drop the *modus vivendi*, as well as the decision immediately following, to submit in its place the Ten Point Note, could only have been made with the President's approval. Roosevelt evidently indicated his approval of both decisions sometime before Hull presented the Ten Points to the Japanese ambassadors in the late afternoon of November 26.

The Ten Point Note, along with the *modus vivendi*, had grown out of the Morgenthau-White proposal, but instead of embodying suggestions for a temporary settlement, it set forth America's maximum demands as a

[30] *Ibid.*

basis for discussion of a permanent agreement.[31] In the form submitted to the Japanese, it was headed "Tentative and Without Commitment" and entitled "Outline of Proposed Basis for Agreement between the United States and Japan." America's demands, however, included complete evacuation of China and Indochina and the abandonment of the Nanking regime. And the tone and content of the note were on the whole so drastic that it is easy to understand why this document was characterized immediately by the Japanese as an ultimatum. At the same time it is hard to understand why Secretary Hull, after all the thought and time spent on a truce, decided to present the most extreme version of America's demands as a response to the Japanese Proposal B. The War and Navy Departments had been consulted about the substance of the *modus vivendi* in a form that included some of the demands listed among the Ten Points, but they had not been consulted about the Ten Points as a separate document.

Most historical accounts of this period regard our presentation of the Ten Point Note as *the* decisive act that closed the negotiations and gave the green light to the Japanese War Plan. It was not so clear at the time to many of our government leaders, either because they were not completely informed as to its contents, or because they were tired of reacting to danger signals, or because they were easily influenced by Secretary Hull's ever-present hope of reopening the conversations. To some the Note was simply a way of keeping the record straight for history that the United States was no "appeaser"; to a few it was even a "magnificent statement"[32] of our position. *The New York Times* described it as a restatement of American principles "to clear the atmosphere." For Army and Navy officers the reports of Japanese military movements loomed larger in the picture than any diplomatic act short of a formal declaration of war.

It would make a neater story if one could believe that a clear perspective on the Ten Point Note and an accurate estimate of the probable Japanese reaction to it would have resulted in an unambiguous warning to the theaters to go on a full alert. For it is always easier to recognize the need for alerting your forces if it is *your* country that is taking a definitely provocative step. But the documents of these critical days in November make clear that history has many candidates for the "initial incident" in

[31] See page 236.
[32] Roosevelt's phrase, as recorded by Stimson, in *Hearings*, Part 11, p. 5435.

the last moments of tension before war, and what finally sparks the explosion is largely a matter of accident. When Secretary Hull presented his Ten Point Note, the Pearl Harbor task force had been under way for 24 hours.

THE DECISION TO WARN THE THEATERS

Unfortunately we do not know how much the services knew about American diplomatic moves before sending the November 27 warning messages, or how they learned as much as they did. The record for November 25, 26, and 27 has many gaps. Contemporary accounts, for example, refer to "Hull's decision" of November 26. But Hull's decision was really two decisions: (1) to abandon the *modus vivendi* and (2) to submit the Ten Point Note. The second decision did *not* necessarily follow from the first (even though Hull said he thought of them together). In terms of what was communicated to the services as a basis for alerting the theaters, the second seems today much more alarming.

At least one thing is clear. Secretary Hull submitted the Ten Points without consulting the Army and Navy. The theater warnings were probably sent out without knowledge of this second decision, though very probably with knowledge of the dropping of the *modus vivendi*. The first drafts of the warning, however, were written largely on the basis of Japanese military movements into Indochina or on the basis of assumptions prevailing on November 25. General Marshall, in any case, had not expected the Japanese to accept the terms of the American *modus vivendi*, and neither had Admiral Turner, who drafted the naval warning.

The most precise statement of Army and Navy thinking at this time was recorded in a memorandum to the President dated November 27, signed by General Marshall and Admiral Stark, and drafted by their War Plans Divisions. Admiral Turner remembered starting this draft about November 24; Marshall probably signed it on the 26th, since he left town the afternoon of the 26th and did not return until the evening of the 27th, and Roosevelt saw it and in general approved of it on November 27.[33]

This November 27 memo is, for the most part, a restatement of a November 5 memo, which had grown out of an earlier November crisis,

[33] Cf. letter from Stark to Roosevelt, in *ibid.*, Part 20, p. 4487.

in which China was putting a great deal of pressure on the U.S. government for a warning to Japan and for some air support to keep open the Burma Road. In both memos the services emphasized their need for time[34] and their urgent desire to postpone war in the Pacific, or to somehow "tide the situation over for the next several months."[35] They stated categorically and with emphatic disapproval that the actions that China was recommending to America, "however well-disguised, would lead to war."[36]

The contents of the November 5 memo were worked out at a Joint Board meeting on November 3. The Joint Board was regularly attended by Admiral Stark, General Marshall, their immediate assistants, Admiral Ingersoll and General Bryden, and members of the War Plans staffs. This particular meeting is interesting, by the way, for the glimpse it gives of the military's view of the State Department. Admiral Ingersoll, for example, commented that "the present moment is not the opportune time to get brash," and he was most decidedly not inclined to share the State Department's "impression that Japan could be defeated in military action in a few weeks."[37] There was an undercurrent of suggestion that whatever the State Department did was going to be irresponsible, and the military could only hope that it would not present an ultimatum to Japan.

But more pertinent was the discussion between Marshall and Ingersoll on the risks to the Japanese of any action against the Philippines:

> General Marshall felt that the main involvement in the Far East would be naval and that under this assumption, due consideration should be given to the fact that the Navy was now fighting a battle in the Atlantic. It was his information that the Japanese authorities had not as yet determined the action to be taken under the present situation. The information which he

[34] The intensity with which the Army expressed this need for time is understandable if we look at a memo of a conference held on November 3 among Generals Marshall and Gerow and Colonel Bundy. Marshall "had been paralyzed to find that a shipment of bombs sent at the end of September would not get to Singapore until December 18. It is not only that delay occurs in matters of this sort, but that we do not know *why* it occurs. . . . As General Marshall sees it, we have only begun when an order is issued. He does not want to pester commanders by checking up on them constantly, but there must be some means of knowing how things are progressing before a crisis develops, as in the case of bombs for Singapore." (Notes on Conferences in OCS, II, 424C, Chief of Staff, U.S. Army records, quoted in Cline, *Washington Command Post: The Operations Division*, in the series *United States Army in World War II*, p. 73.)

[35] *Hearings*, Part 14, p. 1065.
[36] *Ibid.*, p. 1061.
[37] *Ibid.*, p. 1064.

had received indicated that the Japanese authorities might be expected to decide upon the national policy by November 5. He then read General Gerow's analysis of the strength of the United States forces in the Far East and emphasized the danger of moving Army Air Forces away from their present station in the Philippines. It was his belief that *as long as the augmented Army Air Force remained in the Philippines, Japanese action against the Philippines or toward the south would be a very hazardous operation.* It was his belief that *by the middle of December, the Army Forces in the Philippines would be of impressive strength, and this in itself would have a deterrent effect on Japanese operations.*

Admiral Ingersoll gave a summary of naval reinforcements scheduled for the Philippines. A stated number of submarine units enroute to the Philippines were now in Guam. Other submarines scheduled for transfer to the Philippines were about to leave Hawaii. With reference to Japanese decision on National policy he felt that United States forces and shipping now being moved to the Philippines might be in danger if a decision adverse to United States interest should be made on November 5th. General Marshall emphasized the point that *Japan could hardly take the risk of military operations with a powerful air and submarine force directly on the flank of their supply lines,* and that when United States power is sufficiently developed in the Philippines, we would then have something to back up our statements. Until powerful United States forces had been built up in the Far East, it would take some very clever diplomacy to save the situation. It appeared that the basis of U.S. policy should be to make certain minor concessions which the Japanese could use in saving face. These concessions might be a relaxation on oil restrictions or on similar trade restrictions [author's italics].[38]

This view of the great risk to Japan of an attack on the Philippines, or an attack to the south which would have to bypass the Philippines, evidently persisted in the War Department until the time of the attack. It was a view strongly shared by Admiral Stark.

The November 27 memo set forth the risks of alternative courses of action for Japan in some detail. We reproduce the entire memo below:

November 27, 1941

MEMORANDUM FOR THE PRESIDENT

Subject: Far Eastern Situation

If the current negotiations end without agreement, Japan may attack: the Burma Road; Thailand; Malaya; the Netherlands East Indies; the Philippines; the Russian Maritime Provinces.

[38] *Ibid.*

There is little probability of an immediate Japanese attack on the Maritime Provinces because of the strength of the Russian forces. Recent Japanese troop movements all seem to have been southward.

The magnitude of the effort required will militate against direct attack against Malaya and the Netherlands East Indies until the threat exercised by United States forces in Luzon is removed.

Attack on the Burma Road or Thailand offer Japanese objectives involving less risk of major conflict than the others named, and clearly within the means available, if unopposed by major powers. Attack on the Burma Road would, however, be difficult and might fail. If successful, the Chinese Nationalist Government might collapse. Occupation of Thailand gains a limited strategic advantage as a preliminary to operations against Malaya or the Netherlands East Indies, might relieve internal political pressure and to a lesser extent, external economic pressure. Whether the offensive will be made against the Burma Road, Thailand, or the Philippines cannot now be forecast.

The most essential thing now, from the United States viewpoint, is to gain time. Considerable Navy and Army reinforcements have been rushed to the Philippines but the desirable strength has not yet been reached. The process of reinforcement is being continued. Of great and immediate concern is the safety of the Army convoy now near Guam, and the Marine Corps' convoy just leaving Shanghai. Ground forces to a total of 21,000 are due to sail from the United States by December 8, 1941, and it is important that this troop reinforcement reach the Philippines before hostilities commence. *Precipitance of military action on our part should be avoided so long as consistent with national policy.* The longer the delay, the more positive becomes the assurance of retention of these islands as a naval and air base. Japanese action to the south of Formosa will be hindered and perhaps seriously blocked as long as we hold the Philippine Islands. War with Japan certainly will interrupt our transport of supplies to Siberia, and probably will interrupt the process of aiding China.

After consultation with each other, United States, British, and Dutch military authorities in the Far East agreed that joint military counteraction against Japan should be undertaken only in case Japan attacks or directly threatens the territory or mandated territory of the United States, the British Commonwealth, or the Netherlands East Indies, or should the Japanese move forces into Thailand west of 100° East or south of 10° North, Portuguese Timor, New Caledonia, or the Loyalty Islands.

Japanese involvement in Yunnan or Thailand up to a certain extent is advantageous, since it leads to further dispersion, longer lines of communication, and an additional burden on communications. However, a Japanese advance to the west of 100° East or south of 10° North, immediately becomes a threat to Burma and Singapore. Until it is patent that Japan intends to advance beyond these lines, no action which might lead to immediate hostilities should be taken.

It is recommended that:

prior to the completion of the Philippine reinforcement, military counteraction be considered only if Japan attacks or directly threatens United States, British, or Dutch territory as above outlined;

in case of a Japanese advance into Thailand, Japan be warned by the United States, the British, and the Dutch governments that advance beyond the lines indicated may lead to war; prior to such warning no joint military opposition to be undertaken;

steps be taken at once to consummate agreements with the British and Dutch for the issuance of such warning [author's italics].

/s/   G. C. Marshall   /s/   H. R. Stark

25-66654-2000[39]

These considerations were the ones to the fore when the warning messages to the theaters were drafted: the need for time and the belief that there would be time because the Japanese would not risk a major attack on the Philippines. If an attack on the Philippines would be risky, then certainly an attack on Pearl Harbor—our strongest fortress, located much farther away from Japanese supply lines—would be a much greater gamble.

Whether the military knew that the current negotiations had ended without agreement is not clear from the wording of the memo. Evidently before presenting it to the President, Stimson had asked General Gerow and Admiral Stark not to recommend any action "at any cost of humility on the part of United States or of reopening the thing which would show a weakness on our part."[40] The word "reopening" would suggest that the negotiations had closed. But Stimson's request evidently necessitated "only minor changes." This exchange took place at the same time as the revision of the Army warning in Stimson's office. (See page 253.)

It appears that to the military our diplomatic maneuvering with Japan was a complicated and dangerous balancing at the edge of war. It was good if it gained time; it was bad if it was obscure or involved threats of military force that we could not back up. In this memorandum of Novem-

39 *Ibid.*, p. 1083.
40 *Ibid.*, Part 11, p. 5435.

ber 27, they were certainly not talking about a *modus vivendi* anymore, but rather of a warning to Japan, and they were setting definite limits to military counteraction. Failure of the negotiations had been anticipated, of course, since November 22, and it was only the part of wisdom to prepare estimates of action for this contingency.

The first we hear of a draft of the November 27 Army warning was at an Army staff conference held at 10:40 A.M. on November 26. The notes for this conference had much in common with the November 27 memo. General Gerow, General Arnold, Colonel Bundy, and Colonel Handy of WPD were present. General Marshall was reported as saying that the "President and Mr. Hull felt the Japanese were dissatisfied with the current conferences and 'will soon cut loose.' "[41] Mark Watson, the official Army historian, who summarized in this way the notes taken at the meeting, gave no further indication of Secretary Hull's views except to say that "both the President and Mr. Hull anticipate a possible assault on the Philippines."[42] General Marshall disagreed:

> General Marshall said he did not see this [assault on the Philippines] as a probability because the hazards would be too great for the Japanese. . . . We know a great deal that the Japanese are not aware we know, and we are familiar with their plans to a certain extent.[43]

However, Marshall pointed out: "We are not justified in ignoring any Japanese convoy that might be a threat to our interests. Thus far we have talked in terms of the defense of the Philippines, but now the question is what we do beyond that."[44]

The convoy mentioned here was the expeditionary force off the coast of Formosa. The second sentence referred to an important change in the theory of Philippine defense that seriously affected the Army warning. General Bryden had written to General MacArthur on November 21, 1941, summarizing our Philippine policy in this way:

> Heretofore, contemplated Army action in the Far East area has been purely of a defensive nature. The augmentation of the Army Air Forces in the Philippines has modified that conception of Army action in this area to include offensive air operations in the furtherance of the strategic defensive

[41] Watson, *Chief of Staff: Prewar Plans and Preparations*, p. 450.
[42] *Ibid.*
[43] *Ibid.*
[44] *Ibid.*

combined with the defense of the Philippine Islands as an air and naval base.[45]

The "offensive air operations" had been detailed in the revised Rainbow Five War Plan that went to MacArthur on the same date (November 21). In this revised plan the Philippine Coastal Frontier had been enlarged to include all the islands in the archipelago rather than Luzon alone, and MacArthur's mission had been increased by three new tasks:

1. Support the Navy in raiding Japanese sea communications and destroying Axis forces.
2. Conduct air raids against Japanese forces and installations within tactical operating radius of available bases.
3. Cooperate with the Associated Powers in the defense of the territories of these Powers in accordance with approved policies and agreements.[46]

With this change in the theory of Philippine defense General MacArthur was to be alerted to get up and go, not merely to defend himself against a direct attack.

At this November 26 Army staff conference, General Marshall indicated that the negotiations had bogged down, but that a break would not necessarily be followed by a Japanese declaration of war. General Gerow spoke after General Marshall, predicting a Japanese advance into Thailand as most likely. He then raised the question of American action after the Japanese had passed the agreed limit of longitude 10°N., latitude 100°E. He also "raised a question of immediate instructions for General MacArthur, and was advised that prior to actual hostilities, General MacArthur should, in cooperation with the Navy, take such reconnaissance and other measures as he felt necessary."[47]

The term "actual hostilities" was suggested by Marshall as a substitute for "state of war" in Gerow's draft. Marshall commented with some realism: "there is war in China and there is war in the Atlantic at the present time, but in neither case is it declared war."[48]

These staff conference notes, imprecise as they were, indicated that the first draft of the Army warning[49] had already been drawn up at least with

---

[45] Quoted by Watson, *ibid.*, p. 440.
[46] Changes in Joint Army and Navy Basic War Plan, Rainbow 5, in Louis Morton, *The Fall of the Philippines*, p. 67.
[47] Watson, *Chief of Staff: Prewar Plans and Preparations*, p. 450.
[48] *Ibid.*
[49] General Gerow was unable to locate a copy of this original draft.

the knowledge that the negotiations were temporarily broken, and against a background of concern about our British and Dutch allies. Hull's estimate that the Japanese would soon "cut loose" and the G-2 information on Japanese convoy movements seem to have provided the central impulse. The notes also suggested that the Army warning was intended primarily for General MacArthur, even though the staff did not agree with the President or Secretary Hull that an assault on the Philippines was likely. Rather, they wanted to alert him to some actions that would go "beyond" defense, since they anticipated a Japanese violation of the "agreed limit."

Some of the assumptions of this original draft very probably remained to muddy the clarity of Stimson's suggestion—which Roosevelt approved— for a "final alert" to MacArthur "to be on the qui vive against any attack."[50] This was the phrase as Stimson recorded it in his diary. Stimson did go to work revising the draft with General Gerow on the morning of November 27, but his changes all emphasized the original tone, in particular by suggesting that the negotiations might not have closed. The first draft was written in WPD without the idea that this was to warn against a direct attack on a U.S. possession. Marshall approved it in this form, left town for maneuvers in North Carolina, and did not return until the message had been sent out. Gerow took the responsibility for the wording, and in its final form it evidently satisfied Stimson, even though Stimson *was* very concerned about an attack on the Philippines. It evidently satisfied Roosevelt too, for he sent a priority message on the 26th to the High Commissioner of the Philippines that stated in part:

A copy of a dispatch will be delivered to you by Admiral Hart which, with *my approval*, the CNO and the COS addressed to the senior Army and Navy commanders in the Philippines. *In addition, you are advised* that the Japanese are strongly re-enforcing their garrison and naval forces in the mandates in a manner which indicates they are preparing this region as quickly as possible against a possible attack on them by U.S. forces. However I am more particularly concerned over increasing opposition of Japanese leaders and by current southward troop movements from Shanghai and Japan to the Formosa area. Preparations are becoming apparent in China, Formosa and Indo-China for an early aggressive movement of some character, although as yet there are no clear indications as to its strength, or whether it will be directed against the Burma Road, Thailand, Malay Peninsula, Neth-

[50] *Hearings*, Part 11, p. 5435.

erlands East Indies or the Philippines. Advance against Thailand seems the most probable. *I consider it possible that this next Japanese aggression might cause an outbreak of hostilities between the U.S. and Japan* [author's italics]....[51]

To return to the morning of November 26, a Joint Board meeting followed this Army staff conference at 11:30 A.M. The minutes of the meeting reflected no discussion of a warning measure or the events leading up to it. But a memo from Gerow to Marshall dated November 27 referred to "the draft message you discussed at the JB meeting."[52] And Admiral Turner testified that the Joint Board did discuss a naval warning draft, and that it was "correct" and "customary" for the minutes to contain no mention of such discussion. A "dispatch of this character," he stated, "while it might be discussed in Joint Board . . . was not the function of the Joint Board to send. It was the business of Admiral Stark and General Marshall. . . . So that customarily, when something of that sort came up that required action, it was not put down in the Joint Board minutes, because then it would look as if the Joint Board had decided to do such and such, which would not be the case."[53]

Whatever the case, War Plans officers of both services were evidently at work on drafts of the warning messages on the afternoon of November 26, and both Army and Navy drafts reflect pretty much the same line of reasoning.

It is easy to get lost in the maze of conflicting testimony about communication between the State Department and the Army and Navy in Washington on the morning of November 26. We have essentially the documents quoted in the text and the testimony of Stark, Marshall, Turner, Gerow, and Schuirmann (Navy liaison man with the State Department). Turner, for example, testified that Schuirmann brought the news of the decision to abandon the *modus vivendi* to Stark at 10:30 A.M. on November 26. Schuirmann testified that he could not remember this, but he knew that he did not bring news about the Ten Point Note at any time. Stark

[51] *Ibid.*, Part 2, p. 950.

[52] *Ibid.*, Part 3, p. 1020.

[53] *Ibid.*, Part 4, p. 1497. Turner's explanation seems rather fantastic, since the Joint Board was primarily a place for discussion rather than action. It was consultative rather than executive, and if it had failed to record its discussions for fear they would suggest power of decision, there would have been no minutes whatsoever.

testified that he remembered something about the Japanese affair being in the hands of the Army and Navy, but could not remember whether he heard this on the 27th or the 28th. Marshall said he would not have known anything before Stimson, because Stimson was his informant on Hull's actions, and Stimson found out about the whole thing being "kicked over" on the morning of November 27. The only conclusion to draw is that diplomatic maneuvers at this moment had become so complex and shifting, and bore so obscure a relation to our own defense preparations in the Pacific and to the vague but ominous MAGIC messages, that the precise timing of the maneuvers was hardly likely to remain fixed in the minds of the military commanders.[54] Our forces in the Far East were being warned because we knew that some major Japanese military and naval units were on the move. As Turner put it, the delivery of the Ten Point Note "had no effect whatsoever on the situation, because they were already on the move."[55]

We can see, for example, what was going on in Stark's mind from a postscript appended to his letter to Kimmel on November 25. These lines were written after the War Council meeting:

> I won't go into the pros and cons of what the United States may do. I will be damned if I know. I wish I did. The only thing I do know is that we may do most anything and that's the only thing I know to be prepared for; or we may do nothing—I think it is more likely to be "anything" [received by Kimmel on December 3].[56]

In short, the surprise for which Stark was steeling himself was what *we* might do. He had somewhat more orderly and definite anticipations as to the course of Japanese action:

> I have been in constant touch with Mr. Hull and it was only after a long talk with him that I sent the message [the November 24 warning] to you a day or two ago showing the gravity of the situation. He confirmed it all in today's meeting, as did the President. Neither would be surprised over a Japanese surprise attack. From many angles an attack on the Philippines would be the most embarrassing thing that could happen to us. There are some here who think it likely to occur. I do not give it the weight others

---

[54] This conclusion is lenient on the military. Actually, Stark's information was usually fuller and more accurate and earlier than Marshall's. There is no reason why it should have been any less so on November 26.

[55] *Hearings*, Part 32, p. 618.

[56] *Ibid.*, Part 16, p. 2225.

do, but I included it because of the strong feeling among some people. You know I have generally held that it was not time for the Japanese to proceed against Russia. I still do. Also I still rather look for an advance into Thailand, Indochina, Burma Road area as most likely.[57]

These assumptions were very close to Marshall's and Gerow's. The November 24 naval dispatch had warned that "a surprise aggressive movement in any direction including attack on Philippines or Guam is a possibility." The November 27 naval warning stated: "an aggressive move by Japan is expected within the next few days. The number and equipment of Japanese troops and the organization of naval task forces indicate an amphibious expedition against either the Philippines, Thai, or Kra Peninsula or possibly Borneo." Both naval warnings mentioned explicitly the possibility of a direct attack on the Philippines, even though Stark personally did not go along with this. Stark also recorded his views in a cable dictated November 24 to the Special Naval Observer in London, in response to a report from the Dutch of a Japanese expeditionary force in the vicinity of Palau which seemed to threaten the Dutch East Indies:

> The CNO does not believe that any large Japanese aggressive force is now prepared for any immediate move from the region under discussion (Palau) but he is concerned over southward troop movements from Shanghai and Japan to Formosa and also apparent preparations in China, Formosa and Indochina for an early aggressive movement of some character. There are no clear indications at present as to the direction or strength of such a movement and the situation should be carefully watched.[58]

Stark testified before the Naval Court of Inquiry that his dispatch of the 24th to Admiral Kimmel had been "largely informatory." "Kimmel had previously taken measures . . . which I considered appropriate. . . . I was trying to acquaint him with the picture as I saw it and that there was a 'possibility' of a surprise attack."[59] He did not expect Kimmel to take any further action on the basis of this dispatch: he used the weak word "possibility" and he used it "advisedly." His sentence "A surprise aggressive movement in any direction . . . is a possibility" does not, of course, convey any new information. He could have sent this particular sentence to the theater at any time during 1941 without changing Kimmel's

[57] *Ibid.*, p. 2224.
[58] *Ibid.*, Part 15, p. 1772.
[59] *Ibid.*, Part 32, p. 49.

expectation. "I wasn't ready," he said, "to go on an all-out at that time. Admiral Kimmel was confronted with problems, and very difficult problems, of training. He was making a so-called health cruise. . . . I didn't feel at that time that he needed to start using everything he had on a war basis, and the word 'possibility' was used advisedly, though I knew the situation was certainly no better, and if anything, deteriorating."[60]

On November 27, however, Stark said he felt that there was no longer hope of delay. Since the 24th two things had happened: (1) negotiations had ceased and (2) he had received the news of the convoy off Formosa. He ascribed his change of estimate entirely to the first development.[61] It seems likely, however, that the news of the Japanese naval movement had as potent an influence on Stark's view of the danger as it had on Roosevelt's. As Kimmel pointed out with some asperity, the newspapers in Honolulu carried news of continuing negotiations during the first week in December.[62] If this point were critical, and if Stark expected Kimmel to rely as usual on his public sources, then he should have notified Kimmel that the appearance of continuing negotiations was a Japanese ruse. However, the gathering signals of Japanese naval and military movements probably formed the main impulse behind the November 27 naval warning.

Beginning on November 27, Stark felt that war was "likely to take place any time." In composing the naval warning, "we pondered almost an entire forenoon" on the phrase, "Japanese aggression is expected within the next few days" rather than "is a possibility" and a good deal over the phrase "this is a war warning," and "we used language which we thought was strong enough to indicate to them that Japan was going to strike."[63] As for leaving out the phrase "in any direction" and listing specifics in the November 27 dispatch, Stark felt that the phrase "in any direction" should have continued to function as a valid warning to any reader of both dispatches. He believed that the specific listing did not limit the

---

[60] *Ibid.*

[61] *Ibid.*, p. 90.

[62] See, for example, the front-page headline in the Honolulu *Advertiser* for December 1: "JAPAN CALLED STILL HOPEFUL OF MAKING PEACE." There was also a full headline on page 5 of the December 2 issue: "JAPAN GIVES TWO WEEKS MORE TO NEGOTIATIONS." Many other columns on Japan during the last ten days before the attack gave ample evidence that the Honolulu reporting was largely speculation done in the dark.

[63] *Hearings*, Part 32, p. 51.

targets, but simply indicated the most probable ones; therefore the dispatch of the 27th included Pearl Harbor. How Stark could have believed that the single phrase "in any direction" should have carried over from a sentence in a less urgent message that had been carefully revised is incomprehensible. How he could have believed that its all-inclusive reference could have conveyed an attack on Pearl Harbor is equally unclear. In Kimmel's mind at any rate, the phrase did not hold over from the 24th to the 27th.

The sentence, "The number and equipment of Japanese troops and the organization of naval task forces indicate an amphibious expedition . . ." was also misleading. It is true that amphibious equipment had been observed aboard the Japanese ships while they were docked at Shanghai. But even the Japanese naval commanders, who estimated their risks somewhat differently than we had surmised, regarded an amphibious expedition against Pearl Harbor as too risky. Read in the context of Stark's listing of targets, this item of intelligence could only confirm the belief that no part of this movement was destined for Pearl Harbor.

Stimson's diary for November 27 recorded the sequence of events and his own participation in the theater warnings as follows:

> A very tense, long day. News is coming in of a concentration and movement south by the Japanese of a large expeditionary force moving south from Shanghai and evidently headed toward Indochina, with a possibility of going to the Philippines or to Burma, or to the Burma Road or to the Dutch East Indies, but probably a concentration to move over into Thailand and to hold a position from which they can attack Singapore when the moment arrives.
>
> The first thing in the morning I called up Hull to find out what his finale had been with the Japanese—whether he had handed them the new proposal which we had passed on 2 or 3 days ago or whether, as he suggested yesterday he would, he broke the whole matter off. He told me now that he had broken the whole matter off. As he put it, "I have washed my hands of it and it is now in the hands of you and Knox—the Army and the Navy." I then called up the President. The President gave me a little different view. He said they had ended up, but they ended up with a magnificent statement prepared by Hull. I found out afterward that this was not a reopening of the thing but a statement of our constant and regular position [the Ten Point Note].
>
> General Arnold came in to present the orders for the movement of two of our biggest planes out from San Francisco and across the Mandated

Islands to Manila. There is a concentration going on by the Japanese in the Mandated Islands and these planes can fly high over them, beyond the reach of their pursuit planes and take photographs.

Knox and Admiral Stark came over and conferred with me and General Gerow. Marshall is down at the maneuvers today and I feel his absence very much. There was a tendency, not unnatural, on the part of Stark and Gerow to seek for more time. I said that I was glad to have time but I didn't want it at any cost of humility on the part of the United States or of reopening the thing which would show a weakness on our part. The main question has been over the message that we shall send to MacArthur. We have already sent him a quasi alert, or the first signal for an alert, and now, on talking with the President this morning over the telephone, I suggested and he approved the idea that we should send the final alert; namely that he should be on the qui vive for any attack and telling him how the situation was. So Gerow and Stark and I went over the proposed message to him from Marshall very carefully; finally got it in shape and with the help of a telephone talk I had with Hull, I got the exact statement from him of what the situation was.[64]

It was this last telephone talk with Hull that resulted in a milder warning being sent to the Army than to the Navy in Honolulu. Hull continued to cling to the hope that something could be done by talking. The Army warning began: "Negotiations with Japan appear to be terminated to all practical purposes with only the barest possibilities that the Japanese Government might come back and offer to continue."[65] Admiral Stark, continuing the naval tradition of more definite statement, had a warning sent to Kimmel and Hart beginning: "This dispatch is to be considered a war warning. Negotiations with Japan toward stabilization of conditions in the Pacific have ceased."[66] Stark did, however, follow up this original warning message with another on November 28 that gave the full text of the Army warning and added the precaution, "Undertake no offensive action until Japan has committed an overt act."[67]

The first Army warning went out sometime during the day of November 27, in time at any rate for General Short to send back his acknowledgment on the same day. General Short's answer was received in Washington at 5:57 A.M. on November 28. It was distributed from the Signal Center to General Marshall, General Gerow, and Secretary Stimson, each of

[64] *Ibid.*, Part 11, p. 5434*f.*
[66] *Ibid.*, p. 1406.

[65] *Ibid.*, Part 14, p. 1328.
[67] *Ibid.*, p. 1407.

whom initialed the copy. Short's answer read: "Report Department alerted to prevent sabotage period Liaison with Navy reurad four seven two twenty seventh."[68]

The Plans Group of WPD at this time had the function not only of preparing and dispatching orders to the theater, but also the responsibility of following up such orders and checking on the adequacy of the measures taken by the theater commanders. As Ray S. Cline has pointed out, however, "the very name of this group reflected its primary function."[69] There was no unit assigned like the later OPD Theater Group to deal exclusively with follow-up on operational orders. General Short's message, read after the attack, seemed to say quite clearly that he was alerted for sabotage and not for anything else. But in the press of work on November 28, neither General Gerow nor any of his aides saw anything to question in the message. It might indeed have seemed unnecessarily officious to question it at the time, in view of the current War Department hypotheses as to the probable targets of Japanese attack. It had been these hypotheses that shaped the November 27 warning dispatch in the first place.

As we have seen in Chapter 1, several other Army agencies also sent warning messages on November 27 and November 28. Both the Army Air Force and G-2 sent messages to General Short underlining the dangers of sabotage.

The first naval warning left Washington just twenty-three minutes before midnight on November 27 and was received by Kimmel on November 28. It did not request a report of measures taken, and there is no record of an answer from Kimmel in the *Hearings*. His last letter before the attack was written on December 2, and it was entirely concerned with the subject of later dispatches from Admiral Stark having to do with reinforcing the outlying islands of Midway and Wake and replacing the Marines by Army troops. Some of Kimmel's remarks, however, were pertinent to the directive to "execute an appropriate defensive deployment preparatory to carrying out the tasks assigned in WPL 46 [the naval war plan providing for the Pacific Fleet to move against the Marshalls]."

[68] *Ibid.*, p. 1330.
[69] *Washington Command Post: The Operations Division*, p. 78.

"Eventually," Kimmel wrote, "this war will require a much greater number of transports and supply ships in the Pacific. We are working on an estimate of the requirements. This estimate, in addition to some thirty or forty transports and an equal number of supply ships, must also include a thirty to fifty percent increase in the fighting strength of the Fleet before we can occupy the Marshalls and Carolines in an advance across the Pacific."[70]

Kimmel also commented apropos of protecting any air fields developed in Fiji and New Caledonia: "I fear we may become so much concerned with defensive roles that we may become unable to take the offensive. Too much diversion of effort for defense will leave us an inadequate force with which to take the offensive."[71]

This was not the writing of an officer who felt he had been warned that an attack on his fleet was just around the corner. This was an officer who had long-range offensive plans connected with a Far Eastern conflict in which he would participate after the British and Dutch had been thoroughly involved. WPL 46 anticipated a period of preparation that would last for at least six months.

As we indicated in Chapter 2, Stark was readying Kimmel to attack the Marshalls, once the Pacific war was in motion: "Execute an appropriate defensive deployment preparatory to carrying out the tasks assigned in WPL 46." In the same spirit the Army thought primarily of readying MacArthur to go to the aid of the British: "Should hostilities occur you will carry out the tasks assigned in revised Rainbow five which was delivered to you by General Brereton."

Before leaving the subject of theater warnings, we might take note here of a passage in a letter dated November 28 from Admiral Stark to President Roosevelt. The letter referred to Roosevelt's general agreement with the Marshall-Stark memo of November 27, and mentioned two "holes" that he wanted filled:

> Was glad you found such general concurrence with the paper Marshall and I sent to you. One of the holes we had plugged with the message I read you for Hart and Kimmel. The other with regard to specifically

[70] *Hearings*, Part 16, p. 2255.
[71] *Ibid.*, p. 2256.

defining an area we will work on in connection with the messages you requested be prepared.[72]

Written communication on these top-secret matters was naturally terse and, for us today, it is somewhat enigmatical. The first hole to have been plugged may have been the caution that Japan commit the first overt act. The original naval warning of the 27th had not contained any such directive. The second message sent out by Stark late on November 28 stated that

> WPL 52 [shooting orders for destroying hostile land, naval, or air forces in the Western Atlantic] is not applicable to Pacific area and will not be placed in effect in that area except as now in force in southeast Pacific sub area and Panama naval coastal frontier. Undertake no offensive action until Japan has committed an overt act. Be prepared to carry out tasks assigned in WPL 46 so far as they apply to Japan in case hostilities occur.[73]

The second hole "with regard to specifically defining an area" may have referred to a message that went to Admiral Hart several days later as a presidential directive, instructing him "as soon as possible" to send out "three small vessels to form a 'defensive information patrol.'" The message continued:

> Minimum requirements to establish identity as U.S. men-of-war are command by a naval officer and to mount a small gun and 1 machine gun would suffice. Filipino crews may be employed with minimum number naval ratings to accomplish purpose which is to observe and report by radio Japanese movements in west China Sea and Gulf of Siam. One vessel to be stationed between Camranh Bay and Cape St. Jacques and one vessel off Pointe de Camau.[74]

The message further authorized the use of the *Isabel* as one of the chartered vessels, and requested a report on all reconnaissance measures being regularly performed by the Army and Navy.[75]

[72] *Ibid.*, Part 20, p. 4487.
[73] *Ibid.*, Part 14, p. 1407.
[74] *Ibid.*
[75] Hart's reply, dated December 2, 1941, read: "My views are as follows: the Jap movement down the Indochinese coast is already defined but it remains to be seen whether aimed against the Malay Peninsula, Borneo, or both. That the British can meet their commitment to guard as far as Cape Padaran and we should use what have left after guarding against descent on Luzon in watching for one on Borneo. Am recalling Isabel from current mission and sending

This patrol had not been instituted by the morning of December 7. The instructions indicated, however, a genuine need for more specific information on Japanese movements off the Indochina coast in the direction of the Gulf of Siam. Admiral Stark's office was naturally keyed to news of Japanese naval movements, and normally such additional reconnaissance would have been at the discretion of Admiral Hart, whose Fleet Intelligence was one of the main sources for such information. But this was a presidential directive, and it has been suggested by some critics that a small American patrol boat, stationed in the path of advancing Japanese forces, might very well have triggered off the first shot of the Pacific war with a suitably small "incident," so that information and the first overt act by the Japanese could be radioed simultaneously to Hart. However, there was nothing in Stark's letter to suggest any other motive than to define more specifically the targets of the Japanese advance. He may have characterized it as a presidential directive only in order to indicate to Hart that he himself was satisfied with Hart's methods of reconnaissance. Langer and Gleason have suggested that the directive was in response to British pressure on the President for cooperation in patrolling the South China Sea and the Gulf of Siam, and their explanation seems the most plausible.

LAST-MINUTE DIPLOMACY AND LAST-MINUTE SIGNALS

While Army and Navy planners were busy revising their warning messages on the morning of November 27, Hull was conferring with his colleagues Hamilton, Hornbeck, and Ballantine on the conference projected for that afternoon between Roosevelt and the Japanese ambassadors. Stanley Hornbeck, Hull's chief adviser on Far Eastern affairs, was

---

toward Padaran. She is too short radius to accomplish much and since we have few fast ships her loss would be serious. Therefore have to recommend against carrying out Isabel's movement though it is improbable that can start any chartered craft within two days. Am searching for vessels for charter that are suitable but cannot yet estimate time required to obtain and equip with radio. Army planes are reconnoitering sector northerly from Luzon and eastward from San Bernardino. Navy planes northwesterly from Luzon, also covering Balabac Strait and joining up with Dutch to cover Mindanao-Halmahera line, effectiveness is problematical but as great effort as available forces can sustain continuously. Two cruisers, two desdivs [destroyer divisions] are deployed well south, remainder surface forces on local or repairing. . . ." (*Ibid.*, Part 6, p. 2670f.)

one of the most articulate exponents of the aid-China faction in the State Department. He

> was urging determination to act by force of arms. The Secretary was point-ing out that the Army felt it would not be ready for another three weeks, that the Navy wanted another three months. Hornbeck pointed out that the Navy had asked for six months last February and the Secretary, through his negotiations, had got them that six months. Now they wanted three more. Hornbeck's idea was that the President ought to stop asking the Navy, and tell it. The Secretary, rather wearily, passed it aside. . . .[76]

Hull continued to hope that somehow he might delay the anticipated explosion. On his advice, the President's conference became another round of polite evasions.

Hornbeck's enthusiasm for a firm U.S. stand against Japan—to the point of forcing the conflict—was based on two convictions: (1) that the Japanese wanted desperately to avoid war with the United States and (2) that if Japan did fight, the war would be short and would end in a complete and easy victory for the United States. A memorandum signed by him on November 27 proclaimed his confidence in terms of three ad-mirably precise wagers that will surely go down in history, along with the optimistic business forecasts of 1929, as a tribute to the chastening un-certainty of social affairs:

> In the opinion of the undersigned, the Japanese Government does not desire or intend or expect to have forthwith armed conflict with the United States. The Japanese Government, while launching new offensive operations at some point or points in the Far East, will endeavor to avoid attacking or being attacked by the United States. It therefore will not order or encourage action by its agents (foremost among which are its armed forces) which, if taken, would lead toward use by the United States of armed force by way of retaliation or resistance. So far as relations directly between the United States and Japan are concerned there is less reason today than there was a week ago for the United States to be apprehensive lest Japan make "war" on this country. Were it a matter of placing bets, the undersigned would give odds of five to one that the United States and Japan will not be at "war" on or before December 15 (the date by which General Gerow has affirmed that he would be "in the clear" so far as consummation of certain disposals of our forces is concerned); would wager three to one that the United States and Japan will not be at "war" on or before the 15th of January (i.e.,

[76] Berle, "Diaries."

7 weeks from now); would wager even money that the United States and Japan will not be at "war" on or before March 1 (a date more than 90 days from now, and after the period during which it has been estimated by our strategists that it would be to our advantage for us to have "time" for further preparation and disposals).... Stated briefly, the undersigned does not believe that this country is now on the immediate verge of "war" in the Pacific.[77]

Nothing could be more explicit. Such assumptions were typical of those held by advocates of immediate entry into war with Japan or of a progressively "tough" policy toward Japan. There is no record, unfortunately, to tell us whether Hornbeck's bets had any takers.

We have seen this same rosy optimism expressed in G-2 reports, and it was no doubt reinforced by the vociferous pro-China faction in the State Department and in Congress. Hornbeck's opinions were frequently equated by the military with State Department policy and were viewed with horror and alarm by the Joint Board of the Army and Navy. While it is true that Hornbeck held a position of authority on Far Eastern affairs, his views did not determine Hull's. It is easy to understand, however, how anyone holding Hornbeck's position would be deaf to the signals coming into the State Department during the first week in December.

A G-2 report of November 27 was the focus of another War Council meeting on November 28. This report had originated in the Far Eastern section and, as we shall see, it struck the one high note of alarm to come out of G-2 before December 7. To Stimson it "amounted to such a formidable statement of dangerous possibilities" that he took it into the President immediately, so that the President would have a chance to read it before the Council meeting at noon.[78]

Stimson recorded the discussion of this meeting in some detail. Besides the President and himself, Stark, Marshall, and Knox were present. Hull reviewed the November 26 note to Japan and emphasized his opinion that "the Japanese were likely to break out any time with new acts of conquest and that the matter of safeguarding our national security was in the hands of the Army and Navy . . . [and] that any plans for our military defense should include an assumption that the Japanese might make the element of surprise a central point in their strategy and also

[77] *Hearings*, Part 5, p. 2089.
[78] *Ibid.*, Part 11, p. 5435.

might attack at various points simultaneously with a view to demoralizing efforts of defense and of coordination."[79]

The meeting then turned to a consideration of the G-2 report:

> The main point of the paper was a study of what the expeditionary force, which we know has left Shanghai and is headed south, is going to do. G-2 pointed out that it might develop into an attack on the Philippines or a landing of further troops in Indochina, or an attack on Thailand or an attack on the Dutch Netherlands, or on Singapore. After the President had read these aloud, he pointed out that there was one more. It might, by attacking the Kra Isthmus, develop into an attack on Rangoon, which lies only a short distance beyond the Kra Isthmus and the taking of which by the Japanese would effectually stop the Burma Road at its beginning. This, I think, was a very good suggestion on his part and a very likely one. It was the consensus that the present move—that there was an expeditionary force on the sea of about 25,000 Japanese troops aimed for a landing somewhere—completely changed the situation when we last discussed whether or not we could address an ultimatum to Japan about moving the troops which she already had on land in Indochina. It was now the opinion of everyone that if this expedition was allowed to get around the southern point of Indochina and to go off and land in the Gulf of Siam, either at Bangkok or further west, it would be a terrific blow at all of the three Powers, Britain at Singapore, the Netherlands, and ourselves in the Philippines. It was the consensus of everybody that this must not be allowed. Then we discussed how to prevent it. It was agreed that if the Japanese got into the Isthmus of Kra, the British would fight. It was also agreed that if the British fought, we would have to fight. And it now seems clear that if this expedition was allowed to round the southern point of Indochina, this whole chain of disastrous events would be set on foot of going.[80]

Out of this discussion on how to prevent the Japanese expedition from landing in the Gulf of Siam there evolved the plan for the President to speak to Congress and at the same time to address a personal appeal or warning to the Emperor of Japan. Notice in the passage that follows that the Council explicitly rejected the notion of striking first. The Japanese were, of course, prepared for such a contingency, since they had reckoned their risks in purely military terms.

> It further became a consensus of views that rather than strike at the Force as it went by without any warning on the one hand, which we didn't think

79 *Ibid.*, Part 2, p. 440.
80 *Ibid.*, Part 11, p. 5435*f.*

we could do; or sitting still and allowing it to go on, on the other, which we didn't think we could do—that the only thing for us to do was to address it a warning that if it reached a certain place, or a certain line, or a certain point, we should have to fight. The President's mind evidently was running towards a special telegram from himself to the Emperor of Japan. This he had done with good results at the time of the Panay incident, but for many reasons this did not seem to me to be the right thing now, and I pointed them out to the President. In the first place, a letter to the Emperor of Japan could not be couched in terms which contained an explicit warning. One does not warn an Emperor. In the second place it would not indicate to the people of the United States what the real nature of the danger was. Consequently, I said there ought to be a message by the President to the people of the United States, and I thought that the best form of a message would be an address to Congress reporting the danger, reporting what we would have to do if the danger happened. The President accepted this idea of a message but he first thought of incorporating in it the terms of his letter to the Emperor. But again I pointed out that he could not publicize a letter to an Emperor in such a way; that he had better send his letter to the Emperor separate as one thing, and then make his speech to the Congress as a separate and a more understandable thing to the people of the United States. This was the final decision at that time, and the President asked Hull and Knox and myself to try to draft such papers.[81]

No record of this meeting mentioned the MAGIC deadline of November 29. Evidently it was not believed to be necessary to act on a warning to Japan before the deadline. Perhaps the receipt of the MAGIC message translated on November 28 that promised a reply to the American Ten Point Note in a few days prompted the conclusion that the Japanese would delay action until the presentation of their reply. Perhaps it had something to do with the way our naval experts were reckoning the sailing time of the Japanese convoys. At any rate, the time from Saturday, November 29, through the morning of December 6 was in good part devoted to drafts and redrafts of a message to Congress and a message to Emperor Hirohito. Stimson, Knox, Hull, and several of Hull's assistants worked on these.

Knox's draft, sent to the President when he was en route to Warm Springs, Georgia, on November 29, bore an accompanying note that "The

[81] *Ibid.*, p. 5436.

news this morning indicates that the Japs are going to deliberately stall for two or three days."[82]

The drafts of these messages made perfectly clear that no one of the authors thought of the deadline or the Japanese expedition or indeed any of the other dangerous possibilities as signaling an immediate direct attack on America or an American possession in the Pacific. True, an attack on the Philippines had been mentioned in the November 28 meeting. And Hull had been alarmed by reports of troop arrivals from Saigon, which the Netherlands minister brought to his attention later that day.[83] But the general assumption seems to have been that the troop shipments for Indochina were a preliminary step toward a later large-scale attack against British and Dutch possessions. The immediate objective would be something less likely to provoke the United States into action—an easier, safer target such as Thailand. In spite of Hull's warning, and their own verbal anticipations of simultaneous attack at various points in the Pacific, the members of the War Council were evidently convinced that Japanese strategists would reason as their American counterparts did. By this reasoning the Japanese did not have the capabilities to carry out a vast network of closely timed attacks in the South Pacific, and they had nothing to gain by immediately involving the United States in a war. Japan should first direct her aggressions at those territories for which the United States would not go to war, no matter with what extremity she might protest their violation, and a policy of gradual encroachment against America's allies would be far more embarrassing to the United States than a direct attack on an American possession.

It is this background that accounts for the tiresome phrasing and rephrasing of the history of Japanese aggressions. The problem was how to arouse the American public to so distant a danger as an attack, say, on the Kra Isthmus. How should we cancel the powerful isolationist argument that we ought not to send our boys overseas to defend British and Dutch imperial interests?

We could draw certain parallels between Hitler's strategy and Japan's, as Knox did; or like Stimson, we could point out how American interests

---

[82] *Ibid.*, Part 19, p. 3508.

[83] *Report of the Joint Committee on the Investigation of the Pearl Harbor Attack, and Additional Views of Mr. Keefe Together with Minority Views of Mr. Ferguson and Mr. Brewster*, p. 396. Hereafter cited as *Majority Report*.

in the Philippines and the Far East were closely involved with the preservation of the Dutch and British position there. But it all sounded dim and academic and there was little agreement in the State Department on where to ask the Japanese to stop. So the drafts simply said that America would have to resort to force and did not go on to say anything definite about where, or when, or how. Hornbeck finally said bluntly that he couldn't draft a message unless he knew what was going into it: was it peace, war, or what? Like everyone else who had had any part in the Japanese-American negotiations, he was "sick and unhappy and disgusted,"[84] and finally with Hull's approval he turned the job of drafting the messages over to Hull's assistant secretary, Adolf A. Berle, who, until that time, had had nothing to do with the Far Eastern picture.

That our principal interest was in delay, and furthermore that the President believed he still had some time, is evidenced by the fact that the message to the Emperor, though composed over the week end of November 29, was not dispatched until 9:00 P.M. on Saturday, December 6. The agenda contemplated after presentation of the message was as follows: The President would wait until Monday night for a reply. If he received no answer he would formally warn Japan on Tuesday afternoon or evening. This warning would be repeated by the British and other powers on Wednesday, but only after the President's warning had surely been delivered to Tokyo and to the Japanese ambassadors in Washington.[85] Evidently it was Hull who stood in the way of a sharp warning any earlier. He continued to mourn the fate of the *modus vivendi* and used his influence to postpone both a public statement to Congress and a message to the Emperor.

But it was not only Hull who was influential in postponing any definite action. There seems to have been a decided break in tension with Roosevelt's departure for Warm Springs on the afternoon of the 28th. MAGIC had indicated a few days of deliberate "stalling" by the Japanese. But more

[84] Berle, "Diaries."

[85] Based on a telegram, probably sent on December 6, from the Australian Minister for External Affairs to the Secretary of State for Dominion Affairs of the United Kingdom. (*Hearings*, Part 11, p. 5166.) The Australian Minister saw President Roosevelt late on Saturday afternoon. (Langer and Gleason, *The Undeclared War, 1940–1941*, p. 928.) The fact that the State Department has no record of this conversation is not unusual, since many of Roosevelt's negotiations were not recorded.

important, the news of the convoy off the coast of Formosa had been absorbed into the general picture of a buildup of troops in Indochina, Hainan, and Formosa, and now we had to wait to see in what directions the troops would move. Hull disappeared over the week end, and Stimson left town to go to his New York dentist the first part of the week.

During these last days our policymakers were occupied primarily with public opinion and the possibility of some desperate last-minute diplomatic remedies. Military details were in the hands of Marshall and Stark. The alerts had been sent, and there was no further discussion of theater warnings. Stimson's time, for example, in addition to that given to Japan, was taken up with a conference on the recent Carolina maneuvers; with discussion of possible action to be taken against the *Chicago Tribune*, which, on December 4, had published one of our most secret war estimates; and with the problem of getting more supplies and big bombers to the Philippines. At a much lower level of information and decisionmaking, there was discussion, between War Plans officers and Far Eastern intelligence experts, about the necessity for further warnings. Both Commander McCollum of ONI and Colonel Sadtler of Signal Intelligence submitted suggested drafts for additional warnings to the theaters. War Plans, however, regarded the November 27 and 28 messages as perfectly adequate, and interpreted the urgency of the Far Eastern experts as stemming from too close a view of MAGIC and too distant a knowledge of the policy level.

President Roosevelt had left for Warm Springs immediately after the War Council meeting on the 28th. He was careful to tell the press that the developing Far Eastern crisis might recall him at any moment. MAGIC on that day was reporting expressions of indignation from the Japanese ambassadors over our Note of the 26th, as well as the reaction of outrage from Tokyo. But it was not until the afternoon of the 30th that Hull telephoned the President and asked him to return in view of two new developments. First, the British ambassador had brought news of his government's having reliable information that the Japanese were about to attack Siam and that this attack would include a seaborne expedition against the Kra Isthmus. Second, Premier Tojo was reported to have released an aggressive statement to a public rally on November 30:

> The fact that Chiang Kai-shek is dancing to the tune of Britain, America, and communism at the expense of able-bodied and promising young men

in his futile resistance against Japan is only due to the desire of Britain and the United States to fish in the troubled waters of East Asia by pitting the East Asiatic peoples against each other, and to grasp the hegemony of East Asia. This is a stock in trade of Britain and the United States.

For the honor and pride of mankind we must purge this sort of practice from East Asia with a vengeance.[86]

Roosevelt returned on December 1, and before he arrived Hull had already talked to the Japanese ambassadors "with a good deal of bark and had given them the devil for what Japan was doing particularly in view of Tojo's statement and their moves in Indochina."[87] The President followed this with a formal request through the State Department to Tokyo asking the Japanese government for an explanation of why it was keeping a larger force in Indochina than had been agreed on with the Vichy government. (This was coincidental with a report from ONI on December 2 of there being twenty-one Japanese troop transports anchored in Camranh Bay.) The reply came on December 5, and explained that the reinforcements were simply a precautionary measure against Chinese troops in bordering Chinese territory. Neither Hull nor the Japanese were deceived by this counterpoint. In the meantime, MAGIC had brought news on December 3 of the order to the Japanese embassies in London, Hong Kong, Singapore, and Manila to destroy code books, as well as indications of the dismay of the ambassadors at the answer to be delivered to Roosevelt's inquiry. An intercept on the Tokyo-Berlin circuit also announced that war with the Anglo-Saxon nations would break sooner than anyone dreamed. Roosevelt requested a copy of this for his own files, in order to study it further.

On December 4, the Netherlands government suggested that Japan be warned not to cross the line between Davao and Waigeo in the direction of the Indies. Bangkok also appealed for an Anglo-American assurance that a Japanese invasion of Siam would meet with armed resistance. Neither of these suggestions drew a commitment from any U.S. representative, although England was more than willing, provided the United States would join her. ONI drew up a report for the President on Decem-

---

[86] *Hearings*, Part 2, p. 441. This is the official Domei News Agency translation, which was more alarmist than the Japanese original. The last phrase is more accurately rendered as "this sort of practice must be removed." (Butow, *Tojo and the Coming of the War*, p. 355.)

[87] Berle, "Diaries."

ber 5, estimating the Japanese forces in Indochina and adjacent areas. This report placed 105,000 Japanese troops in Indochina and strong concentrations of naval forces in Camranh Bay, Saigon, and the Hainan-Formosa area. Finally, on the morning of December 6, the news arrived from American officials in Singapore and from Admiral Hart that three Japanese convoys were rounding Cape Cambodia, believed to be heading for Koh Tron on the western coast of Indochina en route to Bangkok. The same news was wired to Washington from British air reconnaissance in Malaya by way of Ambassador Winant in London. His first message reached the State Department at 10:40 A.M., his second at 3 P.M.[88] At last "the whole chain of disastrous events" was under way.

None of the reports agreed about the size and composition of the three convoys, but it seemed that at least two of them were alarmingly large. It was also not clear whether they would proceed in a northwesterly direction up the coast of Siam or move westward toward Malaya.[89] Evidently the possibility of a landing in Siam caused greater concern in the White House than an anticipated attack on the British holding, since the image of an American public aroused to the defense of Siam was utterly inconceivable. Discussion on this point occupied part of the afternoon of December 6. The War, Navy, and State Departments hastily compiled, at the President's request, estimates of Japanese troops and equipment in Indochina, including the troops aboard the convoys; and the Navy Department was requested to pinpoint the location of all American naval craft in the Far East, as well as all vessels belonging to Japan and to our allies. It was against this background that the final MAGIC messages were received in the State Department and at the White House.

Once again what seems to have been the major cause for alarm was the movement of a Japanese convoy. Our policymakers and military leaders were certainly keyed to react to this sort of stimulus, and they did

---

[88] *Hearings*, Part 14, Exhibit 21, p. 1246*f.*, and Part 15, Exhibit 66, p. 1680*f.*

[89] Compare Lord Alanbrooke's account of the British Chiefs of Staff meeting on this point: "We examined situation carefully, but from the position of the transports it was not possible to tell whether they were going to Bangkok, to the Kra Peninsula, or whether they were just cruising round as a bluff"; quoted in Bryant, *The Turn of the Tide: A History of the War Years, 1939–1943, Based on the Diaries of Field-Marshal Lord Alanbrooke, Chief of the Imperial General Staff*, p. 225.

react, but unfortunately not much beyond the particular stimulus. Reviewing the incidents of this last week, one gets the impression that in dealing with the final Japanese moves, our leaders were impulsive, shortsighted, and heavily influenced by wishful thinking. These attitudes offer one plausible explanation for the drop in tension on the week end of the 29th. MAGIC indicated a few days of grace, some of the convoys put into port, and everyone's energies—with the exception of Secretary Hull's—were turned once more toward other, more immediately pressing, problems, and especially toward Europe and the Atlantic. The assumption was still, as Marshall had put it much earlier, "If we lose in the Atlantic, we lose everywhere." This meant that the Far East simply had to stay quiet. The power of this wish was certainly as effective in limiting the range of our Far Eastern policy as it was in delaying our response to the last-minute military signals.

There seems to be no doubt that with news of the advancing convoy on December 6, members of the War Council at any rate expected war to break between Britain and Japan. There is not much evidence to go on as to how this particular expectation affected the readings of the last-minute MAGIC messages. The only recorded reaction is that of the President. In the presence of Harry Hopkins and Lt. L. R. Schulz, after reading the first thirteen parts of the 14-part message, Roosevelt remarked: "This means war." By that cryptic statement he evidently meant war between Japan and the United States because the United States was going to support Great Britain, and not because Japan was going to attack the United States. Hopkins commented that it was a pity "we could not strike the first blow and prevent any sort of surprise." Roosevelt replied: "No, we can't do that. We are a democracy and a peaceful people. But we have a good record."[90]

The President then tried to get in touch with Admiral Stark by telephone, and, on learning that Stark was attending a performance of *The Student Prince*, decided against calling him out of the theater for fear of alarming the public. He reached Stark later that night, but there is no evidence as to the substance of their conversation.

According to Berle, Army Intelligence brought the same news to the State Department at 7:30 on Saturday evening. Berle described the first

[90] *Hearings*, Part 10, pp. 4661*ff*.

thirteen points as "not only a flat turn-down, but a coarse and gratuitous and insulting message as well. Bad as this was, the accompanying message, likewise intercepted, was worse. The Japanese envoys were to keep this message locked up in their safe and present it only on the receipt of a signal, and during this time the final dispositions were to be completed. In other words, they were to hold up delivering the answer until certain military dispositions were completed."[91] Secretary Hull therefore had the thirteen points and the pilot message on Saturday evening.

Berle's characterization of the first thirteen points as a "flat turn-down" is understandable if we realize that he believed our Ten Point Note to have embodied a "rather general plan for peace in the Pacific" rather than an "ultimatum" of any sort. Also his characterization was dictated the night of December 7, so he may have read into MAGIC some information not in the original messages. Berle had anticipated from the delay in the Japanese reply that "the démarche of Nov. 26 would not be successful." He had spent Saturday afternoon and evening working on Hull's proposed draft of the presidential message to Congress. On Sunday morning too, Berle and the Far Eastern advisers "fussed a little more with the message," and were discussing with Hull the time of presentation to Congress when the Japanese ambassador requested a 1 o'clock appointment with Secretary Hull.

Berle does not mention the fourteenth part of the Japanese reply or the time-of-delivery intercept, both of which were delivered to Hull on Sunday morning. These messages did not stand out then, as they do now, as separate urgent signals. Hull had been at work that morning with Secretaries Knox and Stimson on the message to Congress. Knox's draft came closer than any of the others to being a specific warning to Japan, though the first five points still seem remote from any feeling of imminent attack:

1. We are tied up inextricably with the British world situation.
2. The fall of Singapore and the loss to England of Malaya will automatically not only wreck her far eastern position but jeopardize her entire effort.
3. If the British lose their position the Dutch are almost certain to lose theirs.

91 Berle, "Diaries."

4. If both the British and the Dutch lose their positions we are almost certain to be next, being then practically Japanese surrounded.

5. If the above be accepted, then any serious threat to the British or the Dutch is a serious threat to the United States; or it might be stated any threat to any one of the three of us [is] a threat to all of us. We should therefore be ready jointly to act together and if such understanding has not already been reached, it should be reached immediately. Otherwise we may fall individually one at a time (or somebody may be left out on a limb).[92]

And finally,

6. I think the Japanese should be told that any movement in a direction that threatens the United States will be met by force. The President will want to reserve to himself just how to define this. The following are suggestions to shoot at: Any movement into Thailand; or any movement into Thailand west of 100 degrees east and south of 10 degrees north—this in accordance with the recommendation of the British and Dutch and United States military authorities in the Far East; or any movement against British, Dutch, United States, Free French, or Portuguese territory in the Pacific area.[93]

All the evidence would suggest that the attention of the President and his top advisers was centered on the most effective way to urge Congress that America should join with Great Britain in a war to stop further Japanese aggression. MAGIC did not add anything new to their expectations, because they were expecting an unfavorable reply to their note of November 26. Furthermore, there seems to have been nothing in MAGIC, or any other bit of information, that would have suggested any change in their conception of the most favorable strategy for Japan—namely, to pursue a course of expansion in Southeast Asia without coming into direct conflict with the United States. The premise of all discussion was the belief that Japan's next move would be either against the British or the Dutch, or against Thailand.

Six weeks after Pearl Harbor, Hopkins summarized his memories of Roosevelt's anxiety about the Far East, and his account has the accent of authenticity:

I recall talking to the President many times in the past year and it always disturbed him because he really thought that the tactics of the Japanese would be to avoid a conflict with us; that they would not attack either the

[92] *Hearings*, Part 11, p. 5440.
[93] *Ibid*.

Philippines or Hawaii but would move on Thailand, French Indochina, make further inroads on China itself and possibly attack the Malay Straits. He also thought they would attack Russia at an opportune moment. This would have left the President with the very difficult problem of protecting our interests.

He always realized that Japan would jump on us at an opportune moment and they would merely use the "one by one" technique of Germany. Hence his great relief at the method that Japan used. In spite of the disaster at Pearl Harbor and the blitz-warfare with the Japanese during the first few weeks, it completely solidified the American people and made the war upon Japan inevitable.[94]

Hopkins also set down some other interesting observations of the President on the Japanese-American negotiations.

The President told me about several talks with Hull relative to the loop-holes in our foreign policy in the Far East in so far as that concerned the circumstances on which the United States would go to war with Japan in event of certain eventualities. All of Hull's negotiations, while in general terms indicating that we wished to protect our rights in the Far East, would never envisage the tough answer to the problem that would have to be faced if Japan attacked, for instance, either Singapore or the Netherlands East Indies. The President felt it was a weakness in our policy that we could not be specific on that point. The President told me that he felt that an attack on the Netherlands East Indies should result in war with Japan and he told me that Hull always ducked that question.

I remember when I was in England in February, 1941, Eden, the Foreign Minister, asked me repeatedly what our country would do if Japan attacked Singapore or the Dutch, saying it was essential to their policy to know.

Of course, it was perfectly clear that neither the President nor Hull could give an adequate answer to the British on that point because the declaration of war is up to Congress and the isolationists and, indeed, a great part of the American people, would not be interested in a war in the Far East merely because Japan attacked the Dutch.

. . . .

Apropos of the Roberts report, which indicates that the State Department had given up all hope of coming to an agreement with Japan, it seems to me that hardly squares with the facts. It is true that Hull told the Secretaries of War and Navy that he believed Japan might attack at any moment. On the other hand, up to the very last day, he undoubtedly had hopes that something could be worked out at the last moment. Hull had always been willing to work out a deal with Japan. To be sure, it was the kind of a deal that Japan

[94] Sherwood, *Roosevelt and Hopkins: An Intimate History*, p. 428.

probably would not have accepted but, on the other hand, it was also the type of a deal which would have made us very unpopular in the Far East.

Hull wanted peace above everything, because he had set his heart on making an adjustment with the Japanese and had worked on it night and day for weeks. There was no question that up until the last ten days prior to the outbreak of war he was in hopes that some adjustment could be worked out.[95]

While all these civilian and military leaders awaited December 6 and 7 for news of the next Japanese move, the next piece of "deviltry," it is significant that their anxiety at no time produced a detailed discussion of alternative Japanese strategies. For example, could Japan risk striking at Great Britain without striking at the United States, in view of the Anglo-American alliance? This was a question that the Japanese Imperial Council had discussed at length before adopting the Pearl Harbor attack plan. It had received our attention earlier in 1941, but was not raised now.

A curious kind of numbness seemed to characterize these last moments of waiting, a numbness that was an understandable consequence of long association with signals of mounting danger. The signal picture had been increasingly ominous for some time, and now apparently it added up to something big, but not very definite. It was certainly compatible with the major premise that the Japanese would move next against an ally rather than against the United States directly. There was also a fundamental passivity connected with the avowed policy that the United States could not strike the first blow. The most compelling considerations for the White House on this last week end were how to act properly within the restraints imposed by Congress and the Constitution, and how to move American public opinion. Here on these domestic issues our expectations were centered and our skills were grounded.

CONCLUSIONS

The Washington material from the intelligence viewpoint may be summed up as follows:

(1) The Washington agencies had many more signals than the theaters concerning Japanese activities and intentions.

[95] *Ibid.*, p. 428*f*.

(2) They also had many more signals of American activities and intentions with respect to Japan.

(3) However, this pool of information on the Far East was not unambiguous. It contained a large number of conflicting signals. In particular, with respect to American moves, there was as much noise as there were significant sounds.

(4) Furthermore, no single agency or individual had access to the total mass of information on the Far East.

(5) The Far Eastern information was itself only a small part of a huge body of information that concerned primarily the activities and intentions of European countries. It was the latter, and especially the battle of the Atlantic, that engaged Washington's main attention.

(6) The Atlantic and European focus not only served to distract or lessen the attention that could be given to the Far East, it also resulted in the misreading of Far Eastern signals.

(7) Another important cause for misreading signals was the belief held by some American policymakers that the Pacific Fleet and the Philippines reinforcement were deterrents rather than threats.

(8) While theater intelligence agencies may have been better judges than Washington of the Far Eastern signals, it was simply not practicable to send to the theaters all the information available in Washington.

(9) The fact that this policy of selection resulted in 1941 in the denial of possibly useful information need not be explained by a conspiracy of silence. A less dramatic and more accurate assumption is that the military in Washington were not invariably good judges of what material would be most useful to the theaters. In any case, at the time of drafting the theater warnings, they did not anticipate or warn against an air raid on Pearl Harbor.

5 ▸ WASHINGTON INTELLIGENCE

Now that we have had a glimpse of the complex mass of signals available in Washington, D.C., it is pertinent to inquire what selection of this mass found its way to the central Army and Navy Intelligence agencies. What signals reached Intelligence first and were forwarded to our policymakers? What sorts of signals did Intelligence miss and for what reasons?

At the center of government, Army Intelligence found itself somewhat better informed and closer to operations than Naval Intelligence. But for the most part the role of these two agencies was sadly subordinate. Where they should have been a fountainhead of information, they were very often not even included on the distribution list. Where they should have been vital centers for processing and evaluating all kinds of information, they were either not allowed to evaluate, or their evaluations were seriously limited by uncritical acceptance of current operational hypotheses. The activities of collection and evaluation were also affected by the fact that neither Army nor Naval Intelligence considered its central function to be the detection of a surprise enemy attack. For Army Intelligence (G-2) the detection of subversive activity was the primary function. For Naval Intelligence (ONI) a listing of enemy capabilities was as close as an estimate could come to the delicate question of enemy intentions. Neither agency, therefore, made full use of its sources, and in particular, of its most valuable source, the decoded MAGIC intercepts. Army Intelligence tended to follow and report the desires of the Japanese Army, while the Office of Naval Intelligence followed the moves of the Japanese Navy. These two Japanese services happened to be seriously opposed during 1940 and 1941, with the Japanese Army favoring north-ward expansion, and the Japanese Navy a southward advance.[1] The aims of the two services were reconciled in the summer of 1941, when the Navy won the argument, but apparently news of the reconciliation did not register with our Intelligence services.

In this chapter we shall examine Army G-2 and the Office of Naval Intelligence in some detail. We begin with a look at the people who worked for these agencies to see what sort of experience was required for the job. Then we look at the information that they were able to collect and how they interpreted it.

MILITARY INTELLIGENCE

Structure and People

On December 7, 1941, Gen. Sherman Miles was Chief of Military Intelligence for the Army, with the title Assistant Chief of Staff, G-2. His training in intelligence work dated back to 1912, when he started serving as military attaché to five foreign countries, ending up in Russia during World War I. He also served as an officer attached to the American Peace Commission in 1919. Though his experience included no Far Eastern duty, he had served as Operations officer (G-3) of the Hawaiian Department from 1929 to 1932. From 1934 to 1938 he headed the Plans and Projects Section of the War Plans Division in Washington, and in this capacity he had supervised three overseas departments: the Philippines, Hawaii, and Panama. His duties as head of Army Intelligence began on May 1, 1940, and continued to January 30, 1942. General Miles, therefore, had behind him at least fifteen years of experience in relevant military areas to help him foresee the Pearl Harbor disaster.

During the early years of World War II, as we have already noted, the Army Intelligence Division was beginning to expand. The number of officers on its staff had risen from 22 on September 1, 1939, to 115 when Miles took office, with a projected minimum of 180 officers designed for July 1, 1941. An organization chart of the Washington Division dated October 10, 1941, listed 168 members.[2] According to Miles' testimony

[1] See p. 301.
[2] *Hearings*, Part 34, p. 140.

at the congressional hearings, he estimated the total personnel for MID in Washington to have been between 400 and 450 on December 7, 1941. (See Fig. 3.)

This is a respectably large number for a period when the country was still reluctant to make military appropriations, especially when we remember that it does not include the personnel in Signal Intelligence, who handled the technical processes of decoding and translating intercepted material. (The Signal Corps was quite independent of MID and reported directly to the Chief of Staff, but liaison between its Signal Intelligence Service and Colonel Bratton of MID was close and effective.)

In December, 1941, these 400 to 450 people in MID were organized into an Administrative branch, a Plans and Training branch, an Information Control branch, a Counterintelligence branch, and an Intelligence branch. It is this last branch that interests us primarily. Unfortunately the bearers of most of the names listed for the Intelligence branch in Fig. 3 were never called on, or never appeared, to testify about the events of December, 1941. The record, however, does contain some testimony by witnesses from the Far Eastern section, in particular by its section head, Col. Rufus S. Bratton.

Besides the personnel in Washington, there were military observers and military attachés overseas who were selected by and directly responsible to MID. The observers in the Far East were few (three in Singapore, one in Hong Kong); they were underpaid; and, as might be expected, their information was worth about what was paid for it.[3] MID had military attachés in Thailand, Singapore, Chungking, Hong Kong, Peking, and Tokyo; but the information obtained "on the military side" from the attaché in Tokyo was, as Miles testified, "very limited; the Japanese being extremely close-mouthed."[4] Most military information on Japan actually came out of China, Thailand, and Korea.

MID had no secret agents, though Miles said, "we had started a nucleus of what might be called a secret service under Colonel Clear in Singapore. We had little money to give him, but at least he did make progress tying in with the British Secret Service in the Far East."[5]

[3] Cf. Pettigrew's memo in *Hearings*, Part 18, p. 3439.
[4] *Hearings*, Part 27, p. 56.
[5] *Ibid.*, Part 2, p. 785.

Brig. Gen. Sherman Miles, *Acting Assistant Chief of Staff, G-2*

EXECUTIVE OFFICE

Col. Ralph C. Smith	Lt. Col. Thomas E. Roderick, *Assistant*
2d Lt. E. R. W. McCabe, Jr.	2d Lt. Warren S. Richards

ADMINISTRATIVE BRANCH
Col. Ralph C. Smith

INTELLIGENCE BRANCH
Col. Hayes A. Kroner

MILITARY ATTACHÉ SECTION
Lt. Col. John S. Winslow

American Military Attachés, Missions, Observers aboard, and Language Officers.

FOREIGN LIAISON SECTION
Lt. Col. Lawrence Higgins

Foreign Attachés, Missions, and Officials in the U.S.

COORDINATING SECTION
Lt. Col. B. B. McMahon

Certain special contacts.

FINANCE SECTION
Lt. Col. Robert B. Richards

Finance and property.

PERSONNEL SECTION
Capt. George F. Ashworth

Administration of commissioned officers in G-2, WDGS, and all MI-Reserve officers.

RECORD SECTION
1st Lt. Malcolm Hay, Jr.

Records and files.

TRANSLATION SECTION
Col. Ralph C. Smith

Translations and preparations of dictionaries.

CHIEF CLERK
John S. Calvert

Civilian personnel, classification and employment of applicants for civilian positions, miscellaneous correspondence of Division.

ADMINISTRATIVE SECTION
Lt. Col. M. W. Pettigrew

All administrative matters of Intelligence Branch, Personnel, Cables and Messages, Drafting, Stenographic Pool.

FIELD PERSONNEL SECTION
Capt. H. V. Rohrer

Handles selection of *places* (not personnel) for new observers and attachés. Training of Military Intelligence personnel.

SITUATION SECTION
Lt. Col. Thomas J. Betts

Charge of information bearing on the situation in all parts of world. The heart of the Intelligence Branch. Maintains situation maps both in G-2 and for the Secretary of War. All special studies, etc., emanate from here.

CONTACT SECTION
Col. Harry F. Cunningham

Contact with State, ONI, etc., for military information.

DISSEMINATION SECTION
Col. Fred J. deRohan

Boils down and reports into Tentative Lessons, Special Bulletins, etc., and distributes to service.

SOUTHERN EUROPEAN SECTION
(Formerly Balkans & Near East Section)
Lt. Col. Walton W. Cox

CENTRAL EUROPEAN SECTION
Col. Hamilton E. Maguire

EASTERN EUROPEAN SECTION
Lt. Col. G. B. Guenther

WESTERN EUROPEAN SECTION
Lt. Col. Louis J. Fortier

LATIN AMERICAN SECTION
Col. R. Townsend Heard

Caribbean
Col. E. M. Benitez

Mexican
Lt. Col. Harry M. Gwynn

Central American
Lt. Col. Stuart R. Carswell

West Coast S. America
1st Lt. T. H. Harrell

River Flats S. America
Maj. Wilson L. Townsend

Brazil
Lt. Col. William Sackville

Special Section
Capt. Bob N. Massengale

BRITISH EMPIRE SECTION
Lt. Col. L. J. Compton

FAR EASTERN SECTION
Col. Rufus S. Bratton

Japan
Lt. Col. Carlisle C. Dusenbury
Maj. Wallace H. Moore
2d Lt. J. Bayard Schindel

China
Maj. Frank N. Roberts
1st Lt. Julean Arnold, Jr.
2d Lt. Dwight Edwards

Southeast Asia and Philippine Islands
Maj. Homer A. Stebbins
Maj. Philip N. Taylor

Pacific Islands and Alaska
Maj. John W. Coulter
1st Lt. John B. Broaddus

AIR SECTION
Lt. Col. J. C. Hodgson

FIG. 3. MILITARY INTELLIGENCE DIVISION, WASHINGTON, 1941

COUNTERINTELLIGENCE BRANCH	PLANS AND TRAINING BRANCH	INFORMATION CONTROL BRANCH
Lt. Col. John T. B. Bissell	Lt. Col. Charles Y. Banfill	Maj. W. P. Corderman

COUNTERINTELLIGENCE BRANCH	PLANS AND TRAINING BRANCH	INFORMATION CONTROL BRANCH
ADMINISTRATIVE SECTION Lt. Col. W. A. Holbrook, Jr. General administrative duties for this Branch. Supervision of all activities and policies of the Counterintelligence Branch. **DOMESTIC INTELLIGENCE SECTION** Maj. David G. Erskine Subversive groups and activities. Evaluation of domestic situation. **INVESTIGATING SECTION** Maj. Nicholas S. Beckett Investigation, including personnel, disaffection, subversion, and sabotage within the military establishment. **PLANT INTELLIGENCE SECTION** Maj. W. E. Crist Securing, evaluating, and disseminating intelligence information covering industrial plants, communications, transportation, power and other facilities vital to the national defense program, including labor situation and espionage. Sabotage, strikes, labor agitation. Recommend action on application of aliens for employment in Air Corps or classified contracts. **SAFEGUARDING MILITARY INFORMATION SECTION** Lt. Col. Carter W. Clarke Policies, regulations, and supervisory measures relative to S.M.I. Liaison with Public Relations Bureau on releases. Signal intelligence—Passport control. Supervision of Military Attaché cryptographic security. **SPECIAL ASSIGNMENT SECTION** Capt. Frank B. Nosterman All activities not specifically assigned to other sections. **CORPS OF INTELLIGENCE POLICE SECTION** Capt. Henry Gordon Sheen Procurement and training CIP personnel and promulgation of regulations thereof.	**PLANS AND TRAINING SECTION** Maj. Walter A. Buck Coordination and supervision of all military intelligence activities in the Army. Coordination of G-2 contributions to mobilization and war plans. Review of tables of organization, mobilization plans, war plans, defense projects for G-2. Review of all regulations and manuals having a bearing on military intelligence. Preparation of MI manuals and MID Army Extension Courses not assigned to another agency. Allocation of Reserve intelligence training funds. **GEOGRAPHIC SECTION** Lt. Col. Patrick H. Timothy Formulation of plans and policies governing the collection and compilation of domestic and foreign maps and of geographic information. Procurement, reproduction, and distribution of maps. Preparation of Geographic Chapters of Intelligence Surveys by the research office of the Geographic Section. Guidance in the selection and preparation of maps and charts to accompany Intelligence Surveys. Coordination of Engineer and Air Corps mapping activities. Review of regulations and manuals pertaining to maps, map reading, and map making. Liaison with Federal mapping agencies. Representation on the Federal Board of Surveys and Maps.	Plans and regulations for National Information Control in collaboration with the Navy Department. Training of Information Control Personnel. Liaison with foreign Information Control Organizations. Liaison with other Government Departments on information control matters. **SPECIAL STUDY GROUP** Lt. Col. Percy G. Black

FIG. 3. *continued*

Miles spoke rather wistfully of the large amounts spent on espionage by Great Britain, Germany, and Japan, in contrast to the American practice; but he believed that the American people would not be willing to appropriate money for such a service. In any case, he implied, neither he nor President Roosevelt would approve of spying: "We kept above board."[6]

According to Miles, the most important source for information on Japan was Ambassador Grew's embassy in Tokyo and the reports that he sent to the State Department. These reports, to which Miles claimed he had access, "related almost exclusively to the state of mind of the Japanese people toward the war and their enmity toward the United States."[7] They included only "very indefinite and general" information about Japanese military and naval movements. In fact, on November 17, Ambassador Grew in a telegram to the Department of State had explicitly gone on record to the effect that his staff in Tokyo and his Japanese and American contacts could no longer be relied on to give warning of preparations for surprise attack:

> Referring to Embassy's previous telegram . . . of November 3 . . . emphasizing the need to guard against sudden Japanese naval or military actions in such areas as are not now involved in the Chinese theater of operations. I take into account the probability of the Japanese exploiting every possible tactical advantage, such as surprise and initiative. Accordingly you are advised of not placing the major responsibility in giving prior warning upon the Embassy staff, the naval and military attachés included, since in Japan there is extremely effective control over both primary and secondary military information. We would not expect to obtain any information in advance either from personal Japanese contacts or through the press; the observation of military movements is not possible by the few Americans remaining in the country, concentrated mostly in three cities (Tokyo, Yokohama, Kobe); and with American and other foreign shipping absent from adjacent waters the Japanese are assured of their ability to send without foreign observation their troop transports in various directions. Japanese troop concentrations were reported recently by American consuls in Manchuria and Formosa, while troop dispositions since last July's general mobilization have, according to all other indications available, been made with a view to enabling the carrying out of new operations on the shortest possible notice either in the Pacific southwest or in Siberia or in both.

[6] *Ibid.*, p. 899.
[7] *Ibid.*, Part 27, p. 57.

We are fully aware that our present most important duty perhaps is to detect any premonitory signs of naval or military operations likely in areas mentioned above and every precaution is being taken to guard against surprise. The Embassy's field of naval or military observation is restricted almost literally to what could be seen with the naked eye, and this is negligible. Therefore you are advised, from an abundance of caution, to discount as much as possible the likelihood of our ability to give substantial warning.[8]

Another source for information on Japan and the Far East were the attachés and observers of allied missions in Washington, especially the British. British and Dutch intelligence also released some information to MID, though Miles stresses that they did so reluctantly. His most valuable secret source was MAGIC. There was also some exchange of confidential information with the State Department in Washington. An officer from MID was appointed to maintain contact with the State Department, and during 1940 and 1941 this was done by four successive officers.

"In addition to that," Miles testified, "I personally knew several of the Assistant Secretaries of State and the Under Secretary of State, and at least two or three times went, at his request, to the office of the Secretary of State on intelligence matters."[9] This might be expected to mean that Miles was constantly informed of the progress of negotiations with the Japanese from the American point of view. Actually his information on the negotiations came primarily from the Japanese accounts in MAGIC. Colonel Bratton was more realistic when he said: "It took what I thought was an unreasonably long time for us to get any type of intelligence out of the State Department."[10] In fact, it came more quickly by way of Tokyo.

"With the Navy Department," Miles testified further, "the same liaison existed [as with the State Department], but more in detail. In other words, officers from my Far Eastern Section visited many times a week, perhaps many times a day certain days, the corresponding officers of the office of Naval Intelligence."[11] Miles himself was in constant touch with Captain Wilkinson, the head of ONI. Colonel Bratton was in frequent communication with Commander McCollum, the Naval Intelligence expert on the Far East.

Another source of information might have been the G-2 staffs of overseas departments such as Hawaii. However, these staffs were selected by

[8] *Ibid.*, p. 58.
[10] *Ibid.*, Part 9, p. 4570.
[9] *Ibid.*, Part 2, p. 785.
[11] *Ibid.*, Part 2, p. 785.

their local commanding officers and were responsible only to them. As Miles put it, the relation between Washington G-2 and the overseas G-2's was one of "liaison" only. Exchange of information was entirely a matter of routine or courtesy.

Washington G-2 was most chary of sending out any information that might possibly have been considered "operational" or that might have been construed as a "directive." In Chapter 2 we noted this distinction between "active" and "static" information, and the fact that G-2 estimates for the Chief of Staff contained "active" information and did not go to the overseas G-2's. Since MAGIC, of course, also contained "active" information, even if security had not so dictated, it could not have been sent to the theaters by any G-2 officer. Furthermore the overseas G-2's were under no obligation to acknowledge receipt of the "basic," or "static," information that they did get. As Senator Lucas summed it up, "whatever information you sent to G-2 in Hawaii, as far as the command there is concerned, they could completely ignore and you would have no way of knowing whether they acted intelligently on it or not."[12] General Miles protested, but could only qualify this statement by saying, "that depended on the regulations or policies of the Hawaiian staff, as to how they wanted to use that information."[13] The same was true for information coming out of the theaters to Washington G-2. The local G-2's were under no obligation to send any.

This example within one branch of the Army illustrates how unreliable and how unproductive of information an informal liaison can be. The same can be said for Army-Navy liaison in general during 1941, though there were plenty of testimonials from both services that nothing more cordial and intimate could have been desired. As we noted in the discussion of MAGIC, Miles said repeatedly: "There was a long-standing agreement or policy of complete interchange of information between the Army and the Navy."[14] This was held to be true not only for Washington, but also for all the overseas departments.

The appearance of close-knit communications was of course a shield erected partly for the public, more particularly for inquisitive congressmen.

[12] *Ibid.*, p. 884.
[13] *Ibid.*
[14] *Ibid.*, p. 896.

In spite of the familiar interservice rivalries, an immense loyalty tends to hold the Army and Navy together when they are faced by the common enemy. There is also a normal instinct for self-preservation at work. Intelligence officers, for example, might have been expected to claim that they had close liaison with all the departments within their own service, or else admit to failure in one important aspect of their jobs. And since their reputations depend partly on knowing their way around the various nonmilitary government agencies, it would be surprising if they did not testify in public that they were also privy to these sources of information.

Unfortunately, however, the appearance was frequently taken for the reality by the services themselves, and the testimonials very often mirrored beliefs that did determine action. Colonel Bratton "was told on innumerable occasions by my opposite number in ONI that they were giving all this stuff to the Army" in Hawaii.[15] For this reason he did not jeopardize our codes by sending a separate duplicate message to the Army theater commands about the December 3 order from Tokyo to destroy Japanese codes. He had also been assured that "when the emergency arises the fleet is not going to be there," that is, in the harbor, and that all this espionage on ships in harbor is "a waste of time and effort on the part of the Japanese consul."[16] So Bratton did not waste his time worrying about such Japanese requests to Honolulu: "Nobody in ONI, nobody in G-2, knew that any major element of the fleet was in Pearl Harbor on Sunday morning the 7th of December. We had all thought that they had gone to sea. . . . Because that was part of the war plan, and they had been given a war warning."[17]

Belief in a close liaison, which was utterly unfounded in fact, also characterized Miles' assumption that Admiral Kimmel would show all his messages from Washington to General Short, even though the messages did not carry an explicit directive for him to do so. Miles had lots of company in this belief, including General Short. His own attempts at improving communications in Washington should have undermined this optimism.

[15] *Ibid.*, Part 9, p. 4541.
[16] *Ibid.*, p. 4534.
[17] *Ibid.*

One of the most interesting insights into the way that communication between the services actually functioned is provided by the attempts to form a Joint Intelligence Committee. G-2 and ONI were apparently attempting to mend the break in the link of communications between Intelligence and Operations.

According to Miles' testimony he met with Captain Kirk, then head of ONI, in July of 1941, and they both appeared before the Joint Army and Navy Board on July 16 to present a proposal for integrating Intelligence more closely with the agencies that determined policy. They recommended either that the Chiefs of Naval and Military Intelligence be made members of the Joint Board, or that they be made members of the Joint Planning Committee, which was the committee serving the Board, or that a Joint Intelligence Committee coequal with the Joint Planning Committee be established. The Joint Board recommended that a Joint Intelligence Committee be formed. This committee held its first meeting on October 11, but it did not actually begin to function until the 8th or 9th of December.[18]

The first question that occurs is why there was the delay in meeting between October 11 and December 8. General Miles, under questioning, said that they could not meet without General Gerow's permission. (General Gerow was head of the War Plans Department of the Army.) However, it seems that General Gerow was not really the bottleneck. General Miles finally produced a memorandum from Col. L. L. Montague, formerly secretary to the Joint Intelligence Committee, that revealed:

> There are in the file rough drafts of [papers] . . . by General Gerow and Admiral Turner respectively. These papers indicate a controversy between them as to the scope of the functions of the proposed J.A.N.I.C. [Joint Army-Navy Intelligence Committee].
> General Gerow wished the committee to collate, analyze and interpret information with its implications, to estimate hostile capabilities and probable intentions. Admiral Turner wished to limit it to presentation of such factual evidence as might be available, but to make no estimate or other form of prediction. . . . Admiral Turner won.[19]

18 *Ibid.*, Part 2, p. 786.
19 *Ibid.*, p. 911.

Within his own service, Admiral Turner had already won this argument with respect to ONI. The memo went on to point to another bureaucratic delaying device that was just as effective as a theoretical difference about the scope of intelligence:

> The Joint Army-Navy Intelligence Committee was not fully activated until 1941 because until then the head of the foreign branch office of Naval Intelligence was unable to obtain agreement within the Navy Department as to the office space to be provided. Except for this difficulty the committee might have been activated by the first of December.[20]

General Miles had a further scheme for opening up avenues of information. Beginning in April, 1941, he started to discuss ways and means of establishing liaison with the nine cabinet departments, including the War Department; finally in September he obtained written approval for establishing within each department an office specifically designed for disseminating information to other departments and within each department.[21] Whether this setup actually started to function or whether it simply ended with some signatures of approval is not clear. In any case, if it started to function in September, it did not result in any great harvest of information for MID. General Miles had a better relationship with Army War Plans than his opposite number in the Navy had with Naval War Plans, but he was often not informed directly or immediately of important policy decisions or of action taken upon the intelligence information available. "I . . . never did know," he testified, "what the Secretary of State or the President was saying to the Secretary of War or the Chief of Staff."[22]

Under Senator Ferguson's insistent and aggressive questioning, Miles was made to seem a fool, completely left out of everything. However, if he was uninformed, the responsibility did not lie with him. In private rather than public communications he showed himself aware of the need for a close relationship between Operations and Intelligence. His efforts were expended in a commendable direction; unfortunately they were consistently blocked.

[20] *Ibid.*
[21] *Ibid.*, p. 786*f*.
[22] *Ibid.*, p. 967.

Functions

What was Washington's conception of the duties and functions of the Military Intelligence Division in 1941? According to Army Regulations (1940), MID had the following general duties[23]:

The Military Intelligence Division is charged, in general, with those duties of the War Department General Staff which relate to the collection, evaluation and dissemination of military information.

The MID is specifically charged with the preparation of plans and policies and the supervision of all activities concerning—

1. Military topographical surveys and maps, including their acquisition, reproduction and distribution (except special situation maps prepared by G-3).

2. The custody of the War Department map collection.

3. Military attachés, observers and foreign-language students.

4. Intelligence personnel of all units.

5. Liaison with other intelligence agencies of the Government and with duly accredited foreign military attachés and missions.

6. Codes and ciphers.

7. Translations.

8. [crossed out]

9. Censorship in time of war.

10. Safeguarding of military information.

Supplementing this description in his testimony, Miles said: "Military intelligence was specifically concerned, particularly concerned, and practically solely concerned so far as the General Staff went with anti-subversive precautions and operations."[24] He later amended this under questioning to include some other duties, such as reporting "from time to time as to the situation of the armies throughout the world as viewed in the eyes of the Army, and what the enemy was doing."[25] This amendment brought his view of military intelligence somewhat closer to the definition offered by Senator Ferguson, who believed that an intelligence agency should be operated primarily to "determine when war might come" and "where war might come," and to determine "the strength that the prospective enemy might have to pursue this."[26] Miles allowed these as estimable goals, but in reality, he said, they were far beyond the fondest hopes or ability of his agency to realize: "I do not think any Intelligence

[23]*Ibid.*, Part 14, p. 1419.   [24]*Ibid.*, Part 2, p. 829.
[25]*Ibid.*, p. 905.   [26]*Ibid.*, Part 7, p. 3184.

officer ever thought that he could be sure of picking up a convoy or attack force or task force in Japan before it sailed and know where it was going. That was beyond our terms of efficiency."[27] General Russell asked, had "The G-2 people . . . eliminated investigations in Japan proper and other Japanese territory to determine probable action on the part of the Japanese Army and Navy?" Miles replied: "We had not eliminated it. As Mr. Grew says, it was the principal task of the Embassy, particularly of the military and naval part of the Embassy. What I say is just what Mr. Grew says, that we never dreamed that we could rely on getting that information. It would have been almost a military intelligence miracle had we been able to spot a task force in forming and have known before it sailed where it was going."[28]

In terms of responsibility Miles based his action on the first definition we have quoted—that of MID as an antisubversive agency. When he insisted on extra directives to Honolulu, it was to reinforce or to clarify the precautions against sabotage. As he explained in some detail:

> In the summer of 1939 the President issued a directive to all bureaus . . . to keep out of anti-sabotage and anti-espionage work, except three that were to do it all, FBI, ONI, and MID. After I took MID in May of 1940, I began to build up the counter-intelligence part of it . . . . by the summer of 1941 I had gotten myself into a position where it was definitely established that counter-subversive activity of all kinds was G-2's responsibility and solely G-2's responsibility. I shared the responsibility for measures against an effort to attack by a possible enemy with Operations and with War Plans, because I was supposed to give information on which their orders were based. But I shared with nobody the responsibility for counter-subversive measures.[29]

It was therefore countersubversive measures that occupied Miles' attention. A secondary activity of his agency was the collection and evaluation of information on the enemy's intentions to attack from without. The amount of emphasis to be given this activity was determined by the head of G-2, and his attitude was bound to have an effect on the collection effort. This may explain some of the deficiencies in estimating foreign policy that we found to be characteristic of G-2 in our study of the earlier alerts.

[27] *Ibid.*, Part 27, p. 62.
[28] *Ibid.*
[29] *Ibid.*, p. 66.

Late MID Estimates

Let us take a look at the material that MID had collected on Japan and the Far East just before the surprise attack and see to what uses it was put. An obvious starting point is the series of estimates for the Chief of Staff that came out over the signature of Sherman Miles between November 1 and December 6. Government practice being what it is, it is probable that Miles had nothing to do with their composition. It is not even certain that he read all of them. However, they were issued by his office and they represent certain major hypotheses of MID at the time.

The memos for the first half of November were concerned with weighing the evidence for the likelihood of a Japanese drive into Yunnan Province to cut off the Burma Road supply line to China. Chiang Kai-shek himself, his ambassador, and the aid-China advocates in the State Department were all pressing hard for an official U.S. protest against such action, as well as for direct aid to China in the form of American aircraft. The War and Navy Departments naturally took the line that direct aid might very well involve the United States immediately in war with Japan, an objective that they regarded as highly undesirable. They also viewed with alarm the possibility of further warnings to Japan unless they could be backed up by military force. The Army again went on record to say that it needed more time to complete its preparations in the Philippines, and the Navy again reminded the White House that the Pacific Fleet had been reduced, rather than increased, during 1941.

This background of War Department policy was probably influential in determining the tone and content of the MID estimates for November 1 and November 13 on the likelihood of a Japanese invasion of Yunnan. They pointed out in considerable detail the difficulties of the terrain, the fact that Japan was already overextended in China, and that at the then-current rate of Japanese troop reinforcement in Indochina, she would need from one to three months to prepare an invading force. If the Army wanted more time, this estimate provided it with at least a month. The only firm prediction, however, had the familiar ring of the tautology: "The rate of Japanese advance on Kunming . . . will depend on the degree of Chinese resistance. . . ." At the same time, if the Japanese did advance, both memos acknowledged that such a move would be unfortunate: "A Japanese offensive into Yunnan from Indo-China would be an extremely difficult operation but if it were successful in closing the supply route from Burma it would be a serious blow to China's power and will to resist."[30]

A more general MID estimate of November 2 recalled the phrasing of most of the memos written since the July Embargo Act. Our Far Eastern economic policy was still regarded as the prime deterrent to war with Japan. Japan, it was confidently assumed, wished to avoid armed conflict with the ABD (American-British-Dutch) powers. She was "militarily over-extended on the mainland of Asia, economically weak, and psychologically aware of the fact that her economic structure is crumbling." Therefore her "most probable line of action . . . will be to continue her efforts to secure a relaxation of American economic pressure, while completing her plans and arranging her forces for an advance in the direction which will be most fruitful of quick results."[31] What this direction would be was not stated in the body of the memo, but a number of possible directions were positively ruled out. The Japanese would not attack Siberia, Singapore, Thailand, the Philippines, Hong Kong, the Netherlands East Indies, or Yunnan. At least not "at present."

This commitment did not extend very far into the future, but it *was* definite. It was still guided by the optimism that had characterized the October predictions of MID and that, we remember, was based on the Army belief in the deterrent effect of U.S. embargoes and the program to reinforce the Philippines. This optimism remained, with one exception (in the estimate of November 27), the dominant note of the last five weeks of peacetime analysis. The main difference between the October and November estimates was simply that the Siberian front did not receive as much attention. There was a larger amount of evidence listed in November pointing to activity in Southeast Asia.

After the report of November 13 about Yunnan, nothing is recorded until November 25 and 26. On these dates scattered signals began to filter into MID from the Office of Naval Intelligence: an increase in Japanese air and surface patrols over U.S. shipping routes to Australia, an increase in troop movements into Hainan and Indochina, and strong naval forces gathering in preparation for operations off Southeast Asia and off

---

[30] *Ibid.*, Part 14, p. 1362.
[31] *Ibid.*, p. 1363.

Palau and the Marshalls. In particular, a cable from Shanghai to ONI on November 21 reported:

> Intense activity at Woosung since the 15th. Unusual number of ships present including former merchant craft of 10,000 tons and up. Wednesday 10 transports sailed, eight of which carried troops. Same day 32 additional ships, similar type, anchored in lower Whangpoo. Landing boats included in outgoing equipment. . . .[32]

G-2 commented: "Movement of troops from Central China believed directed toward Hainan and Indo-China. No evidences of heavy concentration on Taiwan (Formosa)."[33] (Stimson had been sent this report on the afternoon of November 25. He sent it immediately to President Roosevelt, but for some reason the message never arrived. He informed the President of the news over the telephone the next day, whereupon the President "fairly blew up." This report was to become a significant signal in the State Department and the White House.)

In compiling and expanding on some of this information in an over-all estimate of the Far Eastern situation on November 27, MID sounded a note of alarm:

> . . . it appears evident that the Japanese have completed plans for further aggressive moves in Southeastern Asia. These plans will probably be put into effect soon after the armed services feel that the Kurusu mission is a definite failure. A task force of about five divisions, supported by appropriate air and naval units has been assembled for the execution of these plans. This force is now enroute southward to an as yet undetermined rendezvous.
>
> This Division is of the opinion that the initial move will be made against Thailand from the sea and overland through Southern Indochina. It is further believed that the Japanese are uncertain of the reaction of the ABD powers to this move and therefore have organized in sufficient strength to cope with any opposition they might initially encounter from those powers in the South China Sea.[34]

This last paragraph was certainly not consistent with the belief that had prevailed until this time that Japan wanted at all costs to avoid war with the ABD powers. There was a real feeling of the imminence of a clash between Japan and the United States or Great Britain or the

[32] *Ibid.*, p. 1365.
[33] *Ibid.*
[34] *Ibid.*, p. 1368.

Netherlands. This estimate may have been written with some knowledge of the theater warning messages of the same day, and the evidence listed had a cumulative effect of great urgency.

The memo of November 27 started with the least alarming news, that between eighteen and twenty-four infantry divisions and eight armored brigades from the Russian Far Eastern Army had been identified on the western front. This reduction in Russian forces might mean an increase in the "possibility of a Kwantung Army offensive thrust against Siberia," although "such a move is not believed imminent at present."[35] The rest of the evidence concerned Japanese movements: 24,000 troops withdrawn from North and Central China and dispatched on transports from a port near Shanghai; a naval task force organized at Taiwan and Hainan on its way to an unknown concentration point; Japanese land forces in the Mandates increased in the previous six months from 5000 to 15,000; British reports of Japanese aerial reconnaissance over British Pacific Islands and North Malaya; reports from Bangkok and North French Indochina indicating that Japanese Foreign Office officials expected an outbreak of hostilities in the near future; Japanese troops then in Indochina numbering at least 70,000, with aircraft totaling 157; large quantities of equipment imported in excess of current needs (here the report gave number and types of tanks, guns, cars, gas masks, boats, etc.); on the island of Hainan, 50,000 troops; "a reliable source reported on November 25 . . . Japanese plans for an invasion of Thailand about December 1, including seizure of Isthmus of Kra; . . . up to the evening of November 26, the Japanese Ambassador had been unable to make the Secretary of State yield to Japanese proposals and demands and in consequence the Japanese hopes for an appeasing settlement by the United States are very slim"[36]; and finally evidence that the Japanese were prepared to use chemical and bacteriological warfare. It is interesting that the one comment about our State Department should have been made from the Japanese point of view, with only the word "appeasing" to indicate the American viewpoint. This is probably explained by the fact that most of MID's information on State Department policy came from the decoded material sent to Tokyo by the Japanese ambassadors in Washington.

[35] *Ibid.*, p. 1366.
[36] *Ibid.*, p. 1367.

The estimates of November 29 and December 5 did not have this same urgency. They considered the four theaters of war—Atlantic, Eastern (Russian), Middle Eastern, and Far Eastern—and concluded that the Allied powers had four months in which "neither the anti-Axis nor the Axis powers can force a decision": The "anti-Axis powers will have a period of at least four months in which they may strengthen their position in one or more of the four important theaters of war, and in which they may decide upon a regrouping of forces, subject to certain physical limitations, consonant with their chosen long range strategy for the defeat of the Nazis."[37]

In the Far Eastern theater, according to these last reports, the initiative rested with Japan: She "has a multiplicity of strategic objectives; but for a variety of reasons, she cannot concentrate the required forces to attack any of them on a large scale and with assurance of success. A possible exception to the latter statement lies in the contingency of a serious depletion of Russian forces in Eastern Siberia."[38] The objectives were listed as follows[39]:

a. Attack Siberia.

b. Attack Yunnan Province to cut the Burma Road with a view to an early end to the war with China.

c. Occupy Thailand.

d. Through Thailand, attack

1) Burma and the Burma Road.

2) Malaya.

e. Attack the Philippines and Hong Kong, preparatory to a movement on Singapore or the Netherlands East Indies.

f. Contain or isolate the Philippines and Hong Kong and

1) Attack Singapore

a) Directly by sea.

b) In conjunction with a land attack through Thailand and Malaya.

2) Attack the Netherlands East Indies.

g. Bide her time, wait for a better opportunity to pursue any of the above lines of action, hoping that the course of events will turn in her favor.

[37] *Ibid.*, p. 1374.
[38] *Ibid.*
[39] *Ibid.*, p. 1371*f.*

h. Seek a general settlement through American mediation, including an understanding with the United States and Great Britain as to political and economic penetration of southeast Asia and the southwestern Pacific.

i. Reorient her whole foreign policy by withdrawing from the Axis.

Examining these alternatives, MID recognized that (h) and (i) were impossible, short of a complete overthrow of Japan's governing forces. It decided that "the most probable line of action for Japan is the occupation of Thailand." On the role of the United States, it repeated the comforting and now-familiar slogan that "Our influence in the Far Eastern Theater lies in the threat of our Naval Power and the effort of our economic blockade. Both are primary deterrents against Japanese all-out entry in the war as an Axis partner. If we become involved in war with Japan we could launch a serious offensive against her by Naval and Air Forces based on the Philippines and elsewhere in Malaysia."[40]

Elaborating the Japanese analysis in a supporting estimate on December 5, MID pictured a Japan torn between Axis and Allied ties. It was most definitely not the picture of a country on the verge of war with the United States, or even with Great Britain. We quote this analysis at length since it is the last MID statement of any weight reproduced in the *Hearings*:

The Tripartite Pact which Japan signed with Germany and Italy in September, 1940, by implication requires Japan to attack the United States, or any other power, except Russia, not involved in the European war at that time, should it attack either of the Axis partners. The strong Russian resistance to Nazi attack has, however, been a damper to Japanese enthusiasm for her Axis obligations. Although Foreign Minister Togo, who succeeded Toyoda, has announced that there is no change in the foreign policy of Japan, and that Japan will adhere to the Axis alliance, there is evidence that in order to secure a better position for herself, *she might disregard her obligations, and even withdraw from the Axis.* Japan has boundless ambitions in East Asia, but in view of the increasing American and British strength in the Far East, and the continued stalemate in China, she finds herself in a more and more unfavorable strategic position to realize these ambitions. Japanese government leaders are aware of the perils of further military adventures; *they want to avoid a general war in the Pacific.* They wish by every means possi-

[40] *Ibid.*, p. 1378.

ble to inveigle the United States into an agreement "looking toward a peaceful settlement of all outstanding issues between the two countries." This simply means recognition of Japan's territorial and economic gains in Eastern Asia. The result of these conflicting desires is a state of almost desperate indecision. The fact that Japanese newspapers have come out with their most bombastic bluster during the beginning of Mr. Kurusu's conference seeking a peaceful settlement with this country is the best indication of the lack of coordination, the indecision, and the confused general political situation in Japan. There can be no doubt that the army hotheads, the Black Dragon Society, and other intransigents will oppose most strenuously any major concessions by their present government leaders. Thus the chief obstacle to successful negotiations by Mr. Kurusu or any other envoy has been the fact that although Premier Tojo is an army man, he cannot be said to control the army, the navy, or the ultranationalistic secret societies. Until such control is assured, no agreements through negotiations can be successfully carried out. The Kurusu conference can now be said definitely to have ended in failure because of the extreme position taken by the Japanese Government in regard to concessions which they felt could be made in the Far Eastern area.

Without their previous enthusiasm and behind uncertain leadership, the Japanese are continuing in the path as to what they believe is their divinely appointed destiny without being sure as to where that destiny will take them. As a matter of fact, there is evidence that the people of Japan are becoming more and more alarmed and apprehensive; they fear that the present course is taking them into a major war with not just one power, but with a combination of powers. In her present situation, if Japan goes to war, her people will enter it desperately rather than confidently [author's italics].[41]

What is the explanation for the striking difference in content between the memos of November 27 and 29? Perhaps the lapse of two days actually caused a relaxation of tension. It is more likely, however, especially in view of other evidence concerning MID's level of information, that there were two sets of writers at work. The November 29 memo was entitled a "Brief Periodic Estimate of the Situation, December 1, 1941–March 31, 1942," whereas the November 27 memo belonged to a series entitled "Recent Developments in the Far East." In the three-month estimates it is common to find large sections of prose taken verbatim from the text of the preceding estimate, with only an occasional insertion or deletion. Such composition acquires a kind of life of its own; it resists

[41] *Ibid.*, p. 1381*f.*

the addition of up-to-the-minute material, particularly if that material is of a radically different nature so as to change the basic hypotheses of the text. The November 27 material would have changed the whole text, because if its reasoning were correct—that Japan would start a war in the Pacific as soon as the Kurusu mission was definitely known to be a failure —then the time had arrived and it would have been utterly inconceivable that Japan would withdraw from the Axis, or that the Allied powers would have four months' time for maneuvering.

The November 27 estimate may have come out of the Far Eastern section with very little change. As Miles testified, this section "consistently rated higher for many, many months the probability of war with Japan than did the Intelligence Branch of the Division or myself. They would have been less than human and certainly less than efficient if they had not."[42] The Far Eastern estimates, however, usually were tempered as they passed through the estimating section and then through the head of the Intelligence branch to Miles: "Now, immediately they got out of the far-eastern section they got into the much bigger picture that we were considering in those days, watching a very desperate war in Europe that seemed to hold possibilities of direct threat to the security of the United States and the whole of the activities of Latin America."[43]

Whatever the reason may have been, the existence of such inconsistencies within one agency at the time of final publication must give rise to some doubts as to the agency's value as an adviser.

These MID estimates, especially those concerning the Far East, had as one important secret source the decoded MAGIC dispatches from Tokyo to Washington and to other Japanese foreign embassies. Miles repeatedly testified that his estimating always took the MAGIC dispatches into account. He and Bratton, the head of the Far Eastern section of MID, were the only ones in Army Intelligence who were privileged to see MAGIC. There is no evidence in the estimates themselves, however, that any of this secret material was actually used except in the estimate of November 27, where two items could be traced directly to MAGIC: the Thailand intrigue and the failure of the U.S.-Japanese negotiations. There were no peaks of alarm in the other estimates to correspond to the peaks in the MAGIC

[42] *Ibid.*, Part 2, p. 817.
[43] *Ibid.*

dispatches. The notices of a November 25 deadline and then of a November 29 deadline, the November 28 prediction of a break in U.S.-Japanese relations, the December 3 orders to destroy major Japanese codes in all the important embassies, the earlier winds-code instructions and the establishment of the hidden-word code, the December 1 message to the Japanese ambassador in Berlin to tell Hitler and Ribbentrop "that there is extreme danger that war may suddenly break out between the Anglo-Saxon nations and Japan through some clash of arms and . . . that the time of the breaking out of this war may come quicker than anyone dreams"—none of these items were anywhere reflected in MID publications. MAGIC appears to have provided only a steady undercurrent of background suspense—like a muted score of the *William Tell Overture* in a Western movie—while knowledge of the existence of this source provided a comfortable feeling that Miles had his finger right on the Japanese pulse.

One can conclude that it is rather unlikely that new matter upsetting previous hypotheses will find its way into a periodic intelligence estimate without a significant time lag. Or one can conclude that these particular analysts had neither the time nor the ability properly to evaluate the MAGIC material. Probably there is some truth in both of these statements —with the one exception of Colonel Bratton's Far Eastern section. We have already mentioned the fact that nobody ever saw the MAGIC messages except for a rapid reading. Most of the writing in MID was done by people of low rank who didn't see MAGIC at all. Miles and Bratton did see it, but except for Bratton, Army recipients of MAGIC held some rather simple formulas about Japanese psychology. It was recognized, of course, that the Japanese were tricky, and that their words could not be trusted. This was believed to apply even to the words they addressed in secret to their own agents. For this reason, the threats and alarms conveyed to the Japanese negotiators, and the notices of deadlines for the termination of their work, were always taken, as Marshall put it, "with a grain of salt."

A similar formula for Japanese espionage, that it was unnecessarily refined and involved endless detail for detail's sake, made it possible for Intelligence experts in both services to ignore Japanese requests to their

Honolulu agents for details on the entry and exit and berthing in harbor of American ships in Pearl Harbor.

Primarily, however, the inefficiency in the use of MAGIC stemmed from the fact that Far Eastern problems seemed much less compelling than Atlantic and European ones. Moreover, Army Intelligence was more interested in the Japanese Army than in the Japanese Navy. Consequently it faithfully followed and reported the traditional desire of the Japanese Army for a Siberian campaign, even after the Army had agreed to the Navy's program of expansion to the south. As we have seen, MID continued to list Siberia high among Japan's objectives as late as November 29. The Far Eastern problems also appeared after July 30 against the background of optimism about the healthy effect on Japanese aggression of the U.S. embargo policy and Philippine defense program. This optimism characterized the entire War Department, and in MID it was reinforced by a focus on counterintelligence rather than attack from without.

Let us look in particular at the way in which this context affected Miles' handling of raw intelligence material. Take, for example, the series of espionage messages that were distributed in the MAGIC folders, including the famous September 24 message dividing Pearl Harbor into five areas. Miles' first reaction was that they were naval messages and therefore of no concern to MID. It was therefore the duty of ONI to evaluate these messages and take action on them.[44] Miles was of course "more interested in the fact that the Japanese were following our ships in our own waters, Panama, Hawaii, and the Philippines"[45] than in what they were tracing in the Dutch East Indies and other places in the Far East. However, his interest was "general"; no "special treatment" was accorded this material and no consideration was given to any precautionary measures against attack at these outposts. According to Miles, there was no way of studying these messages except to look at what they said, and since they said much the same thing about all the places involved, they simply added up to the picture of a detailed and efficient Japanese espionage agency.

[44]*Ibid.*, pp. 859*ff.*
[45]*Ibid.*

Senator Lucas in the course of his questioning of Miles tried to bring out the point that a message from Foreign Minister Togo in Tokyo to Honolulu might have required more analysis or attention than a message from an unknown agent in Honolulu to Tokyo, or that many directives from Tokyo to Honolulu and only one directive from Tokyo to the Panama Canal might have indicated that Tokyo was more interested in Pearl Harbor than in the Canal. Miles denied that any meaning might be attached to this sort of analysis.[46] Similarly he could not see how the place of interception might throw any light on a message.[47]

Miles' rejection of a naval message from the signal picture can be explained in terms of the familiar practice of buck-passing. Or it might be explained by the rivalry between Intelligence agencies about spheres of interest or investigation. Certain material was felt to *belong* to one service rather than another. So Miles may have refrained from any active use of naval material for fear of running into conflict with naval interpretations. Whatever the reason, he did not seriously consider these messages at any time in terms of attack from without. Furthermore his rejection of any kind of formal analysis indicates a mind very much at ease with current War Department interpretations. A willingness to play with material from different angles and in the context of unpopular as well as popular hypotheses is an essential ingredient of a good detective, whether the end is the solution of a crime or an intelligence estimate. This sort of flexibility is probably not good for one's reputation as a sound estimator, since one index to sound judgment is agreement with the hypotheses on which current department policy is based. But intelligence will always be confronted with this choice: whether to be popular or alert.

Information received from British intelligence fell into the same general context in MID. On November 9, for example, a code radiogram from London to G-2 reported:

> The most likely spot where Japanese may be expected to strike is in the Netherlands East Indies. This opinion, from the British Ambassador to Tokyo, holds that as Japan already controls what she needs of the resources of French Indo-China and Thailand she will not proceed against the latter country. To attack British Malaya would be a difficult operation and the rumored Burma Road drive would also be too much of an effort. The Nether-

46 *Ibid.*, p. 891.
47 *Ibid.*, p. 962.

lands East Indies could be assaulted secretly from the Mandated Islands, and would provide the oil which Japan needs. The source reverses his previous view and now believes Japan no longer feels that she must make every effort to avoid war with the United States and this contemplated operation would confront the United States and the British with an accomplished fact.[48]

G-2's comment revealed the same steadfast optimism as that expressed in its November estimates:

> G-2 is of the opinion that while an attack on the Netherlands East Indies is a possibility, it is by no means probable in view of: (1) the action to be expected of the United States and Britain before *even a surprise attack* could be driven home: (2) *the great danger to Japan of trying to by-pass the Philippines and Singapore*: (3) *the knowledge Japanese must have* that the Dutch have prepared their oil installations for immediate demolition, so that it would be a year or more before they could get the oil anyway [author's italics].[49]

G-2's comment on the British ambassador's changing to a more pessimistic belief was that "It is significant that the Ambassador has reversed his former view and no longer believes that Japan will do everything possible to prevent war with the United States. Such a development is not unexpected."[50] This comment was cryptic, but if it had any meaning at all it seemed to say: "Interesting, but how like the British."

The only other piece of information from British intelligence that was recorded in the *Hearings* was a long code radiogram of November 21 that presented "the consensus of all British intelligence services as to Japan, on the basis of all information available up to November 18."[51] The conclusions of the British estimate seemed to agree pretty much with the MID memo of November 29 in selecting Thailand as the "first probable [Japanese] objective involving least risk of major conflict."[52] The tone of the British estimate, however, was much closer to the urgency of the November 27 memo out of Bratton's Far Eastern section: "It is not certain," the British Joint Intelligence summary read, "that Japan has reached a decision to risk conflict with Britain and

---

[48] *Ibid.*, Part 16, p. 2140*f*.

[49] *Ibid.*, p. 2141. The Japanese took care of this contingency by dropping paratroopers who prevented the "immediate demolition."

[50] *Ibid.*

[51] *Ibid.*

[52] *Ibid.*, p. 2143.

U.S.A., but events are driving her to early decision. Japan hopes that present conversations in Washington may provide a way out. The climax of the conversations now reached by Kurusu's arrival and fundamental decision of policy is likely to follow their outcome."[53]

G-2 made no recorded comment on this radiogram, but it seems reasonable to suppose that British urgency, like Bratton's, was tempered as it went through the MID mill. We can gauge the difference between the British and American intelligence estimates for the last part of November by comparing their comments on Japanese troop reinforcements in Indochina. On November 21 American Military Intelligence in Manila forwarded estimates of the increase to MID in Washington, while British intelligence forwarded the same to a British representative in Honolulu.[54] The British report concluded that "Japan envisages early hostilities with Britain and U.S. Japan does not repeat not intend to attack Russia at present but will act in South."[55] The officers concerned in MID, on the other hand, looking at both Manila and Shanghai signals, felt that "unless we receive other information, this is more or less a normal movement, that is, a logical follow-up of their [Japan's] previous notification to the Vichy Government."[56] This opinion of G-2 appeared in a memorandum for the President from the Secretary of War, dated November 26, a date that came uncomfortably close to the announcement of Japan's deadline of November 29.[57]

For MID's use of other MAGIC signals, such as the code burning, we have to rely primarily on Miles' testimony, since Bratton's reactions to Far Eastern events were not the norm for MID as a whole. Let us compare Miles' reconstruction of his estimates for mid-November and December 1, the testimony on his reaction to the last-minute signals, and the action taken by his office in the first week of December. Again we see illustrated the fact that a warning signal is not likely to be heard if its occurrence is regarded as so improbable that no one is listening.

---

[53] *Ibid.*

[54] *Ibid.*, Part 35, p. 203 (Clausen Exhibit), and *Majority Report*, p. 142.

[55] *Majority Report*, p. 142.

[56] *Hearings*, Part 5, p. 2081.

[57] *Ibid.*, Part 20, p. 4476. President Roosevelt "fairly blew up" when he heard about this. Stimson also sent Roosevelt the British estimate of November 21.

Miles summarized his estimate for mid-November in this way:

One thing we felt sure of was that Japan faced a crisis which would almost certainly result in radical action on her part. She had been unsuccessful in her military venture against Russia in 1939 and she had been none too successful in her long and costly war against China. Her military clique was losing face, although gaining power. We were closing in on her economically in our embargoes and other measures, but her radical action might take one or more of many forms. She might give direct aid to her Axis partners by an attack on Russia. She might seek further outlet to the South by a seizure, under some camouflage, of the Dutch East Indies. She might go for the wealth of Hong Kong and the Federated Malay States, or Thailand, or Burma. She might further increase her war efforts against China....

. . . .

Lastly, Japan might add to the enormous burden [of] her already strained military resources by attacking simultaneously the two great naval powers of the world. Only the latter alternative would surely involve the United States. I doubted whether, at that time, we would have gone to war in defense of the Dutch, the Siamese, or even the British in the Far East, and certainly not the Chinese or the Russians.[58]

Miles recalled his estimate for the first week in December as follows:

The crisis that resulted in General Marshall's telegram of November 27 certainly indicated that the possibility of a war between the United States and Japan had very much increased.

By the 3rd of December, when we knew that they were burning their codes, one would have rated that possibility, now well within the realms of probability, now even higher, so that if you are asking me on December 7 I am quite sure in saying that I would have rated quite highly the probability of an involvement immediate, or certainly in the fairly near future, of a Japanese-American war.

I remember on the 6th of December saying goodbye to an old naval friend of mine, Admiral Kincaid, who was leaving to take command of his division of cruisers, and telling him that I hoped he would hurry because I did not know whether he would make it or not.[59]

These estimates were both reconstructions after the event. Even with the benefit of hindsight, the "involvement ... in the fairly near future, of a Japanese-American war" was vague. It did not specify, any more than MAGIC had done, whether the United States or Japan would strike

[58] *Ibid.*, Part 2, p. 817.
[59] *Ibid.*, p. 817f.

the first blow, nor did it specify whether Miles leaned more to a theory of gradual involvement after Japan had struck one of our allies or to a theory of direct Japanese attack on the United States. In the earlier Army hearing he had been equally impartial:

> I thought that very definitely some action by Japan, a pretty radical action, would be taken almost at once but that need not necessarily be an overt and open attack on the United States. . . . There were a good many things Japan could have done if she broke her negotiations in Washington short of open war with the United States; and we were considering all of those possibilities.[60]

During the ten days before the attack Miles had the following information. Though he had not participated in the formulation of either the November 5 or the November 27 memo from Stark and Marshall to the President, he was generally aware that "it was the desire of the War Department Chief of Staff, Secretary of War, that we obtain as much time as possible to increase particularly the forces in the Philippines."[61] He knew the general background of the November 27 warning message —the alarm over the convoy off the coast of Formosa—even though he did not share that alarm. Presumably he had read his Far Eastern section's compilation of danger signals on November 27. He also had some knowledge about the closing of the negotiations. By November 29 he knew through MAGIC that "certain Japanese officials regarded our message of November 26 as a last word or ultimatum in the diplomatic negotiations in Washington."[62] A MAGIC message translated on November 28 had recorded the Japanese ambassadors' shocked reaction to the Ten Point Note: " . . . we were both dumbfounded and said we could not even cooperate to the extent of reporting this to Tokyo."[63] Through MAGIC he also learned some of the last-minute diplomatic details.

It is important to remember that Miles had never been consulted about the *modus vivendi*. He did not know about it or about the Ten Point Note until after Hull's decisions had been made.[64] It was not the custom either to consult him or inform him on State Department matters. (This was clearly illustrated at the time of the imposition of embargoes when *The New York Times* had wind of the news before MID.) However, Miles

---

[60]*Ibid.*, p. 970.   [61]*Ibid.*, p. 805.
[62]*Ibid.*, p. 943.   [63]*Ibid.*, Part 12, p. 182.
[64]*Ibid.*, Part 2, p. 801*f*.

did keep in close touch with General Gerow, the head of War Plans, for Gerow depended on Miles for his intelligence evaluations. It was probably through Gerow, in connection with the theater warnings, that Miles heard on the 27th about Hull's loss of hope in the Japanese-American negotiations. He did not get any notice from the State Department, and he did not attend the Army staff conference of November 26, which met at 10:40 A.M., or the Joint Army-Navy Board meeting at 11:35 A.M.

Miles testified that he had no part in drafting the November 27 warning,[65] though according to General Gerow, he did. Miles said he knew the general content and found it inadequate for alerting his overseas G-2's to the danger of sabotage, and for that reason he sent out to them the additional warning on November 27: "Japanese negotiations have come to practical stalemate stop Hostilities may ensue stop Subversive activities may be expected stop Inform commanding general and Chief of Staff only." He had General Gerow's approval for sending this, since it was compatible with the Marshall warning of the same day. Miles also participated in drafting a similar and more detailed follow-up message on sabotage with General Arnold on November 28.

On the 28th MAGIC brought Miles news of the winds-code setup. He and Bratton made their special arrangements for 24-hour monitoring for this message. November 29, the day of the Japanese deadline, came and went. News of the Japanese buildup in Indochina continued to come in from Manila. On December 2, a report estimated that since November 10, six Japanese divisions (100,000 men) had landed at Haiphong, a port in Northern Indochina, and that the figures had been taken from ship manifests. G-2 accepted these figures "with reserve," commenting that it was "Doubtful that Japanese transports . . . could be checked as indicated," and pointing out that the number was "almost three times the unloading capacity of the port." However, G-2 suggested that the landing might have been made in Southern Indochina and estimated the total number of troops in Indochina then to number 105,000.[66] This conservative estimate itself was alarming.

Miles' next important piece of information was the December 3 MAGIC order from Tokyo to destroy codes. His Far Eastern expert, Colonel

[65] *Ibid.*, p. 829.
[66] *Ibid.*, Part 5, pp. 2079–2081.

Bratton, on receipt of this notice, immediately sent one of his young officers to the Japanese embassy, "to find out if they were burning any papers in their back yard, and he came back and reported . . . that they were."[67] On the same day Bratton and Miles took the precaution of ordering military attachés and observers in the Far East to destroy most of their codes.[68]

On December 5, there was a flurry of excitement in Bratton's office over the reception of a possible winds-code execute. Bratton believed at the time that an authentic execute had been received indicating a Japanese-British break in diplomatic relations. He drafted and sent the message to Honolulu G-2 to contact Rochefort for Tokyo weather broadcasts. Whatever the original motivation may have been, Bratton testified that he did so in order to get Colonel Fielder and Commander Rochefort together, since he had been informed by his opposite number in the Navy, Commander McCollum, that "Rochefort knew everything that we did in Washington."[69] Miles' memory of the incident was dim.

Still another message was drawn up in MID on December 5 for dispatch to the Panama Canal. It was not marked "priority" or "urgent," so it was not sent out until December 7. The routine sending of this message, as well as its content, seems to reflect the usual Army tendency to tone down the alarm of official warnings. The message read: "U.S.-Japanese relations strained. Will inform you if and when severance of diplomatic relations imminent."[70] The last sentence certainly implied that severance was not imminent at that date and suggests that perhaps the Japanese ruse to continue the appearance of negotiating had been partially successful.

On December 6, MID drew up an estimate for the Chief of Staff on Japanese strength in Indochina.[71] This estimate reported 125,000 Japanese troops in the theater (25,000 in the north, 82,000 in the south, and an estimated 18,000 on ships in harbor, specifically on board twenty-one transports in Camranh Bay); 50,000 on Hainan; and 40,000 on Formosa. Other troops, number unknown, were reported en route toward Indochina,

[67] *Ibid.*, Part 9, p. 4576.   [68] *Ibid.*, Part 14, p. 1409.
[69] *Ibid.*, Part 9, p. 4596.   [70] *Ibid.*, p. 4579.
[71] *Ibid.*, Part 14, p. 1384.

south of Shanghai. This report had been requested by the Chief of Staff for the White House.

It was against this general background that Miles received the last-minute signals. He was dining with his wife at the home of Captain Wilkinson, head of the Office of Naval Intelligence, when Kramer brought by his last MAGIC delivery for Saturday, December 6, around 10:30 P.M. At this time Miles read the first thirteen parts of the 14-part message. Earlier in the afternoon he had seen the pilot message announcing the arrival of the fourteen parts. "These 13 parts," he testified at the congressional hearings, "had little military significance. They concluded only with a Japanese refusal to accept the American proposal of November 26 as a basis of negotiations—a result which had been expected and discounted by that time."[72] Later Miles added:

> We were thoroughly prepared and had been for some days to receive an unfavorable reply to the message of November 26. . . . we had received a message and decoded it from Tokyo to the Japanese Ambassador in Washington directing him to put this Japanese reply in the safe when he received it and wait for further instructions on delivery.[73]

So Miles was not particularly alarmed. He directed Colonel Bratton to hold delivery of the thirteen parts until the fourteenth part came in and then deliver the entire message to General Marshall on Sunday morning: "There was no reason for alerting or waking up the Chief of Staff . . . or certainly Secretary Hull, on the night of December 6 that I could see."[74] However, "when we got the 14th part we saw quite a different picture, when we got the 1:00 P.M. message we saw quite a different picture. . . ."[75]

With the receipt of these two final MAGIC signals on Sunday morning, Miles evidently went into action to the extent of trying to get General Gerow of War Plans to meet with General Marshall and himself about sending out an additional warning to the theaters. He seems to have been spurred into action primarily by the last-minute urgency of Colonel Bratton.

Bratton had had no sharp reaction to the fourteenth part of the long Japanese message. This sort of conclusion had been anticipated, and he

[72]*Ibid.*, Part 2, p. 925. [73]*Ibid.*, p. 940.
[74]*Ibid.*, p. 942. [75]*Ibid.*

had already (on December 5) done all he could to make clear to War Plans that he would interpret a break in negotiations to mean that Japan would go to war with the United States. As Bratton pointed out quite correctly, it was important that the fourteenth part had finally arrived and that it did *not* contain a new Japanese counterproposal. But "there was no military significance to its presence in Washington as long as the Japanese Ambassador kept it locked up in his safe."[76] That was the instruction of the pilot message.

About 9 A.M. on Sunday, or shortly before that time, Bratton received a copy of the 1 o'clock message, and his reaction was immediate and "frenzied." He was convinced that it meant "an attack on an American installation in the Pacific" at this hour or very close to it, and he dropped all other duties to contact first General Marshall and General Gerow, both of whom had the authority to send out another warning message, and then General Miles. He reached General Miles around 10 o'clock, but through a series of accidents and delays, he was unable to give the message to General Marshall until the general reached his office at 11:25 that morning. One of the most harrowing scenes of that Sunday was the spectacle of General Marshall absorbed in reading the 14-part message, while Bratton and Miles stood beside his desk, unable to interrupt him. Bratton evidently made one unsuccessful attempt to secure Marshall's attention. When Marshall finally did see the 1 o'clock delivery message, after he had read the entire 14-part message, his reaction was as swift and sure as Bratton's, and it took only a few minutes to draft and dispatch a further alert to the theaters. That final alert, as everyone knows, arrived hours after the attack.

There were other last-minute signals available in Washington, but only one of them reached MID. It was telephoned on December 6 from ONI to G-2 for the attention of Maj. W. A. Holbrook, Jr., of Counterintelligence "to the effect that the Japanese Embassy in Washington, D.C., was reliably reported to have burned a code book and ciphers last night."[77] This information evidently remained in Counterintelligence and was not referred to the Far Eastern section.

[76] *Ibid.*, Part 9, p. 4529.
[77] *Ibid.*, Part 8, p. 4053.

A most important signal that did not reach MID was the information cabled on December 6 from Ambassador Winant in London and also from Admiral Hart to the State, Navy, and War Departments, on the movement of two large convoys en route to Kra. Whether the receipt of these additional signals would have made much difference in MID estimates is doubtful. After the event, Miles and Bratton regarded them as merely confirmatory of existing hypotheses.

Miles' actions certainly showed a commendably high degree of alertness to sabotage. He was much less alert to attack from without, because such alertness was not his major responsibility. Certainly he, like the rest of the Army, felt that war was "on the horizon." "The Army in those days . . ." he testified, "was intensely busy in building itself and training and maneuvering and so forth, and I would not say the Army as a whole were much concerned as to where war was going to break if they could get their troops ready before the break."[78] Miles evidently shared this belief, that the start of the war was not so important as the ability to get in there and fight after the outbreak. His job was simply to see that we didn't lose by sabotage a lot of equipment that should go into the fighting effort.

Colonel Bratton, on the other hand, with his special knowledge and interest in the Far East and his close acquaintance with MAGIC, was alerted to signals of attack from without. His interpretation of the 1 o'clock message depended first on the fact that the disagreeable 14-part message was coming out of the safe; second that it was to be delivered on Sunday, a most unusual day for diplomatic discussion; third that it was to go if possible directly to Secretary Hull; and fourth that it was to be presented at a particular hour of the day. Instruction for presentation at a particular hour had never been received before. We must remember that Bratton also believed at this time that an authentic execute of the winds code had been received on the 5th, indicating an early break with Great Britain, and he knew enough about U.S. military conversations with the Dutch and British to assume further that such a break must also mean a break with the United States. There is a good deal of evidence that Bratton, Colonel Sadtler of SIS, and Commander McCollum of ONI did try on December 5

[78] *Ibid.*, Part 27, p. 69.

to communicate their more urgent interpretations directly to the chiefs of Army and Navy War Plans. But their efforts were unsuccessful because of the poor repute associated with Intelligence, inferior rank, and the province of the specialist, or long-hair. General Gerow, for example, felt that "enemy information of such grave moment would be brought to my attention . . . by the Assistant Chief of Staff, G-2, and not by a Signal Corps Officer."[79] What delicacy, we wonder, prevented him from saying "a mere Signal Corps officer"?

It is true that Bratton, Sadtler, and McCollum were experts, and in general it is healthy to assemble and compare the opinions of experts and place them in a larger world perspective. Unfortunately for Bratton, that larger world perspective could not be contained within Miles' agency as Miles conceived its functions. Whatever realism might have emerged from the Far Eastern section was lost in the competition with the European theater, the hopes for the Philippines, and the central anxiety about sabotage.

NAVAL INTELLIGENCE

Structure and People

On December 7, 1941, Capt. T. S. Wilkinson was head of the Office of Naval Intelligence in Washington. He had been top man in his class (1909), and already had behind him a distinguished record in active service. He was familiar with fleet problems in the Hawaiian area, since he had served with the Hawaiian detachment operating off Hawaii from October, 1939, to May, 1941. During this period, as Chief of Staff to Vice Adm. Adolphus Andrews, he had had some experience in war planning and perhaps, therefore, some acquaintance with predicting enemy intentions. Still one might characterize his training for the office of Chief of Naval Intelligence as rather limited. His previous work in intelligence had been, according to his own statement, attendance at two international conferences on disarmament in 1933 and 1934, and he professed himself to have been surprised at his appointment as head of ONI. He took office on October 15, 1941, which meant that he had less than two months of peace in which to get his bearings.

[79] *Ibid.*, Part 35, p. 92.

Wilkinson was the third naval officer to head ONI during 1941. His immediate predecessor, Capt. Alan G. Kirk, had served from March 1 to October 15. Before Kirk, Capt. Jules James had served for two months, and during 1940 Adm. Walter S. Anderson had held the post. This is a rather rapid turnover for a key job, and there seems to have been no effort to offset the turnover by a careful preparation of candidates for the position. Wilkinson spent only a few days learning about the operation of the office as a whole, and he spent "several hours, perhaps a day" in the Far Eastern section, talking to its chief, Commander McCollum, and to Captain Kirk.[80] He was not shown any MAGIC messages that had come in before he took office. He was not told that MAGIC had been sent to Hawaii in July or at any other time, nor was he ever informed of the separate efforts of Layton and Kimmel to get more information based on the intercepts and more information on U.S. policy. Wilkinson learned only that the existing practice with respect to disseminating MAGIC was one of very tight security. Even granting Wilkinson's evident mental acuity and considerable naval experience, it would be surprising if between October 15 and December 7 he could have become very adept at interpreting the specialized Far Eastern material or very well acquainted with the intelligence needs of the operating forces. The rapid succession of officers occupying the position of Chief and the very perfunctory briefings for the job suggest the inferior role of this office in 1941.[81]

The Office of Naval Intelligence at this time had three main branches: administrative, domestic, and foreign. (See Fig. 4.[82]) Domestic Intelligence was concerned primarily with espionage and counterespionage. The Foreign Intelligence branch was divided into seven geographic sections, of which the Far Eastern was one. Captain W. A. Heard headed the Foreign Intelligence branch and Commander McCollum headed the Far Eastern section. McCollum was an expert Japanese linguist, with many years of service in the Far East and two years as assistant naval attaché

[80] *Ibid.*, Part 4, p. 1736.

[81] Vice Admiral Harry Sanders counters that the length and type of briefings are no measure of the importance of a job, and apparently it was not naval practice to require this sort of preparation. However, there appears to be universal agreement that the prestige of the Office of Naval Intelligence was extremely low.

[82] ONI did not release a chart of its divisions and personnel to the congressional investigating committee. Some naval officers suggest that the organization at this date was rather rudimentary and had not been charted. Figure 4 is based on the testimony of naval witnesses.

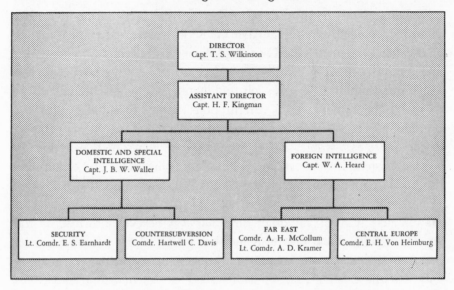

FIG. 4. OFFICE OF NAVAL INTELLIGENCE, WASHINGTON, 1941

in Tokyo. He had headed the Far Eastern Division of ONI from 1933 to 1935 and had returned as head again in September, 1939. He was highly qualified for his post, and evidently Wilkinson respected and trusted his judgment implicitly. McCollum was assisted by two officers, one a Japanese linguist and the other a Chinese specialist, and by four civilian experts on Far Eastern affairs.

The personnel for the entire Office of Naval Intelligence in Washington at the beginning of December, 1941, numbered 230 officers, 175 enlisted men, and 300 civilians. In the naval districts there were about 1000 men in all, of which 10 per cent were civilians. In the foreign posts there were 133 officers and 200 enlisted men who were serving as naval attachés and observers. The naval attachés were located at foreign capitals and the naval observers at main foreign ports. There were 17 observers in the Far East.[83]

Wilkinson testified that he obtained his information "in large part" from these naval attachés and observers. The reports of Fleet Intelligence officers and naval radio units also contained a good deal of information

[83] *Hearings*, Part 4, p. 1846.

relevant for estimating enemy capabilities and movements. Honolulu's two officers, Commander Rochefort of the 14th District Radio Communications unit, and Commander Layton, the Pacific Fleet Intelligence officer, forwarded their material to Washington, and Wilkinson's office received it by way of the Office of Naval Communications and the Office of the Chief of Naval Operations.

Information collected by Intelligence officers assigned to the various naval districts concerned only local espionage, and it was not a part of a district officer's duties to report to Washington. He was "an aide on the staff of the Commandant of the District . . . [and] his command relationships were direct to the Commandant."[84] This command relationship did not seriously impair ONI's use of the district offices to secure information on the activities of local foreign populations, but the district offices were not responsible for, or interested in, collecting material relevant for estimating the probability of an attack from without. According to his own testimony, Captain Mayfield, the 14th District Intelligence officer in Honolulu, had given no thought to this sort of problem.

Within the Office of Naval Operations in Washington, Wilkinson had ready access to Admiral Stark, though he met most frequently with Stark's assistant, Admiral Ingersoll. Ingersoll was apparently Wilkinson's chief source of information on American naval policy, since the relations between Wilkinson and Admiral Turner, the head of Navy War Plans, were something less than cordial. General Miles of MID enjoyed the confidence of General Gerow of Army War Plans and was therefore reasonably well informed on Army planning, but Turner's communications with Wilkinson were held to a minimum. This was not a personal matter. Admiral Turner, as head of Navy War Plans, consistently distrusted Naval Intelligence, no matter who headed the organization.

Another important source of information for ONI was Capt. R. E. Schuirmann, head of the Central Division of the Office of Naval Operations and the Navy's special liaison officer with the State Department. Schuirmann met regularly with Hull's Far Eastern advisers, and he advised Wilkinson "usually of what transpired on the occasions that he was called in conference."[85] His rank, which was equal to Wilkinson's,

[84] *Ibid.*, Part 26, p. 304.
[85] *Ibid.*, Part 4, p. 1771.

certainly enhanced his ability to get information, though it was not high enough for easy access to Secretary Hull. It was only on rare occasions that he communicated directly with the Secretary of State. Hull, we remember, took complete personal charge of the Japanese negotiations, but he kept Hamilton, Hornbeck, and Ballantine up to date on their progress.

On a lower level, Wilkinson had a lieutenant commander, Delaney Hunter of the Naval Reserve, who "went over to the State Department daily and searched through the dispatches there, and was shown dispatches from all parts of the world, and made copies of a number of them and extracts of them which because of code security could not be copied direct, and brought these back."[86] These dispatches, which were *incoming only*, were circulated daily within the Office of Naval Intelligence and the Office of the Chief of Naval Operations.

Wilkinson's office also exchanged information with Army Intelligence and the FBI. He did not mention British or Dutch intelligence among his sources, but evidently he saw as much of this material as General Miles did. By far his most important source on the Far East was the decoded MAGIC material from the Navy's Communications Security unit.

There was no formal channel set up whereby Wilkinson could learn about War Council meetings or meetings in Hull's office. He learned about American policy in the Far East primarily from the newspapers and from reading MAGIC.[87] "Our office," he testified, "was an incoming and receiving office of information from abroad and from the domestic areas. We were not concerned with the outgoing directives for the Fleet nor in fact told of the movements and operations of our own forces . . . . prior to getting into the war we did not know the U.S. side of an argument that was going on."[88]

This dichotomy of incoming and outgoing signals was evidently accepted as normal in 1941 naval circles, though Wilkinson testified that "it did cause some difficulties at times."[89] After the war started, Wilkinson was able to keep his own office posted on U.S. Fleet locations; but before the war, the signal picture that came out of ONI was ideally a picture of Japanese activity revealing no more information on the United States than the Japanese themselves had.

86 *Ibid.*
88 *Ibid.*, p. 1772f. Cf. p. 1778.

87 *Ibid.*, p. 1856f.
89 *Ibid.*, p. 1778.

Functions

According to the written regulations issued on October 23, 1940, the duties of the Foreign Intelligence branch (Op 16 of ONI) were as follows:

1) Secure all classes of pertinent information concerning foreign countries, especially that affecting naval and maritime matters, with particular attention to strength, disposition and probable intentions of foreign naval forces.

2) Evaluate the information collected and disseminate as advisable.

3) Direct the activities of U.S. Naval attachés.

4) Maintain liaison with naval missions.

5) Maintain liaison with foreign naval attachés accredited to the U.S.

6) Maintain liaison with other Government departments for the exchange of foreign information.[90]

With respect to the second regulation, the meaning of the word "evaluate" had been given a precise limitation in April, 1941. At that time Captain Kirk had been head of ONI, and he had had a discussion with Assistant Chief of Naval Operations Ingersoll and War Plans Director Turner concerning the scope of his duties. Kirk felt rather strongly that his job should include "interpreting possible enemy intentions," and that his department should be comparable to G-2 in the War Department and prepare the section of the formal Estimate known as "Enemy Intentions." Admiral Turner felt equally strongly that the War Plans Division should prepare this section of the Estimate and "should interpret and evaluate all information concerning possible hostile nations from whatever source received." Turner believed that the Office of Naval Intelligence was "solely a collection agency and a distributing agency, and was not charged with sending out any information which would initiate any operations on the part of the fleet, or fleets, anywhere." All three officers, Kirk, Ingersoll, and Turner, went to Admiral Stark for the final decision, and Stark "approved the position taken by Rear Admiral Turner."[91] The written instructions remained the same, but the oral instructions from April through December, 1941, made it quite clear that ONI would "evaluate" only in the sense that it would grade the

[90] *Ibid.*, p. 1728.
[91] *Ibid.*, p. 1926.

reliability and consistency of its sources. Kirk's memorandum on this decision of Stark is quite restrained, but the testimony of Turner and Wilkinson recreates the violence of the clash. Wilkinson was bitter about the restrictions placed on himself and his men, while Turner was complacently positive about the wisdom of this course.

With respect to dissemination, Wilkinson's province was the so-called basic, or static, information,

> ... such as the defenses of the country, its economics, the diplomatic relations, the characters and activities and previous careers of its military and naval men, the location of its fleets, the actual movements of its fleets and everything other than the enemy's probable intentions, and such specific information as in itself might give rise or might require action by our fleet, or by our naval forces.[92]

The static picture was primarily historical and statistical, but at any moment the addition of an item of information might change it to an active one, i.e., one demanding an operational order or a command decision. The delicate point at which the static changed to the active was something that the War Plans Division of the Navy had the responsibility of deciding and the responsibility for transmitting to the theaters in the form of directives approved by the Chief of Naval Operations.

The question of who sent what to the operating forces was of course partly a matter of prestige. The static information was dull, safe, old, long term, and primarily based on public sources. Directives were usually based on top-secret sources that concerned either the intentions of the U.S. government or of the enemy and were usually exciting and up to the minute. It was partly the prestige value of the source that determined who would send directives, rather than any zeal for exact definitions of responsibility. Admiral Turner found it very hard indeed to distinguish between types of information, particularly during the congressional hearings when he wanted to put the responsibility on ONI for failing to send some bits of information that his own office had neglected to send out.[93] It was also partly a matter of power. Naval War Plans was traditionally a more powerful agency than Naval Intelligence, and Admiral Turner as

---

[92] *Ibid.*, p. 1730.

[93] All directives to U.S. Fleet units were, of course, subject to the approval of the CNO or Assistant CNO. War Plans functioned in an advisory capacity, though Turner often originated and composed the directives.

its head had no difficulty in monopolizing a function that was necessary to the effective performance of Intelligence.

The attempt to make ONI into a mere collection agency had serious consequences that Naval War Plans refused to acknowledge in 1941; for when the job of collecting information is separated from the job of assessing its meaning, the fundamental motive or incentive for collecting information disappears. Signals and noise are bound to be received and transmitted with equal inattention. It was not only possible, but perfectly proper, for Captain Wilkinson to disregard the meaning of the diplomatic language in the crucial last-minute messages from Japan. It was not his job, but rather the job of Admiral Turner, to understand these messages and act accordingly. All Wilkinson needed to do was to see that somebody in his agency delivered the messages to Turner.

The battle between War Plans and Intelligence was evidently loud enough to be heard in the theater. In a letter to Admiral Stark of February 18, 1941, Kimmel had added this postscript:

> I have recently been told by an officer fresh from Washington that ONI considers it to be the function of Operations to furnish the Commander-in-Chief with information of a secret nature. I have heard also that Operations considers the responsibility for furnishing the same type of information to be that of ONI. I do not know that we have missed anything, but if there is any doubt as to whose responsibility it is to keep the Commander-in-Chief fully informed with pertinent reports on subjects that should be of interest to the Fleet, will you kindly fix that responsibility so that there will be no misunderstanding.[94]

It was not until March 22 that Stark addressed a reply to this request. Stark indicated that he had been given to understand that all available information was being and always had been forwarded to Kimmel, especially with respect to the specific subjects mentioned earlier by Kimmel. "Kirk informs me," Stark wrote, "that ONI is fully aware of its responsibility in keeping you adequately informed concerning foreign nations, and disloyal elements within the United States."[95] The letter omitted any reference to keeping Kimmel informed of current U.S. policy, perhaps because ONI itself was not so informed. Kimmel's phrase "information of a secret nature" was, of course, vague; but Stark's reply

[94] *Hearings*, Part 16, p. 2229.
[95] *Ibid.*, p. 2160.

•

was not, and it was positively misleading. There was some secret information that ONI could send out, but it could send nothing that might change Kimmel's current picture of the situation. Under any reasonable definition of information, this is the same as not being able to send any information at all.

But Kimmel did not drop the subject. On May 26 he addressed a fairly long memorandum to Admiral Stark in which he raised the question of information on American governmental policy and its influence on naval decisions, as well as its relationship to the activities of foreign nations:

> The Commander-in-Chief, Pacific Fleet, is in a very difficult position. He is far removed from the seat of government in a complex and rapidly changing situation. He is, as a rule, not informed as to the policy, or change of policy, reflected in current events and naval movements and, as a result, is unable to evaluate the possible effect upon his own situation. He is not even sure of what force will be available to him and has little voice in matters radically affecting his ability to carry out his assigned tasks. This lack of information is disturbing and tends to create uncertainty, a condition which directly contravenes that singleness of purpose and confidence in one's own course of action necessary to the conduct of military operations.
>
> It is realized that, on occasion, the rapid developments in the international picture, both diplomatic and military, and, perhaps, even the lack of knowledge of the military authorities themselves, may militate against the furnishing of timely information, but certainly the situation is susceptible to marked improvement. Full and authoritative knowledge of current policies and objectives, even though necessarily late at times, would enable the Commander-in-Chief, Pacific Fleet, to modify, adapt, or even reorient his possible courses of action to conform to current concepts. This is particularly applicable to the current Pacific situation, where the necessities for intensive training of a partially trained Fleet must be carefully balanced against the desirability of interruption of this training by strategic dispositions, or otherwise, to meet impending eventualities. Moreover, due to this same factor of distance and time, the Department itself is not too well informed as to the local situation particularly with regard to the status of current outlying island development, thus making it even more necessary that the Commander-in-Chief, Pacific Fleet, be guided by broad policy and objectives rather than by categorical instructions.
>
> It is suggested that it be made a cardinal principle that the Commander-in-Chief, Pacific Fleet, be immediately informed of all important developments as they occur and by the quickest secure means available.[96]

[96] *Ibid.*, p. 2238.

Kimmel's plea was both precise and persuasive. If it reads today some-what like an apologia written with posterity in mind, we must remember that its public in 1941 was limited strictly to the Office of the Chief of Naval Operations, and its primary motive was simply to get more adequate guidance out of Washington. Admiral Halsey, who was not one to mince words, agreed vociferously with Kimmel that they "were operating in the dark" and that Washington knew a lot more than the theater and should have informed the theater.[97]

There was no specific response to Kimmel's memorandum in the selection of letters published in the *Hearings*. However, a paragraph in a letter dated August 19, which was quoted in the course of Wilkinson's cross-examination, said:

> I can readily understand your wish to be kept informed as to the depart-ment policies and decisions and the changes thereto which must necessarily be made to meet the changes in the international situation. This we are trying to do, and if you do not get as much information as you think you should get the answer probably is that the situation which is uppermost in your mind has just not jelled sufficiently for us to give you anything authoritative.[98]

In several later letters also Stark did try to reply to some of the thorny policy questions raised by Kimmel, such as what we would do if England took certain actions in the Far East. Stark's most frequent comment was that he could not get an answer: Instead "I get a smile or a 'Betty, please don't ask me that.' Policy seems to be something never fixed, always fluid and changing."[99]

As we have seen in Chapter 4, Stark's description of our policy as fluid was quite accurate. There was no definite policy to which Roosevelt cared to commit himself explicitly. Stark was honestly puzzled, as were many of Roosevelt's advisers.

However, Stark was located in Washington, at the center of discussion and decision, and his modesty and underestimation of his own opinions were excessive. His professions of ignorance ("One fellow's estimate is as good as another, and I really wonder whether this letter is worthwhile"), combined with the curt assurance that Kimmel was being sent all available

97 *Ibid.*, Part 26, p. 325.
98 *Ibid.*, Part 4, p. 1838.
99 *Ibid.*, Part 16, p. 2177.

information must have given Kimmel a deceptively comforting background for his decision not to interrupt his training program on receipt of the November 27 warning. This situation should also give us pause today. "Fluid" is still a correct, though euphemistic, description of our present foreign policy, and it might be pertinent to ask how many of our theater commanders are currently receiving assurances that their information is full and up to date and to ask further how accurate these assurances can be.

While the battle between War Plans and Intelligence had been noisy during Kirk's early administration of ONI, by the time Wilkinson took charge of the agency, the subordination of Intelligence to War Plans was a *fait accompli*. Admiral Turner, besides keeping to himself the job of evaluating, also kept to himself the results of this work. He had daily strategic estimates made up in his own division, but he did not show them to ONI. None of these estimates was reproduced in the *Hearings*, so we are at liberty to wonder how accurate they may have been. We are in nearly the same position as Captain Wilkinson, who had to learn primarily by way of the lower echelons what went on in Turner's division and what evaluation was put on the intelligence material he turned over to War Plans.

However, our position is somewhat better than Wilkinson's was. For Admiral Turner's predilection for the belief in a Japanese Siberian advance was attested to many times in the course of the congressional hearings. The first published record of his giving a higher probability to the southeastern advance was on November 26. Furthermore, his own analysis of the Navy's comprehensive war plan made clear that most of his attention in any case was given to the defeat of Germany:

> The plan contemplated a major effort on the part of both the principal associated powers against Germany, initially. It was felt in the Navy Department, that there might be a possibility of war with Japan without the involvement of Germany, but at some length and over a considerable period, this matter was discussed and it was determined that in such a case the United States would, if possible, initiate efforts to bring Germany into the war against us in order that we would be enabled to give strong support to the United Kingdom in Europe. We felt that it was incumbent on our side to defeat Germany, to launch our principal efforts against Germany first, and

to conduct a limited offensive in the central Pacific, and a strictly defensive effort in the Asiatic.[100]

With respect to Admiral Kimmel, Turner testified at the same time that "his [Kimmel's] part in the plan was not defensive. It required a limited offensive through the Central Pacific islands. It was realized that Admiral Kimmel did not have at hand all the material and men and organizations to proceed immediately with a strong offensive to the Gilberts or the Marshalls."[101] As we have seen in Chapter 4, the Navy was asking for more time—time to prepare for this offensive, as well as to complete preparations in the Philippines. And the naval draft of the November 27 war warning was quite in keeping with this concept of a limited offensive for Admiral Kimmel, rather than an enemy air attack on his fleet.

In the absence of evidence to the contrary, it is natural to assume that Admiral Turner fitted the ONI material into his own favorite set of hypotheses. He could have disregarded any material that didn't fit, since his hypotheses were not open to scrutiny or discussion by any Intelligence expert. In spite of Stark's assurances, it was not ONI, but War Plans, that was primarily responsible for directives to the theaters, and the theaters suffered accordingly. In addition, ONI itself was seriously affected by its exclusion from the evaluations and policy decisions of War Plans. It was limited even more by the fact that it was not allowed to make its own evaluations. And its usefulness to the Navy was in direct proportion to the use it could make of raw intelligence.

ONI Estimates

For the last crucial weeks there were only three estimates from the Office of Naval Intelligence published in the *Hearings*—those of November 1, November 15, and December 1. All three were entitled "Fortnightly Summaries of Current National Situations" and covered both diplomatic and military aspects. Fortnightly summaries had been issued since December, 1940, and were supplemented by daily summaries until October 24, 1941, when the latter stopped for no apparent reason, perhaps because there was not enough manpower available to handle the paper work. In

[100] *Ibid.*, Part 26, p. 264f.
[101] *Ibid.*, p. 265.

accordance with the policy established by Admiral Turner, the estimates were almost entirely bare of prediction. Stark's directive also posited that "no information be included pertaining to the U.S., British or Dutch military or naval disposition and strengths; nor should reference be made to U.S. war plans or secret diplomatic conversations."[102] Even with these restrictions, however, ONI managed to assemble international developments in a way that made certain inferences fairly easy to draw.

The first of the Japanese diplomatic estimates, on November 1, started with the fall of the Konoye Cabinet on October 16 and continued with a realistic appraisal of the new Premier:

> Lt. General Tojo, Konoye's Minister of War . . . holds the posts of Premier, Minister of War and Minister of Home Affairs. He also reshuffled the membership of the powerful Cabinet Advisory Council to ensure that this body would cooperate with the government. Tojo has thus concentrated enormous power in his own hands, far more than any Premier of modern times. He is jingoistic and anti-foreign, particularly anti-Russian. He has strong pro-Axis leanings.[103]

This appraisal was followed by some comments on Japan's next moves:

> Tojo stated that Japan would seek settlement of the China incident, strengthen her ties with the Axis, and continue her policy of building the Greater East Asia Co-prosperity sphere. An early Japanese attack on Siberia is predicted by many observers, a drive against Thailand by others. Still others think an advance into Yunnan to cut the Burma Road is imminent. However, General Tojo announced that Japan-U.S. conversations will continue. This, together with the fact that a special five-day session of the Diet has been called for November 15, makes it appear probable that Japan will not launch any new attacks at least until after mid-November.[104]

As we have seen, Siberia, Thailand, and Yunnan were also the most frequently mentioned targets in G-2 estimates for the period.

In the November 15 diplomatic estimate, U.S.-Japanese relations were regarded as deteriorating further, and Kurusu's mission was presented as almost hopeless:

> The approaching crisis in U.S.-Japanese relations overshadowed all other developments in the Far East during the period.

102 *Ibid.*, Part 4, p. 1731.
103 *Ibid.*, Part 15, p. 1815.
104 *Ibid.*

Saburo Kurusu, former Japanese Ambassador to Berlin, is flying to Washington with compromise Japanese proposals. No one apparently expects his mission to succeed, the envoy himself expressing extreme pessimism. American spokesmen, including Secretary Knox, have indicated that the U.S. will not budge from her position. Prime Minister Churchill warned that if war breaks out between Japan and America, Britain will declare war on Japan "within the hour." The U.S. is preparing to withdraw the marine detachments from China. The Japanese press continued to rail at Britain and the U.S.

Japan protested to Panama against treatment of Japanese subjects in Panamanian territory. Panama rejected the protest. Japan also protested to Russia against floating mines in the sea of Japan which sank a Japanese passenger vessel in Korean waters.

Russia and Japan reached agreement of demarcation of the Mongolia-Manchukuo border in the Lake Buir Nor area.[105]

On December 1, the diplomatic review was very brief. The Japanese-American negotiations had broken down, and Japanese-Russian relations were characterized as "strained":

> Unless the Japanese request continuance of the conversations, the Japanese-American negotiations have virtually broken down. The Japanese government and press are proclaiming loudly that the nation must carry on resolutely the work of building the Greater East Asia Co-prosperity sphere. The press also is criticising Thailand severely. Strong indications point to an early Japanese advance against Thailand.
>
> Relations between Japan and Russia remained strained. Japan signed a five-year extension of the anti-comintern pact with Germany and other Axis nations on November 25.[106]

On the basis of this prose, there was no way of choosing between an advance into Thailand and a move into Siberia.

The backbone of these brief diplomatic estimates lay in the military and naval summaries. The November 1 military figures stressed disposition of Japanese forces for a possible Russian attack:

> The Japanese forces in Manchukuo, Korea and Inner Mongolia, disposed for attack upon Russia, are reliably reported to have been increased to 684,000. At the same time reinforcements are arriving in Indo-China and it is believed that the garrison in that colony is to be increased from 50,000 to approximately 100,000 men. A large new air base is being established in

105 *Ibid.*, p. 1796.
106 *Ibid.*, p. 1775.

northern Indo-China. The Japanese force at Canton is also being strengthened. The small Japanese garrison at Sharps Peak near Foochow has been
withdrawn. A minor clash near the Siberian-Manchukuo border, in which
both sides suffered casualties, was reported by the Russians but denied by
the Japanese.[107]

On November 15, the military and naval summaries dealt only with
the mounting danger in Indochina, though the tone was not at all urgent
and coincided closely with that of MID estimates for this period:

> Reports of Japanese strength in Indo-China ranged from 43,500 to
> 120,000. It is believed that actually there are about 60,000 Japanese troops
> in Indo-China, whose number is being increased slowly. China fears an
> attack on Yunnan, and Thailand fears attack. Both governments are attempt-
> ing to obtain British-U.S. military (particularly air) support. It does not
> appear that Japan is yet strong enough in Indo-China to attack Yunnan or
> even Thailand.[108]

The December 1 summaries viewed the Indochina situation as serious,
though no indication of attack targets was given:

> Japanese troops, supplies and equipment were pouring into Indo-China
> during the past fifteen days. Units landed at Haiphong were sent south by
> rail to Saigon. Troops were moved quickly through Saigon towards the
> interior and the Thailand border. The arrival of reinforcements continues.
> Japanese army strength now in Indo-China is believed to be about 25,000 in
> Tonking province, and between 70,000 and 100,000 in south Indo-China.
> Naval craft and aircraft also moved south. It is estimated that there are
> about 200 Japanese planes in Indo-China and roughly the same number on
> Hainan Island.[109]

The remarks on the Japanese naval situation were understandably more
detailed. The November 1 estimate noted that the Japanese Navy Department's spokesman had declared that the Japanese Navy "is ready for any
immediate eventuality." It located the Combined Fleet in "home waters"
on normal stations, as well as the Third Fleet, which was normally stationed on the China coast. However, "Fleet aircraft units . . . in considerable strength have moved down to Southern Formosa." (These were the
aircraft pilots in training for the Pearl Harbor and Philippine strikes.)
This part of the estimate ended with the note that "Although troop

[107] *Ibid.*, p. 1825.
[108] *Ibid.*, p. 1805.
[109] *Ibid.*, p. 1783.

transports and cargo ships have been taking troops and supplies to ports in Indo-China, these vessels have not been accompanied by naval escorts."[110]

On November 15, the Japanese Fleet aircraft units that had been sent to South Formosa were reported to have returned to home waters. (This was correct; they were en route to their rendezvous in the Kuriles.) The estimate still placed the Combined Fleet in home waters and "no major units ... off their regular stations." While troop transports and cargo vessels were noted as "continuously moving down to Indo-China ports" with "small naval craft ... providing escort," there was "no indication of any large naval concentration at present in any area." However, naval aircraft in Indochina were being augmented, "drawn not only from Hainan and China coast bases, but probably also from units normally shore-based in Japan." "Accurate numbers," unfortunately, were not available.[111]

The December 1 report on the naval situation was more alarming, even though the major Japanese capital-ship strength and "the greatest portion of the carriers" were still believed to be in home waters:

> Deployment of naval forces to the southward has indicated clearly that extensive preparations are underway for hostilities. At the same time troop transports and freighters are pouring continually down from Japan and northern China coast ports headed south, apparently for French Indo-China and Formosan ports. Present movements to the south appear to be carried out by small individual units, but the organization of an extensive task force, now definitely indicated, will probably take sharper form in the next few days. To date this task force, under the command of the Commander in Chief Second Fleet, appears to be subdivided into two major task groups, one gradually concentrating off the Southeast Asiatic coast, the other in the Mandates. Each constitutes a strong striking force of heavy and light cruisers, units of the Combined Air Force, destroyer and submarine squadrons. Although one division of battleships also may be assigned, the major capital ship strength remains in home waters, as well as the greatest portion of the carriers.
>
> The equipment being carried south is a vast assortment, including landing boats in considerable numbers. Activity in the Mandates, under naval control, consists not only of large reinforcements of personnel, aircraft,

[110] *Ibid.*, p. 1825.
[111] *Ibid.*, p. 1805.

munitions but also of construction material with yard workmen, engineers, etc.[112]

With the naval material added to the military and diplomatic, the picture of a Japanese attack somewhere to the south appears to have been indicated more definitely than any movement into Siberia. Fortunately, for this period there is in the record a memorandum for Captain Wilkinson from Commander McCollum, head of the Far Eastern section of ONI, presenting some of the evidence behind these brief estimates. McCollum here detailed the hypothesis that Japan was planning "an eventual control or occupation of Thailand followed almost immediately by an attack against British possessions, possibly Burma or Singapore."[113] This memorandum was dated December 1; it summarized Army, Navy, and political preparations by Japan from October 1 to November 30, and unlike comparable MID estimates, it assembled a good deal of privileged information, including decoded MAGIC messages.

In the matter of military preparations, McCollum noted that until November 15, shipments out of Shanghai had been largely military supplies—large numbers of landing boats, camouflaged tanks and trucks, and considerable railroad equipment. However,

> *starting about 15 November the character of the shipments underwent a marked change.* From 15 to 21 November large transports took out of Shanghai alone some 24,000 fully equipped veteran troops, while an additional 30,000 were reported as being withdrawn from North China reputedly destined for Formosa. From 21 to 26 November 20,000 troops were landed at Saigon and 4,000 at Haiphong which with 6,000 troops already there were sent South to Saigon and Cambodia by rail. All wharves and docks at Haiphong and Saigon are reported crowded with Japanese transports unloading supplies and men. It is estimated that the following Japanese troops are now in French Indo-China ready and equipped for action.
>
> (a) South and Central Indo-China   70,000
> (b) Northern Indo-China   25,000

The landing of reinforcements continues and additional troops and supplies are undoubtedly available on nearby Hainan Island and more distant Formosa [author's italics].[114]

[112] *Ibid.*, p. 1783.
[113] *Ibid.*, p. 1839.
[114] *Ibid.*, p. 1840.

McCollum listed the high points in Japanese naval preparations as follows:

(a) All possible ships have been recalled to Japan for quick docking and repair check up that has now been completed.

(b) Some additional naval aircraft strength has been sent to the Japanese Mandate Island area.

(c) An air and surface patrol was established on a line between the Marshall Islands and the Gilberts. Guam was placed under air and submarine observation.

(d) The CinC 2nd Fleet organized two task groups, both rather loosely knit organizations; group No. 1 to operate in the South China Area, group No. 2 to operate in the Mandate Islands area. This organization is about finished and the CinC of the 2nd Fleet expects to be in Southern Formosa by 3 or 4 December.

(e) The CinC of the Combined Air Force has just completed an inspection of all outlying naval air groups, particularly those in the Mandates, South China, and Formosa.

(f) Many merchant vessels have recently been taken over by the Navy and at least three of these have been equipped as anti-aircraft ships.[115]

In discussing Japan's political preparations, McCollum pointed out the evacuation of Japanese residents from six different areas:

(a) British India and Singapore
(b) Netherlands East Indies
(c) Philippine Islands
(d) Hong Kong
(e) Australia
(f) The United States, Canada, and South America.

McCollum's cataloguing of espionage activities brought together a significant number of signals. He mentioned that the center of War Intelligence and Espionage covering the Americas was in the process of being shifted from Washington, D.C., to Rio de Janeiro, and that the Japanese embassy at Rio had recently been equipped with a short-wave radio transmitter. He also mentioned the establishment of an espionage net in Thailand and Singapore, including such specific items as the following:

(a) Japanese consulate at Singora is manned by 4 Army Intelligence officers.

[115] *Ibid.*, p. 1840*f*.

(b) A consulate has been established at the northern railhead of Chiengmai.

(c) Army communication personnel and equipment is present at Singora, Bangkok, and Chiengmai.

(d) Four Army and Navy officers under assumed names have been sent to the Embassy at Bangkok. The Ambassador has received instructions not to interfere in the work of these men.

(e) A chain of drug stores manned by intelligence agents is in process of establishment.

(f) Japanese Army doctors under assumed names are in the hospital at Bangkok.

(g) At the end of November 60,000 Bahts were sent in gold to the Ambassador at Bangkok with instructions to hold it for emergency intelligence use.

(h) At least two sabotage agents have been sent into Singapore.[116]

The memo continued with several more general indications:

In French Indo-China the Japanese military has taken over police functions. Many Chinese and Annanese are being summarily arrested. At the end of November Japanese Ambassador Yoshizawa queried his government as to whether he and his staff should take over the governmental functions of French Indo-China or continue to function through the front of the French Government General.

The Consul General at Shanghai has informed his government that all preparations are complete for taking over all physical property in China belonging to British, American and other enemy nationals.[117]

Of special interest today is the next-to-last item:

The Army General Staff sent urgent requests for information ... [on] U.S. and Dutch troop and plane strengths and dispositions in the Philippines and Netherlands East Indies.

Finally McCollum noted the arrival of Ambassador Kurusu to conduct negotiations. In accordance with ONI policy, he deliberately avoided "drawing conclusions in each instance." It is a pity that we thereby lose any idea of the particular weight attached to these different items of intelligence.

On December 1 McCollum presented copies of this memo to a group of officers that included Admirals Stark, Ingersoll, Turner, Brainard, and

116 *Ibid.*, p. 1841.
117 *Ibid.*, p. 1842.

Noyes, and Captain Wilkinson. He read it aloud to them and "pointed out that in [his] opinion war or a rupture of diplomatic relations was imminent, and . . . requested information as to whether or not the fleets in the Pacific had been adequately alerted."[118] Admirals Stark and Turner gave him a "categorical assurance" that "dispatches fully alerting the fleets and placing them on a war basis had been sent."[119] At that time McCollum had seen neither the November 24 nor the November 27 dispatch and, as he commented at the congressional hearings, "I was put in the rather difficult position of not personally knowing what had been sent out to the fleet."[120] He added, "Possibly it was none of my business." However, when the American message went out to U.S. naval attachés to destroy U.S. codes in Tokyo, Peking, Bangkok, and Shanghai, McCollum drafted a dispatch for the operating forces, condensing the December 1 memo and stating "that we felt everything pointed to an imminent outbreak of hostilities between Japan and the United States." He and his chief, Captain Heard, took the dispatch to Captain Wilkinson: "We did it in view of the fact that the function of evaluation of Intelligence, that is, the drawing of inferences therefrom, had been transferred over to be a function of the War Plans Division."[121]

Captain Wilkinson sent McCollum with the draft of his dispatch to Admiral Turner, who "made a number of changes in it, striking out all except the informational parts of it." (The "informational parts" have been quoted beginning on page 328. Do they lead very obviously to an inference of war between Japan and the United States in the next few days—more precisely to the inference that Japan would strike against the United States at the same time that she moved against the Kra Isthmus?)

Admiral Turner then showed McCollum the November 27 warning, and McCollum reacted: "Well, good gosh, you put in the words 'war warning.' I do not know what could be plainer than that, but, nevertheless, I would like to see mine go too."[122] Turner replied: "Well, if you want to send it, you either send it the way I corrected it, or take it back to Wilkinson and we will argue about it." McCollum took it back to

118 *Ibid.*, Part 8, p. 3385.   119 *Ibid.*
120 *Ibid.*, p. 3388.   121 *Ibid.*
122 *Ibid.*

Wilkinson, and from Wilkinson's desk it very probably found its way into the wastebasket.

McCollum had no knowledge of the November 24 and 27 dispatches until this interview with Admiral Turner; and his superior, Captain Wilkinson, was not much better informed. Wilkinson learned "through informal channels" about the dispatches a few days after they had been sent. As he testified, he was "not directly concerned in them." His function, as he conceived it, was to proffer information; there were no instructions requiring Stark or Turner to tell him how they used that information. He knew nothing about the Stark-Marshall memoranda of November 5 and November 27. However, his estimate of the situation seems to have been rather close to theirs. His estimate up to that moment had been that "every evidence indicated an attack in the South China Sea on either Siam or the Kra Peninsula. . . . There were possibilities of attack elsewhere ranging, in fact, from Panama on the Pacific Coast to Hawaii, Guam, Wake and the Philippines. The nearer each of these objectives was to Japan, to our mind the greater the probability of their attack."[123] Wilkinson thought that the Japanese would move south and see how far they could go with "infiltration methods" without precipitating a full-scale war. In his opinion there was "not the slightest" information specifying Hawaii as a point of attack, though it was a possible target in the sense that it was within the Japanese Navy's steaming radius. Wilkinson believed that the Japanese would avoid attacking the Philippines for political reasons, and that they would not attack Hawaii because "they would expose themselves to great danger to whatever force they brought there, and, furthermore, they would be precipitating a war with the United States, which theretofore they had given every indication of attempting to avoid."[124] It did not occur to him to send a warning message to Pearl Harbor specifying danger from a surprise air attack,

> first, because from my service out there and from these letters that had been interchanged throughout the year, it was my belief that Hawaii knew the possibility of an air attack. Second, it did not occur to me because it was not within my province to conclude or derive the enemy functions although naturally I was interested in such matters. And, third, it was my own belief

123 *Ibid.*, Part 4, p. 1754.
124 *Ibid.*, p. 1758.

that an approaching force would be detected before it could get into attack range.[125]

In short, Wilkinson was less concerned and less convinced than McCollum in the last days before the disaster that Japan would risk attacking an American possession.

After November 27 Wilkinson apparently saw no reason to change his estimate on the basis of signals coming into the Office of Naval Intelligence. He knew about the orders for code destruction sent to the major Japanese embassies, and had initiated the cable notifying Admiral Kimmel.[126] He also approved instructions to American naval attachés in the Far East to destroy their codes. He knew about the messages setting up the winds code and about our efforts to intercept an execute. He knew that the Dutch were seriously worried about their possessions in the East Indies and had seen the Dutch alert dispatches. These simply confirmed in his mind the progression of the Japanese movement to the south, which was evidenced also in a December 5 estimate that his office had drawn up for the President, showing ground forces in Indochina and naval forces at Camranh Bay, at Saigon, off the Indochina coast, at Hainan, and at Formosa. Wilkinson knew that Admiral Hart was conducting reconnaissance, along with the British, off the Kra Peninsula, and on December 6 he saw Hart's message, as well as Winant's, reporting Japanese convoy movements off Cambodia Point. Wilkinson believed that the convoys were probably headed for Bangkok rather than for Kra because he was convinced that the Japanese would prefer to take Thailand rather than attack the British; but at the same time, curiously, he believed that the British would enter the war in support of Thailand. As for American participation at that juncture, he "had heard of this imaginary line of 100 degrees east longitude and 10 degrees north latitude and ... had some doubt as to whether we would be able, in the light of the temper of the country, to back that conclusion up."[127] It was against this background that Captain Wilkinson received the last-minute signals.

[125] *Ibid.*, p. 1756*f.*

[126] The original cable ended with the sentence "From foregoing infer that Orange plans early action in Southeast Asia." This was struck out by Ingersoll or Wilkinson. (*Ibid.*, p. 1753.)

[127] *Hearings*, Part 4, p. 1777.

On Saturday, December 6, before leaving his office, Wilkinson had seen the pilot message announcing the impending delivery of the Japanese reply to our Ten Point Note. He was giving a small dinner party at his home that evening, and his guests included General Miles, head of Army Intelligence, and Capt. John R. Beardall, the naval aide who received MAGIC for the President. Commander Kramer arrived about 10:30 or 11 P.M. with the first thirteen parts of the 14-part message, and Wilkinson, accompanied by Miles and Beardall, withdrew with him to study the material. At this time Kramer informed Wilkinson that he had been unable to reach Admirals Stark and Turner by telephone. Evidently Wilkinson then tried to reach them, but without success. There was no great urgency, because no one had expected the Japanese to accept the American proposals, and the first thirteen parts resembled in tone and content many previous messages from Tokyo. All of those assembled at Wilkinson's house "felt that this was a diplomatic message ... that resembled the diplomatic white papers, of which we had often seen examples, that it was a justification of the Japanese position."[128] It meant that the current negotiations would be broken off, as everyone had anticipated, but it did not necessarily mean that diplomatic relations would be ruptured.

Captain Wilkinson went to his office about 8:30 A.M. on Sunday to be sure to be on hand for the fourteenth part. Commander McCollum was already there, since he had relieved the last man on night watch at 8 A.M. The fourteenth part alarmed Wilkinson; he thought that these were "fighting words" and "very serious." He and McCollum went to see Admiral Stark about 9:15 that morning and "advised that the Fleet should be notified, not with any question of an attack on Hawaii in mind, but with the question of imminence of hostilities in the South China Sea."[129]

They then left Stark's office without waiting to see what additional warning might be sent, and returned about 10:40 A.M. with the 1 o'clock delivery message. The only ensuing discussion that Wilkinson could remember concerned the fact that the presentation time was earlier than had been indicated by the pilot message. The mention of an exact hour for delivery and the fact that Sunday was an unusual day for business

128 *Ibid.*, p. 1763.
129 *Ibid.*, p. 1766.

among diplomats did not strike him as ominous, for the pilot message had announced that Tokyo would inform the ambassadors when to present their reply: "The fact that there was a certain time for delivery was not significant to me. . . . I was not familiar with diplomatic language, that the time of presentation is characteristic of an ultimatum rather than an ordinary note, which would not ordinarily be presented at some certain time. . . . In other words, the time element, the fact that they were to deliver it at a certain time, it didn't mean anymore to me than as being a time with respect to negotiations. . . ."[130] The matter, then, was something for the State Department to handle.

If Wilkinson's interpretation of this last-minute signal seems today to have been rather relaxed, we must remember that his responsibility ended with its delivery to Admiral Stark's office. Strictly speaking, if the 1 o'clock message contained any new information, then that would change the strategic picture, and Admiral Turner or the CNO would have to take charge of any new operational directive. If the premise of the November 27 warning message were to be changed from a highly probable Japanese attack on Thailand or a British or Dutch possession to an absolutely certain or highly probable simultaneous attack on a U.S. possession, then that was for Admiral Turner or Admiral Stark to say.

Admiral Turner consistently held that the November 27 naval warning took care of this contingency, and it is true that this message listed first the possibility of an amphibious expedition against the Philippines. (None of the areas mentioned in the dispatch, incidentally, was under Kimmel's jurisdiction.) Turner further maintained that every significant signal received after November 27 was confirmatory or else a matter of "pure information" and therefore the responsibility of ONI. He testified about the 1 o'clock message: "I did not consider that that message and the fact that it appeared to be an ultimatum changed the over-all situation in the least degree, because I was certain in my mind that there was going to be war immediately between the United States and Japan, and this was merely confirmatory."[131] However, a little earlier he had said: "I saw that dispatch in Admiral Stark's office about noon, recognized its very great importance, and asked him if anything had been done about it. He

130 *Ibid.*, p. 1874.
131 *Ibid.*, p. 1924f.

told me that General Marshall was sending a dispatch, and I did nothing further about it because I considered that would cover the situation."[132]

These two statements are not precise enough to be exactly inconsistent. But Admiral Turner's willingness, at this moment of remembered crisis, to relinquish his grasp on the responsibility for sending out new, strategically important information to the operating forces would seem to contrast rather markedly with his general zeal for this responsibility in 1941. Of the first thirteen parts of the 14-part message, he also remarked at the congressional hearings: "I considered the dispatch very important, but as long as those officers Captain Wilkinson, Admiral Ingersoll, and Secretary Knox had seen it, I did not believe it was my function to take any action."[133]

In short, naval reaction to the last-minute signals was not at all frenzied, though it was characterized by some urgency on the part of the Far Eastern specialists, particularly Kramer and McCollum. Captain Wilkinson evidently envisaged a direct attack on the Philippines after reading the final part of the 14-part message, but until that moment he had not anticipated even a direct attack on the British. The fact that Naval Intelligence had so little influence with War Plans and the CNO, and so little responsibility to the operating forces, partly accounted for the lack of alarm. Whatever alarm existed, or whatever perception of a more exactly defined danger, could not and did not, for the same reason, get translated into a warning message. Admiral Turner maintained his rigid authority to the end. Of course one might argue, as Admiral Turner later did, that for those with perception the November 27 message was a warning. But there seems little doubt that if the sender had been more alarmed, the warning itself would have been more alarming.

ESTIMATES AND THE ACTUALITY

In closing this account of Washington's Intelligence agencies, it is interesting to compare American estimates of Japanese capabilities with the actuality. On the whole, American figures were fairly accurate for

---

[132] *Ibid.*, p. 1924.

[133] Similarly, on noting that General Short's alert was for sabotage only and that his response was rather brief, Turner did not speak to General Gerow about it because he "felt if anything was wrong it would be attended to." (*Ibid.*, p. 1960.)

trained troops and reserves and their location; for numbers, types, and organization of ships; for numbers and types of aircraft and their bases; and for numbers of trained air crews and technicians. Navy figures tended to be more conservative than Army ones. (This is curious, since the naval interpretations of the figures were usually more alarming than the Army's.) For example, the December 5 ONI estimate of Japanese troops in Indochina was 105,000 as compared to 125,000 in the Army estimate.[134] The Navy estimated that there were 158 Japanese aircraft based on Formosa and 200 on Hainan, while the Army estimated 400 on Formosa and 200 on Hainan. (Actually, there were 475 on Formosa and 200 on Hainan.) Where the figures erred, they were almost always too low[135]; but the discrepancies in quantities were not so serious as the underestimations of production rate and of various vehicle and equipment performance.

For example, on December 1, Army Intelligence placed Japanese aircraft production at "200 per month for all combat types, both army and navy."[136] The actual rate was 426 per month.[137] It was also usual to consider Japan's pilot training inferior to ours, although their cadets averaged 300 flying hours as compared to 200 for U.S. cadets; their first-line pilots averaged about 600 flying hours; and their carrier pilots, about 800. Our descriptions of the Zero single-engine fighter underestimated its range (800 instead of 900 miles), its speed (250 statute miles per hour instead of 300—it was faster at high altitude than our P-40), and its maneuverability. The majority of U.S. naval officers believed that the sonar gear in Japanese destroyers was inferior, when it was actually four or five times more powerful than our own; and it was commonly believed that their ships were somewhat top-heavy, when they were not. The aircraft capacity of their carriers, the efficiency of their direction-finding stations, etc., were also underestimated. Even the common notion about

---

[134]*Hearings*, Part 14, p. 1384, and Part 15, p. 1838.

[135] In the sources available today, the "actual" figures themselves are unreliable, since the estimates of the *USSBS* and various Japanese authorities are at variance, and even the Japanese authorities disagree with each other. This account uses the *USSBS* figures, though these, too, are regarded as doubtful by Admiral McCollum.

[136]*Hearings*, Part 14, p. 1380.

[137]*USSBS, Japanese Air Power*, p. 28.

poor Japanese eyesight seems to have been an unconscious factor in making performance estimates.[138]

Apart from considerations peculiar to 1941 military thinking, the consistent underestimation of Japanese performance and productive capacity was based on two assumptions: a superior American economy and superior American scientific skill. These assumptions were certainly not confined to Intelligence officers. There is no question that America's economy in 1941 could expand military production much faster than Japan's could. The fact that we underestimated her aircraft production potential by about one-half, therefore, had no serious consequences. However, the smug attitude on American "know-how" had its dangers in 1941, and both assumptions would be questionable today.

Our errors in gauging Japanese skill and ingenuity were matched by equally serious errors on Japan's part in measuring the United States. The Japanese had a vast and efficient network of spies, with a rather high record of accuracy in reporting public and private quantitative data, and a system for tabulating equipment far more refined than ours. In fact, their tally of our equipment in the Philippines as of December 1, 1941, was more accurate than our own. They also had a rather impressive ability to forecast American productive capacity in wartime. However, the Japanese planning staffs did not make full use of this intelligence, especially in the case of the production forecasts, which pointed without question to ultimate American victory in the event of war.

The following chapter describes these war plans and the way the Japanese military conceived of America's role in the Far East.

---

[138] In addition to *USSBS, Japanese Air Power,* see Craven and Cate (eds.), *United States Air Force in World War II: Plans and Early Operations: January 1939 to August 1942,* pp. 79–81. Further information on this subject was obtained by the author in an interview with Adm. Stuart S. Murray on May 20, 1957. There were, of course, individual experts and officers who were not affected by the common prejudices, but apparently their views did not carry weight. For example, by the middle of 1941, ONI had established a 1500-mile range for the Zero (the distance necessary for a round trip between the Salween River bridges and air bases in northern French Indochina, a mission successfully accomplished by the Japanese), but neither the Navy Bureau of Aeronautics nor the Army Air Corps would believe the intelligence reports. (Interview with Admiral McCollum on August 23, 1958.)

6 ▸ THE REALITY BEHIND THE SIGNALS

We have looked in detail at the American signal picture and the American image of Japan. We are ready to ask, What was the Japanese reality? On the basis of the Japanese data made available since the close of the war, how closely did the reality fit the image?

Because of its dramatic character, the Japanese attack on Pearl Harbor has naturally usurped most of the attention and interest of historical discussions on the opening of World War II. In America all sorts of variations have been played on the theme of a "stab in the back" and the perfidy of surprise. Japanese responses to American criticisms have also centered on justification of this particular part of their war plan. They have pointed out, for example, how their secret diplomatic messages were incorrectly interpreted because our decoders had not translated them accurately, or how the Japanese military tampered with Hull's Ten Point Note before delivery to the government so as to change it from a tentative proposal to an "ultimatum," or how an unexpected delay in preparing a smooth copy of their last note was responsible for our being surprised, that they really had intended to present this note as a formal declaration of war.

The point of such exchanges becomes largely irrelevant if the basic Japanese war plan is considered in its entirety. The opening attack at Pearl Harbor accomplished what the Japanese had hoped. It was in fact a complete surprise to the United States. But the basic plan called for a carefully timed *series* of surprise blows that were to be aimed not only at British and Dutch holdings in the Far East, but also at the Philippines,

Guam, and Wake. For some reason the damage done to these other American outposts in the Pacific is not considered in the same category of crime. Apparently because Washington was not in the strict sense surprised by these attacks, they were considered as fair as any war move could be. The Philippines had always seemed to the American military a much more probable target than Pearl Harbor, and news of the attack on Pearl Harbor had of course reached the Philippines and the outlying islands before the air attacks on them began. This last tip-off had *not* been part of the Japanese plan. Ideally the attack on the Philippines should have been committed at the earliest practicable time after the Pearl Harbor strike—at dawn in the Philippines, which came five and one-half hours after dawn at Pearl Harbor. During the interim, Imperial Headquarters was relying on radio jamming to block all broadcasts to the Philippines.

The Japanese war plan provided for the neutralization of the U.S. Fleet at Pearl Harbor, followed immediately by strong simultaneous air attacks against the Philippines and Malaya, with the primary purpose of destroying Allied air power in the Far East. While the landings in the Philippines and Malaya were taking place, troops were to occupy Guam, Wake, Hong Kong, British Borneo, and Thailand, and advance bases were to be established in the Bismarcks, Dutch Borneo, the Celebes, Molucca, and Timor. After Malaya and the Philippines were completely under control, Japanese forces would be partly released to concentrate on the occupation of Java and Burma. This would complete the first phase of the war plan.

Preparations for Phase I began on November 5–7, when operational orders were issued by the Combined Fleet Commander. The Southern Army was formally established on November 6. Naval, ground, and air commanders worked together until November 10 completing details of plans for joint action. All such joint action was entirely a matter of cooperation, and yet the coordination required was extremely complicated.

For example, during the opening hours of the first day of war the Japanese were to strike at 29 separate targets. (See Table 1.) Of these targets, 6 were on Oahu, 10 in the Philippines, 8 along the Malayan coast, and 1 each at Hong Kong, Thailand, Guam, and Wake. Eight of the targets were to receive two waves of aerial attack, each separated by

TABLE 1

TARGETS FOR JAPANESE ATTACK PLANNED FOR
MORNING OF DECEMBER 8, JAPANESE TIME

Location	Number	Description
Pearl Harbor	6	Aerial attack targets, two waves of attack.
Philippines	10	4 aerial attack targets, two waves for 2 targets; 6 landings (only 5 carried out).
Malaya	9	5 aerial attack targets; 3 landings plus inland penetration from Thailand.
Thailand	1	Army march across border to take Bangkok.
Guam	1	Aerial attack target to be followed by landing.
Wake	1	Aerial attack target to be followed by landing.
Hong Kong	1	Aerial attack target to be followed by landing.

TOTAL TARGETS 29

approximately 1 hour. The Malaya, Pearl Harbor, and Philippine attacks were subject to cancellation up to 24 hours before D-day in the event of a successful conclusion of the Japanese-American negotiations. The string of attacks was to go off like a string of Japanese firecrackers: Hong Kong was not to be attacked until notice of the Malayan invasion had been received, and neither Guam nor the Philippines was to be attacked until notice of the Pearl Harbor strike had been received.

The major targets were separated by hundreds, and in some cases thousands, of miles, and these distances had to be covered by attack vehicles ranging in speed from 10 knots for the slowest surface craft to 250 knots for the fastest aircraft. Over 2000 aircraft were involved, about a quarter of them carrier based, the rest land based. There were 169 surface ships and 64 subsurface ships.[1] Regrouping and assembling of fleet and troop units before final departure had to start on November 5–7, or thirty-three days before the attack. The first of the final departures—that of the task force destined for Pearl Harbor—had to occur as early as November 25. (See Table 2.)

[1] The subsurface ships had an average surface speed of 12 knots and an average submerged speed of 3 knots.

TABLE 2

TIMING AND COORDINATION PROBLEMS OF JAPANESE ATTACK ON PEARL HARBOR

Aircraft (land based)	1478
Aircraft (carrier based)	537
Surface craft	169
Submarines	64
TOTAL	2248

Time from initial decision to first bomb drop	33 days
Time from first departure to first bomb drop	20 days
Time from final decision to first bomb drop	24 hr
Aircraft speeds	150–250 kn
Surface craft speeds	10–35 kn
Submarine speeds	12 kn av
Greatest speed difference between vehicles	240 kn

In spite of the complexity of the plans for Phase I, by November 20 agreement between Japanese Army and Navy commanders had been reached, and orders for attack were issued. These orders went only to top officials. For example, most of the Army staff concerned with the main Philippine landings scheduled for December 22 were not informed of their mission. Fleet units and troops for these landings at Lingayen Gulf and Lamon Bay had to start assembling in and near Formosa as early as November 25 for a December 17 departure. Date of departure and destination were not revealed, although these conditions of strict security, which successfully preserved surprise at Pearl Harbor, evidently caused a good deal of confusion, delay, and nervousness after the United States had declared war.

The first phase of the timetable required the invasion forces to complete the occupation of Malaya and the Philippines in fifty days and to secure the whole southern area in ninety days from the start of hostilities. This tight schedule for Phase I had certain tactical advantages, such as reducing Allied chances of moving in reinforcements by denying them forward bases, or presenting the Allies with a staggering *fait accompli.* The first phase was also designed to take place during the months when the weather in Siberia would prevent possible Soviet attack. Bad Siberian weather conditions, combined with favorable weather conditions in South-east Asia, dictated an ideal starting date around November 1, but this had to be postponed until December 8 because of the Japanese government's reluctance to follow the military recommendation for war.

The second and third phases of the war plan called for Japan to under-take a strategic defensive position, exploit the natural resources of their new territories, strengthen the defensive perimeter that would then run from the Kuriles in an arc south around the Marshall and Bismarck islands to Java and Sumatra and back to Burma (see Fig. 5), and wage a war of attrition to destroy the U.S. will to fight. The latter objective was to be accomplished by raids on Allied advance bases. Japan was counting on the pressing demands of the war in Europe, and the rapidity of the first phase of her conquest, to make the Far Eastern situation acceptable to, or at least unchallenged by, the United States.

JAPANESE POLICY PLANNING AND LONG-RANGE ESTIMATES

Tactical planning for Phase I of the war was the exclusive province of the military services. As Admiral Yonai described it, "the Imperial Gen-eral Staff confined its activities to questions of operations" and their decision on such matters was final: "As far as questions of Army opera-tions are concerned, if the Chief of the Army General Staff says that we will do this, that is the end of it; and so far as the Navy operations are concerned, if the Chief of the Navy General Staff says we will do this, that fixes it." "If they can't obtain an agreement," he explained, with tautological finality, "it means there is a lack of unity."[2]

For longer-range considerations, such as whether to go to war in the first place, the members of the government and of the services had to have some meeting of minds; these considerations were matters for approval by the cabinet after discussion in a Liaison Conference composed of mili-tary and government officials. This committee, which was comparable to our War Council, had six regular members: the Prime Minister, the For-eign Minister, the Navy and War Ministers, and the two Chiefs of Staff.

---

[2] *USSBS, Interrogations of Japanese Officials*, Vol. II (Pacific), Interrogation No. 379, November 17, 1945, p. 328.

FIG. 5. JAPANESE STRATEGIC DEFENSIVE PERIMETER: PHASES II AND III OF
JAPANESE PLAN OF ATTACK

The Deputy Chiefs of Staff also usually attended, as well as a couple of invited civilian cabinet members. It is not surprising that the military could sway decision, especially after General Tojo occupied the post of Prime Minister beginning on October 17, 1941. A "unanimous" decision by this body was simply the current euphemism for majority agreement— and the military were in the majority.[3] The Emperor confirmed the Liaison Conference decisions generally by meeting with the same officers, and the full meetings were called Imperial Conferences.[4]

From the point of view of American intelligence, the most important unanimous decisions of the Japanese government centered around the dates of July 2, September 6, October 16, November 5, November 25, November 29, and December 8 (Tokyo time). We shall review these decisions briefly, for with each decision in this sequence, the Japanese government drew closer to war with the United States. From our present vantage the sequence looks quite direct. In 1941, however, American experts, who had access to all but the December 8 decision, tended to credit the moderates in Tokyo with more influence than they actually had. The Japanese method of conducting committee meetings permitted frequent statement of the moderate position, even though such expression bore little relation to the resolutions finally taken.

On July 2, 1941, the Emperor summoned an Imperial Conference to re-examine national policy. The impetus for this conference was the German invasion of Russia on June 22, and German pressure for a Japanese attack on Siberia. Present were the Prime Minister, Prince Konoye; Foreign Minister Matsuoka, who was soon to be replaced; War Minister Tojo, who would head the wartime cabinet; Navy Minister Oikawa; Chief of the Army General Staff Sugiyama; Chief of the Naval General Staff Nagano; the President of the Privy Council; and the Minister of the Interior. Out of this conference came the decision that put the imperial seal of approval on a course that led eventually to war between Japan and America.

---

[3] Maxon, *Control of Japanese Foreign Policy: A Study of Civil-Military Rivalry, 1930–1945*, pp. 149–189.

[4] Chief Cabinet Secretary Sakomizu described the Imperial Conferences as primarily cere-monial. Apparently the agenda and final decisions were arranged beforehand, but everyone "took great pains to make it seem like a Conference." (*Ibid.*, p. 157*f.*)

Prince Konoye recorded this decision in his memoirs as follows[5]:

1. The Imperial Government is determined to follow a policy which will result in the establishment of the Greater East Asia Co-Prosperity Sphere and world peace, no matter what international developments take place. [This Sphere included all British, Dutch, French, and Portuguese possessions in the Far East, and ultimately the Philippines, India, and Australia. It had been defined as the main national objective in July, 1940. Our MAGIC translation of point 1 read: "Imperial Japan shall adhere to the policy of contributing to world peace by establishing the Great East Asia Sphere of Co-prosperity, regardless of how the world situation may change."[6]]

2. The Imperial Government will continue its effort to effect a settlement of the China Incident and seek to establish a solid basis for the security and preservation of the nation. This will involve an advance into the Southern Regions and, depending on future developments, a settlement of the Soviet Question as well. [Our MAGIC translation does not show this second sentence or the third point, which follows. Either these parts were not intercepted, or they were not sent; and it is more probable that they were not sent.]

3. The Imperial Government will carry out the above program no matter what obstacles may be encountered.

The phrases "no matter what international developments take place" and "no matter what obstacles may be encountered" were made more explicit in the summary, which followed in the Imperial decision as recorded by Konoye: "In carrying out the plans outlined . . . we will not be deterred by the possibility of being involved in a war with England and America," and "all plans, especially the use of armed forces, will be carried out in such a way as to place no serious obstacles in the path of our basic military preparations for a war with England and America."[7] However, "the Imperial Government will continue all necessary diplomatic negotiations."[8] This last qualification was a sop to Prince Konoye, who proclaimed his faith in the negotiations while at the same time approving a course of military conduct in Indochina that could only make the work of his diplomats impossible. This summary also was not sent to Washington, or, if sent, was not intercepted.

On the July 2 policy decision, Ambassador Nomura in Washington was informed only of points 1 and 2. By July 8 our government leaders had available to them a MAGIC decode of the message, as well as a few

[5] *Hearings*, Part 20, p. 4018.   [6] *Ibid.*, Part 12, p. 1.
[7] *Ibid.*, Part 20, p. 4019.   [8] *Ibid.*, p. 4018.

details on the southward advance and this vague, though menacing, extract:

> As regards the Russo-German war, although the spirit of the Three-Power Axis shall be maintained, every preparation shall be made at the present and the situation shall be dealt with in our own way. In the meantime, diplomatic negotiations shall be carried on with extreme care. Although every means available shall be resorted to in order to prevent the United States from joining the war, if need be, Japan shall act in accordance with the Three-Power Pact and shall decide when and how force will be employed.[9]

Receipt of this message, followed by the details of the Indochina campaign, resulted, as we have seen, in a series of cables to the Hawaiian Islands. However, our own MAGIC translation was milder than the original, even for the two points regarded as safe for Ambassador Nomura to have. If our leaders had had a copy of the whole policy statement, it is doubtful that Secretary Hull would have so patiently reopened the negotiations after the imposition of embargoes.

July 2, then, figured as a major date in the signal picture.

September 6 was the next major date. Another Imperial Conference reaffirmed the policy decision of July 2 and set an October 15 deadline for the Konoye Cabinet to conclude the negotiations successfully. MAGIC carried no inkling of this deadline.

On October 16 the fall of the Konoye Cabinet occasioned another set of alarm reactions in Washington, which were reviewed in Chapter 2. We had public as well as private news sources for this event and for the formation of a new cabinet under General Tojo.

From October 23 to November 2 the Liaison Conference met in almost continuous session to re-examine its national policy decision of July 2. MAGIC brought us news beginning on November 3:

> The Government has for a number of days since the forming of the new Cabinet been holding meetings with the Imperial headquarters. We have carefully considered a fundamental policy for improving relations between Japan and America, but we expect to reach a final decision in a meeting on the morning of the 5th and will let you know the result at once. This will be our Government's last effort to improve diplomatic relations.[10]

[9] *Ibid.*, Part 12, p. 2.
[10] *Ibid.*, p. 90.

At this Liaison Conference beginning October 23, the following questions were raised:

1. *Is there a prospect of having the United States accept promptly the demands agreed to on September 6?* The answer was, "No."

2. *What would be the consequences to Japan of acceptance of the U.S. memorandum of October 2?* The answer was that "if Japan accepted ... all that had been achieved since the Manchuria Incident would have evaporated, and the established position of Japan in Manchuria and Korea would be prejudiced and Japan would be compelled ultimately to withdraw entirely from the continent."[11]

3. *To what extent can Japan recede from her September 6 decision?* The answer to this was worked out in Proposals A and B, which were presented to the United States and rejected, as we saw in Chapter 3. (Japan's greatest concession, contained in Proposal B, was to withdraw her troops from southern to northern French Indochina and not to advance further into Southeastern Asia or the Southern Pacific area. In return she expected the United States to restore full commercial relations with Tokyo, supply the "required quantity of oil," help Tokyo establish full trade relations with the Dutch East Indies, and stop all aid to China.)

4. *What is the prospect of the European war?* The view of the Foreign Minister was that a German invasion of England would be very difficult and that it was going to be a long war in which Germany might suffer setbacks. The Japanese Army's view was that Germany would definitely be victorious over Russia and England.

5. *Is it possible for Japan to fight either Britain or America separately?* The answer was, "No."

6. *What are the U.S. potential and ability for war?* The answer was about seven to eight times larger than Japan's: "there was no means, it was unanimously agreed, of directly vanquishing the United States in case of war against her."[12]

7. *How can Japan's war potential be built up?* The answer involved methods for increasing financial strength and the production of steel, petroleum, ships, and other munitions. Here the records were brief and vague, for the services guarded their actual production figures very closely.

[11] Togo, *The Cause of Japan*, p. 125*f*.
[12] *Ibid.*, p. 126.

On November 5, as a result of these discussions, at which in typical Japanese fashion contradictions were not resolved but merely stated, the "unanimous" decision was reached to go to war with England, America, and Holland. Negotiations with the United States, however, were to continue, though the limits set by the Army representatives on Japanese concessions were so stringent as to preclude success. The formality of continuing negotiations was a strictly bureaucratic sort of compromise between the views of the members advocating immediate war, and those who wished to avoid war with the United States for a bit longer. It set the deadline forward to November 25 for the Japanese ambassadors in America to accomplish their task, and advanced the opening date for war to December 8. Later the November 25 deadline was changed to November 29, and there was some dispute about how much time to allow between presentation of the Japanese reply to the American Ten Point Note and the hour of the first attack, opinions varying from two and one-half hours to forty-five minutes.

The discussions of the timing of the opening strike on Pearl Harbor show a very nice concern for the delicate adjustment between the necessities of morality and the requisites of surprise. The Japanese wanted us to have what amounted to their declaration of war and their justification for waging war, and they wanted us to receive it before the actual blow— but not so long before that it would be useful. Perhaps the most interesting aspect of these Japanese discussions of timing was their concern for world opinion.

As we have seen in the chapter on MAGIC, our November warnings included the deadlines of the 25th and the 29th, and the entire substance of the Japanese demands and concessions. All that we lacked was the date of December 8, a precise list of targets, and—most important—an ability to estimate correctly Japanese desperation and daring. Signals we had in abundance. But we could not believe that a power as small as Japan would make the first strike against a power as big as the United States. Even in retrospect it is difficult to understand the magnitude and the particular characteristics of Japanese rashness.

Historians have neglected the most striking aspect of the Japanese long-range considerations, i.e., their fuzziness, in contrast to the precision and clarity of the short-range plans. Most of the military and government records were destroyed before the surrender, so that accounts from memory of their projected plans for 1943 and later were naturally some-what vague and conflicting. But the remembered short-range plans are not at all so.

Admiral Yamamoto, who planned the Pearl Harbor attack, would have been a most interesting witness regarding the long-range forecasts, even though his sphere was strictly operational. (He was killed during the war in an aerial ambush.) The few statements attributed to him indicate that he was at first firmly opposed to war with the United States because he thought that defeat was inevitable. In a letter to Ryoichi Sasakawa, he warned that "if hostilities break out between Japan and the United States, it would not be enough for us to take Guam and the Philippines, nor even Hawaii and San Francisco. We should have to march into Washington and sign the treaty in the White House."[13]

After the decision to go to war was made, Yamamoto is reported as saying to Premier Konoye:

> If you tell me that it is necessary that we fight, then in the first six months to a year of war against the U.S. and England I will run wild, and I will show you an uninterrupted succession of victories; I must also tell you that, should the war be prolonged for two or three years, I have no confidence in our ultimate victory.[14]

It is not clear whether Yamamoto at this later date believed that Japan could win in a short war, and that the United States and England would accept a compromise peace on the basis of a destruction of their forces-in-being in the Pacific, or whether he believed that the war would be a long one and Japan's defeat would be inevitable, once the American economy was geared to wartime production and American forces returned to settle the score.

The testimony of Premier Tojo and General Sugiyama was equally vague on the long-range picture. They both assured the Emperor and the cabinet that they would be victorious, but they always added that the question of victory was irrelevant because Japan had to strike immediately or never. Victory, when it was not vague, was figured in terms of forces-

---

[13] Kato, *The Lost War*, p. 89.

[14] Okumiya and Horikoshi, *Zero*, p. 61. Cf. Fuchida and Okumiya, *Midway: The Battle That Doomed Japan*, p. 18.

in-being and a projected time schedule of one year. Only lip service was given to the menace of a U.S. war potential seven to eight times the size of Japan's.[15]

The attitude toward future U.S. strength was very much like that shown in the instructions issued to the Japanese ambassadors in Washington. The ambassadors simply had to "work harder" and try more energetically to persuade Secretary Hull and his advisers. They were not to make any concessions or to change their demands in any way, but simply to expend more effort on the task of persuasion. Similarly, the Army and Navy forces were going to be called on to work harder than ever before for the glory of Japan, but it was the image of an expanding empire and the realization of loudly advertised national goals that provided the incentive. The U.S. war potential loomed in the background as a remote threat only.

Navy Minister Shimada spoke at some length on the subject of risks at the November 1 Liaison Conference:

> In the event of war, the Naval High Command believes that the Navy stands a very good chance of victory in both the early stage operations and the interception operations against the enemy fleet, with the present power ratio. However, should the war continue into its third year ... shortages of war materials and the inadequacy of Japan's industrial potential will then begin to have their effect on the Navy's strength. Under the latter conditions, it would be very difficult for us to have any measure of confidence that we could win.
>
> On the other hand, if we decide to continue diplomatic negotiations and later fail to bring them to a successful conclusion, we will be forced to open hostilities at a great operational disadvantage, caused by the delay. Consequently, though there is a great risk in beginning the war now, we must realize that there is also great risk in depending upon negotiations unless we can be certain of the final outcome. It would seem, therefore, that whether we continue diplomatic negotiations or open hostilities, great risks and difficulties are involved. The risks involved in each case have to be weighed in order to arrive at an estimate of the situation.[16]

This sounds rational enough, but there is no evidence as to how these risks came out on the scales, or whether they were ever actually weighed.

---

[15] There is some evidence also that "careful and conservative estimates" about Japan's economy were definitely discouraged by Japan's Planning Board: "Those responsible were likely to be dismissed or lose their chance for advancement." (Kato, *The Lost War*, p. 169*f*.)

[16] "Political Strategy prior to the Outbreak of War," Part V, p. 1.

(Unfortunately, diplomatic and long-term military risks are hard to measure.) On November 4 and 5 a series of meetings between the military and the government resulted in the decision to go to war with the United States, Great Britain, and the Netherlands. The decision was supported with all kinds of figures indicating that Japan could not hope to keep up with American production of armaments or aircraft, coupled with the frequent repetition that "each day of delay will place us at a greater disadvantage."[17]

The Japanese did have the material for making some relevant long-range predictions. The intelligence estimates released by *USSBS*, for example, show that their assessment of our war potential in aircraft manufacture, shipbuilding, and rate of training of the necessary crews was much more accurate than our own for 1941, 1942, and 1943.[18] The relation between this material and the decision to take on the United States as an opponent is simply not explicable in rational terms. Shigenori Togo, who was Minister of Foreign Affairs in the last peacetime cabinet, and who made a last-minute effort to bring the Japanese-American negotiations to some successful conclusion, complained that the "high command refused to divulge figures on the numbers of our forces, or any facts relating to operations."[19] He "felt keenly the absurdity of our having to base our deliberations on assumptions."[20] While he had a picture of the U.S. forces-in-being and potential from "the numerous published figures on American productive capacity"[21] and fully recognized that "her potential was beyond comparison greater than that of Japan,"[22] he was in the dark about just how the Japanese services were operating. He had "demanded that the high command give its forecast of the outlook for a war"[23] at the November 1 Liaison Conference. Admiral Nagano assured him of victory in the initial stages, but Togo pressed for further assurance on an ultimate victory: "The War Minister responded that victory was certain in the over-all view, and that I could put my fears at rest, trusting in the high command. The Navy Minister repeated that there

[17] *Ibid.*, p. 3f.
[18] *USSBS, Japanese Military and Naval Intelligence Division.*
[19] Togo, *The Cause of Japan*, p. 127.
[20] *Ibid.*   [21] *Ibid.*, p. 126.
[22] *Ibid.*   [23] *Ibid.*, p. 141.

was no cause for pessimism. The Navy Chief of Staff reiterated his confidence in ambushing operations, and said that the Navy would sink the American Fleet as it sailed north from the Central Pacific toward the area of the Mandates."[24] Togo finally came to the conclusion that he "had no alternative to taking on trust the services' assurances."[25] These assurances camouflaged the central unsolved problem: Japan could not win in a long war; yet she had no feasible plan for making sure that the war would be short. Her initial success might discourage us and make us quit, and her leaders could only hope that that was what would happen; but they had no way of depriving us of the means and the will to continue fighting.

In other words, war with the United States was not chosen. The decision for war was rather forced by the desire to avoid the more terrible alternative of losing status or abandoning the national objectives. These objectives, which added up to expansion of the Japanese Empire, had been proclaimed for years—at least since the 1930's. But their feasibility or their compatibility with the goals of other nations was rarely analyzed or even questioned. Step-by-step pursuit of a program of expansion in China, Korea, and Indochina had committed the Japanese to further steps in the same direction; so that stopping at any point always became equivalent to "accepting national humiliation" or "accepting the role of a second-rate power." So, for example, by July, when President Roosevelt suggested neutralizing Indochina and Siam as a last resort before the embargo, matters had already proceeded too far. As Togo put it, "the idea was studied by the Japanese authorities; but our forces could not be withdrawn from southern Indo-China unless the whole southward drive was to be abandoned, the Indo-China move having been based on the 2 July Imperial Conference decision, and the first implementation of the policy of southward advance therein prescribed."[26]

There is no doubt that the less aggressive civilian members of the government were swept along by the military in this headlong progress. Within the Navy any remaining reluctance had been overcome by Army generosity in interservice bargaining about sharing the new resources in

24 *Ibid.*, p. 142.
25 *Ibid.*, p. 143.
26 *Ibid.*, p. 86.

the southeast. In the cabinet, the brilliant and stubborn General Tojo, who had helped to plan the China campaign, had replaced the last weak moderate, Konoye, as Prime Minister. He dominated every discussion and won every argument. He also discouraged whatever tendency there may have been to raise long-term considerations by focusing discussion of the alternatives facing Japan on specific, immediate strategies, even tactics. The question became not whether the United States should be involved as well as Great Britain, but which would be the most effective initial blow—to attack Malaya first and reserve the Philippines for later, or to attack both simultaneously. Such considerations can decide the outcome of a battle, but not of a war.

It is interesting to observe now that Japanese and American estimates of the risks to the Japanese were identical for the large-scale war they had planned, as well as for the individual operations. What we miscalculated was the ability and willingness of the Japanese to accept such risks. As Ambassador Grew had said, "National sanity would dictate against such an event, but Japanese sanity cannot be measured by our own standards of logic."[27]

Our own standards, as we have observed them in military and State Department documents, reckoned the risks to the Japanese as too large, and therefore not likely to be taken. They were too large. But they were going to be taken. And we missed this apparently illogical connection because we did not include in our reckoning any consideration of the alternative of "gradual exhaustion," the danger of encirclement and defeat without having struck a single blow. Our own standards of logic pointed to the easier British and Dutch targets, but the Japanese regarded the American-British-Dutch alliance as a firm one, which committed us to war if the easier targets were attacked. Our own naval standards assumed no more than two carriers for a single seaborne air attack, because we were accustomed to thinking in terms of our own capabilities. Even in the congressional hearings, as late as 1945, with the evidence of six carriers before them, naval witnesses often refer to four carriers because it was beyond the reach of imagination that any naval power would risk its entire heavy carrier strength in one operation. Even if we had played

[27] *Hearings*, Part 14, p. 1056.

out a Japanese war game, we might not have been able to project the daring and ingenuity of the enemy. (The Martin-Bellinger estimate, mentioned in Chapter 1, had specified "one or more carriers.")

This inability to imagine enemy psychology and tactics is, of course, a flaw inherent in most war games; the strategies are as good as the players and, on the whole, are typical of the players rather than of their identities in the game. The American decisionmakers, it has been noted, were rather poor at imagining Japanese intentions and Japanese values. It should be said that the Japanese themselves had essential difficulties with empathy, with projecting American responses to Japanese acts. Most unreal was their assumption that the United States, with ten times the military potential and a reputation for waging war until unconditional victory,[28] would after a short struggle simply accept the annihilation of a considerable part of its air and naval forces and the whole of its power in the Far East.

One of the most interesting examples of the Japanese inability to understand American psychology was a combined political-military game played out by the Japanese during the month of August, 1941.[29] This game, though not so well known as the naval war game played in September,[30] attempted to deal with some long-term considerations. The participants, drawn from the Army, the Navy, and the government ministries, were members of a Total War Research Institute in Tokyo, which the Japanese government had established in October, 1940. The countries represented included Italy and Germany (treated as one), Russia, America, England, Thailand, the Netherlands East Indies, China, Korea, Manchuria, and French Indochina. With fidelity to the actual domestic scene, the players did not represent Japan as simply one team with a single interest, but as a coalition of conflicting interests that had to reach an agreement on major issues. There was, for example, disagreement as to the inevitability of war, the date and manner of beginning the

[28] A reputation established at any rate during World War I. See Kennan, *American Diplomacy, 1900–1950.*

[29] Exhibits 868 and 871 in "Tokyo War Crime Trial Documents," Vol. 16.

[30] Evidence for this game is fragmentary, since the legal staff engaged in research for the Tokyo War Crime Trials was primarily interested in establishing the existence of the sponsor —the Total War Research Institute.

war, the number of adversaries to be engaged, and the economic controls needed to support the war.

In the course of the prewar part of the game, which was projected in time from mid-August to December 15, 1941, the military services succeeded in selling the cabinet the program of southeastern expansion. Japan in this game did not initiate the war with America. Italy and Germany became involved with America first (no details are given in the existing papers), and Japan followed. She played a tactic of diplomatic delay until America declared a neutral sea zone in the Far East and sank a few Japanese ships. These two acts were taken as the trigger for springing the carefully prepared series of surprise attacks on all the Southeastern Asiatic countries, including the Philippines. There was no mention of Pearl Harbor.

The hot-war progress of the game, which was projected through 1943, showed Germany slowly gaining on Russia, enabling Japan to attack Siberia successfully in the autumn of 1942. This corresponded precisely with Japanese Army predictions at the time; so one may speculate that the strings were held here by the Army players. With fidelity also to the actual course of events during 1941, the Army was represented as the most aggressive and influential clique. It won all the cabinet arguments, and its premises prevailed. The conspicuous absence of mention of Pearl Harbor, at that moment under heated debate by the Navy, would indicate that the participants in the game had no inkling of the plan.

This political game, unlike the tactical games played during September at the Naval War College, does not seem to have been an actual testing of alternatives, but rather a sophisticated way of demonstrating or arguing a set of convictions. The favorable prognosis for the Japanese forces, as well as the vagueness with which the outcome of American and British opposition was handled, bear a close relation to the actual arguments presented to the Emperor by General Sugiyama, the Army Chief of Staff. Somehow—with Germany victorious over Russia and England—the United States was going to fade out of the conflict, and the details of the fadeout were irrelevant.

All the evidence seems to indicate that the Japanese decision to go to war with the United States was not clearly faced but rather accepted as the lesser of two evils. It was war with the United States or disintegration as a nation. The objectives of the war and the sort of compromise peace or equilibrium that might have been achieved in the Pacific were never given serious consideration by either policy planners or operational experts.

The calculations of the first phase of the war were detailed and daring, if not rash. They were enormously complex in terms of timing, geographic spread, and close matching of Japanese and U.S. forces-in-being. These calculations called for nearly perfect coordination, and at the time of planning they pressed to the limits of Japanese capacity—in some cases, even beyond them. However, the anticipation of ultimate U.S. acquiescence in the second or third phase hardly deserves to be called "calculation." It would seem that the Japanese undertook this risk wishfully, without thinking it through. Or rather, the risk of doing nothing about the United States, while attacking the British and Dutch, and, still more, the *risk of not attacking* the British and Dutch, seemed overwhelming and unthinkable—the acceptance of status as a tenth-rate power.

It gives one pause to contemplate how slightly the future acted as a curb on this particular aggressor. With all the necessary economic and military data to predict their own defeat, the Japanese never seriously considered restraint in the pursuit of territorial expansion, with which they identified "national honor." The future should hold even less of a threat today for the industrially inferior power. For it is feasible with contemporary weapons for a series of opening clashes with the forces-in-being to decide the outcome of a war.

JAPANESE SHORT-RANGE PLANS

Let us look now in more detail at two of the opening clashes in the Japanese war plan: the Philippine campaign and the Pearl Harbor attack. Consideration of some of the operational details will give us additional insight into the great daring and precise calculations of the Phase I military planners.

The Attack on the Philippines

Brigadier General Koichi Shimada, who served on the staff of the Eleventh Air Fleet at the outbreak of World War II, has given us the most recent authoritative account of the first days of the Philippine campaign.[31] We shall summarize here only certain limited aspects.

Briefly, the Philippine campaign was to open with air attacks by the Army's Fifth Air Group and the Navy's Eleventh Air Fleet, to be followed by landings on the island of Batan,[32] on Luzon, and on Mindanao. The Fifth Air Group was to contribute 72 fighters, 27 twin-engined bombers, 54 light bombers, 27 reconnaissance aircraft, and 12 liaison aircraft, making a total of 192. The Navy's Eleventh Air Fleet was to contribute the majority of the Zero fighters not assigned to the Pearl Harbor attack, 108 in all, plus 13 old-type fighters, 81 new-type bombers, 36 old-type bombers, 15 reconnaissance planes, 24 flying boats, and 27 transport planes, making a total of 304 Navy planes.[33] The respective range of Army and Navy aircraft determined the division of duties. Army aircraft had been designed primarily for a continental war against Russia, which required operation against Soviet targets from land bases in nearby Manchuria. The radius of Army fighters at the time was therefore only 300 miles, and Army bombers carrying a normal bomb load could not travel from Formosa bases to Lingayen Gulf and return. The Navy's Zero fighters, on the other hand, had a radius of 420 miles. The Navy therefore agreed to operate south of the 16th parallel (which runs from Lingayen Gulf to the San Ildefonso Peninsula), while Army air would operate north of that latitude. The Army Air Force was to attack Tuguegarao and Baguio (the summer capital of the Philippines), while the Navy handled Clark and Nichols fields. (See Fig. 6.)

The bulk of the Navy carrier force had been assigned to the Pearl Harbor attack; most of the air support for the Philippine and Malayan invasions would therefore have to come at first from land bases in Formosa and southern French Indochina. Each advance southward would have to be accompanied by the securing of forward air bases for support of the next stage of the invasion, and each advance would have to be made within a certain time limit.

Now the distance from Formosa to targets in the Manila area is a full 550 statute miles. Even the Navy Zeros were not equipped with fuel for

[31] Shimada, "Japanese Naval Air Operations in the Philippine Invasion," pp. 1–17.
[32] Not to be confused with the peninsula of Bataan.
[33] Shimada, "Japanese Naval Air Operations in the Philippine Invasion," p. 3.

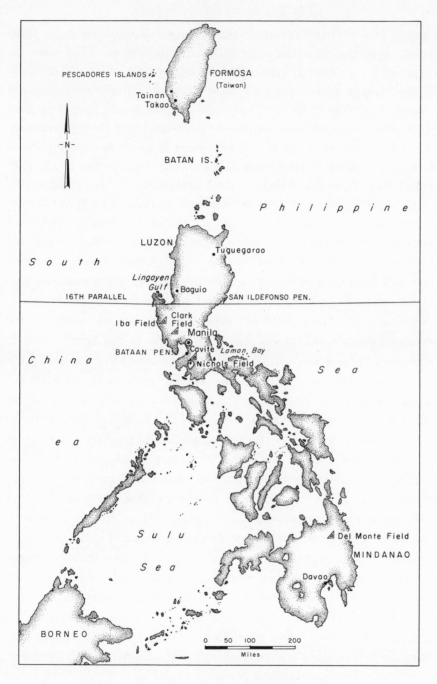

Fig. 6. Planned Points of Attack by Japanese Aircraft in Philippine Invasion, December 8, 1941 (Japanese Time)

a round trip to and from this central target. There were three small carriers available, but they presented many difficulties. They were the *Ryujo*, with a 24-aircraft capacity, the *Zuiko* with a 28-aircraft capacity, and the *Kasuga Maru* with a 23-aircraft capacity. Altogether they could accommodate only 75 aircraft, and some of these would have to be used for combat air patrol. None of the three carriers could launch with more than half its aircraft on deck; and even more serious was the complicated problem of trying to coordinate takeoff from the carriers at sea with takeoff from Formosa, especially since last-minute changes could not be communicated under the strict radio silence necessary to surprise the defending forces. Furthermore there was the risk of forewarning the United States, as the carriers would have to maneuver within range of possible observation to launch the Zeros for the opening attack. Another consideration was the loss of efficiency in splitting naval air maintenance personnel into two groups—one for land bases and one for the carriers.

Obviously the Navy could not depend wholly on the small carriers, nor could they depend on the Zeros for attacks in the Manila area. In September, 1941, it seemed the better part of wisdom to try to find some way to increase the range of the Zeros. The Eleventh Air Fleet transferred its main strength to Formosa and started working on this problem, as well as on training its pilots for aerial combat, strafing, and night flying. In mid-October, Zero pilots also started rehearsing landings and takeoffs from actual flight decks when the small carriers arrived in Formosa. Training for operations both from land bases and from carriers was necessary because the carriers might have to be used if the range of the Zeros could not be improved. This double sort of training continued until early in November, when the decision was finally made to operate primarily from land bases.[34] It was only at this late date that an increase in combat radius to 500 statute miles had been achieved, with a maximum of fifteen minutes over the target. This was still 50 miles short of the radius required for Manila targets. The increase had been accomplished by reducing the engine cruising speed from 1850 to 1650–1700 rpm and by setting the fuel mixture as lean as possible. "The further 50-mile extension in combat radius," as General Shimada explained, "would have to be

---

[34] One small carrier was used for air cover for landings at Davao in the south.

achieved through pilot skill and discipline to insure constant flight speed, especially in night formation flying."[35]

With calculations drawn this close, Navy planners also hopefully included on the agenda the occupation of Batan Island on the morning of D-day. This island, located midway between Formosa and Luzon, would have made a valuable refueling stop for returning Zeros whose pilots had overstayed their time over target.

Besides the difficulties with the carriers, which occasioned the need for increasing the combat radius of the Zero, surprise in the Philippines was going to be much more difficult to achieve than at Pearl Harbor. The attack on Pearl Harbor was to be delivered shortly after dawn on December 7, Hawaii time, which was several hours before dawn of December 8, Philippine time.[36] In order to deliver the Philippine and Pearl Harbor air attacks simultaneously, the Zero pilots would have to bomb the Philippines at night. However, night bombing in China had been very unreliable because of inadequate bombsights; and the planners decided to delay the attack on the Philippines until daylight, when successful bombing would be ensured. Accordingly, "the final plan issued on December 6 for the first attack on Luzon fixed departure time . . . from Formosan bases at 0230 December 8. Fifteen minutes after an 0615 sunrise, Nichols Field was to be hit by one force of 54 bombers and 50 fighters from Takao, and Clark Field by another of 54 bombers and 36 fighters from Tainan."[37]

This meant that if everything went as planned and the coordination was perfect, the Philippine defending force would have at least several hours to receive warning and to react. Imperial General Headquarters was counting on radio jamming to prevent the news of the Pearl Harbor strike from getting through, but naval air planners did not count on the jamming. They expected the defenders to have several hours of warning time, but it was a risk they had to take.

[35] Shimada, "Japanese Naval Air Operations in the Philippine Invasion," p. 5. See also Okumiya and Horikoshi, *Zero,* pp. 80 *ff.,* for a discussion of training for the Philippine air attacks. Night formation flying was necessary because there were no rendezvous devices on the aircraft.

[36] The international date line at the 180° meridian separates Hawaii from the Philippines. All islands lying to the east carry the same date as the Americas; all those to the west carry the same date as Japan and Australia.

[37] Shimada, "Japanese Naval Air Operations in the Philippine Invasion," p. 8.

As we now know, the attack did not come off as planned. Fog held the Japanese pilots on the ground for 6 hours that morning. At the last moment they changed their target from Nichols Field to Iba, in order to destroy the fighters that they assumed would otherwise attack them if they tried to bomb Nichols. Moreover, the Philippine jamming was unsuccessful, and news of Pearl Harbor was received at Manila an hour after the Pearl Harbor attack, at least 3 hours before the planned Philippine attack, and some 9 hours before the actual Philippine attack. But, in spite of the delay, the Japanese pilots achieved a tactical surprise as spectacular as if everything had proceeded on schedule. In some ways the Philippine surprise is even more startling than the more publicized case at Pearl Harbor.

The difficulties experienced by the Japanese Naval Air Force in the Philippine campaign were merely one set among many in the vast preparations for the Southeast Asia war plan. The Japanese Army's original plan for this part of the campaign,[38] for example, had assigned six battalions for advance landings, two full divisions for the main landings, and supporting troops. In the end, General Homma, commander of the 14th Army, had to be content with two divisions, the 15th and the 48th, for the entire operation. His supporting troops consisted of two tank regiments, two regiments and one battalion of medium artillery, three engineer regiments, five antiaircraft battalions, and a number of service units. He would lose to the Indies and the Malaya campaign the 48th Division and many units just as soon as Luzon was occupied. Where he had expected a combined Army-Navy air support of about 600 aircraft, he was finally able to secure 500. The reduction in his forces is easily understandable in view of the enormous requirements for simultaneous landings on D-day, as well as the large number of troops already engaged in the China incident, or held for policing in Manchuria, Korea, Formosa, and Indochina.

There were dangers for the Japanese, then, in the shortage of manpower, inadequate weapons, and a scheduled spread of several hours between bomb release times at Pearl Harbor and Luzon, to say nothing of the risks of unscheduled delays. To these must be added the risks of discovery during at least six weeks before D-day in a project where sur-

[38] Morton, *The Fall of the Philippines*, p. 59.

prise was vitally important. In the case of the Navy, scores of transport vessels were heading south. General Shimada mentioned enormous concentrations during November in the South Formosan port of Takao, and at Mako in the Pescadores. They seemed to him at the time "an almost unmistakable tip-off that a large-scale amphibious move to the south impended."[39]

Ship and troop movements had necessarily to be made weeks in advance, but air reconnaissance missions were held off until very late. The first, on October 25, merely went over Batan Island to determine whether or not there was an airfield there. Reconnaissance of Luzon was held off until November 20, and flights were separated by several days, with every possible precaution taken against detection. The last mission was flown on December 5 to see if there were any changes in the disposition of enemy forces just prior to attack. Weather observation planes were also sent over the waters flanking the east and west coasts of the Philippines beginning on November 25 to get the necessary weather data on the routes to target that the attack planes would fly on December 8. Detailed intelligence data had of course been collected in advance on location of our airfields, number of aircraft, disposition of troops, etc. But last-minute data continued to be received from Manila by way of Tokyo as late as December 6. When all these sources were put together, the Japanese attackers were extremely well informed. They were, in fact, better informed than Washington concerning what equipment and what vehicles were actually ready for use. Shimada summarized as follows the information available on December 6 to the naval air planners on Formosa:

> Most of the enemy surface units and submarines observed in Manila Bay in late November were no longer there. It was estimated that the surface units had moved to southern Philippine waters, while the submarines appeared to be widely scattered. Several submarines had been located by radio to the east of the Philippines and around the Palau islands, and others were believed to be maneuvering off western Luzon near Lingayen Gulf. Also, on several occasions subsequent to early November, American submarines had been reported to the east and west of Formosa.
>
> Most of the enemy's heavy bombers were based on Clark and Nichols, with a few scattered at Nielson, Murphy, Iba, Del Carmen and other minor airfields situated around the two major bases. Starting in mid-November,

[39] Shimada, "Japanese Naval Air Operations in the Philippine Invasion," p. 7.

daily routine air patrols had been carried out over the waters west of Luzon. On December 5 enemy air units in the Philippines had been ordered to a 15-minute stand-by alert.[40]

In addition, Japanese reconnaissance aircraft had obtained detailed photographic coverage of Lingayen Gulf, the beaches on northern Luzon where the Army would land its troops, and the Bataan Peninsula. Photographs of Bataan were forwarded immediately to General Homma's headquarters.

However, while the attackers were extremely well informed, as can be seen from Table 3, their preparations, as well as their espionage activities, made them vulnerable to discovery. The American Intelligence agencies had picked up many of the available signals. Washington knew about most of the naval concentrations to the south. It knew about the amphibious equipment aboard the ships and about troops being moved into Formosa and Southern Indochina. Our State Department had registered appropriate formal protests with the Japanese government. MacArthur's forces had spotted the air reconnaissance over the Philippines, and steps were being taken in Washington for an American flight to make a photographic reconnaissance over some of the Japanese islands in the Marshalls and Carolines. Cryptanalysis officers both in the Philippines and in Washington had copies of Japanese messages sent out of the Philippines giving data on the number, type, and disposition of our defenses.

What our officers did *not* have was, for the most part, crucial last-minute data. They lacked data on enemy intentions deduced from the movements of forces on the way to the target (usually included under "action" intelligence), and they lacked data on the capabilities of the enemy (usually listed under the ironically optimistic heading of "static" intelligence). For even the static capabilities had changed: estimates that had been true in early November were no longer true in early December. In the Philippines the most important case of a swift change in Japanese capabilities was the increase in range of the Zeros, making feasible a round-trip flight to the Philippines from Formosan bases. Our officers had not received this information by December 7. Furthermore, they did not have the "action" intelligence that the carriers had left the Kuriles on November 25, though the earlier estimate by naval traffic

[40] *Ibid.*, p. 9.

TABLE 3

ACTUAL U.S. FORCES IN THE PHILIPPINES ON DECEMBER 8, 1941
(TOKYO TIME) COMPARED WITH JAPANESE ESTIMATE[a]

Actual U.S. Forces	Japanese Estimate of U.S. Forces
45 naval vessels	33 to 48 naval vessels
1 heavy cruiser	1 heavy cruiser
2 light cruisers	2 light cruisers
13 destroyers	15 destroyers
29 submarines	15 to 30 submarines
307 operational aircraft	250 to 300 operational aircraft[b]
107 P-40's	108 P-40's
68 other fighters	79 other fighters and patrol aircraft
35 B-17's	38 bombers
39 other bombers	18 PBY's
58 miscellaneous aircraft (reconnaissance, cargo)	13 reconnaissance aircraft
31,104 U.S. Army troops	20,000 to 25,000 U.S. Army troops
11,988 Philippine scouts	....
19,116 other American troops	....
Majority of troops located on Luzon	Majority of troops located on Luzon
1 division	1 division
1 air unit	1 air unit
1 fortress unit	1 fortress unit
1 battalion of 54 tanks	1 battalion of 54 tanks
....	1 antitank battalion
4 coast artillery regiments	4 coast artillery regiments
1 antiaircraft regiment	1 antiaircraft regiment

[a] Compiled from the following sources: Morton, *The Fall of the Philippines*, pp. 42, 49, and 58; Shimada, "Japanese Naval Air Operations in the Philippine Invasion," *passim*; Craven and Cate (eds.), *United States Air Force in World War II: Plans and Early Operations: January 1939 to August 1942*, pp. 201*ff.*; USSBS, *Japanese Air Power*, p. 6.

[b] Approximate estimate.

analysts that they were somewhere near Japan in a covering position had been correct for mid-November. Nor did they have the last-minute espionage information out of Manila because these messages had not yet been decoded or translated. There were, of course, other last-minute signals with respect to the Pearl Harbor attack that were missed. For the moment, however, the only concern is the Philippine campaign, and the departure of the carriers is mentioned because two of these had originally been designated for the air strike against the Philippines and Malaya.

Access to these late signals might have helped to minimize the surprise of the Philippine defenders. It might, for example, have led them to serious preparation for air attack either from Formosa or from carriers. Even though they missed the signals just mentioned, however, the Philippine defenders did have a good 9 hours of warning—from 2:30 A.M., when news of the Pearl Harbor attack was received by radio, until about 12:30 P.M., when the Japanese struck.[41] Lack of response to the warning was not because of inadequate intelligence. Rather, our defense was simply not prepared for sudden air attack and had no capacity for responding to warning. This was partly a matter of the primitive state of communication and equipment and the lack of coordination of command on the islands; it was also partly a matter of the prevailing belief that the Japanese attack would come in March or April, 1942—a date that corresponded neatly with the date set by military estimates for completion of U.S. Philippine defenses.

But essentially a Japanese air attack was a contingency that had been methodically considered only on paper. The actions to be taken on receipt of warning could not be, or at any rate were not, implemented. For example, after receipt of the November 27 warning message, General Mac-Arthur ordered all heavy bombers transferred to the new southern air base at Del Monte on Mindanao, but by December 7 General Brereton had moved only half of them. B-17's were precious objects then, and the new air base was not yet finished or properly equipped for their use. After November 27 there was evidence of increasing Japanese reconnaissance over the Philippines, and yet no order went out to extend our own reconnaissance over Formosa. According to some accounts (and there is, of course, much conflicting evidence on each of the examples reported here) our reconnaissance was held to two-thirds of the distance between northern Luzon and the southern tip of Formosa to comply with Washington's directive to let Japan commit the first overt act. Urgency about shifting bombers to the south or making a reconnaissance over

---

[41] Morton (*The Fall of the Philippines*, pp. 80–90) gives an excellent summary of the conflicting reports on what happened during these 10 hours. See also Edmonds, *They Fought with What They Had*.

Formosa could not have seemed very great at this time because the Japanese Zero was not supposed to have the radius for successfully attacking Clark Field from Formosan bases. When the attack actually occurred, our forces assumed that the Japanese aircraft were coming in from carriers.

It was partly the lack of photographic reconnaissance information to establish accurate targets that delayed an American counterattack on Formosan bases after receipt of news of the Pearl Harbor attack. Several key airmen at Clark and Nichols Fields urged such an attack, but they could not get permission to schedule the flight until the afternoon of December 8 (Philippine time). Even then that first flight was to be for reconnaissance, and the counterattack was to take place on the morning of December 9. In the meantime there was a good deal of discussion and disagreement on what to do next, how to disperse the aircraft or whether to try to keep them in the air to avoid destruction. As it happened, all but one of the B-17's were on the ground getting fuel and bombs when the Japanese pilots finally reached Clark Field, and they were all destroyed. The aircraft of the 20th Pursuit Squadron were also caught on the ground, having just completed an unsuccessful interception mission and returned for refueling. Our bombers at Nichols Field were not hit on that first day of war only because the initial attack had been diverted to Iba at the last moment to destroy the fighters there. At Iba the destruction was almost as great as at Clark.

This glimpse of some of the operational details of the Philippine campaign invites a healthy respect for the Japanese ability to estimate and accept risks in the immediate future. The Hawaiian operation was, of course, even more daring, and it was preceded by at least a year of secret research, and heated debate, among top Navy planners. Neither Army planners nor any members of the cabinet were informed of this particular operation until the fall of 1941.

The Pearl Harbor Attack

For years, in fact since 1909, the Japanese Fleet had prepared for action against the American Fleet, but the major emphasis had been on training and weapons for a decisive counteroffensive in the waters near Japan *after* the United States had struck in the Pacific. However, by 1939 it became apparent even to the conservative Naval General Staff that the

Japanese Navy might have to deal simultaneously with Dutch, British, *and* American forces, and the threat posed by a large fleet as close as Hawaii was something that had to be reckoned with in new terms. It was Admiral Yamamoto, Commander-in-Chief of the Combined Fleet, a daring gambler and a firm supporter of air power, who proposed the solution that was finally adopted.

Toward the close of 1940, Admiral Yamamoto requested the aid of "a flier, whose past career has not influenced him in conventional operations,"[42] to study the problem of an air attack on Pearl Harbor. Curiously, news of this attack plan reached Ambassador Grew through the Peruvian embassy in January, 1941, and was rejected by him and by our Intelligence agencies as fantastic. Their judgment was the same as that of the Japanese Naval General Staff. Yamamoto selected Rear Adm. Takijiro Ohnishi to make the study, together with another unconventional airman named Minoru Genda. Ohnishi completed a general plan toward the end of April, 1941, and isolated two main obstacles: (1) "the technical difficulties of launching aerial torpedo attacks in Pearl Harbor, which is so shallow that aerial torpedoes launched by ordinary methods would stick to the bottom"[43] and (2) the strategic difficulty that surprise was essential to the operation. Ohnishi at that time figured that his plan had a 60 per cent chance of success. Admiral Fukudome, Chief of the First Bureau of the Naval General Staff, who was let in on the secret, estimated its chance to be only 40 per cent because, as he explained, he took operational difficulties more seriously than did Ohnishi. Evidently Ohnishi himself came around to this point of view by early September, 1941, because at that time, and again in October, he tried to dissuade Admiral Yamamoto from the enterprise. But Yamamoto had by then accepted the decision to go to war with America and only on condition that the Pearl Harbor attack be incorporated in the war plan.

Immediately after the completion of Ohnishi's general plan, in May, 1941, the Japanese Navy started training for the Hawaii operation. The pilots and crews naturally knew nothing about the ultimate goal of their training, and even among top Navy personnel, information concerning the plan was carefully restricted. It is not certain whether Admiral Nagano,

---

[42] Fukudome, "Hawaii Operation," p. 1317.
[43] *Ibid.*, p. 1318.

Chief of the Naval General Staff, was informed in May or later in August.[44] But Yamamoto was making sure that once he presented the plan, there would be no argument on inadequate training. In accordance with his instructions, dive-bombing was practiced at Kagoshima on the southern tip of Kyushu, where the terrain resembled that of Pearl Harbor. Special training in refueling at sea was begun to permit the use of the most secure northern route to the target. Research men went to work on the problem of developing torpedoes for shallow water, and Genda had his air crews practice short and shallow torpedo runs at Saeki.

The date at which the right sort of torpedo was finally developed is not clear. Some testimony indicated success during the summer of 1941; but both Genda and Capt. Mitsuo Fuchida, the pilot who had led the actual attack, said it was not until early November that the problem was finally solved by fixing special fins to regular torpedoes. Fins were also designed to be fitted to 15-inch and 16-inch armor-piercing bombs so that they could penetrate the armor-plated decks of the American ships. These late developments are comparable to the extension of the Zero's range for the Philippine campaign. Admiral Kimmel was as uninformed on these crucial developments as the Philippine air officers were on the range and maneuverability of the Zero.

In a letter from Admiral Stark, dated February 15, 1941, Admiral Kimmel had been assured that

> A minimum depth of water of seventy-five feet may be assumed necessary to successfully drop torpedoes from planes. One hundred and fifty feet of water is desired. The maximum height planes at present experimentally drop torpedoes is 250 feet. Launching speeds are between 120 and 150 knots. The desirable height for dropping is sixty feet or less. About two hundred yards of torpedo run is necessary before the exploding device is armed, but this may be altered.[45]

Kimmel was also informed that the depth of the waters in which torpedoes were launched in the successful attacks at Taranto was 84 to 90 feet, with a few runs at 66- to 72-foot depths. The depth of the water in Pearl Harbor is 30 feet or less, except in the channels, where it is 40 feet.

[44] Nagano denies any knowledge of the Pearl Harbor plan until late in October. ("Tokyo War Crime Trial Documents," p. 10187.)

[45] *Hearings*, Part 33, p. 1283.

A follow-up letter on June 13 from Admiral Ingersoll added some second thoughts:

> Recent developments have shown that United States and British torpedoes may be dropped from planes at heights of as much as three hundred feet, and in some cases make initial dives of considerably less than 75 feet, and make excellent runs . . . . it cannot be assumed that any capital ship or other valuable vessel is safe when at anchor from this type of attack if surrounded by water at a sufficient distance to permit an attack to be developed and a sufficient run to arm the torpedo.[46]

And some third thoughts:

> While no minimum depth of water in which naval vessels may be anchored can arbitrarily be assumed as providing safety from torpedo plane attack, it may be assumed that depth of water will be one of the factors considered by any attacking force, and an attack launched in relatively deep water (10 fathoms [or 60 feet] or more) is much more likely.[47]

Notice the final quiet shift from flat statements of infeasibility (of torpedo bomb drops from altitudes below 250 feet or in water shallower than 75 feet) to the milder assumptions that water depth would be a factor considered by the enemy, and—somewhat stronger—that deep-water attacks were more likely.

This information was forwarded to all fleet commanders in connection with requesting their recommendations on antitorpedo baffles. The commanders were instructed to keep in mind that their ships had to have ample maneuvering room, and that "where a large force such as a fleet is based, the installation of satisfactory baffles will be difficult because of congestion."[48] No light antitorpedo net that could be swiftly and easily installed and removed had been developed by December, 1941, and naval technicians seem agreed that any other type of net would simply not have been practicable at Pearl Harbor. Kimmel and his staff, as well as Admiral Bloch, believed after reading the June communication that "the danger of a successful torpedo attack on Pearl Harbor was negligible."[49] On the basis of their information, their judgment was correct. But once more the objects of static intelligence were to behave dynamically.

In addition to the intensive development of weapons and the actual training of pilots and crews, Yamamoto tested the Pearl Harbor attack

46 *Ibid.*, p. 1318.   47 *Ibid.*
48 *Ibid.*, p. 1317.   49 *Ibid.*, Part 6, p. 2509.

plan as part of a large tactical war game at the Naval War College in Tokyo from September 2 to September 13. Yamamoto acted as head umpire, and Vice Adm. Chuichi Nagumo, who later led the actual attack, played out his part also. At this point, quite a large number of naval men were necessarily let in on the secret. The main purpose of gaming was to work out the best schedule of operations for occupying Malaya, Burma, the Netherlands East Indies, the Philippine Islands, and the Solomon and Central Pacific Islands, and to work out the details of the naval air strike at Pearl Harbor.[50] On the basis of the gaming, they decided to strike simultaneously at Malaya and the Philippines.

As for Pearl Harbor,

> the conclusion reached was that there was an even chance that the main force of the U. S. Fleet would be at anchor in Hawaiian waters and present a good opportunity for attack. However, should the American Fleet be sufficiently alert, it might be necessary to break through enemy opposition. On the other hand, there was a possibility that the sea area north of Hawaii might not be effectively patrolled and it appeared that the best move would be to approach through that area. Should the surprise attack succeed, it was estimated that about two thirds of the American capital ships at anchor in Hawaii would be sunk, and Japanese losses probably would be two or three aircraft carriers.[51]

Since six carriers were used in these games for the Pearl Harbor strike, this meant an estimated loss of 33⅓ to 50 per cent of the large carrier force. To Admiral Nagano and the Navy General Staff the risk was entirely too great. It was only after it became clear in early November that Philippine and Malayan air cover could be provided from land bases in Formosa, and after certain negotiations with the Army Air Force, that they were willing to allot all the large carriers to the Pearl Harbor strike and to add to the task force the necessary tankers for refueling. However, even with the chances for success thus improved, Admiral Yamamoto had difficulty in obtaining the personal approval of Nagano, who with his staff put forward four main objections.

First of all, there was the extreme difficulty of preserving the secrecy

---

[50] "Tokyo War Crime Trial Documents," p. 10210.

[51] "Political Strategy prior to the Outbreak of War," Part V, p. 12. See also Hattori, "Complete History of the Greater East Asia War," Vol. I, pp. 318*ff*.

essential to surprise. The task force was a large one, involving as many as sixty ships,[52] which would have to start out at least a month before the date of attack. The Naval General Staff feared detection en route to the target, either through visual observation by the enemy, or through some inadvertent leak on the part of one of the Japanese participants, or through some accident that might necessitate the transmission of radio dispatches. Furthermore, it was believed that U.S. aircraft regularly patrolled the waters around Oahu, occasionally up to a distance of 600 miles. There was a high probability therefore that the patrol planes would spot the carriers at their launching point 200 miles from the target, at which point it would be too late to turn back.

Second, the Naval General Staff argued that it made more sense to follow orthodox teaching and concentrate all their forces on a decisive engagement in the familiar waters near Japan, where their chances of winning were greater. It was not that the concept of surprise was either novel or repugnant. It was simply that surprise attack had always been conceived in the form of a surprise *submarine* attack at the mouth of Pearl Harbor, closing the entrance and blockading as well as destroying American ships. The carriers and battleships were supposed to do battle close to home. This lag in adapting strategy to the new air weapons is not peculiar to the Naval General Staff but is characteristic of most military organizations. It is all too easy to supply Western parallels.

The third argument was that refueling in the North Pacific was very dangerous and uncertain of accomplishment. The destroyers had to refuel not once, but twice, before reaching Pearl Harbor, and it had been calculated on the basis of weather statistics that there were only seven days per month on the average during which refueling operations would be feasible.[53]

Finally, Admiral Nagano was a close friend of Ambassador Nomura's and was hopeful of success in the Washington negotiations until the last moment. He wanted to avoid anything prior to the deadline that might

---

[52] The task force consisted of 6 of their heavy carriers, plus 8 tankers for refueling, 2 heavy cruisers, 1 light cruiser, 2 battleships, 11 destroyers, 3 submarines, 432 aircraft, and the cream of the Japanese Naval Air Force—in addition to the supply train and the advanced expeditionary submarine force.

[53] According to Adm. Stuart S. Murray, the Japanese overestimated the difficulties of refueling.

jeopardize Nomura's efforts. Even on December 1, when Yamamoto came up to Tokyo on his last visit, Nagano reaffirmed the policy of withdrawing all forces from the Pearl Harbor attack should there be a favorable turn in the negotiations.

All of these objections were overcome. But one has the impression at this historical distance that it was the forceful personality of Admiral Yamamoto rather than any rational argument that finally won over the Naval General Staff. Yamamoto, it appears, was not an enthusiast for the war decision, but if the decision was to be made he argued that the whole plan of conquest in Southeast Asia would be endangered unless the U.S. Pacific Fleet were crushed at the outset. His threat to resign unless the Pearl Harbor attack was incorporated in the larger plan seems to have been the ultimate stimulus to its acceptance.

The reader may have noticed that naval air planning, including the war games previously mentioned, as early as September, 1941, precluded the use of the large carriers for the Philippine attack, since they were assigned to the Pearl Harbor task force. This would seem to indicate, at least among naval air planners, not only a lack of opposition to Yamamoto's plan, but even great confidence that the Naval General Staff and Imperial General Headquarters could be persuaded finally to adopt it. And, of course, training for the big event had begun during the summer of 1941.

Following the tactical war games, there was careful preparation of attack information. Toward the end of October elaborate weather data were collected by two military observers aboard the *Taiyo Maru*, a ship that sailed to Honolulu on the exact route to be followed by the task force, traveling east between Midway and the Aleutians and then cutting south.[54] When they arrived in Honolulu, the two observers also made new aerial photographs of the harbor and picked up some useful items of information. For example, they confirmed the espionage reports that the U.S. Fleet was not assembling at Lahaina and that week ends were still universally honored as times of rest and recreation. Tokyo directed Consul General Nagao Kita in Honolulu to send more detailed and more frequent observations on ship movements, harbor berthings, antitorpedo nets,

[54] Lord, *Day of Infamy*, p. 15*f*.

alert practices, U.S. Army installations, etc. Best known of Kita's instructions is the famous September 24 message, which our radio experts intercepted and passed on to our top military and political leaders in Washington:

> Henceforth we would like to have you make reports concerning vessels along the following lines insofar as possible:
>
> 1) The waters (of Pearl Harbor) are to be divided roughly into five subareas. (We have no objection to your abbreviating as much as you like.)
>
> Area A. Waters between Ford Island and the Arsenal.
>
> Area B. Waters adjacent to the Island south and west of Ford Island. (This area is on the opposite side of the Island from Area A.)
>
> Area C. East Loch.
>
> Area D. Middle Loch.
>
> Area E. West Loch and the communicating water routes.
>
> 2) With regard to warships and aircraft carriers, we would like to have you report on those at anchor, (these are not so important) tied up at wharves, buoys and in docks. (Designate types and classes briefly. If possible we would like to have you make mention of the fact when there are two or more vessels along side the same wharf.)[55]

During September, October, and November, the messages between Kita and Tokyo usually went out in the J-19 code. But on December 2, Kita, on orders from Tokyo, destroyed all but his most simple code, the PA-K2.[56] While J-19 could not be read by anyone in Honolulu, Rochefort's local traffic analysis staff was able to read PA-K2. They began to include in their work the reading of some of these messages during the first week in December. Until that time, all such messages had been forwarded to Washington in the original code. Unfortunately by the time of the last-minute signals, the practice in Rochefort's office had not been established long enough for his men to be processing the material with any speed. For this reason the PA-K2 messages exchanged between Kita and Tokyo on December 5 and 6 were not translated by December 7. What our officers might have done with these messages will always be a fascinating

---

[55] *Hearings*, Part 12, p. 261.

[56] The code message "Haruna," meaning "all major codes destroyed," was sent from Kita to Tokyo on December 2. (*Ibid.*, Part 37, p. 1003.) Messages sent from the Japanese consulate in Honolulu and signed "Kita" are identical with "A intelligence" cited by Fukudome and Fuchida.

subject for speculation, since they included such tantalizing bits of information as the following:

DECEMBER 5—*Honolulu to Tokyo*:

1) During Friday morning, the 5th, the three battleships mentioned in my message #239 arrived here. They had been at sea for eight days.

2) The Lexington and five heavy cruisers left port on the same day.

3) The following ships were in port on the afternoon of the 5th:

8 battleships
3 light cruisers
16 destroyers

Four ships of the Honolulu class and [unreadable] were in dock.

DECEMBER 6—*Tokyo to Honolulu*:

Please wire immediately re the latter part of my #123 the movements of the fleet subsequent to the fourth.

DECEMBER 6—*Honolulu to Tokyo*:

Re the last part of your #123:

On the American continent in October the Army began training barrage balloon troops at Camp Davis, North Carolina. Not only have they ordered four or five hundred balloons, but it is understood that they are considering the use of these balloons in the defense of Hawaii and Panama. In so far as Hawaii is concerned, though investigations have been made in the neighborhood of Pearl Harbor, they have not set up mooring equipment, nor have they selected the troops to man them. Furthermore, there is no indication that any training for the maintenance of balloons is being undertaken. *At the present time there are no signs of barrage balloon equipment.* In addition, it is difficult to imagine that they have actually any. However, even though they have actually made preparations, because they must control the air over the water and land runways of the airports in the vicinity of Pearl Harbor, Hickam, Ford, and Ewa, there are limits to the balloon defense of Pearl Harbor. I imagine that *in all probability there is considerable opportunity left to take advantage for a surprise attack against these places.*

2) *In my opinion the battleships do not have torpedo nets.* The details are not known [author's italics]. . . .

The last of the messages was from Kita to Tokyo and was also dated December 6. It reported:

1) On the evening of the 5th, among the battleships which entered port were [unreadable] and one submarine tender. The following ships were observed at anchor on the 6th:

9 battleships, 3 light cruisers, 3 submarine tenders, 17 destroyers, and

376 The Reality behind the Signals

in addition there were 4 light cruisers, 2 destroyers lying at docks (*the heavy cruisers and airplane carriers have all left*).

    2) It appears that *no air reconnaissance is being conducted by the fleet air arm* [author's italics].[57]

All of these messages were forwarded to the task force, according to Admiral Fukudome.[58] The final message quoted above was the last one on the U.S. Fleet to be received by the Japanese task force. It was sent from Tokyo at 6 P.M. on December 7 and received at 8:50 P.M. on December 7, Tokyo time, or 6:50 A.M. on December 6, Washington time. The word missed was *"Utah,"* and Tokyo added the sentence: "Oahu is quiet and Imperial General Staff is fully convinced of success."

In spite of such evidence, during the postwar interrogations Japanese government officials and military officers consistently played down the role of Japanese intelligence, and particularly the value of last-minute espionage provided by foreign agents. They emphasized a long-term, painstaking collection of historical and statistical data, chiefly from naval attaché reports and foreign books, newspapers, and broadcasts. There is no doubt that such basic research on public data is an important, perhaps an essential, background for the exploitation of more covert material. But this is not to say that data from covert sources do not play a significant role. Here the Japanese accounts were somewhat thin and implausible. They claimed that there was no organized exchange of information between the Army and the Navy. The intelligence departments were always understaffed; photographic reconnaissance was poor, as was its interpretation; pilots were incompletely briefed; maps were unreliable; etc. They claimed that no naval officer received special training in intelligence work, and no special intelligence officers were assigned to ships: the captain was supposed to perform any intelligence duties as part of his job, while on flagships the communications officer was expected to do some evaluating. However, each of the five Japanese fleets did have one intelligence officer assigned to it.

According to Japanese accounts, the Army's intelligence organization was even worse than the Navy's, at least for the Southeastern campaign. Evidently for fighting in Manchuria and Siberia, the Army was adequately

57 *Hearings*, Part 12, pp. 268–270.
58 Fukudome, "Hawaii Operation," p. 1327.

equipped with undercover agents, observation posts, and patrols; but for the extended Southeastern campaign of December, 1941, the Army had only a small untrained intelligence section. The bulk of the data required for invading U.S. and British territories in the Far East was supplied to the Army by the Navy.

It is impossible to reconcile this view of Japanese intelligence with what we now know of Japanese information on U.S. forces and installations as of December, 1941. It is true that their reconnaissance photography during the war left much to be desired, but their estimates for 1941 were amazingly detailed and accurate. Their data were unusually complete and up to date when dealing with types of information that could be gathered at leisure, such as fixed installations and locations of piers, airfields, hangars, barracks, etc. On statistical matters such as numbers of men, types of weapons, and numbers of aircraft and ships, their estimates ran sometimes a bit higher, or lower, than the actuality, but frequently their inventory of our battle order was more accurate than our own.

Their last-minute information was also excellent. For example, they were quite accurately informed on the traffic in and out of Pearl Harbor, thanks to Kita and another consular agent, Takeo Yoshikawa. Yoshikawa spent hours in a restaurant overlooking the harbor, and later claimed that he was sending daily reports to Tokyo from the moment of departure of the task force. The actual count of ships in Pearl Harbor on the morning of December 7 was 86. Among these were 8 battleships, 3 heavy cruisers, 6 light cruisers, 29 destroyers, 5 submarines, and no carriers. Kita's last code message listed 9 battleships, no heavy cruisers, 7 light cruisers, 19 destroyers, 3 submarine tenders, and no carriers.[59] The Japanese claim that they made no use of such last-minute observations is hardly credible. The knowledge that there were no carriers in the harbor almost caused cancellation of the Pearl Harbor strike. Captain Fuchida, who led the strike, recorded his recollection of the conversation aboard the *Akagi* on December 6 (our time) when this message was received.[60]

First of all there was an anxiously careful count and recheck of prior messages giving exits and entrances of specific ships from November 28.

[59] It was this message, and not a commercial U.S. broadcast on December 5 (as originally claimed by the Japanese), that provided the last data on the U.S. Fleet dispositions to be received by Japan.
[60] Fuchida, "I Led the Air Attack on Pearl Harbor," p. 944.

Vice Admiral Nagumo, who was in charge of the task force, discussed with his Intelligence officer Ono, his Chief of Staff Kusaka, and his Operations officer Genda the pros and cons of continuing on the mission in the absence of the carriers. Ono explained on the basis of his reports that there might be three carriers in port, arriving over the week end:

> On 29 November . . . *Enterprise* left harbor accompanied by two battleships, two heavy cruisers and twelve destroyers [actually 3 heavy cruisers and 9 destroyers]. The two battleships returned on the 6th, but the rest have not yet come back. *Lexington* came in on the 29th and left with five heavy cruisers on the sixth [actually with 3 heavy cruisers and 5 destroyers]. Thus *Enterprise* ought to return today. *Saratoga* is under repair at San Diego, and *Wasp* is in the Atlantic. But *Yorktown* and *Hornet* belonging to the Pacific Fleet must be out here. They may have arrived with *Enterprise* today.[61]

Chief of Staff Kusaka, "always strong for statistical studies," argued, however, that eight battleships made as good a prize as three carriers: "There is only a slight chance that carriers may enter the harbor on Saturday, and it seems unlikely that battleships would leave on Saturday or Sunday. We may take it for granted that all eight battleships will be in the harbor tomorrow. . . . I think we should attack Pearl Harbor tomorrow."[62] Nagumo fell in with this view and on the evening of December 6 issued the following estimate of the enemy situation:

> 1. Enemy strength in the Hawaiian area consists of eight battleships, two carriers, about ten heavy and six light cruisers. The carriers and heavy cruisers seem to be at sea, but the others are in the harbor. Those operating at sea are most likely in the training area south of Maui; they are not in Lahaina.
> 2. Unless an unforeseen situation develops tonight, our attack will be launched upon Pearl Harbor.
> 3. So far there is no indication that the enemy has been alerted, but that is no reason to relax our security.[63]

Commander Ono's radio communication unit on board the *Akagi* also collected some relevant last-minute information by paying close attention to the commercial Hawaiian broadcasts:

> Admiral Nagumo and his staff felt that they could sense from these broadcasts whether or not the Forces on Oahu had an inkling of the impending

[61] *Ibid.*
[62] *Ibid.*, p. 944f.
[63] *Ibid.*, p. 945.

attack. They felt they could judge the tenseness of the situation. . . . Since KGU and DGMB [Honolulu commercial radio stations] were going along in their normal manner, Nagumo felt that our forces were still oblivious to developments.[64]

Another useful function of Commander Ono's office had been to intercept messages from U.S. patrol aircraft for several days prior to the attack: "They [the Japanese] had not broken the code, but they had been able to plot in . . . [the] positions [of U.S. patrol aircraft] with radio bearings and knew the number of patrol planes in the air at all times and that they were patrolling entirely in the southwestern sector from Oahu."[65] This type of information was available only as the task force came near enough to Pearl Harbor to intercept the messages.

A two-aircraft reconnaissance flight preceded the attack. At 5:30 A.M. one aircraft took off from the cruiser *Tone* and another from the cruiser *Chikuma*. They reported that the fleet was in harbor, as expected, and that the carriers were not in Lahaina and could not be located. Five midget submarines, launched between 3:30 and 5:30 A.M. from the advance submarine guard of the main expedition, were supposed to send in further confirmation of the U.S. carrier locations.

Precisely matching the careful collection of preattack information were the security precautions and deceptive techniques surrounding this part of the attack plan. The rendezvous point for the task force was in the remote northern islands, in Hitokappu Bay off Etorufu Island, where it was least likely to be observed even by Japanese citizens. Elaborate measures were taken to conceal the purchase of cold-weather clothing and equipment for this rendezvous point, as well as for the voyage over the northern route. Dumping of waste or garbage into the waters of the Kuriles was strictly forbidden; everything had to be burned or disposed of on shore. Beginning on November 10, direct radio communication between ships of the task force was forbidden. At the same time deceptive communications were undertaken by the main force in the Inland Sea and in Kyushu to indicate to the outside world that the task force was still in training in Kyushu. This impression was reinforced by allowing large

[64]*Hearings*, Part 13, p. 427.
[65]*Ibid*.

numbers of shore leaves in Tokyo and Yokohama for men of the Yoko-
suka Naval District.

As we have mentioned, only top naval planning officers were privy to
the Pearl Harbor attack plan in the first place. It is doubtful that Army
officials other than the Chief of Staff and his deputy heard more than
rumors until October, or that the Army and Navy cabinet ministers heard
about it much before December 1.[66] The Minister of Finance, the Minister
of Agriculture, the Minister of Communications, and the Foreign Minister
were never apprised of the plan. Members of the crew participating in
the attack were unaware of their destination and were briefed for the
first time only after the port of departure had been cleared.

Similar precautions were enforced for other aspects of the attack to the
south. Many of the troop and ship movements had been necessarily public,
but their final destinations remained unclear to the Allies until very
shortly before D-day, and Japanese troop units were sometimes left in
the dark almost as long. For example, Army commanders in north French
Indochina had been issued authentic plans for large-scale attacks on the
Chinese air base at Kunming, as cover for the actual march into Thailand
and Malaya. The Kunming plans were not formally canceled until December 3, 1941.[67] American citizens in Japan proper and members of the U.S.
embassy staff in Tokyo had their suspicions allayed by a November 25
Foreign Office announcement that the *Tatsuta Maru* would sail on December 2 for Los Angeles and Balboa to evacuate Japanese residents from
the United States and Panama: "The announcement was greeted with
relief, on the assumption that a final break was unlikely while Japan's
crack liner was at sea."[68] We saw earlier the smoke screen provided by
newspaper announcements of continuing Japanese-American negotiations.

From a glance at the details of these operations against the Philippines
and against Pearl Harbor, it is apparent that Japanese short-term planning for the opening days of the war was extremely skillful. The matching
of forces-in-being for an extended series of targets was daring and even
brilliant. Intelligence reports on their enemy were detailed and accurate,

[66]Japanese testimony on this point is conflicting. For a recent scholarly appraisal, see
Butow, *Tojo and the Coming of the War*, p. 375.

[67]*USSBS, Japanese Air Power*, p. 8.

[68]Tolischus, *Tokyo Record*, p. 304.

and the numerous security precautions were carefully observed. Japanese ingenuity and care in these opening campaigns were rewarded by spectacular success for the first six months of war.

From the American point of view, it is apparent that these opening campaigns involved bold and massive movements of men, aircraft, ships, and supplies. Japanese physical preparations were easily capable of detection and, in fact, were detected by our Intelligence agencies in most instances. The American image of the total Japanese reality was not, of course, exact. It had not measured the immense daring and skill of the enemy. It had missed some highly significant last-minute signals. But still our information system had provided the major clues to the Japanese war plans.

This brings us back to a question that we asked in our opening pages. With all the information available, why were our political and military leaders surprised on December 7? More precisely, why were they surprised at the specific attacks on American possessions? For they were not taken unawares in one sense: they did look for an eruption soon in the Far East; they did expect Japan to make one or more aggressive moves on that first week end in December—perhaps against Thailand, perhaps against one of America's allies.

A number of answers to this question of surprise have been suggested in the course of this study. Let us collect and arrange these now, and demonstrate their application to the problem of intelligence today.

7 ▸   SURPRISE

If our intelligence system and all our other channels of information failed to produce an accurate image of Japanese intentions and capabilities, it was not for want of the relevant materials. Never before have we had so complete an intelligence picture of the enemy. And perhaps never again will we have such a magnificent collection of sources at our disposal.

RETROSPECT

To review these sources briefly, an American cryptanalyst, Col. William F. Friedman, had broken the top-priority Japanese diplomatic code, which enabled us to listen to a large proportion of the privileged communications between Tokyo and the major Japanese embassies throughout the world. Not only did we know in advance how the Japanese ambassadors in Washington were advised, and how much they were instructed to say, but we also were listening to top-secret messages on the Tokyo-Berlin and Tokyo-Rome circuits, which gave us information vital for conduct of the war in the Atlantic and Europe. In the Far East this source provided minute details on movements connected with the Japanese program of expansion into Southeast Asia.

Besides the strictly diplomatic codes, our cryptanalysts also had some success in reading codes used by Japanese agents in major American and foreign ports. Those who were on the distribution list for MAGIC had access to much of what these agents were reporting to Tokyo and what Tokyo was demanding of them in the Panama Canal Zone, in cities along the east and west coasts of the Americas from northern Canada as far south as Brazil, and in ports throughout the Far East, including the Philippines and the Hawaiian Islands. They could determine what installations, what troop and ship movements, and what alert and defense measures were of interest to Tokyo at these points on the globe, as well as approximately how much correct information her agents were sending her.

Our naval leaders also had at their disposal the results of radio traffic analysis. While before the war our naval radio experts could not read the content of any Japanese naval or military coded messages, they were able to deduce from a study of intercepted ship call signs the composition and location of the Japanese Fleet units. After a change in call signs, they might lose sight of some units, and units that went into port in home waters were also lost because the ships in port used frequencies that our radios were unable to intercept. Most of the time, however, our traffic analysts had the various Japanese Fleet units accurately pinpointed on our naval maps.

Extremely competent on-the-spot economic and political analysis was furnished by Ambassador Grew and his staff in Tokyo. Ambassador Grew was himself a most sensitive and accurate observer, as evidenced by his dispatches to the State Department. His observations were supported and supplemented with military detail by frequent reports from American naval attachés and observers in key Far Eastern ports. Navy Intelligence had men with radio equipment located along the coast of China, for example, who reported the convoy movements toward Indochina. There were also naval observers stationed in various high-tension areas in Thailand and Indochina who could fill in the local outlines of Japanese political intrigue and military planning. In Tokyo and other Japanese cities, it is true, Japanese censorship grew more and more rigid during 1941, until Ambassador Grew felt it necessary to disclaim any responsibility for noting or reporting overt military evidence of an imminent outbreak of war. This careful Japanese censorship naturally cut down visual confirmation of the decoded information but very probably never achieved the opaqueness of Russia's Iron Curtain.

During this period the data and interpretations of British intelligence were also available to American officers in Washington and the Far East, though the British and Americans tended to distrust each other's privileged information.

In addition to secret sources, there were some excellent public ones. Foreign correspondents for *The New York Times*, *The Herald Tribune*, and *The Washington Post* were stationed in Tokyo and Shanghai and in Canberra, Australia. Their reporting as well as their predictions on the Japanese political scene were on a very high level. Frequently their access to news was more rapid and their judgment of its significance as reliable as that of our Intelligence officers. This was certainly the case for 1940 and most of 1941. For the last few weeks before the Pearl Harbor strike, however, the public newspaper accounts were not very useful. It was necessary to have secret information in order to know what was happening. Both Tokyo and Washington exercised very tight control over leaks during this crucial period, and the newsmen accordingly had to limit their accounts to speculation and notices of diplomatic meetings with no exact indication of the content of the diplomatic exchanges.

The Japanese press was another important public source. During 1941 it proclaimed with increasing shrillness the Japanese government's determination to pursue its program of expansion into Southeast Asia and the desire of the military to clear the Far East of British and American colonial exploitation. This particular source was rife with explicit signals of aggressive intent.

Finally, an essential part of the intelligence picture for 1941 was both public and privileged information on American policy and activities in the Far East. During the year the pattern of action and interaction between the Japanese and American governments grew more and more complex. At the last, it became especially important for anyone charged with the responsibility of ordering an alert to know what moves the American government was going to make with respect to Japan, as well as to try to guess what Japan's next move would be, since Japan's next move would respond in part to ours. Unfortunately our military leaders, and especially our Intelligence officers, were sometimes as surprised as the Japanese at the moves of the White House and the State Department. They usually had more orderly anticipations about Japanese policy and conduct than they had about America's. On the other hand, it was also true that State Department and White House officials were handicapped in judging Japanese intentions and estimates of risk by an inadequate picture of our own military vulnerability.

All of the public and private sources of information mentioned were available to America's political and military leaders in 1941. It is only fair to remark, however, that no single person or agency ever had at any given moment all the signals existing in this vast information network. The signals lay scattered in a number of different agencies; some were decoded, some were not; some traveled through rapid channels of communication, some were blocked by technical or procedural delays; some never reached a center of decision. But it is legitimate to review again the general sort of picture that emerged during the first week of December from the signals readily at hand. Anyone close to President Roosevelt was likely to have before him the following significant fragments.

There was first of all a picture of gathering troop and ship movements down the China coast and into Indochina. The large dimensions of this movement to the south were established publicly and visually as well as by analysis of ship call signs. Two changes in Japanese naval call signs—one on November 1 and another on December 1—had also been evaluated by Naval Intelligence as extremely unusual and as signs of major preparations for some sort of Japanese offensive. The two changes had interfered with the speed of American radio traffic analysis. Thousands of interceptions after December 1 were necessary before the new call signs could be read. Partly for this reason American radio analysts disagreed about the locations of the Japanese carriers. One group held that all the carriers were near Japan because they had not been able to identify a carrier call sign since the middle of November. Another group believed that they had located one carrier division in the Marshalls. The probability seemed to be that the carriers, wherever they were, had gone into radio silence; and past experience led the analysts to believe that they were therefore in waters near the Japanese homeland, where they could communicate with each other on wavelengths that we could not intercept. However, our inability to locate the carriers exactly, combined with the two changes in call signs, was itself a danger signal.

Our best secret source, MAGIC, was confirming the aggressive intention of the new military cabinet in Tokyo, which had replaced the last moderate cabinet on October 17. In particular, MAGIC provided details of some of the preparations for the move into Southeast Asia. Running counter to this were increased troop shipments to the Manchurian border in October.

(The intelligence picture is never clear-cut.) But withdrawals had begun toward the end of that month. MAGIC also carried explicit instructions to the Japanese ambassadors in Washington to pursue diplomatic negotiations with the United States with increasing energy, but at the same time it announced a deadline for the favorable conclusion of the negotiations, first for November 25, later postponed until November 29. In case of diplomatic failure by that date, the Japanese ambassadors were told, Japanese patience would be exhausted, Japan was determined to pursue her Greater East Asia policy, and on November 29 "things" would automatically begin to happen.

On November 26 Secretary Hull rejected Japan's latest bid for American approval of her policies in China and Indochina. MAGIC had repeatedly characterized this Japanese overture as the "last," and it now revealed the ambassadors' reaction of consternation and despair over the American refusal and also their country's characterization of the American Ten Point Note as an "ultimatum."

On the basis of this collection of signals, Army and Navy Intelligence experts in Washington tentatively placed D-day *for the Japanese Southeastern campaign* during the week end of November 30, and when this failed to materialize, during the week end of December 7. They also compiled an accurate list of probable British and Dutch targets and included the Philippines and Guam as possible American targets.

Also available in this mass of information, but long forgotten, was a rumor reported by Ambassador Grew in January, 1941. It came from what was regarded as a not-very-reliable source, the Peruvian embassy, and stated that the Japanese were preparing a surprise air attack on Pearl Harbor. Curiously the date of the report is coincident roughly with what we now know to have been the date of inception of Yamamoto's plan; but the rumor was labeled by everyone, including Ambassador Grew, as quite fantastic and the plan as absurdly impossible. American judgment was consistent with Japanese judgment at this time, since Yamamoto's plan was in direct contradiction to Japanese naval tactical doctrine.

PERSPECTIVE

On the basis of this rapid recapitulation of the highlights in the signal picture, it is apparent that our decisionmakers had at hand an impressive amount of information on the enemy. They did not have the complete list of targets, since none of the last-minute estimates included Pearl Harbor. They did not know the exact hour and date for opening the attack. They did not have an accurate knowledge of Japanese capabilities or of Japanese ability to accept very high risks. The crucial question then, we repeat, is, If we could enumerate accurately the British and Dutch targets and give credence to a Japanese attack against them either on November 30 or December 7, why were we not expecting a specific danger to *ourselves?* And by the word "expecting," we mean expecting in the sense of taking specific alert actions to meet the contingencies of attack by land, sea, or air.

There are several answers to this question that have become apparent in the course of this study. First of all, it is much easier *after* the event to sort the relevant from the irrelevant signals. After the event, of course, a signal is always crystal clear; we can now see what disaster it was signaling, since the disaster has occurred. But before the event it is obscure and pregnant with conflicting meanings. It comes to the observer embedded in an atmosphere of "noise," i.e., in the company of all sorts of information that is useless and irrelevant for predicting the particular disaster. For example, in Washington, Pearl Harbor signals were competing with a vast number of signals from the European theater. These European signals announced danger more frequently and more specifically than any coming from the Far East. The Far Eastern signals were also arriving at a center of decision where they had to compete with the prevailing belief that an unprotected offensive force acts as a deterrent rather than a target. In Honolulu they were competing *not* with signals from the European theater, but rather with a large number of signals announcing Japanese intentions and preparations to attack Soviet Russia rather than to move southward; here they were also competing with expectations of local sabotage prepared by previous alert situations.

In short, we failed to anticipate Pearl Harbor not for want of the relevant materials, but because of a plethora of irrelevant ones. Much of the appearance of wanton neglect that emerged in various investigations of the disaster resulted from the unconscious suppression of vast congeries of signs pointing in every direction except Pearl Harbor. It was difficult later to recall these signs since they had led nowhere. Signals that are characterized today as absolutely unequivocal warnings of surprise air attack on Pearl Harbor become, on analysis in the context of December, 1941, not merely ambiguous but occasionally inconsistent with such an attack. To recall one of the most controversial and publicized examples, the winds code, both General Short and Admiral Kimmel testified that if they had had this information, they would have been prepared on the morning of December 7 for an air attack from without. The messages establishing the winds code are often described in the Pearl Harbor literature as Tokyo's declaration of war against America. If they indeed amounted to such a declaration, obviously the failure to inform Honolulu of this vital news would have been criminal negligence. On examination, however, the messages proved to be instructions for code communication after normal commercial channels had been cut. In one message the recipient was instructed on receipt of an execute to destroy all remaining codes in his possession. In another version the recipient was warned that the execute would be sent out "when relations are becoming dangerous" between Japan and three other countries. There was a different code term for each country: England, America, and the Soviet Union.

There is no evidence that an authentic execute of either message was ever intercepted by the United States before December 7. The message ordering code destruction was in any case superseded by a much more explicit code-destruction order from Tokyo that was intercepted on December 2 and translated on December 3. After December 2, the receipt of a winds-code execute for code destruction would therefore have added nothing new to our information, and code destruction in itself cannot be taken as an unambiguous substitute for a formal declaration of war. During the first week of December the United States ordered all American consulates in the Far East to destroy all American codes, yet no one has attempted to prove that this order was equivalent to an American declaration of war against Japan. As for the other winds-code message, provided an execute had been received warning that relations were dangerous between Japan and the United States, there would still have been no way on the basis of this signal alone to determine whether Tokyo was signaling Japanese intent to attack the United States or Japanese fear of an American surprise attack (in reprisal for Japanese aggressive moves against American allies in the Far East). It was only after the event that "dangerous relations" could be interpreted as "surprise air attack on Pearl Harbor."

There is a difference, then, between having a signal available somewhere in the heap of irrelevancies, and perceiving it as a warning; and there is also a difference between perceiving it as a warning, and acting or getting action on it. These distinctions, simple as they are, illuminate the obscurity shrouding this moment in history.

Many instances of these distinctions have been examined in the course of this study. We shall recall a few of the most dramatic now. To illustrate the difference between having and perceiving a signal, let us return to Colonel Fielder, whom we met in Chapter 1. Though he was an untrained and inexperienced Intelligence officer, he headed Army Intelligence at Pearl Harbor at the time of the attack. He had been on the job for only four months, and he regarded as quite satisfactory his sources of information and his contacts with the Navy locally and with Army Intelligence in Washington. Evidently he was unaware that Army Intelligence in Washington was not allowed to send him any "action" or policy information, and he was therefore not especially concerned about trying to read beyond the obvious meaning of any given communication that came under his eyes. Colonel Bratton, head of Army Far Eastern Intelligence in Washington, however, had a somewhat more realistic view of the extent of Colonel Fielder's knowledge. At the end of November, Colonel Bratton had learned about the winds-code setup and was also apprised that the naval traffic analysis unit under Commander Rochefort in Honolulu was monitoring 24 hours a day for an execute. He was understandably worried about the lack of communication between this unit and Colonel Fielder's office, and by December 5 he finally felt that the matter was urgent enough to warrant sending a message directly to Colonel Fielder about the winds code. Now any information on the winds code, since it belonged to the highest classification of secret information, and since it was therefore automatically evaluated as "action" information, could not be sent through normal G-2 channels. Colonel Bratton had to figure out another way to get the information to Colonel Fielder. He sent this message: "Contact Commander Rochefort immediately thru Commandant Fourteenth Naval District regarding broadcasts from Tokyo reference weather." Signal Corps records establish that Colonel Fielder received this message. How did he react to it? He filed it. According to his testimony in 1945, it made no impression on him and he did not attempt to see Rochefort. He could not sense any urgency behind the lines because he was not expecting immediate trouble, and his expectations determined what he read. A warning signal was available to him, but he did not perceive it.

Colonel Fielder's lack of experience may make this example seem to be an exception. So let us recall the performance of Captain Wilkinson, the naval officer who headed the Office of Naval Intelligence in Washington in the fall of 1941 and who is unanimously acclaimed for a distinguished and brilliant career. His treatment of a now-famous Pearl Harbor signal does not sound much different in the telling. After the event, the signal in question was labeled "the bomb-plot message." It originated in Tokyo on September 24 and was sent to an agent in Honolulu. It requested the agent to divide Pearl Harbor into five areas and to make his future reports on ships in harbor with reference to those areas. Tokyo was especially interested in the locations of battleships, destroyers, and carriers, and also in any information on the anchoring of more than one ship at a single dock.

This message was decoded and translated on October 9 and shortly thereafter distributed to Army, Navy, and State Department recipients of MAGIC. Commander Kramer, a naval expert on MAGIC, had marked the message with an asterisk, signifying that he thought it to be of particular interest. But what was its interest? Both he and Wilkinson agreed that it illustrated the "nicety" of Japanese intelligence, the incredible zeal and efficiency with which they collected detail. The division into areas was interpreted as a device for shortening the reports. Admiral Stark was similarly impressed with Japanese efficiency, and no one felt it necessary to forward the message to Admiral Kimmel. No one read into it a specific danger to ships anchored in Pearl Harbor. At the time, this was a reasonable estimate, since somewhat similar requests for information were going to Japanese agents in Panama, Vancouver, Portland, San Diego, San Francisco, and other places. It should be observed, however, that the estimate was reasonable only on the basis of a very rough check on the quantity of espionage messages passing between Tokyo and these American ports. No one in Far Eastern Intelligence had subjected the messages to any more refined analysis. An observer assigned to such a job would have been able to record an increase in the frequency and specificity of Tokyo's requests concerning Manila and Pearl Harbor in the last weeks before the outbreak of war, and he would have noted that Tokyo was not displaying the same interest in other American ports. These observations, while not significant in isolation, might have been useful in the general signal picture.

There is no need, however, to confine our examples to Intelligence personnel. Indeed, the crucial areas where the signals failed to communicate a warning were in the operational branches of the armed services. Let us take Admiral Kimmel and his reaction to the information that the Japanese were destroying most of their codes in major Far Eastern consulates and also in London and Washington. Since the Pearl Harbor attack, this information has frequently been characterized by military experts who were not stationed in Honolulu as an "unmistakable tip-off." As Admiral Ingersoll explained at the congressional hearings, with the lucidity characteristic of statements after the event:

> If you rupture diplomatic negotiations you do not necessarily have to burn your codes. The diplomats go home and they can pack up their codes with their dolls and take them home. Also, when you rupture diplomatic negotiations, you do not rupture consular relations. The consuls stay on.
>
> Now, in this particular set of dispatches that did not mean a rupture of diplomatic negotiations, it meant war, and that information was sent out to the fleets as soon as we got it. . . .[1]

The phrase "it meant war" was, of course, pretty vague; war in Manila, Hong Kong, Singapore, and Batavia is not war 5000 miles away in Pearl Harbor. Before the event, for Admiral Kimmel, code burning in major Japanese consulates in the Far East may have "meant war," but it did not signal danger of an air attack on Pearl Harbor. In the first place, the information that he received was not the original MAGIC. He learned from Washington that Japanese consulates were burning "almost all" of their codes, not all of them, and Honolulu was not included on the list. He knew from a local source that the Japanese consulate in Honolulu was burning secret papers (not necessarily codes), and this back yard burning had happened three or four times during the year. In July, 1941, Kimmel

[1] *Hearings*, Part 9, p. 4226.

had been informed that the Japanese consulates in lands neighboring Indochina had destroyed codes, and he interpreted the code burning in December as a similar attempt to protect codes in case the Americans or their British and Dutch allies tried to seize the consulates in reprisal for the southern advance. This also was a reasonable interpretation at the time, though not an especially keen one.

Indeed, at the time there was a good deal of evidence available to support all the wrong interpretations of last-minute signals, and the interpretations appeared wrong only *after* the event. There was, for example, a good deal of evidence to support the hypothesis that Japan would attack the Soviet Union from the east while the Russian Army was heavily engaged in the west. Admiral Turner, head of Navy War Plans in Washington, was an enthusiastic adherent of this view and argued the high probability of a Japanese attack on Russia up until the last week in November, when he had to concede that most of Japan's men and supplies were moving south. Richard Sorge, the expert Soviet spy who had direct access to the Japanese Cabinet, had correctly predicted the southern move as early as July, 1941, but even he was deeply alarmed during September and early October by the large number of troop movements to the Manchurian border. He feared that his July advice to the Soviet Union had been in error, and his alarm ultimately led to his capture on October 14. For at this time he increased his radio messages to Moscow to the point where it was possible for the Japanese police to pinpoint the source of the broadcasts.

It is important to emphasize here that most of the men that we have cited in our examples, such as Captain Wilkinson and Admirals Turner and Kimmel—these men and their colleagues who were involved in the Pearl Harbor disaster—were as efficient and loyal a group of men as one could find. Some of them were exceptionally able and dedicated. The fact of surprise at Pearl Harbor has never been persuasively explained by accusing the participants, individually or in groups, of conspiracy or negligence or stupidity. What these examples illustrate is rather the very human tendency to pay attention to the signals that support current expectations about enemy behavior. If no one is listening for signals of an attack against a highly improbable target, then it is very difficult for the signals to be heard.

For every signal that came into the information net in 1941 there were usually several plausible alternative explanations, and it is not surprising that our observers and analysts were inclined to select the explanations that fitted the popular hypotheses. They sometimes set down new contradictory evidence side by side with existing hypotheses, and they also sometimes held two contradictory beliefs at the same time. We have seen this happen in G-2 estimates for the fall of 1941. Apparently human beings have a stubborn attachment to old beliefs and an equally stubborn resistance to new material that will upset them.

Besides the tendency to select whatever was in accord with one's expectations, there were many other blocks to perception that prevented our analysts from making the correct interpretation. We have just mentioned the masses of conflicting evidence that supported alternative and equally reasonable hypotheses. This is the phenomenon of noise in which a signal is embedded. Even at its normal level, noise presents problems in distraction; but in addition to the natural clatter of useless information and competing signals, in 1941 a number of factors combined to raise the usual noise level. First of all, it had been raised, especially in Honolulu, by the background of previous alert situations and false alarms. Earlier alerts, as we have seen, had centered attention on local sabotage and on signals supporting the hypothesis of a probable Japanese attack on Russia. Second, in both Honolulu and Washington, individual reactions to danger had been numbed, or at least dulled, by the continuous international tension.

A third factor that served to increase the natural noise level was the positive effort made by the enemy to keep the relevant signals quiet. The Japanese security system was an important and successful block to perception. It was able to keep the strictest cloak of secrecy around the Pearl Harbor attack and to limit knowledge only to those closely associated with the details of military and naval planning. In the Japanese Cabinet only the Navy Minister and the Army Minister (who was also Prime Minister) knew of the plan before the task force left its final port of departure.

In addition to keeping certain signals quiet, the enemy tried to create noise, and sent false signals into our information system by carrying on elaborate "spoofs." False radio traffic made us believe that certain ships were maneuvering near the mainland of Japan. The Japanese also sent to individual commanders false war plans for Chinese targets, which were changed only at the last moment to bring them into line with the South-eastern movement.

A fifth barrier to accurate perception was the fact that the relevant signals were subject to change, often very sudden change. This was true even of the so-called static intelligence, which included data on capabilities and the composition of military forces. In the case of our 1941 estimates of the infeasibility of torpedo attacks in the shallow waters of Pearl Harbor, or the underestimation of the range and performance of the Japanese Zero, the changes happened too quickly to appear in an intelligence estimate.

Sixth, our own security system sometimes prevented the communication of signals. It confronted our officers with the problem of trying to keep information from the enemy without keeping it from each other, and, as in the case of MAGIC, they were not always successful. As we have seen, only a very few key individuals saw these secret messages, and they saw them only briefly. They had no opportunity or time to make a critical review of the material, and each one assumed that others who had seen it would arrive at identical interpretations. Exactly who those "others" were was not quite clear to any recipient. Admiral Stark, for example, thought Admiral Kimmel was reading all of MAGIC. Those who were not on the list of recipients, but who had learned somehow of the existence of the decodes, were sure that they contained military as well as diplomatic information and believed that the contents were much fuller and more precise than they actually were. The effect of carefully limiting the reading and discussion of MAGIC, which was certainly necessary to safeguard the secret of our knowledge of the code, was thus to reduce this group of signals to the point where they were scarcely heard.

To these barriers of noise and security we must add the fact that the necessarily precarious character of intelligence information and predictions was reflected in the wording of instructions to take action. The warning messages were somewhat vague and ambiguous. Enemy moves are often subject to reversal on short notice, and this was true for the Japanese. They had plans for canceling their attacks on American possessions in the Pacific up to 24 hours before the time set for attack. A full alert in the Hawaiian Islands, for example, was one condition that might have caused the Pearl Harbor task force to return to Japan on December 5 or 6. The fact that intelligence predictions must be based on moves that are almost always reversible makes understandable the reluctance of the intelligence analyst to make bold assertions. Even if he is willing to risk his reputation on a firm prediction of attack at a definite time and place, no commander will in turn lightly risk the penalties and costs of a full alert. In December, 1941, a full alert required shooting down any unidentified aircraft sighted over the Hawaiian Islands. Yet this might have been interpreted by Japan as the first overt act. At least that was one consideration that influenced General Short to order his lowest degree of alert. While the cautious phrasing in the messages to the theater is certainly understandable, it nevertheless constituted another block on the road to perception. The sentences in the final theater warnings—"A surprise aggressive move in any direction is a possibility" and "Japanese future action unpredictable but hostile action possible at any moment"—could scarcely have been expected to inform the theater commanders of any change in their strategic situation.

Last but not least we must also mention the blocks to perception and communication inherent in any large bureaucratic organization, and those that stemmed from intraservice and interservice rivalries. The most glaring example of rivalry in the Pearl Harbor case was that between Naval War Plans and Naval Intelligence. A general prejudice against intellectuals and specialists, not confined to the military but unfortunately widely held in America, also made it difficult for intelligence experts to be heard. McCollum, Bratton, Sadtler, and a few others who felt that the signal picture was ominous enough to warrant more urgent warnings had no power to influence decision. The Far Eastern code analysts, for example, were believed to be too immersed in the "Oriental point of view." Low budgets for American Intelligence departments reflected the low prestige of this activity, whereas in England, Germany, and Japan, 1941 budgets reached a height that was regarded by the American Congress as quite beyond reason.

*   *   *

In view of all these limitations to perception and communication, is the fact of surprise at Pearl Harbor, then, really so surprising? Even with these limitations explicitly recognized, there remains the step between perception and action. Let us assume that the first hurdle has been crossed: An available signal has been perceived as an indication of imminent danger. Then how do we resolve the next questions: What specific danger is the signal trying to communicate, and what specific action or preparation should follow?

On November 27, General MacArthur had received a war warning very similar to the one received by General Short in Honolulu. MacArthur's response had been promptly translated into orders designed to protect his bombers from possible air attack from Formosan land bases. But the orders were carried out very slowly. By December 8, Philippine time, only half of the bombers ordered to the south had left the Manila area, and reconnaissance over Formosa had not been undertaken. There was no sense of urgency in preparing for a Japanese air attack, partly because our intelligence estimates had calculated that the Japanese aircraft did not have sufficient range to bomb Manila from Formosa.

The information that Pearl Harbor had been attacked arrived at Manila early in the morning of December 8, giving the Philippine forces some 9 or 10 hours to prepare for an attack. But did an air attack on Pearl Harbor necessarily mean that the Japanese would strike from the air at the Philippines? Did they have enough equipment to mount both air attacks successfully? Would they come from Formosa or from carriers? Intelligence had indicated that they would have to come from carriers, yet the carriers were evidently off Hawaii. MacArthur's headquarters also pointed out that there had been no formal declaration of war against Japan by the United States. Therefore approval could not be granted for a counterattack on Formosan bases. Furthermore there were technical disagreements among airmen as to whether a counterattack should be mounted without advance photographic reconnaissance. While Brereton was arranging permission to undertake photographic reconnaissance, there was further disagreement about what to do with the aircraft in the meantime. Should they be sent aloft or should they be dispersed to avoid destruction in case the Japanese reached the airfields? When the Japanese bombers arrived shortly after noon, they found all the American aircraft wingtip to wingtip on the ground. Even the signal of an actual attack on Pearl Harbor was not an unambiguous signal of an attack on the Philippines, and it did not make clear what response was best.

PROSPECT

The history of Pearl Harbor has an interest exceeding by far any tale of an isolated catastrophe that might have been the result of negligence or stupidity or treachery, however lurid. For we have found the roots of this surprise in circumstances that affected honest, dedicated, and intelligent men. The possibility of such surprise at any time lies in the conditions of human perception and stems from uncertainties so basic that they are not likely to be eliminated, though they might be reduced.

It is only to be expected that the relevant signals, so clearly audible after an event, will be partially obscured before the event by surrounding noise. Even past diligence constructs its own background of noise, in the form of false alarms, which make less likely an alarm when the real thing arrives: the old story of "cry wolf" has a permanent relevance. A totalitarian aggressor can draw a tight curtain of secrecy about his actions and thus muffle the signals of attack. The Western democracies must interpret such signals responsibly and cautiously, for the process of commitment to war, except *in extremis*, is hedged about by the requirements of consultation. The precautions of secrecy, which are necessary even in a democracy to keep open privileged sources of information, may hamper the use of that information or may slow its transmission to those who have the power of decision. Moreover, human attention is directed by beliefs as to what is likely to occur, and one cannot always listen for the right sounds. An all-out thermonuclear attack on a Western power would be an unprecedented event, and some little time (which might be vital) would surely have to pass before that power's allies could understand the nature of the event and take appropriate action.

There is a good deal of evidence, some of it quantitative, that in conditions of great uncertainty people tend to predict that events that they want to happen actually will happen. Wishfulness in conditions of uncertainty is natural and is hard to banish simply by exhortation—or by wishing. Further, the uncertainty of strategic warning is intrinsic, since an enemy decision to attack might be reversed or the direction of the attack changed; and a defensive action can be taken only at some cost. (For example, at Pearl Harbor, flying a 360-degree reconnaissance would have meant sacrificing training, would have interrupted the high-priority shipment program to the Philippines, and would have exhausted crews and worn out equipment within a few weeks.) In general, an extraordinary state of alert that brings about a peak in readiness must be followed by a trough at a later date. In some cases the cost of the defensive actions is hard to estimate and their relevance is uncertain. Therefore the choice of action in response to strategic warning must also be uncertain. Finally, the balance of technical and military factors that might make an attack infeasible at one time can change swiftly and without notice to make it feasible at another. In our day such balances are changing with unprecedented speed.

Pearl Harbor is not an isolated catastrophe. It can be matched by many examples of effective surprise attack. The German attack on Russia in the summer of 1941 was preceded by a flood of signals, the massing of troops, and even direct warnings to Russia by the governments of the United States and the United Kingdom, both of whom had been correctly informed about the imminence of the onslaught. Yet it achieved total surprise.[2] Soviet arguments current today that Stalin and Marshal Zhukov, his Chief of the General Staff, knew and failed to act have obvious parallels with the accusations about President Roosevelt's conspiracy of silence. These Soviet reinterpretations of history aim not only to downgrade Stalin, but also to establish that Soviet leaders were not *really* surprised in 1941, and the Soviet Union can therefore count on adequate warning in any future conflict.[3] But the difficulties of discerning a surprise attack on oneself apply equally to totalitarian and democratic states.

The stunning tactical success of the Japanese attack on the British at Singapore was made possible by the deeply held British faith in the impregnability of that fortress. As Captain Grenfell put it, newspapers and statesmen like their fortresses to be impregnable. "Every fortress," he wrote, "that has come into the news in my lifetime—Port Arthur, Tsing Tao, the great French defensive system of the Maginot Line—has been popularly described as impregnable before it has been attacked. . . . One way or another it became a virtually accepted fact in Britain and the

---

[2] I am grateful to William W. Kaufmann of the M.I.T. Center for International Studies for permission to read his unpublished paper, "Operation Barbarossa," which deals with the background of the German surprise attack.

[3] For a recent Russian view of the Pearl Harbor attack and its lessons on the "launching of aggression by imperialist states," see Maj. Gen. N. Pavlenko, "Documents on Pearl Harbor," *Voenno-Istoricheskii Zhurnal* (*Military-Historical Journal*), No. 1, January, 1961, pp. 85–105. I am indebted for this reference to John Thomas of the Institute of Defense Analysis and to Arnold Horelick, Soviet analyst of The RAND Corporation.

Dominions that Singapore was an impregnable bastion of Imperial security."[4] Yet the defenses of Singapore were rendered useless by military surprise in the form of an attack from an unexpected, northerly direction.

More recently, the Korean War provided some striking examples of surprise. The original North Korean attack was preceded by almost weekly maneuvers probing the border. These regular week-end penetrations built up so high a level of noise that on June 25, 1950, the actual initiation of hostilities was not distinguished from the preceding tests and false alarms. The intervention of the Chinese, at a later stage of the Korean War, was preceded by mass movements of Chinese troops and explicit warnings by the Chinese government to our own, by way of India, that this was precisely what they would do if we crossed the 38th parallel. Nonetheless, in important respects, we were surprised by the Chinese Communist forces in November, 1950.[5]

How do matters stand with reference to a future thermonuclear aggression by a totalitarian power? Would such an attack be harder or easier to conceal than the Japanese aggression against Pearl Harbor? There have been many attempts in recent years to cheer us with the thought that the H-bomb has so outmoded general war that this question may appear unimportant. However, such attempts to comfort ourselves really beg the question. The question is, Will it be possible in the future for a totalitarian power so to conceal an impending attack on the forces that we have disposed for retaliation as to have a high probability of virtually eliminating them before they receive warning or have time to respond to it? In this connection it is important to observe that there is no cause for complacency. In spite of the vast increase in expenditures for collecting and analyzing intelligence data and in spite of advances in the art of machine decoding and machine translation, the balance of advantage seems clearly to have shifted since Pearl Harbor in favor of a surprise attacker. The benefits to be expected from achieving surprise have increased enormously and the penalties for losing the initiative in an all-out war have grown correspondingly. In fact, since only by an all-out surprise attack could

[4]Grenfell, *Main Fleet to Singapore*, p. 64.

[5]For a succinct and lucid account, see "Strategic Surprise in the Korean War," an unpublished paper by Harvey DeWeerd of The RAND Corporation and the National Security Studies Program, University of California at Los Angeles.

an attacker hope to prevent retaliation, anything less would be suicidal, assuming that some form of attack is contemplated by one major power against another.

In such a surprise attack a major power today would have advantages exceeding those enjoyed by the Japanese in 1941. It is a familiar fact that with the ever-increasing readiness of bomber and missile forces, strategic warning becomes harder and harder to obtain; and with the decrease in the flight time for delivery of massive weapons of destruction, tactical warning times have contracted from weeks to minutes. It is no longer necessary for the aggressor to undertake huge movements of troops and ships in the weeks immediately preceding an all-out war, such as we described in our account of the Japanese war plan. Manned bombers capable of delivering a blow many times more devastating than anything dreamed of by the Japanese might be on their way from bases deep inside their homeland without yielding any substantial intelligence warning; they might conceivably follow routes that, by avoiding detection or at least identification among the friendly and unknown traffic appearing on radars, would be unlikely to give even any considerable tactical warning. Submarines might be kept on station several hundred miles off our coast during years of peace and might launch ballistic missiles on the receipt of a prearranged signal. Finally, intercontinental ballistic missiles might be kept for years at a high degree of readiness, and, if there were enough of them, they might be launched after simply being "counted down," with no further visible preparation. Total flight time for such rockets between continents might be less than fifteen minutes and radar warning less than that. Most important, such blows, unlike those leveled by the Japanese at Pearl Harbor, might determine the outcome not merely of a battle, but of the war itself. In short, the subject of surprise attack continues to be of vital concern. This fact has been suggested by the great debate among the powers on arms control and on the possibilities of using limitation and inspection arrangements to guard against surprise attack. The very little we have said suggests that such arrangements present formidable difficulties.

This study has not been intended as a "how-to-do-it" manual on intelligence, but perhaps one major practical lesson emerges from it. We cannot *count* on strategic warning. We *might* get it, and we might be able to take useful preparatory actions that would be impossible without it. We certainly ought to plan to exploit such a possibility should it occur. However, since we cannot rely on strategic warning, our defenses, if we are to have confidence in them, must be designed to function without it. If we accept the fact that the signal picture for impending attacks is almost sure to be ambiguous, we shall prearrange actions that are right and feasible in response to ambiguous signals, including signs of an attack that might be false. We must be capable of reacting repeatedly to false alarms without committing ourselves or the enemy to wage thermonuclear war.

It is only human to want some unique and univocal signal, to want a guarantee from intelligence, an unambiguous substitute for a formal declaration of war. This is surely the unconscious motivation of all the rewriting of Pearl Harbor history, which sees in such wavering and uncertain sources of information as the winds code and all of the various and much-argued MAGIC texts a clear statement of Japanese intent. But we have seen how drastically such an interpretation oversimplifies the task of the analyst and decisionmaker. If the study of Pearl Harbor has anything to offer for the future, it is this: We have to accept the fact of uncertainty and learn to live with it. No magic, in code or otherwise, will provide certainty. Our plans must work without it.

APPENDIX

During 1941 General Short had revised his alert procedures. A tentative draft of the revision was printed on July 14, and copies were forwarded to the War Department in Washington for comment. Marshall dictated his first comments on October 10.[1] By November 5 the final procedures had been settled on and reprinted, and copies of the so-called Standing Operating Procedure were distributed locally and were once again forwarded to Washington.

We reproduce below the entire section of alerts of the November 5 document as it appears in the *Hearings*. Since this revision led to some confusion on December 7, a few comments are in order here.

In the tentative draft General Short had worked out three different alert phases, numbered 1, 2, and 3. Number 1 was a full alert. It required "the occupation of all field positions by all units, prepared for maximum defense of Oahu and the Army installations on outlying islands."[2] Number 2 was an alert "against sabotage and uprisings" and also against "attacks from hostile sub-surface, surface and aircraft."[3] Number 3 was an alert "against acts of sabotage and uprisings within the islands, with no threat from without."[4] In the final draft Short reversed these numbers so that his full alert became Number 3 and his sabotage alert, Number 1. This meant that his numerals no longer corresponded to the degrees of alert in the Navy's "conditions," for the Navy's condition Number 1 was the full alert. The naval procedure was to go into condition Number 1

[1] *Hearings*, Part 3, p. 1080.   [2] *Ibid.*, Part 15, p. 1655.
[3] *Ibid.*, p. 1441; cf. p. 1657.   [4] *Ibid.*, p. 1657.

and taper off if the danger of attack receded. Short's procedure was to select an alert appropriate to the danger indicated.

General Herron, Short's predecessor, regarded the change as an unnecessary refinement

> that the training men put over on General Short when he came out there. I told him I would not do any such thing. There was only one kind of alert, and that was a total alert, and then I would do it in accordance with the situation. But the training men liked refinements, and they recommended three kinds because the Navy had three kinds. But they did not get to the real point of the thing. The Navy has three kinds, but the all-out alert is the number one always. Now they ease up into two and three; but these young men did not know that, and when Short came out they put over the three and got them reversed, so that Short went into the Number 1 which was sabotage. It did not seem to him a very important change, I don't suppose, and it turned out to be vital.[5]

The change in numerals caused confusion locally at the time of the November 28 alert preceding the Pearl Harbor attack. But in spite of Herron's objections to degrees of alert, there does seem to be good reason for a flexible alert system under circumstances of frequent alarms, as was the case in 1941, and as is the case in any period of cold war. In order for this flexibility to be exploited, however, it is necessary for both the central command and the theaters to be informed of the detailed procedure, particularly if the alert system is not uniform for all theaters. Short's system of three alerts was evidently unique for the Army at the time. His final draft, it is claimed, did not reach the War Department until after the December 7 attack. Marshall had not seen it at the time he sent his last warning message. However, he did know that Short had three alert phases under consideration; and when Short replied to Marshall's November 27 warning, he said that he was alerted against sabotage. He did not use a number to designate the alert, so there could have been no confusion on that score. His message, if read by someone familiar with his tentative operating procedure, could have meant only one thing: that he was on his lowest alert, for sabotage and for sabotage only.

[5] *Ibid.*, Part 27, p. 125*f*.

STANDING OPERATING PROCEDURE[6]

Hawaiian Department

[*November 5, 1941*]

Section II—Alerts

13. All defense measures are classified under one of the three (3) Alerts as indicated below. Operations under any Alert will be initiated by a Department order, except in case of a surprise hostile attack. See paragraph 15 f. (8) below.

14. *Alert No. 1.*—a. This alert is a defense against acts of sabotage and uprisings within the islands, with no threat from without.

b. At Department Headquarters, all General and Special Staff Sections will continue with their usual duties at their present stations, pending further orders.

c. Department Troops will carry on their normal training, pending instructions from this Headquarters.

d. Each Infantry Division will:

(1) Suppress all civil disorders, including sabotage, in its assigned sector.

(2) Maintain one (1) infantry battalion with motor transportation sufficient to transport it, prepared to move on one (1) hour's notice.

(3) Protect the Schofield Barracks Reservation and all vital installations (except those on garrisoned Army and Navy Reservations) in its assigned sector, not protected by the Territorial Home Guard.

* * * * *

e. The Hawaiian Coast Artillery Command will:

(1) Protect all seacoast and antiaircraft armament, searchlights, observation and fire control installations, and other elements of the seacoast and antiaircraft defense.

(2) Protect all vital installations on posts and reservations of the command.

* * * * *

f. The Hawaiian Air Force will:

(1) Protect all vital installations on posts on Oahu garrisoned by air forces.

(2) Assist in defense of air fields on outlying islands by cooperation of local base detachments with District Commanders. See paragraph 14 g. below.

g. The District Commanders, assisted by the air corps detachments within the districts, will:

Defend the air fields and vital installations thereat against acts of sabotage, and maintain order in the civil community.

[6]*Ibid.*, Part 15, pp. 1440–1444.

i. The Station Complements of Hickam, Wheeler and Bellows Fields, under command of the Hawaiian Air Force, will assist in the protection of all vital installations on their respective posts.

* * * * *

15. *Alert No. 2.*—a. This alert is applicable to a condition more serious than Alert No. 1. Security against attacks from hostile sub-surface, surface, and aircraft, in addition to defense against acts of sabotage and uprisings, is provided.

b. At Department Headquarters, only the G-2 and G-3 Sections will be required to operate on a 24-hour basis. All other sections of the General and Special Staffs will continue with their normal schedule.

c. Department Troops will carry on their normal training, pending instructions from this Headquarters.

d. Each Infantry Division will:

(1) Suppress all civil disorders, including sabotage, in its assigned sector.

(2) Maintain available all units at fifty per cent (50%) of their present strength, except those required under (3), (4) and (5) below.

(3) Maintain one (1) infantry battalion with motor transportation sufficient to transport it, prepared to move on one (1) hour's notice.

(4) Protect the Schofield Barracks Reservation and all vital installations (except those on garrisoned Army and Navy Reservations) in its assigned sector, not protected by the Territorial Home Guard.

* * * * *

(6) Place 240 mm howitzers in position, establish the necessary guards and, when directed place ammunition at positions.

(7) Release Field Artillery units manning seacoast armament (155 mm guns) to Hawaiian Coast Artillery Command. See paragraph 15 e. below.

* * * * *

e. The Hawaiian Coast Artillery Command, and attached Field Artillery will:

(1) Occupy initial seacoast and antiaircraft defense positions, except that railway batteries will remain at Fort Kamehameha or where emplaced.

(2) Release the 53d AA Brigade to the Interceptor Command for operational control.

(3) Protect all seacoast and antiaircraft armament, searchlights, observation and fire control installations, and other elements of the seacoast and antiaircraft defense.

(4) Protect all vital installations on posts and reservations of the command, except Fort Shafter. For Fort Shafter, see paragraph 15 k. (1) below.

(5) Support Naval Forces within range of seacoast armament.

(6) Prevent approach of and landing from hostile vessels.

(7) Coordinate all seacoast intelligence agencies.

(8) Coordinate seacoast defense with the Inshore Patrol.

(9) Protect the Radio Beacon on Sand Island.

(10) Provide Army personnel required to operate the Harbor Control Post.

f. The Hawaiian air force will:

(1) Maintain aircraft and crews in condition of readiness as directed by this headquarters. See paragraph 17.

(2) Release without delay all pursuit aircraft to the Interceptor Command.

(3) Prepare aircraft for dispatch to fields on outlying islands and upon arrival thereat, disperse on fields.

(4) Disperse bombers with crews.

(5) Disperse pursuit planes with crews to bunkers.

(6) Protect all vital installations on posts on Oahu garrisoned by air forces.

(7) Assist in defense of air fields on outlying islands by cooperation of local base detachments with District Commanders. See paragraph 15 g. below.

(8) In case of surprise hostile attack:

(a) Release to Navy for operational control all bombers in condition of readiness "A". The bomber commander will report to the Commander of Patrol Wing Two.

(b) Receive all available shore based Naval and Marine Corps fighter planes in appropriate condition of readiness and release them to the Interceptor Command for operational control.

g. The District Commanders, assisted by the air corps detachments within the districts, will: Defend the air fields and vital installations thereat against acts of sabotage, hostile attacks, and maintain order in the civil community.

*   *   *   *   *

i. The Department Signal Officer will:

(1) Insure occupation of all battle stations by the Aircraft Warning Service and then release it to the Interceptor Command.

(2) Insure that joint Army-Navy communications are in readiness for immediate employment.

j. The Interceptor Command will: Coordinate and control the operations of pursuit aircraft, antiaircraft artillery (including available Naval and Marine Corps AA Artillery), the Aircraft Warning Service, and attached units, and will provide for the coordination of antiaircraft measures of units not under military control, to include:

(1) Arrival and departure of *all* friendly aircraft.

(2) The coordination of the antiaircraft fire of Naval ships in Pearl and/or Honolulu Harbors.

(3) Transmission of appropriate warnings to all interested agencies.

k. Station Complements:

(1) The Fort Shafter Complement, under the supervision of the Department Provost Marshal, will protect all vital installations on Fort Shafter and, in

addition thereto, will provide a guard for the rear echelon of Department Headquarters and Tripler General Hospital.

(2) The Hickam, Wheeler and Bellows Fields Complements, under command of the Hawaiian Air Force, will assist in the defense of their respective posts against sabotage, air and ground attacks.

* * * * *

16. *Alert No. 3.*—a. This alert requires the occupation of all field positions by all units, prepared for maximum defense of Oahu and the Army installations on outlying islands.

b. At Department Headquarters:

(1) All sections of the forward echelon *** will occupy their stations at forward command post, prepared to operate on a 24-hour basis.

(2) All sections of the rear echelon *** will continue their usual duties at their present stations. Blackout instructions will be complied with.

c. Department Troops will remain in condition of mobile readiness at their permanent stations, pending instructions from this headquarters.

d. Each Infantry Division will:

(1) Defend its assigned sector on Oahu.

(2) Protect all vital installations (except those on garrisoned Army and Navy Reservations) in its assigned sector, not protected by the Territorial Home Guard.

* * * * *

(5) Place 240 mm howitzers in position.

(6) Release Field Artillery units manning seacoast armament (155 mm guns) to Hawaiian Coast Artillery Command. See paragraph 16 e. below.

* * * * *

e. The Hawaiian Coast Artillery Command, and attached Detachment Field Artillery will:

(1) Occupy initial seacoast and antiaircraft positions.

(2) Support Naval forces within range of seacoast armament.

(3) Prevent approach of and landing from hostile vessels.

(4) Support the Infantry Divisions.

(5) Coordinate all seacoast intelligence agencies.

(6) Coordinate seacoast defense with the Inshore Patrol.

(7) Provide the Army personnel required to operate the Harbor Control Post.

(8) Release the 53d AA Brigade to the Interceptor Command for operational control.

(9) Protect all vital installations on posts and reservations of the command, except Fort Shafter. For Fort Shafter, see paragraph 16 1. (2) below.

(10) Protect all seacoast and antiaircraft armament, searchlights, observation and fire control installations, and other elements of the seacoast and antiaircraft defense.

f. The Hawaiian Air Force will:

(1) Destroy enemy aircraft.

(2) Carry out bombing missions as directed.

(3) Cooperate with Naval air forces.

(4) On Oahu, defend all posts garrisoned by air forces against sabotage, air and ground attacks.

(5) Assist in defense of air fields on outlying islands by cooperation of local base detachments with District Commanders. See paragraph 16 h. below.

(6) Arm all planes, except that normally *bombs* will not be loaded on ships dispatched to outlying islands.

(7) Prepare aircraft for dispatch to fields on outlying islands and upon arrival thereat, disperse on fields.

(8) Disperse bombers with crews.

(9) Disperse pursuit planes with crews to bunkers.

(10) Perform observation, command and photographic missions.

(11) Release without delay all pursuit aircraft to the Interceptor Command.

* * * * *

h. The District Commanders of Hawaii, Maui (includes Molokai) and Kauai Districts, assisted by the air corps detachments present within the districts, will:

Defend the air fields against acts of sabotage, hostile attacks, and maintain order in the civil community.

* * * * *

j. The Interceptor Command will coordinate and control the operations of pursuit aircraft, antiaircraft artillery (including available Naval and Marine Corps AA Artillery), the aircraft warning service, and attached units, and will provide for the coordination of antiaircraft measures of units not under military control to include:

(1) Arrival and departure of *all* friendly aircraft.

(2) The coordination of the antiaircraft fire of Naval ships in Pearl and/or Honolulu Harbors.

(3) Transmission of appropriate warnings to all interested agencies.

k. The Department Signal Officer will:

(1) Insure occupation of all battle stations by the Aircraft Warning Service and then release it to the Interceptor Command.

(2) Insure that joint Army-Navy communications are in readiness for immediate employment.

(3) Be prepared to assume control over essential civilian communications.

l. Station Complements—

(1) The Schofield Barracks Complement will protect all vital installations on the Schofield Reservation.

(2) The Fort Shafter Complement, under the supervision of the Department Provost Marshal, will protect all vital installations on Fort Shafter and, in addition thereto, will provide a guard for the rear echelon of Department Headquarters and Tripler General Hospital.

(3) The Hickam, Wheeler and Bellows Field Complements, under command of the Hawaiian Air Force, will assist in the defense of their respective posts against sabotage, air and ground attacks.

ABBREVIATIONS AND SPECIAL NAMES

ABCD—American-British-Chinese-Dutch
ADB (ABD)—American-Dutch-British
adees (Adees)—Addressees
AGMC—Adjutant General Message Center
AWS—Aircraft Warning Service (Army)
Cardiv—Carrier Division
C.I.—Counterintelligence
C in C (CinC)—Commander-in-Chief
Cincaf (CinCAF)—Commander-in-Chief, Asiatic Fleet
Cinclant—Commander-in-Chief, Atlantic Fleet
Cincpac (CinCPAC)—Commander-in-Chief, Pacific Fleet (U.S. Fleet, 1941)
Cincus—Commander-in-Chief, U.S. Fleet
CNO—Chief of Naval Operations
CNS—Chief of Naval Staff (British)
Com—Command
COS—Chief of Staff, U.S. Army
D.C.A.—Defensive Coastal Area
DIP—Diplomatic intelligence (derived from MAGIC)
D.N.I.—Director of Naval Intelligence
FBI—Federal Bureau of Investigation
FCC—Federal Communications Commission
G('s)—Divisions of the War Department in 1940–41
G-1—Army Personnel Division
G-2—Army Intelligence Division
G-3—Army Mobilization and Training Division
G-4—Army Supply Division
G-5—Army War Plans Division
GCT—Greenwich Civil Time

HSCAB—Headquarters Separate Coast Artillery Brigade

IFF—Identification, Friend or Foe

JD—Japanese Diplomatic (code)

JN-25—Japanese Naval (code)

JPC—Joint Planning Committee

J-series—American term for group of Japanese codes; for example, the J-17 (K6) code

LA—American term for a simple Japanese code

MAGIC—American term for all Japanese diplomatic codes and ciphers

MID—Military Intelligence Division, U.S. Army

N.E.I.—Netherlands East Indies

ONI—Office of Naval Intelligence

OPD—Operations Division, U.S. Army; became title of WPD after March, 1942

Opnav—Office of Naval Operations

Orange—U.S. code term for Japan

OSS—Office of Strategic Services

PA-K2—American term for a simple Japanese code

Patwing—Patrol wing

PBY—Patrol bomber; Y designates the builder

Pncf—Pacific Naval Coastal Frontier

Pnncf—Pacific Northern Naval Coastal Frontier

Psncf—Pacific Southern Naval Coastal Frontier

PURPLE—American term for the top-priority Japanese diplomatic cipher

RCA—Radio Corporation of America

reurad—Regarding your radiogram

SIS—Signal Intelligence Service

SOPA—Senior Officer Present Afloat

Spenavo—Special Naval Observer (in London)

SWPA—Southwest Pacific Area

USN—U.S. Navy

USSBS—United States Strategic Bombing Survey

WDCSA—Chief of Staff, U.S. Army

WPD—War Plans Division, U.S. Army; changed to OPD after March, 1942 (U.S. Navy also had a War Plans Division)

WPL—War Plan

BIBLIOGRAPHY

BOOKS, MANUSCRIPTS, AND GOVERNMENT DOCUMENTS

Beard, Charles A., *American Foreign Policy in the Making, 1932–1940*, Yale University Press, New Haven, 1946.

———, *President Roosevelt and the Coming of the War, 1941*, Yale University Press, New Haven, 1948.

Berle, Adolf A., Jr., "Diaries" (unpublished manuscript in the possession of the diarist).

Brereton, Lewis H., *The Brereton Diaries*, W. Morrow & Co., Inc., New York, 1946.

Bryant, Arthur, *The Turn of the Tide: A History of the War Years, 1939–1943, Based on the Diaries of Field-Marshal Lord Alanbrooke, Chief of the Imperial General Staff*, Doubleday and Co., Garden City, New York, 1957.

Butow, Robert J. C., *Tojo and the Coming of the War*, Princeton University Press, Princeton, 1961.

Byas, Hugh, *Government by Assassination*, Alfred A. Knopf, New York, 1942.

Churchill, Winston S., *The Grand Alliance*, Houghton Mifflin Co., Boston, 1950.

Cline, Ray S., *Washington Command Post: The Operations Division*, in the series *United States Army in World War II*, Washington, D.C., 1951.

Conn, Stetson, and Byron Fairchild, *The Framework of Hemisphere Defense*, in the series *United States Army in World War II*, Washington, D.C., 1960.

Craigie, Sir Robert Leslie, *Behind the Japanese Mask*, Hutchinson & Co., Ltd., London, 1945.

Craven, Wesley F., and James L. Cate (eds.), *United States Air Force in World War II: Plans and Early Operations: January 1939 to August 1942*, University of Chicago Press, Chicago, 1948.

Davis, Forrest, and Ernest K. Lindley, *How War Came*, Simon and Schuster, New York, 1942.

Edmonds, Walter D., *They Fought with What They Had*, Little, Brown & Co., Boston, 1951.

Feis, Herbert, *The Road to Pearl Harbor*, Princeton University Press, Princeton, 1950.

Foote, Alexander, *Handbook for Spies*, Doubleday and Co., Garden City, New York, 1949.

Foreign Relations of the United States: Japan, 1931–1941, Department of State Publication No. 2016, United States Government Printing Office, Washington, D.C., 1943. 2 vols.

Fuchida, M., and M. Okumiya, *Midway: The Battle That Doomed Japan*, Naval Institute Publication, Annapolis, Maryland, 1955.

Grenfell, Russell, *Main Fleet to Singapore*, Faber & Faber, Ltd., London, 1951.

Grew, Joseph C., *Ten Years in Japan*, Simon and Schuster, New York, 1944.

———, *Turbulent Era: A Diplomatic Record of Forty Years, 1904–1945*, ed. by Walter Johnson, Vol. II, Houghton Mifflin Co., Boston, 1952.

Hart, Thomas, "Narrative of Events Leading up to War" (photostatic copy in the Office of the Chief of Military History).

Hattori, Takushiro, "Complete History of the Greater East Asia War," Vol. I (typescript in the Office of the Chief of Military History).

Hearings before the Joint Committee on the Investigation of the Pearl Harbor Attack, 79th Congress, United States Government Printing Office, Washington, D.C., 1946. 39 vols.

Hearings on American Aspects of the Richard Sorge Spy Case, based on testimony of M. Yoshikawa and Maj. Gen. C. A. Willoughby, Hearings before the Committee on Un-American Activities, August 9, 22, and 23, 1951, Washington, D.C., 1951.

Huie, William Bradford, *The Case against the Admirals*, E. P. Dutton and Co., New York, 1946.

Hull, Cordell, *The Memoirs of Cordell Hull*, The Macmillan Company, New York, 1948. 2 vols.

Ickes, Harold L., *The Lowering Clouds*, Vol. III of *The Secret Diary of Harold L. Ickes*, Simon and Schuster, New York, 1954.

Ind, Allison, *Bataan, the Judgment Seat: The Saga of the Philippine Command of the United States Army Air Force, May, 1941, to May, 1942*, The Macmillan Company, New York, 1944.

"Judgment," Judge Advocate, Department of the Army, International Military Tribunal for the Far East, November, 1948 (mimeo.).

Karig, Walter, and Welbourn Kelley, *Battle Report: Pearl Harbor to Coral Sea*, Farrar and Rinehart, New York, 1944.

Kase, Toshikazu, *Journey to the Missouri*, Yale University Press, New Haven, 1950.

Kato, Masuo, *The Lost War*, Alfred A. Knopf, New York, 1946.

Kaufmann, William W., "Operation Barbarossa" (unpublished manuscript in the possession of the author).

Kennan, George F., *American Diplomacy, 1900–1950*, University of Chicago Press, Chicago, 1951.

Kimmel, Husband E., *Admiral Kimmel's Story*, Henry Regnery Co., Chicago, 1955.

King, Ernest J., and Walter Muir Whitehill, *Fleet Admiral King: A Naval Record*, W. W. Norton and Co., New York, 1952.

Koehler, Hansjuergen, *Inside the Gestapo: Hitler's Shadow over the World*, Pallas Publishing Co., Ltd., London, 1940.

Langer, William L., and Everett S. Gleason, *The Challenge to Isolation*, Harper, New York, 1952.

———, *The Undeclared War, 1940–1941*, Harper, New York, 1953.

Lord, Walter, *Day of Infamy*, Henry Holt and Co., New York, 1957.

Mashbir, Sidney Forrester, *I Was an American Spy*, Vantage Press, Inc., New York, 1953.

Matloff, Maurice, and Edwin M. Snell, *Strategic Planning for Coalition Warfare, 1941–1942*, in the series *United States Army in World War II*, Washington, D.C., 1953.

Maxon, Yale Candee, *Control of Japanese Foreign Policy: A Study of Civil-Military Rivalry, 1930–1945*, University of California Press, Berkeley, 1957.

Meissner, Hans-Otto, *The Man with Three Faces*, Rinehart and Co., New York, 1956.

Millis, Walter, *This Is Pearl!* W. Morrow & Co., Inc., New York, 1947.

Morgenstern, George, *Pearl Harbor: The Story of the Secret War*, Devin-Adair Co., New York, 1947.

Morison, Elting, *Turmoil and Tradition: A Study of the Life and Times of Henry L. Stimson*, Houghton Mifflin Co., Boston, 1960.

Morison, Samuel Eliot, *The Rising Sun in the Pacific: 1931–April 1942*, Vol. III of *History of United States Naval Operations in World War II*, Little, Brown & Co., Boston, 1950.

Morton, Louis, *The Fall of the Philippines*, in the series *United States Army in World War II*, Washington, D.C., 1953.

Nomura, Kichisaburo, "Diary of Admiral Kichisaburo Nomura, 1 June–31 December, 1941," trans. by K. Kurosawa, July 18, 1946 (mimeo.).

Okumiya, Masatake, and Jiro Horikoshi, with Martin Caidin, *Zero*, E. P. Dutton and Co., New York, 1956.

Payne, Robert, *The Marshall Story: A Biography of General George C. Marshall*, Prentice-Hall, Inc., New York, 1951.

"Political Strategy prior to the Outbreak of War," Part V, Document No. 152, Office of the Chief of Military History (mimeo.).

Rauch, Basil, *Roosevelt from Munich to Pearl Harbor*, Creative Age Press, New York, 1950.

Report of the Joint Committee on the Investigation of the Pearl Harbor Attack, and Additional Views of Mr. Keefe Together with Minority Views of Mr. Ferguson and Mr. Brewster, United States Government Printing Office, Washington, D.C., 1946.

Roosevelt, Elliott, and Joseph P. Lash (eds.), *F.D.R.: His Personal Letters: 1928–1945*, Vol. II, Duell, Sloan and Pearce, New York, 1950.

Sakai, Saburo, with Martin Caidin and Fred Saito, *Samurai: The Personal Story of Japan's Greatest Living Fighter Pilot*, E. P. Dutton and Co., New York, 1957.

Seth, Ronald, *Secret Servants: A History of Japanese Espionage*, Farrar, Strauss, and Cudahy, New York, 1957.

Sherwood, Robert E., *Roosevelt and Hopkins: An Intimate History*, Harper, New York, 1948.

Shigemitsu, Mamoru, *Japan and Her Destiny*, trans. by Oswald White, Hutchinson & Co., Ltd., London, 1958.

Tansill, Charles C., *Back Door to War: The Roosevelt Foreign Policy, 1933–1941*, Henry Regnery Co., Chicago, 1952.

Terret, Dulany, *The Emergency*, Vol. I of *The Signal Corps*, in the series *United States Army in World War II*, Washington, D.C., 1956.

Theobald, Robert A., *The Final Secret of Pearl Harbor*, Devin-Adair Co., New York, 1954.

Togo, Shigenori, *The Cause of Japan*, Simon and Schuster, New York, 1956.

"Tokyo War Crime Trial Documents," International Military Tribunal for the Far East, Harvard Law School Treasure Room Collection (mimeo.).

Tolischus, Otto D., *Tokyo Record*, Reynal and Hitchcock, New York, 1943.

United States Strategic Bombing Survey: Interrogations of Japanese Officials, Reports, Pacific War, No. 72, Vols. I and II, Naval Analysis Division, Washington, D.C., 1946; *Japanese Air Power*, Military Analysis Division, Washington, D.C., July, 1946; *Japanese Military and Naval Intelligence Division*, Japanese Intelligence Section, G-2, Washington, D.C., 1946; *Summary Report* (Pacific War), Washington, D.C., 1946.

The War with Japan, Part I (December, 1941, to August, 1942), Department of Military Art and Engineering, United States Military Academy, West Point, New York, 1950.

Watson, Mark S., *Chief of Staff: Prewar Plans and Preparations*, in the series *United States Army in World War II*, Washington, D.C., 1950.

Willoughby, C. A., *Shanghai Conspiracy*, E. P. Dutton and Co., New York, 1952.

ARTICLES IN BOOKS, NEWSPAPERS, AND MAGAZINES

Ballantine, Joseph W., "Mukden to Pearl Harbor," *Foreign Affairs*, Vol. 27, July, 1949, pp. 651–664.

Burtness, Paul S., and Warren U. Ober, "Research Methodology: Problem of Pearl Harbor Intelligence Reports," *Military Affairs*, Vol. 25, Fall, 1961, pp. 132–145.

Current, Richard N., "How Stimson Meant To 'Maneuver' the Japanese," *Mississippi Valley Historical Review*, Vol. 40, June, 1953, pp. 67–74.

DeWeerd, Harvey, "Strategic Surprise in the Korean War" (unpublished paper in the possession of the author).

Ellsberg, Daniel, "Uncalculated Risks and Wishful Thinking" (unpublished paper in the possession of the author).

Fioravanza, Giuseppe, "The Japanese Military Mission to Italy in 1941," *U.S. Naval Institute Proceedings*, Vol. 82, January, 1956, pp. 24–31.

Fuchida, Mitsuo, "I Led the Air Attack on Pearl Harbor," *U.S. Naval Institute Proceedings*, Vol. 78, September, 1952, pp. 939–952.

Fukudome, Shigeru, "Hawaii Operation," *U.S. Naval Institute Proceedings*, Vol. 81, December, 1955, pp. 1315–1332.

Higgins, Trumbull, " 'East Wind Rain,' " *U.S. Naval Institute Proceedings*, Vol. 81, November, 1955, pp. 1198–1205.

"Japanese Naval Intelligence," *The ONI Review*, Vol. 1, July, 1946, pp. 36–40.

Kiralfy, Alexander, "Japanese Naval Strategy," in *Makers of Modern Strategy*, ed. by Edward Mead Earle, with the collaboration of Gordon A. Craig and Felix Gilbert, Princeton University Press, Princeton, 1943, pp. 457–484.

Kittredge, Tracy B., "United States Defense Policy and Strategy, 1941," *U.S. News and World Report*, December 3, 1954, pp. 53–63 and 110–139.

May, Ernest R., "The Development of Political-Military Consultations in the United States," *Political Science Quarterly*, Vol. 70, June, 1955, pp. 161–180.

Miles, Sherman, "Pearl Harbor in Retrospect," *Atlantic Monthly*, Vol. 182, July, 1948, pp. 65–72.

Morton, Louis, "The Japanese Decision for War," *U.S. Naval Institute Proceedings*, Vol. 80, December, 1954, pp. 1325–1337.

———, "Pearl Harbor in Perspective," *U.S. Naval Institute Proceedings*, Vol. 81, April, 1955, pp. 461–468.

Pavlenko, N., "Documents on Pearl Harbor," *Voenno-Istoricheskii Zhurnal* (*Military-Historical Journal*), No. 1, January, 1961, pp. 85–105.

Sansom, Sir George, "Japan's Fatal Blunder," *International Affairs*, Vol. 24, October, 1948, pp. 543–554.

Shimada, Koichi, "Japanese Naval Air Operations in the Philippine Invasion," *U.S. Naval Institute Proceedings*, Vol. 81, January, 1955, pp. 1–17.

Ward, Robert E., "The Inside Story of the Pearl Harbor Plan," *U.S. Naval Institute Proceedings*, Vol. 77, December, 1951, pp. 1272–1281.

Welles, Sumner, "Far Eastern Policy Before Pearl Harbor," Chap. 3 of *Seven Decisions That Shaped History*, Harper, New York, 1950 and 1951.

Wilds, Thomas, "How Japan Fortified the Mandated Islands," *U.S. Naval Institute Proceedings*, Vol. 81, April, 1955, pp. 401–408.

Yoshida, Shigeru, "Memoirs," *Asahi* (*Asahi Evening News*), August, 1955, particularly August 2, 1955, trans. by A. M. Halpern.

Yoshikawa, Takeo, "Top Secret Assignment," *U.S. Naval Institute Proceedings*, Vol. 86, December, 1960, pp. 27–39.

INDEX